# ON THE
# FIELDS OF GLORY

# THE NAPOLEONIC LIBRARY

Other books in the series include:

## 1815: THE RETURN OF NAPOLEON
Paul Britten Austin

## CHARGE!
Great Cavalry Charges of the Napoleonic Wars
Digby Smith

## LIFE IN NAPOLEON'S ARMY
The Memoirs of Captain Elzéar Blaze
Introduction by Philip Haythornthwaite

## THE MEMOIRS OF BARON VON MÜFFLING
A Prussian Officer in the Napoleonic Wars
Baron von Müffling

## WATERLOO LECTURES
A Study of the Campaign of 1815
Colonel Charles Chesney

## WATERLOO LETTERS
A Collection of Accounts From Survivors of the
Campaign of 1815
Edited by Major-General H. T. Siborne

www.frontline-books.com/napoleoniclibrary

# ON THE FIELDS OF GLORY

## THE BATTLEFIELDS OF THE 1815 CAMPAIGN

Andrew Uffindell

and

Michael Corum

Frontline Books

*On the Fields of Glory: The Battlefields of the 1815 Campaign*

A Greenhill Book

First published in 1996 by Greenhill Books, Lionel Leventhal Limited
www.greenhillbooks.com

This edition published in 2015 by

Frontline Books
an imprint of Pen & Sword Books Ltd,
47 Church Street, Barnsley, S. Yorkshire, S70 2AS
For more information on our books, please visit
www.frontline-books.com, email info@frontline-books.com
or write to us at the above address.

ISBN: 978-1-84832-820-4

CIP data records for this title are available from the British Library

Printed and bound by CPI Group (UK) Ltd, Croydon, CR0 4YY

# CONTENTS

*List of illustrations*   7
*List of diagrams and drawings*   9
*List of maps*   10
*Key to maps*   11
*Acknowledgements*   13

**Part One: The road to Waterloo**

1   The 1815 campaign: the first battles   17
2   On the field of honour: Waterloo today   33

**Part Two: Wellington's sector**

3   Morning 18 June: from Waterloo to the front line   47
4   The defence of Hougoumont   64
5   The eastern wing: victory from the jaws of defeat   74
6   The panorama: prepare to receive cavalry!   85
7   The centre of the line: La Haie Sainte falls   117
8   Evening 18 June   132

**Part Three: Napoleon's sector**

9   Morning 18 June: the last review   145
10   The assault on Hougoumont   157
11   The main attack: triumph then disaster   163
12   Marshal Ney's massed cavalry onslaught   175
13   The Guard goes into action   187

**Part Four: Blücher's sector**

14   The Prussian march to the battlefield   201
15   IV Corps and II Corps under fire   213
16   I Corps in action   228

**Part Five: Brussels**

17   Brussels in June 1815   245
18   The British monument at Evere cemetery   261

## Part Six: The last shots of the 1815 campaign

| | | |
|---|---|---|
| 19 | The Battle of Wavre | 271 |
| 20 | Aftermath | 303 |
| 21 | Echoes of Waterloo | 320 |

## Appendices

| | | |
|---|---|---|
| 1 | Orders of battle | 337 |
| 2 | Museum addresses and opening times | 349 |
| 3 | Sources | 351 |
| | *Index* | *353* |

Captain Edward Kelly, 1st Life Guards, slays a French cuirassier

# LIST OF ILLUSTRATIONS

Illustrations 1, 3, 4, 6, 10, 15, 19, 20, 22–24, 32, 34, 35, 40, 47 and 52 are reproduced by courtesy of the Anne S.K. Brown Military Collection, Brown University, Rhode Island, U.S.A.

## Pages 97–112

1 Napoleon's headquarters of Le Caillou
2 Le Caillou as it is today
3 The last review: Napoleon is acclaimed by his Guard and a detachment of cuirassiers
4 Napoleon discusses Wellington's position with Lieutenant-General François Haxo
5 Chantelet farm: Ney's headquarters on the eve of Waterloo
6 The British Guards close the North Gate of Hougoumont
7 The same place today
8 The North Gate today, seen from outside of the farm
9 The south face of the building block today
10 French infantry attack the gate of the Gardener's House
11 The garden of Hougoumont: the monument to French soldiers
12 Looking west from Hougoumont to the building block
13 Look west along the road on the crest of Wellington's ridge
14 Wellington's far eastern wing, from the French side of the valley
15 The Scots Greys and Inniskillings attack Napoleon's battery
16 The Waterloo re-enactment of 1995: French cavalry waiting to charge
17 The 1995 re-enactment: grenadiers of Napoleon's Imperial Guard under fire
18 The Wounded Eagle monument
19 The guardsmen lie dead in formation after their last stand
20 Wellington and Blücher meet by chance near La Belle Alliance
21 La Belle Alliance today
22 The battlefield after the fighting
23 The village of Waterloo after the battle
24 Wounded soldiers arrive at the Place Royale in Brussels
25 The same place today
26 The Grand'Place in Brussels
27 The British Waterloo monument at the Evere cemetery, Brussels

## Pages 273–88

28 The Chapelle St Robert
29 The Farm de la Kelle
30 Paris Wood
31 Prussian infantry at the 1995 re-enactment
32 General Bülow issues orders during the battle
33 The area from which the Prussian IV Corps saw French cavalry charging against Wellington
34 Prussian infantry storm into Plancenoit village
35 Plancenoit village in flames
36 Plancenoit village from the north
37 Plancenoit church today
38 The Prussian monument north of Plancenoit
39 The Chapelle Jacques north-east of the battlefield
40 The pursuit after Waterloo
41 The Bridge of Christ at Wavre
42 The Farm de la Bourse at Limal
43 The River Dyle near Bierges mill
44 The monument to Maurice Gérard near Bierges mill
45 The site of the Porte de Bruxelles at Namur
46 Namur: looking north over the city from the citadel
47 British Royal Horse Artillery galloping into action
48 The tomb of Alexander Cavalié Mercer
49 Strijtem château
50 Commemoration of the King's German Legion in Bexhill
51 Barrack Hall, Bexhill
52 The fall of La Haie Sainte
53 The courtyard as it is today
54 Re-enactors of the 2nd Light battalion, King's German Legion
55 View from the crossroads at the centre of Wellington's front line south along the Brussels road

# LIST OF DIAGRAMS AND DRAWINGS

| | | |
|---|---|---:|
| 1 | Wellington at Waterloo | *title page* |
| 2 | Captain Edward Kelly, 1st Life Guards, slays a French cuirassier | 6 |
| 3 | Sir Alexander Gordon is carried from the battlefield | 12 |
| 4 | The summit of the Lion Mound | 32 |
| 5 | The Royal Chapel at the town of Waterloo | 63 |
| 6 | The garrison of Hougoumont | 65 |
| 7 | Hougoumont farm in 1815 and today | 68 |
| 8 | The ruins of Hougoumont, viewed from the garden | 73 |
| 9 | Mont St Jean farm | 116 |
| 10 | The battle at la Haie Sainte | 122 |
| 11 | La Haie Sainte | 131 |
| 12 | Napoleon at Waterloo | 156 |
| 13 | Hougoumont: the ruins of the château | 162 |
| 14 | French infantry attack | 174 |
| 15 | A square of Brunswick infantry repel French cuirassiers | 186 |
| 16 | Marshal Ney at the head of the Guard | 197 |
| 17 | Napoleon interrogates a Prussian prisoner | 212 |
| 18 | Plancenoit Church | 219 |
| 19 | Field Marshal Blücher | 227 |
| 20 | Residence of the Duke and Duchess of Richmond | 247 |
| 21 | Wellington's residence in the rue Royale, Brussels | 260 |
| 22 | French command structure, 18 June | 272 |
| 23 | Wellington and his staff at Waterloo | 352 |

# MAPS

| | | |
|---|---|---|
| 1 | The 1815 campaign: the positions of the three armies on the night of 14/15 June | 19 |
| 2 | Napoleon's invasion of 15 June | 21 |
| 3 | The battles and manoeuvres of 16 June | 23 |
| 4 | Strategic situation: night of 17/18 June | 28 |
| 5 | The battlefield of Waterloo: 11.30 am, 18 June | 38 |
| 6 | Wellington's sector of the battlefield today | 59 |
| 7 | Hougoumont today, showing the dispositions of the initial garrison | 66 |
| 8 | The impact of the French main attack | 76 |
| 9 | The onset of the French cavalry charges | 87 |
| 10 | Maj-Gen Adam's brigade enters the front line | 118 |
| 11 | Repulse of the Middle Guard | 134 |
| 12 | Napoleon's sector of the battlefield today | 146 |
| 13 | The assault on Hougoumont | 158 |
| 14 | The attack by d'Erlon's I Corps | 166 |
| 15 | Aftermath of the repulse of d'Erlon's I Corps | 169 |
| 16 | The attack by Lt-Gens Foy and Bachelu | 181 |
| 17 | Last stand of the Old Guard | 192 |
| 18 | Blücher's army leaves its bivouacs around Wavre: 18 June | 202 |
| 19 | The Prussian march to the battlefield of Waterloo | 205 |
| 20 | The route of the Prussian IV and II Corps today | 208 |
| 21 | The Prussian entry on to the battlefield: 4.30 pm | 214 |
| 22 | The Prussian dispositions towards 8.00 pm | 223 |
| 23 | Plancenoit today, showing the dispositions during the final Prussian assault | 224 |
| 24 | The scene of the Prussian–Nassau clash: the area around Papelotte | 229 |
| 25 | Battle of Wavre: afternoon, 18 June | 290 |
| 26 | Battle of Wavre: evening, 18 June | 292 |
| 27 | Battle of Wavre: morning, 19 June | 293 |
| 28 | Wavre and Bierges today | 296 |
| 29 | Marshal Grouchy's retreat from Wavre: 19 June | 304 |
| 30 | The fighting around Namur: 20 June | 307 |
| 31 | Namur today | 312 |
| 32 | Bexhill-on-sea today | 331 |

# KEY TO MAPS

| | | | | |
|---|---|---|---|---|
| ■ | French | ⊞ | Regiment | |
| ☐ | Allies | ☐ | Brigade | |
| ☐ | Infantry | | | |
| ◪ | Cavalry | ☐ | Division | |
| ı|ı | Artillery | | | |
| ◊ | Skirmishers | ☐ | Corps | |
| ☐ | Company | | | |
| ◪ | Squadron | ☐ | Army | |
| ☐ | Battalion | | | |

Examples:

Durutte  ■  Durutte's French infantry division

16  (Prussian) 16th infantry brigade

1/95th  ☐  1st battalion, (British) 95th Rifles

◪  Brigade of cavalry (from the Prussian I Corps)

The authors and publishers have done their best to ensure the accuracy of all the information in this book; however, they can accept no responsibility for any loss, injury or inconvenience sustained by any traveller as a result of information or advice contained in this book.

This book includes enough maps to enable visitors to find their way easily around the battlefield and to visualise the actions that occurred in its various sectors. However, those enthusiasts who wish to undertake intensive exploration of the 1815 campaign area are advised to take with them a copy of the Michelin 1:200,000 scale map of Belgium (Oostende–Brussel–Liège) for use in conjunction with this book. They should also obtain the relevant 1:25,000 scale maps produced by the Belgian Institut géographique national. These are on sale at good book shops in Belgium.

Wellington's mortally wounded ADC, Sir Alexander Gordon, is carried from the battlefield

# ACKNOWLEDGEMENTS

This book has been a team effort in the fullest sense. We are grateful to all those who have helped with its production. In particular we wish to acknowledge the assistance given by the staff of the Bodleian and Codrington libraries in Oxford. We are also grateful to the staff of the British Library, especially those of the Manuscripts Department. We appreciate the help given by the excellent staff of Waterloo's tourist information office.

Scores of other friends have contributed information, advice and encouragement, including David Chandler, Guy and Janine Delvaux, Geoffrey Ellis, Lucien Gerke and Bernard Gott.

We have been fortunate to benefit from the expertise and encouragement of societies as well as individuals. We wish to record our debt to the Napoleonic Society of America. We are grateful to our re-enactment friends in the Napoleonic Association and the French 21st Line infantry.

We wish to pay tribute to the Bexhill Hanoverian Study Group, which has undertaken a massive research project into the presence of Wellington's King's German Legion in Bexhill during the Napoleonic wars. Under the patronship of Lady Elizabeth Longford, the Study Group is thriving and this book has benefitted immensely from its discoveries. We are grateful to all its members, but especially to Philip Offord, Fred Rye, Major Ronald Gardner (retired) and the late James Wilkes.

We owe a particular debt to Philip Haythornthwaite for reading through three successive drafts of the manuscript. We much appreciate his enthusiastic encouragement and expert advice. Ian Heath kindly edited the manuscript of this book and we gratefully acknowledge his help. For invaluable assistance in obtaining suitable illustrations, we wish to thank Peter Harrington of the Anne S.K. Brown Military Collection.

Furthermore, we are grateful to all the staff of Greenhill Books who contributed to this project, especially to Lionel Leventhal. Finally, but by no means least, we are grateful to our families for their invaluable assistance.

Andrew Uffindell
Michael Corum
1996

# PART ONE:
# THE ROAD TO WATERLOO

# 1

# THE 1815 CAMPAIGN:
# THE FIRST BATTLES

Over Paris the night sky was beginning to lighten in the east. It was Monday 12 June 1815. The Emperor Napoleon was leaving to join his Army of the North which he had painstakingly assembled in secret in the north-east of France ready to invade the United Netherlands, an amalgamated Belgium and Holland under the House of Orange. General Armand Caulaincourt, the Duke of Vicenza, described the scene:

> The clock struck three, and daylight was beginning to appear. 'Farewell, Caulaincourt,' said the Emperor, holding out his hand to me. 'Farewell – we must conquer or die' ... With hurried steps, he passed through the apartments, his mind being evidently absorbed by melancholy ideas. On reaching the foot of the staircase, he cast a lingering look around him, and then threw himself into his carriage.
>
> When the carriage was out of sight, and the rattling of the wheels was no longer audible, the most gloomy feelings overwhelmed me. The silence which pervaded the capital seemed to bode evil. I went down into the garden, and walked about, but without being able to calm the inward agitation that preyed upon me. A mass of flame seemed to be gathering on the horizon; I heard the howling of the storm ...[1]

Three days later, in the early hours of 15 June, French light cavalry crossed the frontier into the southern half of the United Netherlands, present-day Belgium. Napoleon's objective was to seize Brussels and bowl over the two armies that stood before it: the Duke of Wellington's Anglo-Dutch-German composite force and Prince Gebhard Leberecht von Blücher's Prussian troops.

For Napoleon was pitted against the whole of Europe. In 1814 he had been forced by treachery and an invasion of France to abdicate. King Louis XVIII had taken Napoleon's throne but soon antagonised French public opinion. The restored Bourbon monarchy sought to put the clock back to the Ancien Regime, negating the Revolution and the glorious days of Napoleon's Empire. 'All France regrets me and wants me', Napoleon judged. In March 1815 he returned with just 1000 troops from the Italian island of Elba to regain the throne of France. Soldiers flocked to his standard. Royalists panicked. On 19 March, Louis XVIII departed from Paris for exile at Ghent in the United Netherlands. The next day Napoleon entered his capital in triumph.

Representatives of the European states were assembled at the Congress of Vienna to discuss the post-Napoleonic world. They were aghast at his return. To them, Napoleon on the French throne meant war, social upheaval and national humiliation. Russia, Great Britain, Prussia, Austria, Spain, Portugal, Sweden and some of the German states mobilised for war. Vast armies marched towards the eastern frontiers of France. An invasion was planned for July.

But Napoleon had decided to strike a pre-emptive blow. He would take out the two northernmost armies, those of Wellington and Blücher. This would demoralise the hostile coalition, invigorate his troops and consolidate France behind him. Success would give him Belgium, many of whose people loathed their enforced union with Holland and would flock to join Napoleon's armies.

Napoleon rapidly covered the seventy-five miles from Paris to Laon where he passed the night of 12/13 June. The next day, he advanced another forty miles northwards, to Avesnes, and on 14 June completed the final fifteen miles to Beaumont. Meanwhile, Napoleon's Army of the North was carrying out the last stages of its move into position between Beaumont and Philippeville, immediately south of the frontier. The army had accomplished this move in strict secrecy. Napoleon had closed the frontiers to every carriage and every letter. He had masked the troop movements by trebling the strength of advance posts of the frontier fortresses near the North Sea coast, such as Dunkirk. Napoleon wished to deceive the Duke of Wellington into thinking the main French thrust would strike near Tournai or Mons. In fact, Napoleon was going to launch his entire army at the junction of Wellington and Blücher's armies, at the town of Charleroi.

Napoleon's Army of the North was just 124,000 men strong. Wellington and Blücher had a combined strength of 210,000. Nevertheless, the allies would need time to assemble their armies from their extensive cantonments and to unite in order to bring their full numerical superiority to bear. Napoleon confidently believed he could win by a surprise attack. He would divide his two foes by seizing a central position between them, preventing them from supporting each other. He would hurl back or destroy their outposts and any formations which ventured to fight.

In order to guard the whole length of the Franco-Belgian border and to feed their armies without oppressing any one area, Wellington and Blücher's armies covered a front of one hundred miles, from Courtrai in the west to Liège in the east. Wellington's headquarters were in Brussels, where his Reserve Corps was also stationed. The remainder of his troops, the I and II Corps and the Cavalry Reserve, were cantoned to the west and south-west. South and east of Brussels

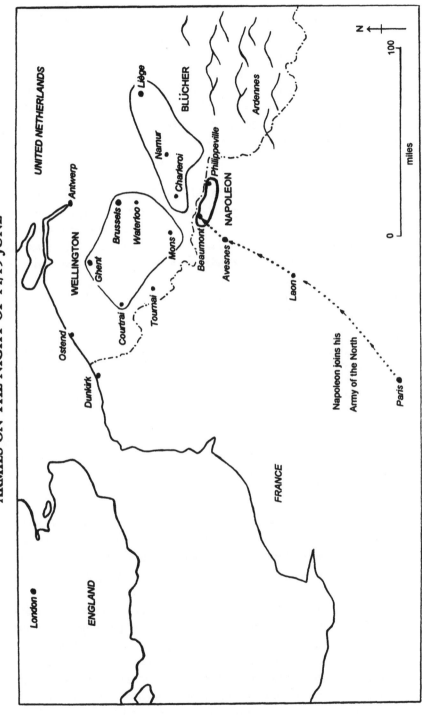

THE 1815 CAMPAIGN: THE POSITIONS OF THE THREE
ARMIES ON THE NIGHT OF 14/15 JUNE

stood the four corps of Blücher's Prussian army. Blücher's headquarters were at first in Liège, later in Namur, which was thirty miles nearer the frontier.

Napoleon's exuberant troops seemed, and felt, invincible. In the early hours of 15 June they advanced to attack their foe. 'An army of 120,000 men is hurling itself on the Low Countries,' Lieutenant-General Baron Maximilien Foy noted in his diary later that day. 'The Emperor wants to strike a great blow before the Russians arrive on the Rhine. The moment of going into action was chosen to perfection. The troops demonstrate not patriotism, not enthusiasm but a real rage for the Emperor against his enemies. No one can put the triumph of France in doubt.'[2] Never has an army marched off more confident of victory.

The first shots were soon exchanged. The French light cavalry spearheading the invasion in the centre cut up and drove back the Prussian outposts along the frontier. Everywhere the French received a rapturous welcome from the local people. This was not merely an invasion but a liberation. The inhabitants of Wallonia, the southern half of Belgium, were French-speaking and generally regarded Napoleon as a liberator from Dutch rule and welcomed the relief from Prussian exactions of food and lodging. Lieutenant Barral of the Imperial Guard fondly remembered the scenes of joy:

> The Belgians were hard put to it to know how fully to express their happiness at seeing us. When we passed through some villages the inhabitants danced and gave us flowers and sprays of foliage. Everywhere, it was truly a surge of emotion. At the hamlet of Nalinnes a peasant girl pressed a small bouquet of roses tied with a ribbon in the French colours into my hand. I gave her a military salute and then a kiss. First of all I attached the flowers to the pommel of my sword but as that hindered me when giving orders I slid them into the interior pocket of my tunic. At Waterloo a musket-ball struck me full on the chest, piercing the uniform but the blow was softened by the calyx of roses. God bless the pretty girl of Nalinnes![3]

Although some of Napoleon's troops had set off late, the invasion was not running far behind schedule. By noon, Charleroi was in French hands and their troops were pouring over on to the north bank of the River Sambre. By a massive, surprise onslaught, Napoleon had secured a bridgehead and could now concentrate on pressing home his thrust on Brussels.

Napoleon wanted to divide and rule his two foes. His seizure of Charleroi at the junction of Wellington and Blücher's armies gave him command of a central position between them. Now he sought to hammer the French army like a wedge even further into the gap. The preliminary target was the strategic chaussée between Nivelles in the west and Namur in the east. This was the only lateral, paved road linking Wellington and Blücher's armies south of Brussels. If Napoleon could cut this road, Wellington and Blücher would have great

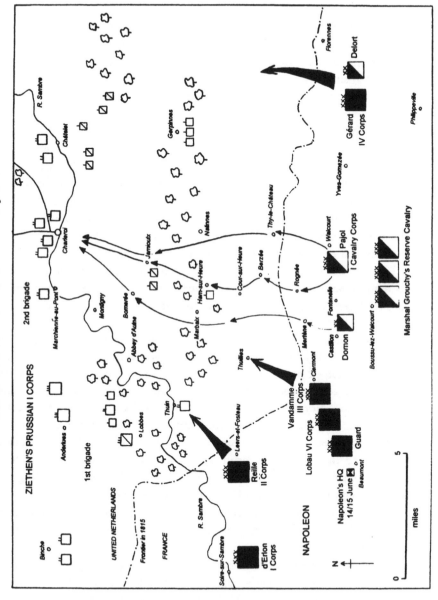

NAPOLEON'S INVASION OF 15 JUNE

difficulty in uniting to defend Brussels. Any march across the wet and hilly countryside lying north of the Nivelles–Namur chaussée would be slow and exhausting.

As it crossed the Sambre, the French army began to form into two wings and a reserve. The left wing was to advance due north from Charleroi and try to cut the strategic lateral chaussée at Quatre Bras. The right wing would advance north-east and cut the road at Sombreffe. The left wing would be responsible for repelling and holding at bay Wellington's advanced guard. The right wing would deal similarly with Blücher's forward formations. The reserve – the VI Corps, part of the Reserve Cavalry and the Imperial Guard – would come into action on whichever wing required support.

Napoleon sat outside the Belle-Vue tavern beneath the northern walls of Charleroi as exuberant French troops passed by. 'Go on, go on, my children!' he encouraged them. 'Advance! Advance!'[4] The inhabitants of Charleroi were acclaiming him too. 'Thank you, children, thank you!' he told them. 'But withdraw from here because today or tomorrow there will be a big battle in this place.' As Napoleon spoke, the local people were strewing the ground before him with flowers, particularly with scores of intensely red poppies. Soon the earth seemed already to be splashed with drops of blood.[5]

Just then Marshal Michel Ney rode up and added to the colourful scene with his flaming hair. 'Hey, the lion!' exclaimed the French soldiers, delighted to have the legendary 'bravest of the brave' amongst them. 'Hey, the red lion! Ah, it is the Redhead!'[6]

Napoleon had at first been reluctant to employ Ney in this campaign, for Ney had deserted him in 1814 and served the restored Bourbon monarchy until Napoleon regained power in France in March 1815. Nevertheless, Napoleon was short of good subordinate commanders. Although not gifted with intellectual genius, Ney was a tough veteran adored by his troops. At the last moment, on 11 June, Napoleon summoned him to join the army.[7]

Napoleon now gave Ney command of the left wing; Marshal Grouchy commanded the right. Ney thrust up the Brussels road but was unable to occupy the crossroads at Quatre Bras that night. A brigade of Wellington's Nassau troops repulsed French Guard Lancers who tried to reach it.

On the right wing, the Prussian I Corps under Lieutenant-General Count Hans von Ziethen halted Grouchy's advance south of Fleurus. The Nivelles–Namur road had not been cut.

Dawn on 16 June heralded a beautiful, hot day. Napoleon did not expect to fight a major battle at this early stage. He believed that the shock of his surprise invasion of 15 June had caused Wellington and Blücher to retreat: Wellington towards Ostend and Blücher towards Prussia.

Instead, Blücher sought to concentrate his army around the village of Ligny, 2000 metres south-west of Sombreffe. This decision surprised Napoleon, for the

# THE BATTLES AND MANOEUVRES OF 16 JUNE

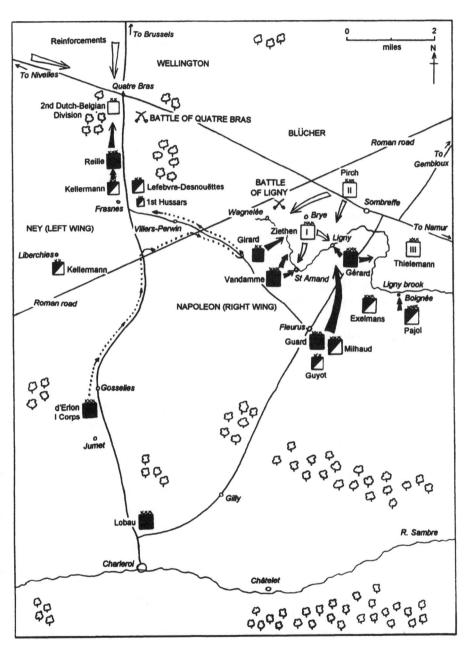

allies had not yet had time to mass their units from scattered cantonments. By noon, Blücher would only have three of his four corps at Ligny; the fourth had delayed marching from its quarters fifty miles away at Liège when hostilities commenced. Wellington would have only one division at Quatre Bras until 3.00 pm. He had reacted slowly to Napoleon's offensive and had not hurried to move his units eastwards to support Blücher at Ligny. Until the early morning of 16 June Wellington had imagined that the attack on Charleroi was a feint. Wellington had believed that Napoleon's real strike would fall further west.

Blücher accepted battle at Ligny for three reasons. Firstly, he wished to delay, blunt or even check Napoleon's thrust towards Brussels. Secondly, he wished to gain time to enable his ally Wellington to concentrate his chronically disunited army. Thirdly, Wellington promised, over-optimistically as it turned out, that in the course of the afternoon of 16 June he would mass most of his army at Quatre Bras, six miles north-west of Ligny. Wellington intended then to overthrow the French left wing and to come to join Blücher at Ligny against the bulk of Napoleon's army.

It was not until 3.00 pm that Napoleon had massed his right wing and reserve at Ligny. His formations had become strung out in the course of the long marches of 15 June. The Prussians had deployed 83,000 men and 224 guns north of the Ligny brook, which flowed all along the front line. The French were 63,000 men and 230 guns strong.

Ligny proved to be a battle of firepower and attrition. Napoleon inflicted severe casualties on the Prussians with his artillery. His infantry attacked Ligny village in the centre but particularly the villages of St Amand, La Haye, Le Hameau and Wagnelée on the western flank. These escalating attacks gradually extended the battle westwards and absorbed the Prussian II Corps, which constituted Blücher's reserve. The fighting was among the bitterest of the Napoleonic wars and raged under a hot sun. Lieutenant Barral of Napoleon's Guard commented wryly that: 'never have I been so cold as in Russia, so hot as at Ligny and never have I been so soaked as on the eve of Waterloo.'[8]

Meanwhile Napoleon sent a direct order to Lieutenant-General Jean-Baptiste Drouet, Count d'Erlon, commander of the French I Corps. D'Erlon was part of the French left wing under Marshal Ney who at this moment was contesting the crossroads of Quatre Bras with Wellington's mustering army. Nonetheless, Napoleon ordered d'Erlon to march across country and to fall on Blücher's left flank at Ligny. At the same time, Napoleon intended to break through the Prussian line at Ligny village with his Imperial Guard. Hopefully this two-pronged master stroke would cut off and annihilate a large portion of Blücher's army in the Wagnelée-St Amand sector.

However, d'Erlon headed in the wrong direction and emerged at 5.30 pm behind the French lines, heading for Fleurus. This caused the French left wing to panic. Using his last reserves, Blücher promptly hurled two ferocious counter-attacks at Wagnelée, La Haye and St Amand. The Prussians were beaten back only after Napoleon detached his Young Guard to the sector.

D'Erlon then turned round and retraced his steps to rejoin Marshal Ney. Owing to poor staff work, Ney had not been informed that Napoleon had summoned d'Erlon to Ligny. Ney assumed that d'Erlon had marched off on his own initiative. Faced with increasing numbers of Wellington's troops at Quatre Bras, Ney had sent a desperate recall to d'Erlon. As it was, d'Erlon was too late to intervene in either Ligny or Quatre Bras and this fiasco cost Napoleon a decisive victory. It was the single most important cause of his eventual defeat.

At 7.30 pm, amidst a thunderstorm and gathering darkness, Napoleon finally sent in his Imperial Guard. As the 1st Grenadiers ran along a corpse-strewn street of Ligny, they saw a Guard battery following in their wake. The heavy wheels of the cannon and the hooves of the horses trampled and crushed the bodies mercilessly and caused them seemingly to spring to life again by an elastic movement. The guardsmen found it appalling to contemplate.[9]

The Guard attack captured Ligny village and hurled back the Prussians but failed to destroy them. The Prussians managed to establish a rearguard line to cover their retreat. Blücher was almost captured in the final cavalry charges but escaped badly bruised. Ligny was a French victory but not a decisive one, for the French lost 10–12,000 men and were too exhausted to pursue immediately. Prussian losses were between 20,000 and 25,000 plus 22 guns.

Meanwhile, Marshal Ney had been striving desperately to contain Wellington at Quatre Bras, six miles to the north-west. Wellington initially held the crossroads with a single division but received reinforcements throughout the battle. By the close at 8.30 pm he was numerically superior to Ney and launched an offensive which regained nearly all the ground he had once held.

Ney had been unable to seize Quatre Bras and detach troops along the chaussée to outflank Blücher at Ligny. Nevertheless, he had done well to prevent Wellington reinforcing the Prussians. Neither Wellington nor Ney had gained a victory. 'Day without result! A drawn battle!' lamented Major Lemonnier-Delafosse, a French ADC.[10] Around 9000 casualties lay strewn over the battlefield. Assistant-Surgeon William Gibney of the 15th Hussars surveyed the striken battlefield on the morning of 17 June:

> It was a painful sight, and exhibited only too distinctly the horrors of war. Dead men and horses, mixed up indiscriminately, were scattered about the field. Clotted blood in small pools, and corpses besmeared with blood, their countenances even now exhibiting in what agonies many had departed. Caps, cuirasses, swords, bayonets, were strewn everywhere. Houses, fields, roads, cut up and injured by artillery; drums, waggons, and parts of uniforms lying about; whilst every house or cottage near was full of wounded and dying; and this was only the commencement of the war.[11]

Similar sights met the eye at Ligny. Sergeant Hippolyte de Mauduit of the French 1st Grenadiers described the battlefield's appearance on the morning of 17 June:

> Ligny was no longer an abode for living people: it was a vast, bloody necropolis, where thousands of victims of human strife still awaited the funeral rites which should preceed their burial. It was 6.00 am ... Already the sun was rising above the hill of Sombreffe and was extending its faint rays into the valley of Ligny and St Amand. The white mist of burnt powder had disappeared and was replaced by that which follows a rainy night. But this mist in its turn would soon dissipate under the sun, so as to remove the ethereal shroud which covered this scene of desolation.[12]

In the villages lying along the valley of the Ligny brook the French and Prussian losses had been approximately equal. A dead French skirmisher remained lodged between two branches of a tree from which he had sniped at his foe. Elsewhere, a French grenadier had been killed as he tried to climb into a house; his corpse lay across a window frame with his head, smashed by a shot, hanging inside the room. His musket lay at his feet.[13] Nevertheless, the really sickening sights lay on the exposed slopes occupied by the Prussian battalions north of the brook. Here Blücher's men had been pounded mercilessly by Napoleon's artillery and had taken severe losses. Sergeant Hippolyte de Mauduit was horrified:

> A vast number of corpses, of men and horses, were scattered here and there, horribly mutilated by shells and cannon-balls. This scene was of a different sort to that of the valley where almost all of the dead had at least preserved a human form, for canister, musket-balls and the bayonet were practically the only instruments of destruction used there. Here, in contrast, it was limbs and scattered body parts, detached heads, torn out entrails and disembowelled horses. Further away, on the plateau not far from our regiment, whole ranks were lying on the ground.[14]

Napoleon had won the first rounds of the campaign. Blücher was forced to retreat from Ligny. In the course of 17 June he rallied his mauled forces thirteen miles to the north, at Wavre, where they were joined by the fresh IV Corps just arrived from Liège. Prussian morale remained steadfast. Captain Fritz of the Westphalian Landwehr Cavalry remembered how Blücher 'rode alongside the troops, exchanging jokes and banter with many of them, and his humour spread like wildfire down the columns. I only glimpsed the old hero riding quickly past, although I should dearly have liked to have expressed to him my pleasure at his fortunate escape.'[15]

The Prussians were fortunate that Napoleon waited until 11.00 am on 17 June before sending Marshal Grouchy and the French right wing in pursuit.

Napoleon imagined his victory at Ligny had knocked Blücher out of the campaign and that he needed simply to rest his troops before marching them to Brussels. Thus the Prussians enjoyed over twelve hours' freedom from pursuit. When Grouchy did set off, he took time to pick up their trail.

Blücher established his headquarters for the night of 17/18 June in Wavre. At 5.00 pm his army's reserve ammunition waggons arrived in the town to the relief of the high command. I and II Corps had expended practically all their ammunition at Ligny and without resupply would have been useless as fighting formations.

In their bivouacs, the Prussian troops seized the opportunity to clean their weapons and prepare for battle. For Blücher's defeat at Ligny had not in the slightest dampened his ardour. If anything, it had made him more determined than ever to fight. 'I shall immediately lead you against the enemy,' he declared in a general order to the army. 'We shall beat him, because it is our duty to do so.'[16]

Blücher's inexhaustible energy and determination had crystallised and focused on the one aim of linking up with the Duke of Wellington. It had become an obsession. In the morning of 17 June, Wellington had informed Blücher that he was pulling back from Quatre Bras to maintain contact with Blücher and to avoid being outflanked by Napoleon. Wellington would retreat to a ridge at Mont St Jean, two and a half miles south of the village of Waterloo, where he would give battle if he could count on the support of at least one Prussian corps.[17] Blücher replied at 6.00 pm: 'I shall not come with two corps only, but with my whole army.'[18]

Wellington received this fine promise late in the evening, by which time he had repeated his request for Prussian assistance. His letter reached Wavre towards 11.00 pm. Blücher thereupon sent the Duke details of the Prussian plan: IV Corps would march at daybreak, followed by II Corps, towards the Anglo-Dutch-German army. I and III Corps would be ready to follow. Only the exhaustion of the troops prevented an earlier start.[19] This welcome message of aid would reach the Duke in the early morning of 18 June.[20]

Blücher's chief-of-staff, Lieutenant-General Count Augustus von Gneisenau, resented Wellington's failure to support the Prussians at Ligny as he had promised. Gneisenau was worried lest Wellington put up a half-hearted fight and then slip away to Ostend to embark for England, leaving the isolated Prussians to face Napoleon's entire army. Even if Wellington did fight resolutely, the Prussian army faced tremendous obstacles. Gneisenau was responsible for marching over 60,000 men along narrow, muddy, hopelessly congested tracks. Between Wavre and Wellington lay the steep, marshy valley of the River Lasne. Crossing this natural obstacle would be a formidable operation; if French troops happened to be guarding it, the Prussian advance would be almost impossible. Nevertheless, Blücher had promised Wellington

# STRATEGIC SITUATION: NIGHT OF 17/18 JUNE

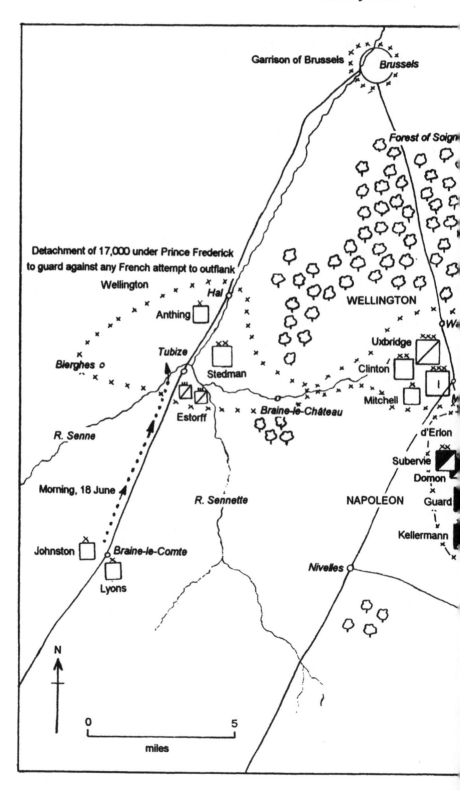

Garrison of Brussels

Brussels

Forest of Soign

Detachment of 17,000 under Prince Frederick
to guard against any French attempt to outflank
Wellington

WELLINGTON

Hal

Anthing

Tubize

Uxbridge

W

Bierghes o

Clinton

Stedman

Mitchell

Estorff

Braine-le-Château

R. Senne

d'Erlon

Subervie

Morning, 18 June

R. Sennette

NAPOLEON

Domon

Guard

Kellermann

Johnston

Braine-le-Comte

Nivelles

Lyons

N

0        5
miles

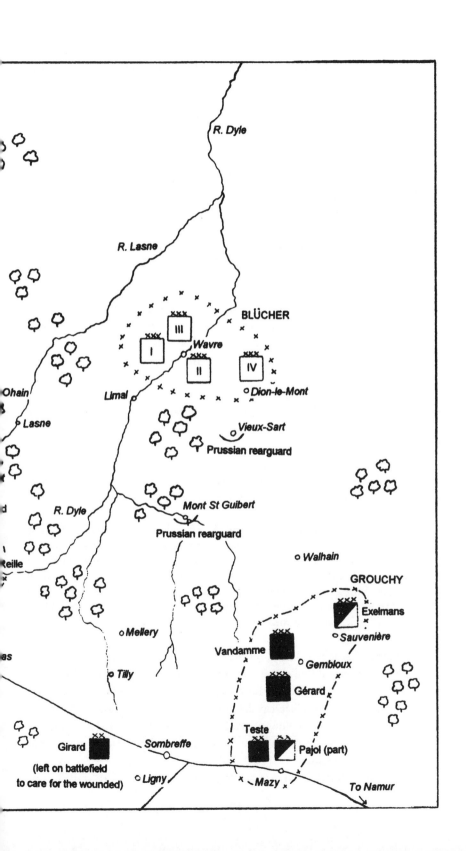

Prussian support and nothing would daunt the old warrior or make him break his word.

Wellington's rearguard had arrived from Quatre Bras at Mont St Jean at 6.00 pm in atrocious weather. Lord Uxbridge, Wellington's cavalry commander, described how he conducted the retreat along the final stages:

> The Royals, Inniskillings, and Greys manoeuvred beautifully, retiring by alternate squadrons, and skirmished in the very best style; but finding that all the efforts of the Enemy to get upon our right flank were vain, and that by manoeuvring upon the plain, which was amazingly deep and heavy from the violent storm of rain, it only uselessly exhausted the horses, I drew these Regiments in upon the *chaussée* in one column, the Guns falling back from position to position, and from these Batteries, checking the advance of the Enemy.[21]

At one stage, a staff officer called on Lieutenant-Colonel John, Earl of Portarlington, commander of the 23rd Light Dragoons, to push on past a section of the road dangerously exposed to French gunfire. The gallant earl pointedly ordered his men to walk and replied 'the 23rd Dragoons should never trot before an enemy.'[22]

Wellington himself welcomed Uxbridge's men as they arrived at the position he had selected on the shallow ridge of Mont St Jean. 'Thus ended', Uxbridge commented nonchalantly later, 'the prettiest Field Day of Cavalry and Horse Artillery that I ever witnessed.'[23]

It was 6.30 pm. To the south, Napoleon had arrived with his advanced guard. The French had suffered just as badly as their foes during the pursuit. Lieutenant Jacques Martin of the 45th Infantry of I Corps wrote that:

> A storm, such as I had never seen the like of, suddenly unleashed itself on us and on the whole region. In a few minutes the road and the plain were no more than a swamp which became still more impracticable for the storm persisted and lasted the rest of the day and the whole night. Men and horses sank into the mud up to their knees. The growing darkness prevented troops from seeing each other, battalions mingled and each soldier marched as best he could and where he could. We no longer formed an army but a real crowd.[24]

From the inn of La Belle Alliance, on the eastern edge of the main road leading to Brussels, Napoleon stared ahead through the misty, soaked atmosphere. The French 7th Hussars under Colonel Baron Marcellin de Marbot were skirmishing with the last of the English cavalry and beyond were masses of troops. Napoleon did not expect Wellington to halt. He thought he had knocked the Prussians out of the campaign and that Wellington, isolated, would scamper to England as fast as possible.

So Napoleon ordered four horse artillery batteries to open fire while Count

Edouard Milhaud's IV Cavalry Corps deployed ready to charge, in order to trick Wellington's artillery into revealing their numbers and positions. The Emperor's servant, Mameluke Ali, vividly described the scene:

> We found ourselves on high ground dominating the vast valley bordered to the north by the curtain of the Forest of Soignes. The grey horizon did not allow the naked eye to see clearly. We noticed only an English rearguard followed by some French troops on our left where from time to time some cannon-shots were being fired, of which we saw the smoke. We were at the end of the day. Shortly after the Emperor had finished examining the whole plain with his telescope, there came the flash of an immense line of fire and almost immediately afterwards the sound of guns. It was the English artillery, which showed the vast front of their army drawn up in battle order. There was only one salvo, then we heard no more than some shots fired to the left, as much by our advanced guard as by the retreating enemy rearguard.[25]

So Wellington was going to stand and fight after all. The ridge opposite the French was aglow with innumerable bivouac fires, so much so that it seemed the Forest of Soignes was on fire.

# Notes

1. A Caulaincourt, *Recollections of Caulaincourt, Duke of Vicenza* (1838), v.1, p.183
2. M. Foy, *Vie militaire* (1900), pp.269–70
3. G. Barral, *L'Epopée de Waterloo* (1895), pp.118–19
4. *Ibid*, p.127
5. *Ibid*, p.126
6. *Ibid*, p.128
7. N. Bonaparte, *Correspondance de Napoléon 1er* (1869), v.28, pp.314–15
8. G. Barral, *L'Epopée de Waterloo* (1895), p.163
9. H. de Mauduit, *Les derniers jours de la grande armée* (1848), v.2 p.101; G. Barral, *L'Epopée de Waterloo* (1895), p.142
10. M. Lemonnier-Delafosse, *Souvenirs militaires* (1850), p.363
11. R. Gibney ed., *Eighty years ago or the recollections of an old army doctor* (1896), pp.180–1
12. H. de Mauduit, *Les derniers jours de la grande armée* (1848), v.2, pp.100–1
13. *Ibid*, v.2, pp.103–4
14. *Ibid*, v.2, pp.108–9
15. A. Brett-James, *The hundred days* (1964), p.86
16. W. Siborne, *History of the Waterloo campaign* (1990), p.189
17. C. Ollech, *Geschiche des Feldzuges von 1815 nach archivalischen Quellen* (1876), pp.180–9
18. W. Siborne, *History of the Waterloo campaign* (1990), pp.174, 188
19. Strictly speaking, this written message was sent to Baron Carl von Müffling, Wellington's Prussian liaison officer; Müffling then informed Wellington of the contents of the message. See O. von Lettow-Vorbeck, *Napoleons Untergang 1815* (1904), v.1, p.365
20. Lady Elizabeth Longford (*Wellington: the years of the sword* [1972], p.444) skilfully examines the question of the precise hour at whch this message reached Wellington: at 2.00 or 6.00 am. Henri Houssaye assumed that Blücher's second message reached Wellington by 3.00 am on 18 June as he was awake at that hour to write two letters (quoted in J. Gurwood ed., *The dispatches of the Duke of Wellington* [1838], v.12, pp.476–7). Nevertheless, it can not be proven that it was the arrival of Blücher's message which woke the Duke, for Wellington had also risen at 3.00 am on 17 June.

In any case, Wellington already knew Blücher would be coming to his assistance on 18 June as he had received Blücher's previous message in the late evening of 17 June. The message which arrived either at 2.00 or 6.00 am was merely a confirmation giving more details. Wellington was certainly not waiting all night to learn whether he could stand and fight at Waterloo or whether he would have to retreat and abandon Brussels.

According to Lieutenant Henry Duperier of the 18th Hussars, Sir Hussey Vivian's hussars patrolled on the night of 17/18 June as far east as the village of Ohain, where they met a Prussian patrol. At 3.00 am a Prussian officer reached the hussars with a verbal dispatch from Blücher to Wellington. The officer was brought to Vivian and then taken to Wellington: BL Add. MSS 34, 703/90. If Duperier was correct in stating that this message was verbal not written, then Blücher clearly sent more than one message in the early hours of 18 June; the second of these – the verbal message – may have been the one which according to Lord Fitzroy Somerset arrived at 6.00 am.

21. H. Siborne ed., *The Waterloo letters* (1983), p.7
22. *Ibid*, p.96
23. *Ibid*, p.7
24. J. Martin, *Souvenirs d'un ex-officier* (1867), p.280
25. M. Ali, *Souvenirs du mameluck Ali sur l'empereur Napoléon* (1926), pp.109–10

The summit of the Lion Mound

# 2

# ON THE FIELD OF HONOUR: WATERLOO TODAY

Waterloo! Its name thunders across the ages. Its memory is evoked year after year in regimental messes. Here history was made. Here modern Europe rose out of the flames like a phoenix.

From whichever point of the compass you approach, the first you see of the battlefield today is the green Lion Mound towering over the golden cornfields. On a clear day it is visible from the top of the tower of Brussels Town Hall, eleven and three-quarter miles to the north.[1] The mound was built between 1823 and 1826 on the spot where the Dutch Prince of Orange was wounded towards 6.45 pm. The prince's father, King William I of the United Netherlands, wanted a monument to commemorate the victory over Napoleon. The size of the mound signifies the importance of the battle while the lion, symbol of both the Netherlands and Britain, rests one paw on a globe.

The lion, weighing 28 tons, was cast in nine pieces of iron and assembled on the summit.[2] Like Nelson's Column in Trafalgar Square, it defiantly faces the French. Sadly, this provoked some disgraceful incidents near the beginning of the twentieth century and one morning, local people awoke to find the pedestal had been painted in the blue, white and red of French national colours. On another occasion someone tried to explain away Napoleon's defeat by decorating the monument with a verse: 'Here treason triumphed by chance. Instead of this lion, there should be a fox.'[3] On 3 July 1919 *The Times* reported that Monsieur Pepin, a socialist deputy, had asked the Belgian Government to order the lion to be turned to the north in recognition of the French role in liberating Belgium in World War One. Twenty-seven days later the paper added that the Finance Minister had correctly rejected this proposal but had also stated incorrectly that the lion's attitude held no hostile suggestion.

Three hundred thousand cubic metres of earth were collected to construct the mound. This soil, alas, was taken from the battlefield itself, thus altering the centre of Wellington's position entirely. The Duke was not pleased. 'They have ruined my battlefield,' he exclaimed.[4] Fortunately, earth was taken only from a rough rectangle bordered by the road atop the ridge to the north, the Brussels road to the east, La Haie Sainte to the south and the mound itself to the west.

The Reverend William Falconer visited Waterloo in 1825 and described how the work on the Lion Mound disgracefully disturbed the sleep of the dead:

> A great deal of earth is of course collected from the parts close around and to serve their purpose they have lately levelled the rising ground where the Duke stood during the contest. It was about there I picked up a human rib just disturbed from its resting-place. I left it where I found it, but the next day in passing over the same ground to go to Namur it was gone; some one amongst the numerous visitors to the place more curious than myself had probably secured it as a relic.[5]

Another eyewitness dwelt on the imposing scenes occurring on the mound itself:

> There is a double carriage road winding round it, in a spiral form, and supplying an easy means of ascent for carriages to the very top; and by this road the materials have been, and are, conveyed to complete the work. In the centre is a shaft of brick-work, which has been carried up from the bottom, and is still going on. It is to be 60 feet higher than the top of the mound, making the whole height 260 feet. It is intended for a pedestal, to receive a lion, 21 feet long, and 12 feet high, which is ready to put up when the work is ready. This mound has been 18 months in hand, and is to be completed in six more, and from what has been already done, little doubt remains that it will be so. For the first twelve months 2,000 men, 600 horses, and as many carts as could be kept at work, were employed on it, and the number has only been reduced as the termination of this great undertaking approaches. At present, as the works are going on, at the top it has a pleasing appearance, from the great number of horses, carts, and people ascending and descending by the winding road.[6]

The Lion Mound is now the most famous battlefield monument in the world. When the earth mound was in danger of collapse in 1923, the Belgian Administration of Roads and Bridges immediately stepped in to save it.[7] It had become too great a tourist attraction to be allowed to fall into disrepair. On 13 April 1926 *The Times* reported that 'because of the Great War it was thought Waterloo and its memories might no longer attract. This belief has been proved to be wrong. The number of visitors to Waterloo is still as great as in pre-war days; and is even said to have increased. Cars full of foreign visitors can be seen every day making the trip from Brussels to Waterloo.'

The battlefield does not attract merely the countrymen of the victors. In 1912, a French writer asserted that 'the battlefield of Waterloo has become an almost obligatory pilgrimage for the French visiting Belgium.'[8] Seven years later the Belgian authors Jules Delhaize and Winand Aerts explained why so many Frenchmen visited the scene of Napoleon's defeat: 'there are some defeats which do not tarnish the glory of an army any more than they diminish a people. Waterloo is one of these.'[9]

Today, over 300,000 visitors climb the Lion Mound each year. Most use the two hundred and twenty-six stone steps but around 1900 one young man did successfully ride a horse up the steep grassy slope.[10]

Entrepreneurs have exploited these hordes of tourists and pilgrims by setting up a ramshackle collection of souvenir shops and cafés around the foot of the mound. You will even find a small waxworks museum containing lifesize wax models of the famous generals of the battle.

All these shops and exhibitions are interesting but you will benefit most from a visit to the new Visitors' Centre. This is one of the best improvements made to the battlefield in recent times. It enables visitors to fix in their minds the chronology of the battle and the geography of the battlefield before exploring the actual ground on foot. A dramatic audio-visual presentation uses a video-laser and a ten square metre model of the battlefield to describe the course of the fight. You then proceed into another room to watch a short film evoking the tumultuous past lying beneath the peaceful scenery of the present. The film intersperses dramatic scenes of hosts of re-enactors in Napoleonic uniforms with children playing Cowboys and Indians in the farms of the battlefield.

At the end of the audio-visual displays, climb the two hundred and twenty-six steps up the Lion Mound. You can see practically the entire battlefield from here. Most of it is still farmed by the local people and changes still occur. Efforts to preserve the battlefield for posterity were first made soon after the turn of the century by enthusiasts in Britain and Belgium. Houses were being built on the historic site and Brussels was so near that Waterloo seemed likely to be obliterated by developers and speculators. On 18 June 1913 Colonel Henry Knollys demanded in *The Times* 'will it not be a bitter pang for us if Hougoumont be cut down, razed, ploughed up, and disguised into a nursery garden with convenient adjacent piggeries?'

The result was the creation of joint British and Belgian committees to raise money to acquire the building rights on the battlefield. The Fourth Duke of Wellington and Field Marshal Earl Roberts were the joint treasurers of the fund. They appealed in *The Times* on 28 May 1914: 'is it too much to ask the British people to take such steps that their sons may not find the Field of Waterloo, the tomb of the valiant, obliterated by rows of villa residences and trim suburban avenues?'

It would have been too expensive simply to buy the field, as the Americans did step by step with their Civil War battlefield of Gettysburg. However, on 26 March 1914 a Belgian law forbade any construction or demolition within an area of 1347 acres. Nevertheless, the battlefield has been threatened several times since. In 1929 a convent was built at the eastern end of Wellington's ridge. It is still there today, as are three modern houses on the western edge of the Brussels road south of La Haie Sainte. In 1933 socialist deputies tried in vain to pass a bill to permit the construction of workmen's dwellings on the battlefield.

The most serious threat came in the early 1970s when planners tried to build a motorway across the field; they were seen off by a vigorous defence conducted by, amongst others, the Eighth Duke of Wellington and Field Marshal Sir Gerald Templer.

Thus the 1914 Protection of the Battlefield Law has helped to prevent the worst excesses of property developers and hopefully will be more rigorously enforced in future. At present, the guardians of the battlefield consist of a few amateur historical societies working independently of each other. Ideally, responsibility for the battlefield ought to lie with a professional body set up by either the Belgian Government or the European Union to preserve such historic sites. Such a body would have the authority to impose penalties on those who disregard the 1914 Law. It would also be able to co-ordinate the activities of the historical societies who are erecting monuments and memorial plaques on the battlefield.

The battlefield is small. The fate of Europe was decided in just six square miles. From the foot of the Mound, a road runs due east along a ridge to a crossroads and then on into the distance. The same road runs south-west from the Mound towards the opposite horizon. This was Wellington's front line.

In front, Wellington had three bastions on which he anchored his army. The cluster of buildings to the south-west is Hougoumont, a fortified château and farm complete, in 1815, with a wood and an orchard. Four light companies of the British 1st, 2nd and 3rd Guards plus a Nassau battalion and two hundred Hanoverians formed its initial garrison.

Immediately south of the crossroads stands the farm of La Haie Sainte, which is smaller than Hougoumont but still a formidable strongpoint. It was held by over three hundred crack soldiers of the 2nd Light battalion, King's German Legion.

Finally, 2500 metres to the east of the Mound, on Wellington's extreme left flank, a Nassau brigade held the village of Smohain and the farms of Papelotte, La Haye and Frichermont. You can distinguish Papelotte by the belvedere above its entrance gate.

In his front line Wellington stationed artillery batteries and, between Hougoumont and the crossroads, the British 1st (Guards) Division and the Anglo-German 3rd Division. East of the crossroads stood Lieutenant-General Sir Thomas Picton's British 5th Division and Major-General Count van Bij-landt's Dutch-Belgian brigade.

To the north were the reserves: infantry, Lord Uxbridge's cavalry and numerous batteries. Mont St Jean farm, 650 metres north of the crossroads, was at the centre of the reserves and served as a field hospital.

Across the valley, Napoleon's army formed up from 10.00 am. It had rained all the previous night and Napoleon had postponed the opening of the battle in the hope the ground would dry sufficiently to enable his artillery to manoeuvre more easily. Now his troops took up their battle positions in a magnificent, colourful display of might. Martial music and cheering drifted over to Wellington's awestruck troops. Lieutenant-General Count Honoré Reille's II Corps formed the French left flank and faced Hougoumont. Lieutenant-General Count Drouet d'Erlon's I Corps stood on the opposite side of the Brussels road. In between the positions of these two corps you can see the inn of La Belle Alliance.

In reserve Napoleon placed the III Cavalry Corps and the Guard heavy cavalry behind II Corps. Behind I Corps were the IV Cavalry Corps and the Guard light cavalry. On the Brussels road itself were Lieutenant-General the Count of Lobau's VI Corps and two attached light cavalry divisions and the Imperial Guard infantry and artillery.

The exact strengths of the opposing armies are unknown. Waterloo occurred on the fourth day of the 1815 campaign and nobody even at the time knew precisely how many casualties had already occurred. Historians disagree even about the strengths before the campaign opened. Nevertheless, it is clear that at Waterloo Napoleon and Wellington each had around 70,000 troops, with Napoleon probably enjoying a superiority of a few thousand. However, Wellington was seriously outgunned, possessing approximately one hundred fewer artillery pieces.[11]

Napoleon's troops were more experienced than most of Wellington's units and their devotion to their Emperor bordered on fanaticism. Nevertheless, French morale was brittle, as the troops feared betrayal by royalists intent on restoring King Louis XVIII to the French throne. In a crisis, the French army was likely to panic; it possessed elan and courage but lacked resilience.

Wellington himself had written that he had 'an infamous army'.[12] Just 30,000 of his men were British and his other troops from the Netherlands and the German states of Hanover, Brunswick and Nassau were often unsteady. Wellington could not hope to fight anything but a defensive battle; for him, Waterloo was a matter of holding out until Blücher's Prussians could arrive in ever increasing numbers to turn the tide.

The battle began at 11.30 am. Elements of the French II Corps assaulted Hougoumont. This was a diversionary attack but Wellington refused to be drawn off balance and fed in only enough reinforcements to hold off the French.

Napoleon's main attack at 2.00 pm in the eastern sector of the battlefield was preceded by a massive artillery bombardment by eighty guns. D'Erlon's I Corps marched in four enormous columns against Picton's division. In support, infantrymen contended for La Haie Sainte and Papelotte. West of the Brussels road advanced a cavalry brigade of breastplated French cuirassiers.

# THE BATTLEFIELD OF WATERLOO: 11.30 AM, 18 JUNE

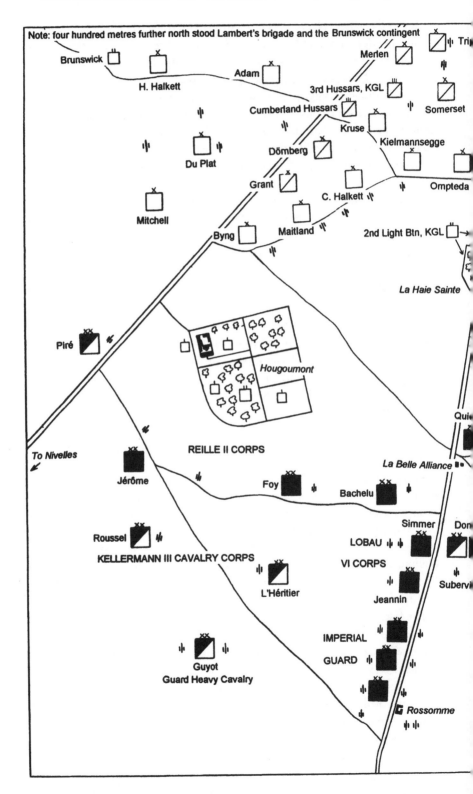

Note: four hundred metres further north stood Lambert's brigade and the Brunswick contingent

Brunswick

H. Halkett

Adam

Merlen

Tri

3rd Hussars, KGL

Somerset

Cumberland Hussars

Kruse

Du Plat

Dömberg

Kielmannsegge

Grant

C. Halkett

Ompteda

Mitchell

Byng

Maitland

2nd Light Btn, KGL

La Haie Sainte

Piré

Hougoumont

Qui

To Nivelles

REILLE II CORPS

La Belle Alliance

Jérôme

Foy

Bachelu

Roussel

Simmer

Don

LOBAU

KELLERMANN III CAVALRY CORPS

VI CORPS

Subervi

L'Héritier

Jeannin

IMPERIAL

Guyot

GUARD

Guard Heavy Cavalry

Rossomme

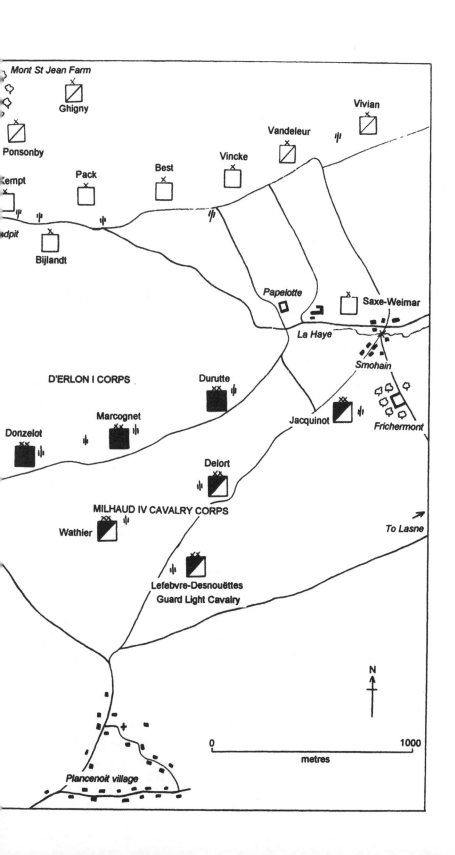

Initially d'Erlon's I Corps made progress but was then halted by musketry and cut to pieces by two heavy brigades of British cavalry. The French attack was completely repulsed, although the British horsemen charged too far and were badly mauled by French lancers.

Another French attempt to seize La Haie Sainte failed at 3.30 pm. Massed French cavalry charges and murderous artillery bombardments ensued but Wellington held out by moving up reinforcements. Fighting continued all along the line but the heaviest attacks were now falling on Wellington's centre, at either side of the location of the Lion Mound.

At 4.30 pm the first Prussians, the head of General von Bülow's IV Corps led by Blücher in person, entered the fray against Napoleon's right flank. Soon Blücher had 16,000 men in action; by 8.00 pm this figure would have increased to 40,000. The village of Plancenoit, whose church spire you can see in the distance to the south-east, was soon in flames. The French VI Corps and elements of the Guard defended the village against ferocious attacks.

La Haie Sainte finally fell at 6.30 pm, heralding an all-arms attritional attack along the whole of Wellington's front line. This caused immense losses but eventually failed.

Napoleon played his final card at 7.30 pm. His last reserve, the formidable Imperial Guard, struck Wellington's line at the foot of the Lion Mound and met with utter defeat.

Wellington then ordered a general advance which swept forward into the valley. The Prussians burst through in the east and Waterloo was over. Wellington had lost 15,000 men and Blücher 7000. The true number of French casualties will never be known but their scale was horrific. Approximately 30,000 Frenchmen were killed or wounded and another 8000 captured. Thousands more deserted after Waterloo.

Such is the outline of the battle. To discover what it was like for the soldiers who fought there, you must follow the events at ground level. Three tours are detailed below. Each explores one army's sector of the battlefield: first Wellington's side of the valley, then Napoleon's and finally Blücher's march from Wavre and the area he fought in at Waterloo.

Whether you manage to undertake all three tours will depend on the time available. However, you will gain a balanced view of the battle by touring the sectors of all three armies and those who have hitherto relied on only British, or French, or German histories will be shown fresh perspectives.

But from whichever angle you view the battlefield, it will be deceptively peaceful. 'The field of Waterloo today resembles any other stretch of country,' wrote the great French novelist Victor Hugo.[13] Yet beneath the surface lie over 10,000 dead soldiers; Waterloo is one vast graveyard.[14] Here friend and foe sleep in peace side by side until the trumpet shall awaken them on Judgement Day. Over this battlefield hangs the calm, powerful stillness of the cemetery.

But whereas the fallen of the two world wars repose beneath pristine rows of gravestones, the dead of Waterloo lie in unmarked mass graves. No reverential burial, no military honours, no last salute honoured the dead of 1815. Hurried, shabby, anonymous burial and then oblivion was their cruel fate.

Here are the dead. Beneath your feet, beneath the shimmering wheat fields gently stirring in the summer breeze, beneath the flaring red poppies, beneath the peace of today they lie. 'The very ground was hallowed,' wrote a tourist just one month after the battle, 'and it was trod by us with respect and gratitude.'[15]

In contrast to today, the horror was readily apparent in the weeks immediately after the battle. Miss Charlotte Waldie recalled how she followed a long line of burial pits:

> The effluvia which arose from them, even beneath the open canopy of heaven, was horrible; and the pure west wind of summer, as it passed us, seemed pestiferous, so deadly was the smell that in many places pervaded the field. The fresh-turned clay which covered those pits betrayed how recent had been their formation. From one of them the scanty clods of earth which had covered it had in one place fallen, and the skeleton of a human face was visible. I turned from the spot in indescribable horror, and with a sensation of deadly faintness which I could scarcely overcome.[16]

The slaughter sickened even hardened soldiers. A British tourist, Captain William Frye, visited the battlefield on 22 June, 'but on arrival there the sight was too horrible to behold. I felt sick in the stomach and was obliged to return. The multitude of carcases, the heaps of wounded men with mangled limbs unable to move, and perishing from not having their wounds dressed or from hunger ... formed a spectacle I shall never forget.'[17]

Even those who had fought in the battle were appalled afterwards. In the early hours of 19 June, Captain Alexander Cavalié Mercer, commander of 'G' Troop, Royal Horse Artillery, awoke from a doze to find the battlefield bathed in an eerie moonlight:

> The night was serene and pretty clear; a few light clouds occasionally passing across the moon's disc, and throwing objects into transient obscurity, added considerably to the solemnity of the scene. Oh, it was a thrilling sensation thus to stand in the silent hour of the night and contemplate that field – all day long the theatre of noise and strife, now so calm and still – the actors prostrate on the bloody soil, their pale wan faces upturned to the moon's cold beams, which caps and breastplates, and a thousand other things, reflected back in brilliant pencils of light from as many different points!
>
> Here and there some poor wretch, sitting up amidst the countless dead, busied himself in endeavours to staunch the flowing stream with which his life was fast ebbing away. Many whom I saw so employed that night were, when morning dawned, lying stiff and tranquil as those who had departed earlier.

From time to time a figure would half raise itself from the ground, and then, with a despairing groan, fall back again. Others, slowly and painfully rising, stronger, or having less deadly hurt, would stagger away with uncertain steps across the field in search of succour. Many of these I followed with my gaze until lost in the obscurity of distance; but many, alas! after staggering a few paces, would sink again on the ground, probably to rise no more. It was heart-rending – and yet I gazed![18]

Sergeant Tom Morris of the British 73rd Foot was prowling nearby in search of water to quench his raging thirst:

By the light of the moon I picked my way among the bodies of my sleeping, as well as of my dead comrades; but the horrors of the scene created such a terror in my mind, that I could not muster courage to go by myself, and was turning back to take my brother along with me, when on passing where a horse was lying dead on its side, and a man sitting upright with his back against the horse's body, I thought I heard the man call to me, and the hope that I could render him some assistance overcame my terror. I went towards him, and placing my left hand on his shoulder, attempted to lift him up with my right; my hand, however, passed through his body, and I then saw that both he and his horse had been killed by a cannonball.[19]

A cannon-shot had torn away the back of the head of Driver Crammond of 'G' Troop, Royal Horse Artillery. Only his face remained; his eyes stared at his surviving comrades and drove them to distraction.[20] Elsewhere a British officer was startled to find a motionless French drummer propped up against some corpses and watching his every move. The officer's hair began to creep; he moved away and then approached the drummer from the side. It was only then that the officer found the man had been killed by a musket-ball; he later admitted that 'the whole incident discomposed me more than the fighting we had been engaged in the day before. It was the weakness which usually follows excitement.'[21]

Lieutenant Frederick Pattison of the 33rd Foot came across a French gunner sitting against a wheel of a broken gun carriage. The gunner was bare-headed and 'his large blue eyes seemed fixed on me, and wore even in death a living expression. His right hand was raised as if under great excitement, and for a second I imagined him to be yet alive, and in the act of enthusiastically exclaiming, "Vive l'Empereur".'

Lieutenant Pattison passed on:

In further examination of the dead, who were scattered over the field like sheathes cut down by the hand of the reaper, I was struck with the diversity of expression still lingering on the countenances of those around me. From the distortion of their faces ... many of them must have had a terrible struggle 'with the king of terrors;' others, from the placidity of their expression, seemed as if they had sunk into refreshing slumber. The separation between soul and body in their case must have been instantaneous.[22]

Captain William Tomkinson of the 16th Light Dragoons likened the forward slope of the ridge between Hougoumont and La Haie Sainte to the breach of a fortress carried by assault.[23] The same image occurred to Major Harry Smith:

I had been over many a field of battle, but with the exception of one spot at New Orleans, and the breach of Badajos, I had never seen anything to be compared with what I saw. At Waterloo the whole field from right to left was a mass of dead bodies. In one spot, to the right of La Haye Sainte, the French Cuirassiers were literally piled on each other; many soldiers not wounded lying under their horses; others, fearfully wounded, occasionally with their horses struggling upon their wounded bodies. The sight was sickening, and I had no means or power to assist them.[24]

Lieutenant Edmund Wheatley found a dead soldier at the edge of the Brussels high road: 'his head, his hands and knees, bent up to his chest, were forced into the mud and he looked like a frog thrusting itself into the slimy puddle.' A short distance away, an enormous cuirassier lay face down in a pool of his own blood.[25] Looters were at work and amassed fortunes from the money, jewels, uniforms and weapons they stole. They even extracted the teeth from corpses for use in dentures. False teeth would be known for years as Waterloo teeth.[26] A Belgian woman cut off the fingers of a wounded Prussian officer in her haste to gain the rings he wore, while a Prussian looter had earlier tried to snatch something from a wounded British ensign.[27] The young ensign protested that it was a present from his mother but the Prussian stabbed him to death. Soon corpses exposed to the sun turned black and swelled up. The stench of decomposing flesh was unbearable.

Waterloo was one vast, human tragedy. Nothing conveys the intense suffering and piercing sense of loss more than the countless scraps of paper littering the battlefield immediately after the fight. One letter picked up from the ground began 'my dear husband'. Another was addressed to a French soldier: 'mon cher fils', my dear son. The father regretted his son had been unable to obtain his discharge but looked forward to embracing him again.[28] Elsewhere lay a notebook given by 'Alexandrine to her Auguste.' Inside, she had written, 'I love you, I love you always.'[29]

Those who sleep beneath the cornfields died in the midst of strife. They choked on blood, screamed in agony, sobbed in fear. The last sounds they heard were the mournful wailing of bagpipes, the intense rattling of drums, the awful crash of musketry. Now they sleep in peace.

They have no splendid, prestigious grave, nor even a simple wooden cross. A few are honoured by monuments but most are unknown, unrecognised, unheeded by the tourists who pass by today. This book is written as a tribute to these ordinary men, boys and women who made the supreme sacrifice at Waterloo.[30]

# Notes

1. G. Barral, *Itinéraire illustré de l'épopée de Waterloo* (1896), p.56, which is confirmed by the Belgian guidebooks published by Ward, Lock and Co. at the turn of the century. The Lion Mound used to be visible from trains between Groenendael and La Hulpe stations, over five miles to the north-east: L. Navez, *Le champ de bataille et le pays de Waterloo en 1815 et actuellement* (1908), p.27

2. J. Logie, *Waterloo: l'évitable défaite* (1989), p.124

3. L. van Neck, *Waterloo illustré* (1903), pp.202–3

4. W. Fraser, *The Waterloo Ball* (1897), p.50

5. *The Times*, 28 June 1937

6. *The Times*, 28 October 1825

7. *The Times*, 20 July 1923

8. Anon, *A propos du champ de bataille de Waterloo* (1912), p.9

9. J. Delhaize and W. Aerts, *Waterloo: études relatives à la campagne de 1815 en Belgique* (1915) [actually published in 1919]

10. L. van Neck, *Waterloo illustré* (1903), p.202

11. Many historians have given more precise statistics and some have even confidently specified the exact numbers down to the last man. However, such figures are impossible to prove and are not wholly relevant. Napoleon probably had 266 guns and Wellington about 161 guns.

12. E. Longford, *Wellington: the years of the sword* (1972), p.402

13. V. Hugo, *Les Misérables* (1985), p.316

14. H. Bernard, *Le duc de Wellington et la Belgique* (1983), p.240; another 3000 or 4000 soldiers were mortally wounded: J. Logie et al., *L'Europe face à Napoléon* (1990), p.143

15. J. Simpson, *A visit to Flanders in July 1815* (1816), p.80

16. C. Eaton, *Waterloo Days* (1888), pp.130–1

17. W. Frye, *After Waterloo. Reminiscences of European travel 1815–1819* (1908), p.27

18. C. Mercer, *Journal of the Waterloo campaign* (1985), pp.182–3

19. T. Morris, *Recollections of military service in 1813, 1814, and 1815* (1845), p.157

20. C. Mercer, *Journal of the Waterloo campaign* (1985), p.185

21. Anon, 'Operations of the Fifth or Picton's Division in the campaign of Waterloo', in *United Service Magazine* (June 1841)

22. F. Pattison, *Personal recollections of the Waterloo campaign* (1870), pp.39–40

23. W. Tomkinson, *The diary of a cavalry officer in the Peninsular and Waterloo campaigns 1809–15* (1894), p.316

24. G. Moore Smith ed., *The autobiography of Sir Harry Smith* (1910), p.275

25. C. Hibbert ed., *The Wheatley diary* (1964), p.72

26. D. Howarth, *A near run thing* (1968), p.207

27. C. Dalton, *The Waterloo roll call* (1978), p.278

28. *The Times*, 4 Jan 1890

29. E. Longford, *Wellington: pillar of state* (1972), p.5

30. Some British soldiers described finding dead Frenchwomen on the battlefield. For instance, Volunteer Charles Smith of the 1st battalion, 95th Rifles, was helping to bury the dead on 19 June when he found a dead young Frenchwoman dressed in an officer's uniform (G. Moore Smith ed., *The autobiography of Sir Harry Smith* [1910], p.279). See also H. Ross-Lewin, *With the Thirty-Second in the Peninsular and other campaigns* (1904), p.273: 'after the attack was repulsed two Frenchwomen were found dead on the field. I saw one of them; she was dressed in a nankeen jacket and trousers, and had been killed by a ball which had passed through her head.' Marie Tête-du-bois, a cantinière with the 1st Grenadiers of Napoleon's Guard, was another female casualty of Waterloo (H. Lachouque, *The anatomy of glory* [1961], p.483).

# PART TWO: WELLINGTON'S SECTOR

# 3

# MORNING 18 JUNE: FROM
# WATERLOO TO THE FRONT LINE

Start your tour of Wellington's sector of the battlefield in the town of Waterloo, two and a half miles north of the battlefield. At the centre of Waterloo, you will find the Wellington museum on the eastern edge of the Brussels road opposite the domed church. The museum is in an inn which had been built in 1705 and where Wellington established his headquarters for the nights before and after the battle. In *The Times* of 22 August 1890, Sir William Fraser, son of a Waterloo veteran, announced that 'the little inn at Waterloo ... where the Duke slept before and after the conflict is, after being for many years lived in by a recluse and shut to the world, again open ... I hope that the Hotel Wellington may entertain many generations of visitors.' It certainly has.

The building came under threat in the 1950s; the then owners wished to sell it and the site seemed set to become a petrol station. There was even talk of Wellington's inn being rebuilt stone by stone in the United States of America. Fortunately, the late Count Jacques-Henri Pirenne founded the Friends of the Wellington Museum in 1954 and launched a determined campaign to save the building. As a result, in 1958 the Belgian State joined with the Province of Brabant and the Municipality of Waterloo to buy the house. The preservation of the museum was confirmed in 1981 when it became a listed building.[1]

The relics and displays in the museum provide the visitor with a first-rate visual understanding of Waterloo. A set of illuminated maps contains some minor errors but sets out the phases of the battle well. The tourist will do well to study them deeply before walking over the battlefield. Recently, a museum curator, Lucien Gerke, set up a section to describe the local history of Waterloo from prehistoric to modern times; one of the exhibits is a map showing the scores of places worldwide named after the battle.

Among the relics you will see is the table on which Wellington began his victory despatch a little after 3.30 am on 19 June.[2] He finished it later that day at Brussels. Many who fought at the battle, and also several historians, later criticised the despatch for not praising deserving individuals sufficiently. Instead, they had to be content with: 'the army never, upon any occasion, conducted itself better. The division of Guards ... set an example which was followed by all; and there is no officer nor description of troops that did not behave well.'

The Duke was terse at the best of times and can hardly be blamed for not writing more when so emotionally and physically drained by the terrible whirlwind campaign. He was also suffering from the trauma of losing so many close friends and of realising how nearly he had lost his own life in the battle. 'The hand of Almighty God has been upon me this day,' he exclaimed when realising how few of his staff had survived the maelstrom of fire unhurt.[3] Besides, he had a host of other matters to attend to, including refitting his mauled army and setting it on the march to Paris. The Waterloo despatch was balanced, to the point and noble in its modesty. Miss Charlotte Waldie, an Englishwoman who visited the battlefield in July 1815, pointed out that perhaps only one victory despatch was conciser than Wellington's. However, Julius Caesar's 'I came, I saw, I conquered' was not so unassuming.[4]

Wellington handed his completed despatch to his ADC, Major Henry Percy, to convey to England, and Percy placed it in a purple sachet given him by a lady at the Duchess of Richmond's Ball on 15 June. The Ball had been cut short as British officers hurried to join their units and march to check Napoleon's invasion. Ironically, when Percy reached London on the evening of 21 June, he interrupted another Ball. He had already informed the British cabinet of the victory and now he drew up in his carriage in St James's Square where the Prince Regent was attending Mr and Mrs Edmund Boehm's Ball. Dashing upstairs, Percy laid the two French eagle standards captured in the campaign at the Prince's feet and announced, 'Victory, Sir! Victory!' All the assembled guests immediately deserted their hosts and rushed to the Foreign Office or Horse Guards to learn whether their relatives were casualties. The Prince Regent had hysterics and had to be revived with first water and then wine thrown in his face.

Another of the relics you can see in the museum is the bed in which Wellington's mortally wounded ADC, Colonel Sir Alexander Gordon, died on the night following the battle. In 1817 his family erected a stone column to his memory between La Haie Sainte and the crossroads. In fact, Gordon had been further west, near the present location of the Lion Mound, when his thigh was shattered as he helped the Duke rally Brunswick infantry towards 6.30 pm.[5]

Dr John Hume amputated Gordon's leg on the battlefield and at first recovery seemed likely. At 10.00 pm Wellington returned to his headquarters after the battle to find Gordon there. 'Thank God you are safe', the wounded man exclaimed and before he lost consciousness he heard Wellington inform him of the victory.[6] Gordon died unexpectedly in Hume's arms at 3.30 am and the doctor deliberated whether to disturb the Duke immediately:

I decided to see if he was awake; and going up stairs to his room, I tapped gently at the door, when he told me to come in. He had, as usual, taken off all his clothes, but had not washed himself; and as I entered the room he sat up in his bed, his face covered with the dust and sweat of the previous day, and extended his hand to me, which I took and held in mine, whilst I told him of Gordon's death, and related such of the casualties as had come to my knowledge. He was much affected. I felt his tears dropping fast upon my hands, and looking towards him, saw them chasing one another in furrows over his dusty cheeks. He brushed them suddenly away with his left hand, and said to me, in a voice tremulous with emotion, 'Well, thank God! I don't know what it is to lose a battle, but certainly nothing can be more painful than to gain one with the loss of so many of one's friends.'[7]

The garden behind the museum contains several tombstones of British officers, including Major Arthur Heyland, commander of the 40th Foot and Lieutenant-Colonel Sir Henry Ellis, of the 23rd Royal Welsh Fusiliers. You will also find a small tomb which used to contain the amputated leg of Lord Uxbridge, Wellington's cavalry commander.

Uxbridge was wounded by one of the last French cannon-shots of the battle, as he was riding with the victorious Wellington into the valley. According to legend, Uxbridge promptly exclaimed, 'By God, sir, I've lost my leg!' Wellington is said to have glanced down, murmured 'By God, sir, so you have', and resumed his calm scrutiny of the French dispositions through his telescope. This is probably a myth that arose out of Wellington's supposed coldness towards Uxbridge who, in 1809, had eloped with the Duke's sister-in-law. In fact Wellington had laughed off the affair. At Waterloo, he supported his wounded cavalry chief until some Hanoverians arrived to carry Uxbridge off the field. The two old warriors remained firm friends until Wellington's death in 1852.

Uxbridge's leg was amputated in the house of Monsieur Hyacinthe Paris, at 214 Chaussée de Bruxelles. The gallant earl made no sound during the excruciatingly painful operation except to remark that the saw was not very sharp. Anaesthetics were yet to make their appearance in the realm of medicine, yet the doctors noted Uxbridge's nerves and pulse were unshaken.

'I have had a pretty long run,' he remarked afterwards. 'I have been a beau these forty-seven years and it would not be fair to cut the young men out any longer.'[8] Uxbridge's courage impressed two people especially. England's Prince Regent created him Marquis of Anglesey while Monsieur Paris placed the amputated limb in a tomb in his garden with a flowery inscription. An English visitor is said to have scribbled another couple of lines: 'Here lies the Marquis of Anglesey's limb; The Devil will have the remainder of him.'[9] Another version reads: 'Here lies the Marquis of Anglesey's leg; Pray for the rest of his body, I beg.'[10] The tomb was transferred to the grounds of the Wellington Museum in March 1991 as it was impossible to preserve it in its original location.[11]

Directly opposite the museum is the domed Royal Chapel, built by the Spanish Governor General of the Low Countries in the vain hope that King Charles II of Spain would produce an heir. It was consecrated in 1690. Pass through the chapel and enter the adjoining Church of St Joseph. This church was greatly extended after the battle and reached its present dimensions only in the 1850s. Inside the church, the walls bear dozens of emotionally moving memorial tablets. Most of them are to British officers but others are to Netherlanders. Another, added in 1989, is dedicated to the memory of the slain soldiers of the French Army.

These plaques, like the pristine rows of gravestones at Normandy or Ypres, are silent yet powerful reminders of the waste and suffering of war. They tell, too, of sublime heroism and sacrifice. The grief of relatives and comrades is recorded in gratitude and dignity. All the tablets echo the thoughts of Miss Charlotte Waldie, who visited the battlefield in July 1815 and wept that: 'alas! those for whom I mourned sleep in death – and in vain for them are the tears, the praise, or the gratitude of their country: but though their bodies may moulder in the tomb, and their ashes, mingled with the dust, be scattered unnoticed by the winds of winter, their names and deeds shall never perish – they shall live for ever in the remembrance of their country.'[12]

A story lies behind each of these tablets. For instance, read the inscription on the first one to the right of the entrance, to the three slain officers of the 15th Hussars, including young Lieutenant Henry Buckley. Assistant-Surgeon William Gibney of the regiment recounted in later years how he discovered the dying lieutenant in the village of Waterloo, not far from where you are standing:

> To my great grief, I came across my dear young friend, Lieutenant Buckley of my regiment. He had received a bullet wound in the stomach, the missile had passed through his liver and came out through his back causing great haemorrhage. I hurriedly dressed the wound and gave him all the hopes possible, but did not conceal my misgivings. It was a melancholy sight to find a youth of his age, perhaps nineteen or twenty, cut off in the very opening of life, and this his first battle. He had done his duty, and acted as bravely as the oldest soldier, and now dying, he behaved and spoke as became a Christian.[13]

Another plaque commemorates Lieutenant William Robe of 'H' Troop, Royal Horse Artillery. He was only twenty-four years old but Waterloo was his thirty-third action. A fellow artillery officer wrote to Lieutenant Robe's father that:

> As to the fall of your son, and my esteemed friend, I can only say that few young men have left this life more sincerely regretted, and his exertions on the 18th will ever endear his memory to all who witnessed his noble conduct on that

day ... About five o'clock on the 18th your son received a mortal wound, and about the same time the following day he died at the village of Waterloo, after twice having taken leave of me in the most friendly and affectionate manner. I was too ill to ask him any questions; indeed, I was so distressed when I saw him at his last moments, that I could only shake him by the hand, and in the course of a few minutes he expired. His remains were interred in a beautiful spot of ground in the village of Waterloo, where I intend to raise a monument to his memory.[14]

Three fallen officers of the 1st (King's) Dragoon Guards are also remembered, including the regimental commander, Lieutenant-Colonel William Fuller, and Major John Bringhurst. The third officer, Captain George Battersby, was only twenty-five and fell in the final clashes of the battle. The regiment also lost Captain Henry Graham, Lieutenants Francis Brooke and Thomas Shelver and Cornet the Hon. Henry Bernard. Except for Bernard, whose body could not be found, all these officers were buried in a common grave near the western wall of La Haie Sainte. A survivor of the battle, Lieutenant John Hibbert, lamented that the best officers had been killed and that the regiment would never be the same again.[15]

Grieving brothers and sisters placed a tablet in the chapel to Alexander Hay, Esquire of Nunraw, who fell gloriously as an eighteen-year-old cornet in the 16th Light Dragoons. He is known to have died on the French side of the valley in the evening but his body was never found.[16]

The plaque sacred to the memory of the fallen officers and men of the 30th Foot evokes scenes of intense carnage. Ensign Edward Macready was one of the regiment's lucky survivors and recalled how the 30th and 73rd Foot recoiled in disorder during the French Guard attack in the evening of Waterloo:

> The cries from men struck down, as well as from the numerous wounded on all sides of us, who thought themselves abandoned, were terrible. An extraordinary number of men and officers of both regiments went down almost in no time. [Lieutenant Edmund] Prendergast of ours was shattered to pieces by a shell; [Captain Alexander] McNab killed by grape-shot, and [Ensigns John] James and [James] Bullen lost all their legs by round-shot.[17]

Major Thomas Walker Chambers of the 30th Foot fell, tragically, to one of the very last shots of the battle. He was standing in a small cluster of British officers, who were congratulating each other on the achievements of the day and speculating on their promotion prospects. One of these officers, Lieutenant Frederick Pattison of the 33rd Foot, recalled how Major Chambers expected to be made a lieutenant-colonel:

> We all acquiesced in this, and congratulated him on his anticipated promotion. While engaged in this social conversation, our attention was directed to

some desultory firing going on in front. A few shots having passed close by us (in passing they made a sharp whistling noise), I quitted my friends saying, 'I will go and see what those fellows are about.' On getting to a rising ground close to the circle [of officers] I had just quitted, I saw a few straggling skirmishers firing towards the Brigade. On a shot passing close to my left, I involuntarily turned round, when I saw poor Chambers leave his friends, advance towards me, put his hand to his breast, and immediately expire. This sad event was the cause of great regret, as Chambers was much liked and respected in his Regiment and by all who knew him.[18]

Another memorial plaque is dedicated to the slain officers of the British and King's German Legion artillery. Among the names is that of Captain Samuel Bolton, commander of a foot artillery battery. Lieutenant William Sharpin vividly recalled Bolton's death during Napoleon's Middle Guard attack in the evening:

> Captain Bolton at the time he was killed was on horseback. I was standing on his left side with my hand on his stirrup talking with him. The shot from a French Battery at that time flew very thick amongst us, and one passed between me and Bolton, upon which he coolly remarked that he thought we had passed the greatest danger for that day; but scarcely were the words uttered before another ball, which I saw strike the ground a little in front of us, hit him in the left breast. The shot having first severely wounded the horse in the left shoulder caused the animal to stagger backwards, thereby preventing my catching poor Bolton as he fell from his horse.[19]

The same plaque commemorates the renowned Major William Norman Ramsay, who was slain in command of 'H' Troop, Royal Horse Artillery. He was the hero of the horse artillery for his exploit at the Battle of Fuentes d'Onoro on 5 May 1811 during the Peninsular war. Finding himself cut off, Ramsay had led his guns in a desperate charge through French cavalry to safety. At Waterloo, a fatal shot cruelly terminated this brilliant career; Sir Augustus Frazer, the commander of the Royal Horse Artillery, described how, 'in a momentary lull of the fire, I buried my friend Ramsay, from whose body I took the portrait of his wife, which he always carried next [to] his heart. Not a man assisted at the funeral who did not shed tears. Hardly had I cut from his head the hair which I enclose, and laid his yet warm body in the grave, when our convulsive sobs were stifled by the necessity of returning to renew the struggle.'[20] Three weeks later, Ramsay's remains were disinterred from the battlefield and later laid to rest near Edinburgh, at Inveresk churchyard in Midlothian.

Lieutenant-Colonel Charles Canning, one of Wellington's ADCs, died in the square formed by the British 30th and 73rd Foot. His only concern was for the safety of the Duke. Lieutenant-Colonel Dawson Kelly of the staff described how

'I found Colonel Canning in the greatest possible agony. He had received a musket shot in the centre of the abdomen, and, although perfectly collected, he could hardly articulate from pain. We raised him, however, to a sitting position by placing knapsacks round him, but a few minutes terminated his existence.'[21]

Among those who fell in the 3rd battalion of the 1st (Royal Scots) Regiment of Foot was Ensign James Grant Kennedy, who was killed while carrying his regiment's King's Colour. He was only sixteen. He was wounded once but continued to advance until struck again, this time mortally. A sergeant of the Royal Scots tried to take the Colour but even in death the ensign refused to relax his grip on the flag pole. The sergeant lifted both the corpse and Colour on to his shoulder and carried his precious burden back to the regiment. According to regimental tradition, a French officer gallantly ordered his men to cease firing until the sergeant regained safety.[22] One of James Kennedy's fellow ensigns, Alexander Robertson, was also slain. His brother, Lieutenant John Robertson, had died during the Peninsular war and the grief-striken mother and sisters of the two brothers were granted pensions. The Royal Scots still treasure a snuff box made from the metal plates taken from the cross belts of the regiment's officers killed at Quatre Bras.[23]

The tablet to the officers of the 33rd Foot is especially poignant. Lieutenant Basil Jackson of the Royal Staff Corps described how he was on the battlefield of Quatre Bras on the morning of 17 June, shortly before Wellington commenced his retreat to his Waterloo position:

My attention being attracted by a group of persons near the wood of Bossu, I crossed over to see what they were about. On getting near I recognised the red facings [collars and cuffs] of the 33rd, and having some acquaintances in that regiment, I at once rode up to the party, and became witness of a most affecting and impressive scene. On the ground was extended the tall form of a departed comrade, covered by his military cloak, around which were standing, bareheaded, three or four officers; two soldiers were leaning on their spades, wherewith a shallow grave had been dug. One of the officers was endeavouring, in broken accents, to read our beautiful Burial Service, another, ... [Captain Ralph] Gore, stood motionless as a statue, with eye fixed on the cloaked mass at his feet; young [Lieutenant Thomas] Haigh, a boy of eighteen summers, was crying like a child; even the hardy soldiers were powerfully affected.

I needed not to be told whose body lay shrouded by the mantle; its length – the mourners – their grief – all told the tale but too plainly. Throwing myself from my horse, I too became a mourner. When the reader ceased I cast an inquiring look towards Haigh, who, stooping, drew back from the corpse a portion of its covering, and, as I expected, disclosed to my gaze the pale and beautifully chiselled features of [Lieutenant] Arthur Gore. Poor fellow! But two short weeks before, chancing to pass through a village in which the 33rd lay cantoned, I there fell in with my old and valued Marlow acquaintance, one of the finest and handsomest samples of British youth in the Service. That evening we had a joyous and harmless carouse; we were all old Marlow men, the eldest of whom was scarcely twenty, who only three years before, were contending at foot-ball in the college field ...

What must have been the anguish of that fine lad's mother, when the sad tidings reached her, that all her fond hopes had thus been nipped in the bud! I waited to see the last shovel-full of earth piled over his remains, dropped a tear upon the grave, and departed.[24]

Young Lieutenant Thomas Haigh's awakening to the harsh realities of war was all the more brutal in that his brother, Captain John Haigh, had also fallen in action at Quatre Bras. Lieutenant Frederick Pattison described how Captain Haigh was encouraging the soldiers of the 33rd:

The words were vibrating on his lips, when a cannonball hit him on the abdomen, and cut him nearly in twain. He fell on his back; the separation between soul and body was most appalling. His eyes strained as if they would leap from their sockets, and the quiver of the lip with the strong convulsion of his whole frame, showed unquestionably how unwilling his spirit was to be driven in this ruthless way from her clay tenement. His poor brother who was standing by was thrown into a terrible state of grief and anguish. Expressing his feelings by the wringing of his hands, and, shedding a flood of tears over the lifeless body, he cried aloud with a bitter lamentation, 'Oh! my brother; Oh! my poor brother; my dear brother! Alas! alas! my poor old father!' Were I to live a thousand years this scene could never be effaced from my mind.[25]

Sadly, Lieutenant Thomas Haigh was shot through the neck at Waterloo and died on 19 June. The 33rd lost four other officers in the campaign. Lieutenant John Boyce died at Quatre Bras, shortly after telling a friend, 'Pat, I feel certain I shall be killed.' At Waterloo, the 33rd were lying down to shelter from the French artillery fire when a missile, probably a fragment of a shell, killed Lieutenant James Hart instantly. Henry Buck and John Cameron both fell during the French Guard attack in the evening of 18 June.[26] The Duke of Wellington had commanded the 33rd for nearly ten years from 1793 and shortly after his death in 1852 the 33rd was designated The Duke of Wellington's Regiment. Its present Colonel-in-chief is the Eighth Duke.

One memorial lists the Netherlands officers killed at Waterloo and at Quatre Bras. Among them is Lieutenant A. Hardt of the 1st battalion, 2nd Nassau Infantry. Wounded at Hougoumont farm, Lieutenant Hardt perished tragically in the inferno started by French howitzer shells.[27]

Captain Count Camille Duchastel de la Howarderie of the 8th (Belgian) Hussars came from an ancient noble family and was killed by a cannon-ball which struck his chest late in the evening of 18 June. His two brothers, Counts Adolphe and Albéric, also served in the Belgian cavalry at Waterloo but survived. Lieutenant-Colonel Coenegracht, commander of the 1st (Dutch)

Carabiniers, died from wounds received in the battle and the commander of the 3rd (Dutch) Carabiniers, Lieutenant-Colonel Lechleitner, also fell in action. Another noteworthy casualty of Waterloo was the commander of the 3rd battalion, 2nd Nassau Infantry, Major Hechmann, who was mortally wounded by a French cannon-ball early in the battle.

Also listed on the Netherlands memorial is 1st Lieutenant Baron van Haren. A separate plaque records that he served as adjutant to Major-General Count van Bijlandt and died at Waterloo just three days short of his twenty-second birthday. Baron Henri-Georges Perponcher, commander of the 2nd Dutch-Belgian Division, recorded that: 'I particularly deplore the loss of the First Lieutenant of the general staff, van Haren, a young man who had joined the army as a volunteer and gave the fairest promise; he was struck by a cannonball whilst in the act of executing a manoeuvre.'[28] Lieutenant van Haren's father had similarly made the supreme sacrifice on 18 September 1793.[29]

Leave the cool interior of the church, and return under the dome of the chapel, past the marble bust of the Duke of Wellington, down the steps and on to the busy Brussels highroad outside. Turn right and you will be walking south towards the battlefield of Waterloo. The field is two and a half miles away. On 18 June 1815, the Brussels road was a *via dolorosa* indeed. Assistant-Surgeon William Gibney was horrified:

> Nothing could exceed the misery exhibited on this road, which, being the highpave, or I might say the stone causeway leading to Brussels, was crowded to excess with our wounded and French prisoners, shot and shell meanwhile pouring into them. The hardest heart must have recoiled from this scene of horror; wounded men being rewounded, many of whom had received previously the most frightful injuries. Here a man with an arm suspended only by a single muscle, another with his head horribly mangled by a sabre cut, or one with half his face shot away, received fresh damage.[30]

For weeks after the battle, all along the road tourists found skeletons of unburied horses, scattered remains of uniforms, swords, belts and other relics. Most of these items had belonged to wounded soldiers being transported north out of the fighting in waggons. Many men died along the route; their bodies were thrown out to lessen the crush inside.[31]

During the battle, the road was crammed not just with wounded but by deserters who had found the firing line too hot for their liking. An entire regiment of Hanoverian cavalry, the Duke of Cumberland's Hussars, fled the field *en masse* and spread panic all the way to Brussels by falsely announcing that Napoleon had won.

Then there were the shell-shocked men produced by every battle. Captain William Verner of the 7th Hussars remembered a lifeguardsman, far from the front line, who repeatedly fired off his carbine. This added to the woes of the physically injured, whose horses continually jerked in terror as they bore their injured riders along the painful twelve miles of road to Brussels.[32]

As you approach the battlefield from the north, you will soon see the Lion Mound. You pass through the village of Mont St Jean which, although a full thousand metres north of the front line, had its share of the horrors of war. A British staff officer, Lieutenant Basil Jackson, wrote:

> Death in every varied form had by this time become so familiar to my sight that I scarce noticed the bodies which lay in my path; nevertheless I can well remember feeling rather a sickening sensation on perceiving the remains of a Brunswick soldier, apparently those of quite a lad, lying partially buried in mire on the high road close to the houses of Mont St Jean. A heavy wheel had passed over the head and crushed it flat, leaving the brains scattered about. No person thought it worth while to pull the body aside, any more than one would think of withdrawing a dead cat or dog from the street.[33]

Just after passing through the village of Mont St Jean, you find Mont St Jean farm on the east of the road, 650 metres north of Wellington's front line. Surgeons were at work at various points to the rear of the army, and after the battle wounded men were tended practically everywhere. Even the Church of St Etienne at Braine-l'Alleud, one and a quarter miles west of the battlefield, served as a hospital. On the exterior wall of the church, at the foot of the tower, a plaque records that 'this church served as a hospital on the day after the battle of 18 June 1815. The inhabitants of Braine-l'Alleud kindly came to help the wounded.' Inside the tower, the same words adjoin a bas-relief depicting Simon Cyrene helping Jesus bear his cross.

However, Mont St Jean farm was the most important field hospital. A plaque on the wall to the right of the entrance gate records:

> In memory of Deputy Inspector Gunning, principal medical officer of the 1st Corps, the surgeons and other members of the field hospital which was established in this farm to care for the wounded of the battlefield 18th June 1815. This tablet was erected in 1981 by the Royal Army Medical Corps.

The farm was originally owned by the Hospitallers, a military order of Christian warriors, but was almost entirely rebuilt in 1778. In spite of its historical significance, it was threatened briefly with demolition in 1906.[34] Twenty years later, its entrance gateway tower was knocked down but then rebuilt using the old stones and bricks.[35] In 1992 the tower, shaken by an earthquake, was again demolished; hopefully it will soon be restored.

No farm can have been the scene of such intense human suffering as that of Mont St Jean. Wounded men poured in to receive preliminary treatment before they set off again further north to Waterloo or Brussels. Lieutenant George

Simmons of the 95th Rifles was treated at the farm: 'a good friend of mine [Assistant-Surgeon James Robson], instantly came to examine my wound. My breast was dreadfully swelled. He made a deep cut under the right pap, and dislodged from the breast-bone a musket-ball. I was suffocating with the injury my lungs had sustained.'[36]

Medical knowledge was primitive in 1815 and the usual practice was to drain blood from the wounded man. Not surprisingly, immediately after Lieutenant Simmons received this treatment, he recalled, 'I now began to feel my miseries.' In a field hospital of today he would receive a blood transfusion.

So chaotic was the situation that the surgeons at Mont St Jean fully expected the French to break through at any moment. Cannon-balls were already hitting the farm. So those wounded who could be moved were immediately evacuated to safety further north. Legend says that one of the few people to remain voluntarily was the farmer's wife who insisted on staying to guard her chickens.

Lieutenant Simmons demanded that a hospital sergeant tell him if he was going to be left at the farm. A fellow rifleman, Lieutenant Elliot Johnston, crawled over to comfort him with these noble words: 'George, do not swear at the fellow; we shall soon be happy; we have behaved like Englishmen.'

Nevertheless, both the lieutenants were eventually placed on horseback and led north. Lieutenant Johnston was killed instantly when hit by a French cannon-ball bouncing up the cobbled road on which he was riding. Lieutenant Simmons made it out of the danger zone to Brussels but suffered excruciating pain: 'the motion of the horse made the blood pump out, and the bones cut the flesh to a jelly', he wrote. At Brussels, he would be bled repeatedly both by the knife and by leeches. He made a full recovery against all the odds and died in 1858 aged 72.

Nearly all the men wounded in a limb had to endure amputation, as doctors had no other method of preventing gangrene or tetanus. Anaesthetics were unheard of at the time and many amputees did not survive the shock of the operation. Most bore it with remarkable fortitude. One plucky French soldier seized his amputated leg and tossed it in the air with a shout of 'Long live the Emperor!' Lord Fitzroy Somerset, Wellington's military secretary, was operated on by Dr John Gunning and was so unshaken that he called out: 'Hallo! don't carry away that arm till I've taken off my ring.'[37]

Britons joked at the blunt saw their surgeon was using: 'take your time, Mr Carver.'[38] Some men did moan how much they suffered: 'ah! je souffre, je souffre beaucoup, beaucoup, beaucoup.' A neighbour would reply: 'ah! ah! you sing well!' John Haddy James of the 1st Life Guards stated that:

> The silent suffering of the greater part of the sufferers was a thing I shall not forget. When one considers the hasty surgery performed on such an occasion, the awful sights the men are witness to, knowing that their turn on that blood-

soaked operating table is next, seeing the agony of an amputation, however swiftly performed, and the longer torture of a probing, then one realises fully of what our soldiers are made.[39]

The surgeons accomplished wonders given the state of contemporary medical science and the floods of men descending on them. One of their cruellest tasks, wrote William Gibney, was 'to be obliged to tell a dying soldier who had served his king and country well on that day, that his case was hopeless, more especially when he was unable to realise the same for himself, and then to pass on to another, where skill might avail.'[40]

The agonies of the wounded at Waterloo equalled those of the Crucifixion. Raging thirst found no relief. Provision for the wounded was woefully inadequate and the little water to be found was tinged with human blood.[41] William Gibney noticed that 'the agony of some was so terrible, that they prayed to be killed outright than endure excruciating torture.'[42]

South of Mont St Jean farm, you arrive at Wellington's crossroads, in the centre of his army's front line. The Duke reached this spot towards 6.30 am on 18 June before touring his line before the battle began. Ensign Rees Gronow of the 1st Guards recalled that the Duke and his staff 'all seemed as gay and unconcerned as if they were riding to meet the hounds in some quiet English county.'[43] Assistant-Surgeon John Haddy James of the Lifeguards thought they looked 'entirely unconcerned and as smart as if they were riding for pleasure.'[44] Indeed, Wellington was wearing comfortable civilian clothes: white buckskin breeches, boots, a blue coat, a gold sash and a cocked hat bearing the cockades of Britain, Spain, Portugal and the Netherlands. He was a field marshal of each of these four countries. Whenever it rained he put on a blue cape: 'I had it on and off fifty times because I never get wet if I can help it.'[45]

As was his custom, the Duke carefully inspected his front line before the battle began. His troops had spent a terrible night in the open amidst pouring rain. Lieutenant William Hay of the 12th Light Dragoons, on the far eastern end of the line, found he had sunk six or eight inches into the watery clay overnight. Captain William Tomkinson of the 16th Light Dragoons was in the same brigade as William Hay:

> With the horses moving about to get their backs to the rain, and the men walking to feed them and light fires, the clover soon disappeared and the whole space occupied by the 16th became one complete puddle. (It was knee-deep at daylight). I lay down in my cloak, and having been up at 2 a.m. on the morning of the 17th, and occupied through the whole of the day, I slept for two or three hours.[46]

Experienced veterans had contrived to obtain a little comfort by sleeping on a makeshift bed of straw or branches and covering themselves with blankets

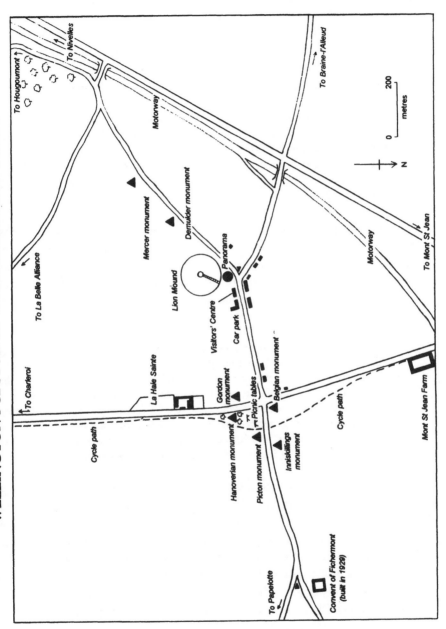

WELLINGTON'S SECTOR OF THE BATTLEFIELD TODAY

smeared with clay. It kept them warm and relatively dry. At last bugles had sounded the reveille. 'If I look half as bad as you do, I must be a miserable looking object', commented Captain William Verner to a fellow officer of the 7th Hussars.[47] Nearly everyone was drenched and covered with mud from head to foot. British redcoats noticed that the water had caused the red dye to run from their jackets and stain their white equipment belts. It looked uncannily like blood.

Sergeant Duncan Robertson of the 92nd Highlanders commented that:

> I never felt colder in my life; every one of us was shaking like an aspen leaf. An allowance of gin was then served out to each of us which had the effect of infusing warmth into our almost inanimate frames, as before we got it, we seemed as if under a fit of ague. We remained on the ground till about six o'clock, when we were ordered to clean ourselves, dry our muskets, try to get forward, and commence cooking.[48]

All along the line men were talking, so that a constant murmuring arose, like the roar of the sea on a rocky coast. This was punctuated by a steady popping as advanced posts fired their muskets to clear them of the old charges that had been in the barrels all night. One British officer noted with fascination how the entire terrain seemed to be in motion for it was covered with a moving mass of human beings:

> Soldiers cleaning their arms and examining the locks, multitudes carrying wood, water, and straw from the village and farm of Mont St. Jean; others making large fires to dry their clothes, or roasting little pieces of meat upon the end of a stick or ramrod, thrust among the embers; a few bundles of straw had been procured, upon which the officers were seated. Though nearly ankle-deep in the mud, they were generally gay, and apparently thinking of everything but the approaching combat, which snapped the thread of existence of so many of them, deprived a few of legs and arms, and disabled many for life.[49]

Guards officers such as Ensign Gronow were eating cold pies and drinking champagne. Their servants had brought these from Brussels; but for most of the men there was but a biscuit or two and some gin. Corporal John Shaw, a giant prizefighter in the ranks of the 2nd Life Guards, was drinking heavily. He was destined to die and would be last seen surrounded by foes, fighting to the end using his helmet as a club after his sword broke.[50]

Assistant-Surgeon John Haddy James of the 1st Life Guards described the moving scenes as the men, unshaven and blue with cold, prepared for the battle everyone knew was to come:

> Everyone was covered with mud, and it was with the greatest difficulty that the men managed to get fires lit, some breakfast cooked, and their arms cleaned

and their ammunition dried. Several hours passed quietly, the weather improved and later the sun came out. Nothing was to be heard except dropping shots now and then, principally from straggling parties of our own troops discharging their pieces, and at intervals the drums of different regiments beating along the line. A few alterations were made in the position of the troops, but mostly we were waiting and still.[51]

At 10.00 am Wellington's forces were treated to a magnificent display of martial grandeur as Napoleon's army formed up to the south. Napoleon hoped to intimidate Wellington's watching troops. Lieutenant Archibald Hamilton of the Scots Greys noted in his diary how the Emperor 'appeared in the front of his troops and the loudest cheering began on the left of the French and ran along their whole line. I confess I never before felt so disheartened; it had evidently a powerful effect upon all present.'[52] Lieutenant Edmund Wheatley of Colonel Christian von Ompteda's brigade saw a raw English soldier white faced and quivering with fear.[53]

Colonel Best, commander of a Hanoverian infantry brigade on the eastern wing, was examining the French army through his telescope: 'we could clearly perceive with our glasses the French Emperor passing down the Line from right to left haranguing his soldiers by whom he was received with loud shouts of "vive l'Empereur".'[54] Corporal John Dickson of the Scots Greys was on picket duty in front of his regiment and thus was able to behold the colourful scene on the other side of the valley. Walk a couple of hundred metres along the cobbled road eastwards from Wellington's crossroads. It was from this sector of the front line that Dickson watched the French troops parading to the south:

It was daylight, and the sun was every now and again sending bright flashes of light through the broken clouds. As I stood behind the straggling hedge and the low beech-trees that skirted the high banks of the sunken road on both sides, I could see the French army drawn up in heavy masses opposite me. They were only a mile from where I stood; but the distance seemed greater, for between us the mist still filled the hollows. There were great columns of infantry, and squadron after squadron of Cuirassiers, red Dragoons, brown Hussars, and green Lancers with little swallow-tail flags at the end of their lances. The grandest sight was a regiment of Cuirassiers dashing at full gallop over the brow of the hill opposite me, with the sun shining on their steel breastplates. It was a splendid show. Every now and then the sun lit up the whole country. No one who saw it could ever forget it ...

There was a sudden roll of drums along the whole of the enemy's line, and a burst of music from the bands of a hundred battalions came to me on the wind. I seemed to recognise the 'Marseillaise,' but the sounds got mixed and lost in a sudden uproar that arose. Then every regiment began to move. They were taking up position for the battle.

On our side perfect silence reigned; but I saw that with us too preparations were being made ... A battery of artillery now came dashing along the road in fine style and passed in front of me ... Then a strong brigade of Dutch and Belgians [under Major-General van Bijlandt] marched up with swinging, quick step, and turned off at a cross-road between high banks on to the plateau on the most exposed slope of our position. They numbered at least three thousand men, and looked well in their blue coats with orange-and-red facings.[55]

# Notes

1. We are grateful to Lucien Gerke for kindly providing this information about the Wellington Museum.

2. For the history of this table, see *The Times*, 22 August 1890. It was bought by Sir William Fraser in 1889 as he feared it might cross the Atlantic. He later donated it to the museum: T. Fleischman, *Le quartier général de Wellington à Waterloo* (1956), p.36

3. E. Longford, *Wellington: the years of the sword* (1972), p.484

4. C. Eaton, *Waterloo Days* (1888), p.125

5. A. Brett-James, *The hundred days* (1964), p.154

6. E. Longford, *Wellington: the years of the sword* (1972), p.484

7. W. Pitt Lennox, *Three years with the Duke of Wellington in private life* (1853), pp.217–18

8. Marquess of Anglesey, *One-Leg* (1963), p.150

9. *Ibid*, p.151

10. C. Dalton, *The Waterloo roll call* (1978), p.12

11. For more details on the transfer of this tomb, see an excellent booklet: J. Godwin, *Beaudesert, the Pagets and Waterloo* (1992). The author is leading the campaign to persuade the Belgian authorities not to permit the demolition of Monsieur Paris' house, which is theatened by plans for a new access road.

12. C. Eaton, *Waterloo Days* (1888), p.158

13. R. Gibney ed., *Eighty years ago, or the recollections of an old army doctor* (1896), pp.201–2

14. C. Dalton, *The Waterloo roll call* (1978), p.276

15. M. Mann, *And they rode on* (1984), p.79

16. H. Siborne ed., *The Waterloo letters* (1983), pp.108, 122

17. E. Macready, 'On a Part of Captain Siborne's History of the Waterloo Campaign', in *United Service Magazine* (1845, Part I)

18. F. Pattison, *Personal recollections of the Waterloo campaign* (1870), pp.38–9; we have changed Pattison's incorrect spelling, 'Chalmers', to 'Chambers'. See also BL Add. MSS 34,707/482.

19. H. Siborne ed., *The Waterloo letters* (1983), p.229

20. F. Duncan, *History of the Royal Regiment of Artillery* (1873), v.2, p.427

21. H. Siborne, *The Waterloo letters* (1983), p.342

22. I. Fletcher, *Wellington's regiments* (1994), p.138; A. Muir, *The First of foot* (1961), pp.11–12

23. A. Muir, *The First of Foot* (1961), p.11

24. 'Recollections of Waterloo by a staff officer' in *United Service Magazine* (1847, Part III). According to Lieutenant Frederick Pattison of the 33rd, a cannon-ball splashed Arthur Gore's brains over the shakos of the regiment's officers. However, Jackson states that Arthur Gore's face was intact; the two accounts are not wholly irreconciliable.

25. F. Pattison, *Personal recollections of the Waterloo campaign* (1870), pp.7–8

26. *Ibid*, pp.8, 26–7, 31

27. D. Boulger, *The Belgians at Waterloo* (1901), p.63

28. *Ibid*, p.49

29. We are grateful to Guy Delvaux for kindly supplying a translation of the Flemish inscription on this plaque.

30. R. Gibney ed., *Eighty years ago, or the recollections of an old army doctor* (1896), pp.195–6

31. C. Eaton, *Waterloo Days* (1888), p.123

32. E. Richardson, *Long forgotten days (leading to Waterloo)* (1928), p.383

33. 'Recollections of Waterloo by a staff officer', in *United Service Magazine* (1847, Part III)

34. *The Times*, 10 July 1906

35. *The Times*, 11 November 1926
36. G. Simmons, *A British rifle man* (1986), p.367
37. J. Sweetman, *Raglan: from the Peninsula to the Crimea* (1993), pp.65–6
38. R. Gronow, *The reminiscences and recollections of Captain Gronow 1810–1860* (1984), p.193
39. J. Vansittart ed., *The journal of Surgeon James* (1964), pp.35–6
40. R. Gibney ed., *Eighty years ago, or the recollections of an old army doctor* (1896), pp.196–7
41. H. O'Donnell, *Historical records of the 14th Regiment* (1893), p.353
42. R. Gibney ed., *Eighty years ago, or the recollections of an old army doctor* (1896), pp.200–1
43. R. Gronow, *The reminiscences and recollections of Captain Gronow 1810–1860* (1984), p.186
44. J. Vansittart ed., *The journal of Surgeon James* (1964), p.31
45. E. Longford, *Wellington: the years of the sword* (1972), p.452; M. Glover and U. Pericoli, *The armies at Waterloo* (1973), p.98
46. W. Tomkinson, *The diary of a cavalry officer in the Peninsular and Waterloo campaigns, 1809–1815* (1894), p.287
47. E. Richardson, *Long forgotten days (leading to Waterloo)* (1928), p.378
48. MacKenzie MacBride ed., *With Napoleon at Waterloo* (1911), p.159
49. 'Operations of the Fifth or Picton's Division in the campaign of Waterloo', in *United Service Magazine* (June 1841), p.176
50. T. Morris, *Recollections of military service in 1813, 1814 and 1815* (1845), p.146
51. J. Vansittart ed., *The journal of Surgeon James* (1964), p.31
52. J. Ponsonby, *The Ponsonby family* (1926), p.218
53. C. Hibbert ed., *The Wheatley diary* (1964), p.64
54. BL Add MSS 34,704/278–9
55. MacKenzie MacBride ed., *With Napoleon at Waterloo* (1911), pp.139–40

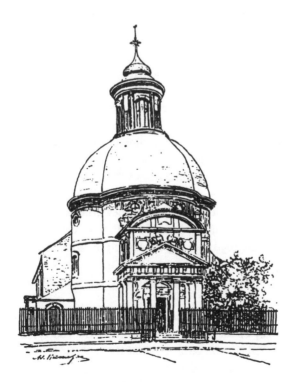

The Royal Chapel at the town of Waterloo

# 4

# THE DEFENCE OF HOUGOUMONT

Suddenly, at 11.30 am, gunfire crashed out on the western sector of the battlefield. The shots came from around the farm of Hougoumont, an extensive complex of enclosures covering 1600 square metres. In the north-west corner stood a building block, to the east of which were a walled garden and then an orchard. The southern half of the enclosures contained a wood.

The garrison received reinforcements throughout the day but consisted initially of four light companies of the British 1st, 2nd and 3rd Guards, the 1st battalion, 2nd Nassau Infantry, and over 200 Hanoverian sharpshooters. These Nassauers and Hanoverians were green-coated German light troops who had been detached from their parent brigades to strengthen the garrison of Hougoumont.[1]

The two light companies of the British 1st Guards occupied the orchard while that of the 2nd Guards garrisoned the building block and the walled garden. The light company of the 3rd Guards stood immediately west of the buildings but was ready to withdraw into them if hard pressed. The Nassau battalion comprised six companies. Two of these, and the Hanoverian sharp-shooters, defended the wood as a first line of defence. Another three Nassau companies occupied the walled garden while the grenadier company helped the 2nd Guards to garrison the building block.[2]

Today, both the wood and orchard of the farm have vanished and many of the buildings were destroyed in the battle. Nevertheless, Hougoumont remains the most evocative point of the battlefield. Park at the Lion Mound and walk south-west along the road running the length of Wellington's ridge. Pass the road branching off to the right over the A202 motorway and continue along the approach track, which sweeps round to the North Gate of the farm's building block.

Visitors are free to pass through the North Gate into the courtyard but must respect the privacy of the tenant farmers. Enter the courtyard and all around you stand memorials to the bitter strife of the past. Stone tablets fixed to the walls are dedicated to the various units who fought here. On the wall of the Great Barn, the large building just inside the North Gate, is one to the Royal

---

### The garrison of Hougoumont

---

*Initial garrison*
- Light company, 2/1st Guards *(in orchard)*
- Light company, 3/1st Guards *(in orchard)*
- Light company, 2/2nd Guards *(in building block and garden)*
- Light company, 2/3rd Guards *(in lane west of building block)*
- 1st battalion, 2nd Nassau Infantry *(in wood, orchard, garden and building block)*
- 1st company, Feld-Jäger Corps (Hanoverians) *(in wood)*
- One hundred picked men from Lüneburg and Grubenhagen Light battalions (Hanoverians) *(in wood)*

*Reinforcements*
- Seven companies, 2/2nd Guards *(in building block and garden)*
- 2/3rd Guards *(in orchard)*
- 2nd Line battalion and three light companies from Colonel du Plat's King's German Legion Brigade *(in orchard)*
- Salzgitter Landwehr battalion (Hanoverians) *(in orchard)*
- Brunswick Advanced Guard battalion, Leib battalion and 1st Light battalion *(in lane northwest of building block and then helped clear the wood of French troops)*

---

Waggon Train which kept the garrison supplied with vital stocks of ammunition. A British ADC, Captain Horace Seymour, described later how:

> Late in the day of the 18th, I was called to by some Officers of the 3rd Guards defending Hougoumont, to use my best endeavours to send them musket ammunition. Soon afterwards I fell in with a private of the Waggon Train in charge of a tumbril on the crest of the position. I merely pointed out to him where he was wanted, when he gallantly started his horses, and drove straight down the hill to the Farm, to the gate of which I saw him arrive. He must have lost his horses, as there was a severe fire kept on him. I feel convinced to that man's service the Guards owe their ammunition.[3]

Without this ammunition, Hougoumont would probably have fallen. Wellington's central outpost of La Haie Sainte was lost to the French owing to a shortage of rounds.

On the outside of the farm of Hougoumont, on the wall adjoining the North Gateway, another plaque commemorates the men of the 3rd (Scots) Guards. The bulk of the battalion remained in reserve on the ridge north of the farm until 2.00 pm when it reinforced the defenders of Hougoumont orchard. However, from the very start of the battle the light company of the 3rd Guards fought in and around the building block. Initially, it stood in the lane running along the western side of the Great Barn. Around 12.30 pm a French infantry

## HOUGOUMONT TODAY, SHOWING THE DISPOSITIONS OF THE INITIAL GARRISON

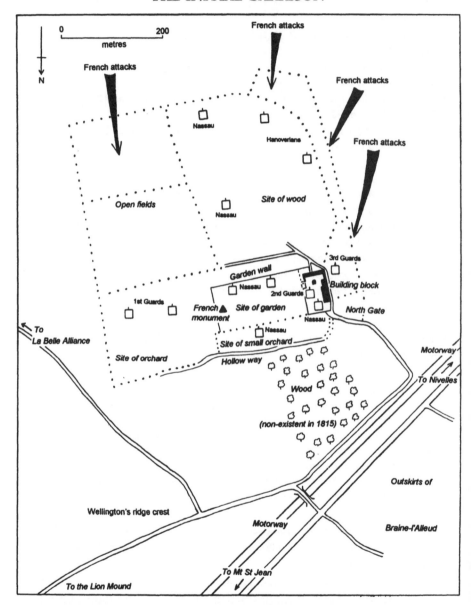

brigade attacked the company and after a bitter struggle drove it back along the lane towards the North Gate. The guardsmen raced to enter the courtyard and secure the gateway behind them. They were too late.

The leading French skirmishers burst through the gate, led by the gigantic Sub-Lieutenant Legros, known by his comrades as 'the Smasher'. It was a desperate moment. Seven Nassau grenadiers were soon prisoners and the garrison desperately tried to contain the inrush of French troops by firing from the windows of nearby buildings. Lieutenant-Colonel James Macdonell, the senior British officer on the scene, gathered a band of powerful men and heaved the wooden gates shut by brute force. The handful of French troops trapped inside the courtyard was soon wiped out. Those who were not killed were taken prisoner, including a drummer boy who had lost his drum. 'The Smasher' lay dead still holding a sapper's axe in his hand.[4]

The farm walls either side of the gate are much lower than they used to be; the defences were hence much more formidable in 1815 than they appear today. Nevertheless, one solitary Frenchman did attempt to climb over the now shut North Gate to open it from the inside for his comrades. A well aimed shot put an abrupt end to the plucky try.

The Duke of Wellington later commented that 'the success of the battle ... turned upon the closing of the gates of Hougoumont.'[5] He sent seven companies of the 2nd (Coldstream) Guards from reserve on the main ridge to drive off the French milling around outside the north face of the farm and to join the garrison. Major Alexander Woodford led this reinforcement and recalled how outside the farm he clashed with the French 1st Light infantry under Colonel Despans de Cubières. The colonel, who wore his arm in a sling after being injured at the Battle of Quatre Bras two days earlier, now fell seriously wounded. Instantly, British officers flung themselves in front of their troops to prevent them from continuing to fire at the stricken colonel. De Cubières survived and later became Governor of Ancona in Italy. He never forgot the chivalry of the British and became Major Woodford's firm friend.[6]

Woodford led his reinforcement into the farm by a side door, on the western face of the building block, into the Great Barn. The doorway is now bricked up but its outline is still visible.

Note the small chapel standing isolated in the middle of the courtyard. This chapel used to adjoin a large château, which was destroyed by fire started by French howitzers towards 2.45 pm. Private Matthew Clay of the 3rd Guards, just twenty years old, was in one of the upper rooms of the château, shooting from the lofty windows at the French troops around the farm. Soon the building was on fire but, as Clay recalled, 'our officer placed himself at the entrance of the room and would not allow anyone to leave his post until our position became hopeless and too perilous to remain. We fully expected the floor to sink with us every moment, and in our escape several of us were more or less injured.'[7]

Miss Charlotte Waldie, who visited Hougoumont in July 1815, was appalled by the desolation of the once fine château:

Its broken walls and falling roof presented a most melancholy spectacle: not melancholy merely from its being a pile of ruins but from the vestiges it

## Hougoumont Farm in 1815

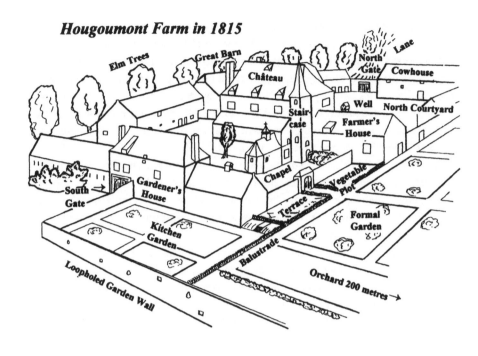

## Hougoumont Farm Today

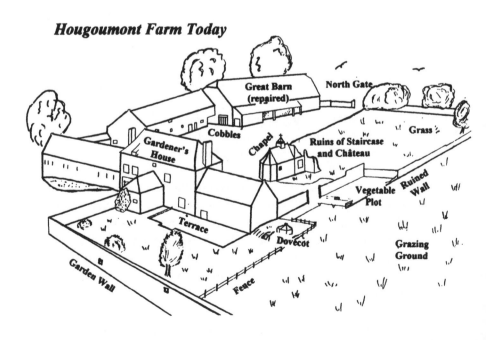

presented of that tremendous and recent warfare by which those ruins had been caused. Its huge blackened beams had fallen in every direction upon the crumbling heaps of stone and plaster, which were intermixed with broken pieces of the marble flags, the carved cornices, and the gilded mirrors, that once ornamented it.[8]

The walls of the gutted building were unsafe and had to be pulled down soon after the battle. Nonetheless, a small portion of the ruins still adjoins the chapel. The chapel survived the inferno raging around it by a miracle. It was left standing intact in the midst of destruction just as St Paul's Cathedral survived the blitz on London in 1940. If you enter the chapel, note the wooden crucifix hanging on the wall. It used to hang immediately above the door, and as the flames reached up through the doorway they charred the feet before dying away. Sadly, in the decades immediately after the battle an English tourist cut off one of the legs as a souvenir.[9] Scores of other visitors also came as vandals, not pilgrims, and covered the interior of the chapel with graffiti.

The flames gutted many of the buildings to the north, east and west of the chapel. The roofs collapsed but the walls remained standing and kept the French infantry out. Ensign George Standen of the 3rd Guards remembered the nightmarish scene: 'during this time the whole of the barn and cart house were in flames. During the confusion three or four Officers' horses rushed out into the yard from the barn, and in a minute or two rushed back into the flames and were burnt.'[10]

Wounded men screamed hideously as they were burned to death; the fire was so fierce it repelled most rescue attempts. Private William Wheeler of the 51st Light infantry watched Hougoumont from his regiment's position 400 metres to the north-west: 'so fierce was the combat that a spectator would imagine a mouse could not live near the spot.'[11] After the battle he visited the farm and found to his horror that 'many who had been wounded inside or near the building were roasted, some who had endeavoured to crawl out from the fire lay dead with their legs burnt to a cinder.'[12]

The Duke of Wellington had noticed the fire at Hougoumont farm from the main position to the north. He wrote a characteristically precise and beautifully composed order in pencil on a piece of ass's skin; these skins could be wiped clean and used for new orders. This particular message was never erased and you will find it preserved in the Wellington Museum at Apsley House, London:

> I see that the fire has communicated from the Hay Stack to the Roof of the Chateau.
>
> You must however still keep your Men in those parts to which the fire does not reach.
>
> Take care that no Men are lost by the falling in of the Roof, or floors: after

they will have fallen in occupy the Ruined walls inside of the Garden; particularly if it should be possible for the Enemy to pass through the Embers in the Inside of the House.

On the outside of the chapel are two plaques. One, of stone, is to the memory of the soldiers of the two light companies of the 1st Guards. These men defended Hougoumont orchard under Lieutenant-Colonel Alexander, Lord Saltoun, with the help of elements of the 1st battalion, 2nd Nassau Infantry. The pitifully few survivors of Lord Saltoun's force were relieved towards 2.00 pm by the 3rd Guards and were told by their brigade commander, Major-General Peregrine Maitland, that 'your defence saved the army: nothing could be more gallant. Every man of you deserves promotion.'[13]

The chapel also bears a bronze plaque with the inscription: 'visitors are earnestly requested to tread this chapel with respect for within its walls on the memorable 18th June 1815 many of the brave defenders of Hougoumont passed to their rest.'

Walk round the chapel and to the east a gate opens into what used to be a fine formal garden with walks, rose bushes and a balustrade but which is now open grazing ground. A loopholed wall borders the southern and eastern limits of the garden. The stone framed loopholes were made when the wall was built, others were knocked out on the eve of the battle by the guardsmen but these have since been bricked up. Lieutenant-Colonel Macdonell worked all the night of 17/18 June collecting wood to construct rough wooden platforms to enable his men to fire over the wall. Major Alexander Woodford of the Coldstreamers recalled that 'the platforms did not extend all the way, as in some cases the bank was high enough to enable the men to fire over the walls.'[14]

The garden was held by British guardsmen and three companies of Major Büsgen's 1st battalion, 2nd Nassau Infantry.[15] The defenders who lined the interior of the garden wall slaughtered the French infantrymen who desperately tried to crawl their way over. Look through one of the loopholes. A wood used to stand south of the garden and of the building block. Its northern edge was lined with a thick bullfincher hedge about thirty metres from you. In their first attack the French infantry seized the wood from Nassau and Hanoverian light troops and then poured out of it to dash across the open space in front of you. The only cover was a sparse line of apple trees which have now disappeared.

After their repulse from the wall the French returned to the wood only to find that Wellington had ordered Captain Robert Bull's howitzer battery to fire shrapnel shells over the British guards to burst right over the heads of the French in the wood. The French suffered immense losses and thereafter contented themselves with blazing away from the cover of the wood at the garden wall. This resulted only in the diminution of their ammunition.

At the eastern end of the garden stands a monument to the French soldiers who died at Hougoumont with such sublime heroism. It was unveiled in 1913 and is crowned by an eagle, the symbol of Napoleon's empire. Below is engraved the coveted medal of the legion of honour. A tribute by the Emperor is inscribed on the stone: 'the earth seemed proud to bear so many brave men.'[16] The monument's location is inappropriate since very few Frenchmen entered the garden. Captain William Tomkinson of the light dragoons inspected Hougoumont next morning and found that 'three or four French infantry had so far succeeded that they had got to the top of the wall, and were there killed, falling into the garden.'[17]

Also in the garden, on the southern wall near the building block, is a plaque to the memory of Captain Thomas Crawfurd, 3rd Guards, killed at the farm. Nearby, in the shade of the wall, two peaceful tombstones mark the initial resting places of Captain John Lucie Blackman of the Coldstream Guards and Edward Cotton of the 7th Hussars. Captain Blackman fell in action; Cotton survived Waterloo, returned to act as a guide to the battlefield and died in 1849. The bodies of both these men were removed a century ago to rest in the crypt of the British Army monument which was unveiled in 1890 at the new Brussels cemetery of Evere.

Before leaving the garden, walk north until you descend into a shallow ravine. This is the hollow way, which ran all along the northern edge of Hougoumont. The portion east of the garden proved of inestimable value to the British and Germans who sheltered in it whenever driven out of the orchard. Major Francis Hepburn, commanding the 3rd Guards here, wrote that the friendly 'hollow way ... served us as a rallying point more than once during the day.'[18]

The French were never able to storm the hollow way and, under a flanking fire from the eastern section of the garden wall, evacuated the orchard once more.

Now leave the interior of the farm and go round the west of the building block to visit the southern face. A small extension has been added to the Gardener's House where the garden wall joins it, but otherwise little has changed. Note the plaque to the Coldstream Guards fixed to the wall of this extension. The French infantry fiercely assaulted the Gardener's House and strove to break down its arched gate. This gate opens on to a passageway leading under the top floor of the house and into the farm's southern court-yard. The failure of the French assault on this gate was largely due to the Coldstreamers who fired down from the now blocked-up windows of the house and from the garden wall. To the south of the Gardener's House a plaque at the corner of the garden wall commemorates Brigadier-General Baron Pierre-François Bauduin, the slain commander of the leading French infantry brigade.

To every visitor, the significance of Hougoumont is clear. It was a formidable post which, held by just 3500 British and Germans, tied up 9000 French attackers. 'No troops but the British could have held Hougoumont', Wellington concluded, 'and only the best of them at that.'[19]

The fighting at Hougoumont caused around 5000 casualties, most of them French. Miss Charlotte Waldie described the grisly surroundings of the farm a month after the battle:

> At the outskirts of the wood, and around the ruined walls of the Chateau, huge piles of human ashes were heaped up, some of which were still smouldering. The countrymen told us, that so great were the numbers of the slain, that it was impossible entirely to consume them. Pits had been dug, into which they had been thrown, but they were obliged to be raised far above the surface of the ground. These dreadful heaps were covered with piles of wood which were set on fire, so that underneath the ashes lay numbers of human bodies unconsumed.[20]

A painting by Denis Dighton depicts one such mass grave dug immediately south of the Gardener's House. Scarlet poppies bloomed all over the graves soon after the battle. Near the wood, Miss Waldie walked through patches of corn as tall as herself:

> Among them I discovered many a forgotten grave, strewed round with melancholy remnants of military attire. While I loitered behind the rest of the party, searching among the corn for some relics worthy of preservation, I beheld a human hand, almost reduced to a skeleton, outstretched above the ground, as if it had raised itself from the grave. My blood ran cold with horror, and for some moments I stood rooted to the spot, unable to take my eyes from this dreadful object, or to move away: as soon as I recovered myself, I hastened after my companions, who were far before me, and overtook them just as they entered the wood of Hougoumont.[21]

Today it is hard to imagine the bitterness of the fighting that once raged at peaceful Hougoumont, or the scenes of horror which reigned after the strife. Yet Hougoumont leaves a profound impression on every visitor and as you depart you will notice many tourists taking a last look back at the historic farm.

# Notes

1. The Nassau battalion came from Prince Bernhard of Saxe-Weimar's brigade on the far eastern flank. The Hanoverians came from Major-General Count Kielmannsegge's brigade in the centre and consisted of fifty men from the Lüneburg Light battalion, fifty from the Grubenhagen Light battalion and the 1st company of the Field-Jäger Corps: J. Pflugk-Harttung, *Belle-Alliance* (1915), pp.60, 77

2. British historians state that only guardsmen held the building block. This is untrue. Major Büsgen, the commander of the 1st battalion, 2nd Nassau Infantry, reported that: 'I immediately took what seemed to me to be the necessary defensive dispositions: I occupied the buildings with the grenadier company ...': Bericht des 1. Bataillons des nassauischen 2. Regiments uber seinen Anteil an der Schlacht bei Belle-Alliance: J. Pflugk-Harttung, *Belle Alliance* (1915), pp.207–9

3. H. Siborne, *The Waterloo letters* (1983), pp.19–20

4. H. de Mauduit, *Les derniers jours de la grande armée* (1848), v.2, p.321; Bericht des 1. Bataillons des nassauischen 2. Regiments uber seinen Anteil an der Schlacht bei Belle-Alliance: J. Pflugk-Harttung, *Belle Alliance* (1915), pp.207–9

5. E. Cotton, *A voice from Waterloo* (1913), p.303

6. H. Siborne, *The Waterloo letters* (1983), p.262; *Illustrated London News* (12 April 1879)

7. 'Adventures at Hougoumont', in *Household Brigade Magazine* (1958), p.41

8. C. Eaton, *Waterloo days* (1888), p.139

9. C. Schepers, *Waterloo: a guidebook to the battlefield* (1892), p.22

10. H. Siborne ed., *The Waterloo letters* (1983), pp.268–9

11. B. Liddell Hart ed., *The letters of Private Wheeler* (1951), p.172

12. *Ibid*, p.174

13. R. Gronow, *The reminiscences and recollections of Captain Gronow 1810–1860* (1984), p.199

14. H. Siborne ed., *The Waterloo letters* (1964), p.265

15. D. MacKinnon, *Origins and services of the Coldstream Guards* (1833), v.2, p.215; Bericht des 1. Bataillons des nassauischen 2. Regiments uber seinen Anteil an der Schlacht bei Belle-Alliance: J. Pflugk-Harttung, *Belle Alliance* (1915), pp.207–9

16. *The Times*, 23 June 1913

17. W. Tomkinson, *The diary of a cavalry officer in the Peninsular and Waterloo campaigns, 1809–1815* (1894), p.307

18. H. Siborne ed., *The Waterloo letters* (1983), p.266

19. Lord Chalfont ed., *Waterloo: battle of three armies* (1979), p.90

20. C. Eaton, *Waterloo days* (1888), p.138

21. *Ibid*, p.137

The ruins of Hougoumont, viewed from the garden. The chapel stands in the centre and the Gardener's House on the left

# 5

# THE EASTERN WING: VICTORY FROM THE JAWS OF DEFEAT

Return to the Lion Mound and walk on to the eastern sector of the field on the far side of Wellington's crossroads. This was the scene of Napoleon's second attack of the day. This sector of the field is well preserved. The only major change has been the erection of Fichermont Convent 750 metres east of the crossroads. This was built in 1929 in spite of the 1914 Protection of the Battlefield Law. The cobbled, open road along the ridge from the crossroads towards the convent used to be a dirt track enclosed on either side by hedges. Today, near the eastern end especially, bright red poppies grow amidst the grass on the verges. Along the 600 metre front formed by this track were Sir James Kempt and Sir Denis Pack's two British brigades of Lieutenant-General Sir Thomas Picton's 5th Division and the Dutch-Belgian infantry of Major-General van Bijlandt. These troops were lying down to shelter from the French pre-assault barrage by eighty guns.

'One could almost feel the undulation of the air from the multitude of cannon-shot,' wrote Lieutenant Edmund Wheatley.[1] 'A furious fire of artillery from the whole line opposite to Picton's burst upon us,' recalled a British officer. 'The greater part, fortunately, went over our heads, carrying one off here and there. This fire was much too high; the old hands said it was meant to intimidate, as usual.' Nonetheless, the French shells did 'considerable execution among us.'[2] Sergeant Duncan Robertson of the 92nd Highlanders agreed that, sheltered by the ridge, his unit suffered little from roundshot but much from the high trajectory howitzer shells.[3]

While Bijlandt's five battalions were drawn up in line immediately behind the hedged track, Picton's men were stationed in columns one hundred metres further north, where the lower ground offered more shelter. The 95th Rifles, however, were partly on the crest of the ridge west of Bijlandt's brigade and partly in a sandpit opposite the garden of La Haie Sainte. Thus Wellington had two defence lines in this sector; there was simply insufficient ground for both the British and Netherlands battalions to form in a single line along the ridge crest. The two lines allowed Wellington to offer a deeper, tougher and more flexible resistance, as one observant British officer noted:

> I had just time, while we awaited the attack, to get a glimpse of Sir Thomas Picton's disposition; it was the most beautiful thing imaginable, and the ground admitted of its being displayed to advantage; all the modern improvements acquired by experience in the Peninsula ... were here brought into play. Some of the regiments [under Bijlandt] deployed and formed line, and were to charge, others [the British redcoats] followed in their rear, at quarter distance columns, ready to deploy and support the charge, or take the place of those in front, if baulked or defeated, or to throw themselves into squares instantaneously, if threatened by cavalry; and, in short, to conform to the movements of those in front.[4]

Wellington had ridden over from the Hougoumont sector to direct operations in person against the impending French main attack. The massed bombardment ceased and soon French infantry were assaulting La Haie Sainte farm, whose whitewashed walls you can see to the south-west from the ridge crest. Other French infantrymen skirmished around Papelotte and Smohain to the east. A brigade of cuirassiers rode forward to the west of La Haie Sainte in support of the operation. In between Papelotte and La Haie Sainte four heavy columns, about 180 men wide and up to twenty-four ranks deep, now marched straight towards the ridge crest. The advance of the columns was staggered so that they would strike Wellington's line in succession, from west to east.[5] Wellington's batteries were sending cannon-balls hurtling down the length of these packed formations.

Lieutenant Johnny Kincaid of the 95th Rifles saw the French columns appear over the crest of a small knoll you can still see in the fields immediately east of the Hanoverian monument. 'They received such a fire from our first line, that they wavered, and hung behind it a little; but, cheered and encouraged by the gallantry of their officers, who were dancing and flourishing their swords in front, they at last boldly advanced.'[6]

The leading columns inclined slightly to the east and ascended the ridge up to the hedged track. There they halted to deploy.[7] In the Napoleonic era, French columns usually tried to deploy when they came up to their foe in order to maximise their firepower. The approach march was made in column as columns were easy to manoeuvre; the disadvantage of columns was that only the front ranks could bring their muskets to bear. Time passed as the French officers gallantly led their companies out.

All this while, the French front ranks were exchanging heavy fire at close range with Bijlandt's Dutch-Belgian brigade on the ridge crest. Lieutenant Chrétien Scheltens of the Belgian 7th Infantry described how 'our battalion opened fire as soon as our skirmishers had come in. The French column

## THE IMPACT OF THE FRENCH MAIN ATTACK

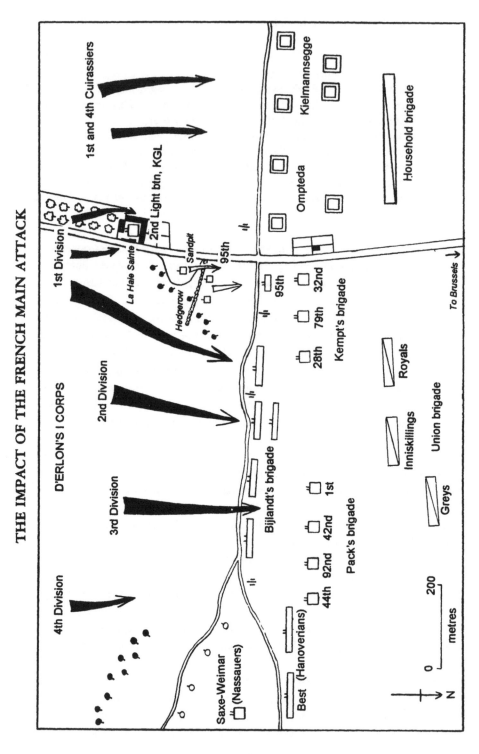

D'ERLON'S I CORPS

1st and 4th Cuirassiers

1st Division

2nd Division

3rd Division

4th Division

2nd Light btn, KGL

La Haie Sainte

Sandpit

Hedgerow

95th

Kielmannsegge

Ompteda

Household brigade

To Brussels

95th

32nd

79th

28th

Kempt's brigade

Royals

Inniskillings

Union brigade

Greys

Bijlandt's brigade

1st

42nd

92nd

44th

Pack's brigade

Saxe-Weimar
(Nassauers)

Best (Hanoverians)

0    200

metres

N

imprudently halted and began to deploy. We were at such close quarters that Captain Henry l'Olivier, commanding our grenadier company, was struck on the arm by a musketball, of which the wad, or cartridge paper, remained smoking in the cloth of his tunic.'[8]

Note the stone monument at the north-east corner of Wellington's cross-roads. This was erected in 1914 in memory of those 'Belgians who died on 18 June 1815 fighting for the defence of the flag and the honour of arms.' A bronze relief fixed to the face of the memorial shows a shot-torn flag and a shield depicting the Belgian lion. Many individuals, particularly officers, of Bijlandt's brigade fought heroically against superior numbers but presently the bulk of the Dutch-Belgians began, understandably, to fall back from the ridge crest. Lieutenant James Hope was with the 92nd Highlanders in the second line and described how 'the Belgians, assailed with terrible fury, returned the fire of the enemy for some time with great spirit.' He saw how they then 'partially retired from the hedge [along the ridge crest]. At the entreaty of their officers, the greater part of them again returned to their posts, but it was merely to satisfy their curiosity, for they almost immediately again retired without firing a shot. The officers exerted themselves to the utmost to keep the men at their duty, but their efforts were fruitless.'[9]

Bijlandt and his chief-of-staff, Colonel Zuylen van Nyevelt, were both wounded. Lieutenant Van Haren of the brigade staff was killed and Lieutenant-General Baron Henri de Perponcher, Bijlandt's divisional commander, had two horses shot dead beneath him. The bulk of the Dutch-Belgian brigade had recoiled in disorder under the impact of the massive French columns. The fugitives were met with a volley of hisses and cries of 'shame!' as they passed Picton's British troops in the second line.[10]

Ensign William Mountsteven of the 28th Foot stated bluntly that the Netherlands 'infantry ran away in an extraordinary manner, as if by word of command, for they still kept their formation in column, yet ... I saw their officers cutting at them with their swords to make them halt. They nearly ran over the Grenadiers of the 28th, who were so enraged that they were with difficulty prevented from firing into them.'[11] Nevertheless, some of Bijlandt's men were still on the ridge crest and trading fire with the French; one British officer recalled in admiration how 'a fine old Belgian Colonel, having a cocked-hat like the sails of a windmill, followed the movements, with his gallant little band, of our division the whole day – always in the thickest of the fire.'[12]

Now Lieutenant-General Sir Thomas Picton's British battalions advanced from the rear up to the track on which you are standing to join the remnants of Bijlandt's battered brigade. While the 44th Foot and 92nd Highlanders remained in reserve, the remaining battalions formed line and clashed with the French columns. Above the crashing volleys of musketry came the sound of wailing bagpipes from the 79th (Cameron) and 42nd (Black Watch) Highlanders.

It was a desperate struggle. The large French columns, with their wide frontage of over 150 men, could match the firepower of the numerically weak British lines. Lieutenant-General Sir Thomas Picton, a tough veteran with years of experience, was roaring for a bayonet charge: 'Charge! Hurrah! Hurrah!' He turned to a staff officer, Captain Horace Seymour, and added 'rally the Highlanders!'[13] Suddenly, he fell from his horse, shot dead through the brain. He had already been wounded two days before at the Battle of Quatre Bras by a musket-shot which broke two ribs but he concealed the fact from all but his servant. Horace Seymour remembered Picton's death clearly: 'when Sir Thomas fell, my horse also came down, and in extricating myself I found I was close to the General, from whose trousers' pocket a Grenadier of the 28th was endeavouring to take his spectacles and purse, which I gave to his A.D.C.'[14]

A memorial stone to Picton stands east of the crossroads, next to the picnic tables. According to Ensign George Keppel, he was 'a strong-built man with a red face, small black eyes, and large nose.'[15] Picton was wearing civilian clothes, a shabby greatcoat and dusty top hat and carried an umbrella instead of a sword. At the Battle of Bussaco in 1810 he had fought in a red nightcap.[16] Despite, or perhaps because of, his eccentricity, Picton enjoyed immense popularity among his troops. This rough tongued Welshman was one of the most formidable of Wellington's generals. Although the Duke disliked Picton's rough manners, he respected his professionalism: 'I found him a rough, foul-mouthed devil as ever lived, but he always behaved extremely well. No man could do better in different services I assigned to him.'[17]

Picton was as brave as a lion but the long years of combat strain had been catching up on him. In the last year of the Peninsular war he had begged Wellington, 'my Lord, I must give up. I am grown so nervous, that when there is any service to be done it works upon my mind so, that it is impossible for me to sleep at nights. I cannot possibly stand it, and I shall be forced to retire.'[18]

With the intuition of a veteran, Picton had sensed he was destined to die at Waterloo. Before leaving England he lay down in a newly dug grave with the exclamation 'why, I think this would do for me.' It happened to be exactly the right size. Later, witnesses noted his brooding silence as he sailed to join the army and watched the white cliffs at Ramsgate fade into the distance. His remains have rested at St Paul's Cathedral since 1859, while the misshapen musketball which killed him is on display at London's National Army Museum.

The French numerical superiority began to tell. They had nearly 10,000 men against just over 4000. D'Erlon's I Corps had not hitherto been engaged in the campaign whereas Picton's and Bijlandt's battalions had borne the brunt of the Battle of Quatre Bras two days earlier and had taken heavy casualties. Wellington himself later confessed to anxiety at this point:

A column of French was firing across the road at one of our regiments. Our people could not get at them to charge them, because they would have been disordered by crossing the road. It was a nervous moment. One of the two forces must go about in a few minutes – it was impossible to say which it might be. I saw about two hundred men of the 79th, who seemed to have had more than they liked of it. I formed them myself about twenty yards from the flash of the French columns, and ordered them to fire.[19]

In the east, the leading ranks of the French third column attained the ridge crest and pushed across the track. The 1st (Royal Scots) and 42nd Highlanders seem to have advanced against the French columns only to be compelled, like Bijlandt's men earlier, to retire from the ridge crest.[20] Then Lieutenant James Hope heard his brigade commander, Major-General Sir Denis Pack, exclaim to the Gordon Highlanders: 'ninety-second, you must charge! All the troops in your front have given way!'[21] Hope found it a 'not very encouraging address', yet 'the regiment responded with cheers, and then advanced to measure bayonets with their enemies. For some time the latter appeared resolved to give us a meeting, but on arriving within 30 paces of them, the whole column completely panic struck, wheeled to the right about, and in the utmost confusion attempted to escape.'[22]

At this moment, Wellington's cavalry commander, Lord Uxbridge, launched his decisive counter-attack with 2000 British heavy horsemen. The Household Brigade under Major-General Lord Edward Somerset advanced from Wellington's second line to charge French cuirassiers west of the crossroads.[23] Shortly afterwards Major-General the Hon. Sir William Ponsonby's ADC raised his cocked hat as a signal to unleash the Union Brigade on the eastern side of the Brussels highroad. The general and his ADC had been watching the progress of the infantry clash from the ridge crest and had perfectly judged the correct moment for the cavalry's intervention. Ponsonby's three regiments, the English Royals, the Irish Inniskillings and the Scots Greys, advanced eagerly from their reserve postions behind the ridge. 'We had several killed and wounded at this moment from small shot,' recalled Lieutenant Charles Wyndham of the Scots Greys, 'and our remark ever since that memorable day was the extraordinary manner in which the bullets struck our swords as we ascended.'[24]

Lieutenant Chrétien Scheltens of the Belgian infantry recalled how 'the English cavalry arrived to take part in the fray. It passed like a whirlwind along the wings of our battalion, several of our men being knocked down by the horsemen. The battalion, which had to cease firing, for the cavalry were in front, immediately crossed the road and advanced.' A British infantry officer later wrote:

I remember a dreadful confusion, thick smoke, horses and men tumbling headlong; soldiers receiving their death wounds, springing up and falling down dead! ... Then a great body of French soldiers in disorder, throwing down their arms and accoutrements, and calling out 'Prisonniers! prisonniers!' driven on by the cavalry, coming towards us ...

The solid mass [of French infantry] I had seen twenty minutes before was there no more, and had now become a defenceless crowd. French officers were brought up from the hollow in great numbers, delivering up their swords. One of our privates brought up *two*, pushing them before him with his bayonet. They were hatless, and had a flushed and vexed kind of look. They came and delivered their swords to our Colonel, and were sent to the rear.[25]

Picton's infantry were pushing across the hedged track on to the forward slopes of the ridge. Lieutenant Robert Belcher took the regimental colour of the 32nd Foot from the hands of Ensign John Birtwhistle who had just been severely wounded. Ahead, a mounted French officer fell to the ground under his shot horse. By the time the Frenchman had struggled free, Belcher was close to him. Suddenly the reckless French officer confronted Belcher and snatched the colour. It was all over in seconds. The Covering Colour-Sergeant, Christopher Switzer, thrust his pike into the officer's chest while Private Lacy fired at point blank range. Captain William Toole had called out to 'save the brave fellow' but the gallant Frenchman lay dead at Belcher's feet.

Captain Alexander Kennedy Clark had charged with the 1st (Royal) Dragoons 200 metres or so east of the crossroads and soon collided with the French infantry:

From the nature of the ground we did not see each other until we were very close, perhaps eighty or ninety yards. The head of the Column appeared to be seized with a panic, gave us a fire which brought down about twenty men, went instantly about and endeavoured to regain the opposite side of the hedges; but we were upon and amongst them before this could be effected, the whole Column getting into one dense mass, the men between the advancing and retiring parts getting so jammed together that the men could not bring down their arms, or use them effectively, and we had nothing to do but continue to press them down the slope.[26]

Captain Kennedy Clark and Corporal Francis Stiles seized the treasured eagle standard of the French 105th Line infantry which is now on display at the National Army Museum at London. To the east, the Irish howl of the 6th (Inniskilling) Dragoons struck fear into the opposing ranks which were knocked over like bowling pins.[27] Further east, the Scots Greys had charged through the 92nd Highlanders to cut up the French. 'Scotland for ever!' roared the elated Gordons. Corporal John Dickson of the Greys noticed his friend Pipe-Major Alexander Cameron of the 92nd standing on a hillock and calmly playing 'Johnny Cope, are ye waukin' yet?' Then his ears echoed with the frenzied battle cry of the Highlanders urging him on: 'Go at them, the Greys! Scotland for ever!'

'My blood thrilled at this', Dickson wrote, 'and I clutched my sabre tighter. Many of the Highlanders grasped our stirrups, and in the fiercest excitement dashed with us into the fight.' The astounded French had no time to form square and although some 'were fighting like tigers', they could not prevent the Greys destroying the column in under three minutes. 'One could hardly believe, had he not witnessed it, that such complete destruction could have been effected in so short a time,' wrote Lieutenant Robert Winchester of the Gordons.[28]

Thomas Creevey, a civilian, visited the field after the battle and discovered that 'just close up to within a yard or two of a small ragged hedge which was our own line, the French lay as if they had been mowed down in a row without any interval.'[29] Whole ranks of French infantry laid down their muskets in surrender. Many of these Frenchmen then ran away and escaped to their own lines. Some who had been spared by the British horsemen fired at their saviours. Captain Kennedy Clark saw a man aiming at him and only saved his life by a sudden turn of his head; the musket-ball took off the tip of his nose.[30] The adjutant of the Inniskillings, Michael Clusky, was not so fortunate. A French soldier on his knees coolly took aim in the midst of an infantry column and shot him through the head.[31]

'It was one of the finest charges ever seen,' decided Captain William Tomkinson as he watched from the ranks of the 16th Light Dragoons.[32] Sergeant Charles Ewart of the Greys carried off the eagle of the 45th Line infantry after a desperate fight. 'How terrible they are, these Grey Horses,' declared Napoleon in amazement as he observed the Scots Greys helping to destroy his main attack.[33]

The charge, having succeeded so brilliantly at first, went out of control. The British cavalry's discipline was poor. They reached the bottom of the valley in front of you and commenced ascending the ridge occupied by the Great Battery. 'Then we got among the guns, and we had our revenge,' remembered Corporal Dickson. 'Such slaughtering! We sabred the gunners, lamed the horses, and cut their traces and harness. I can hear the Frenchmen yet crying "Diable!" when I struck at them, and the long-drawn hiss through their teeth as my sword went home ... The artillery drivers sat on their horses weeping aloud as we went among them; they were mere boys, we thought.' The wild dragoons put up to forty guns out of action. From where you are standing on the crest of Wellington's ridge, one of Picton's officers watched in increasing alarm:

> I had now sufficient time and leisure to admit of my peeping into the valley, and there I saw a sight which rivetted my attention, and I may say chained every faculty. The entire valley presented a scene of scattered and individual combats between the isolated of both armies, principally cavalry ... On the other side, detachments from a French column, drawn up in their

position, were ... destroying and taking prisoners such of our cavalry as had ventured too far, particularly the Scots Greys, – those terrible 'chevaux gris' [grey horses], who, by their ill-timed impetuosity, lost many men and horses. Flushed with their victory, they galloped up by twos and threes, and even singly, as if in defiance. An officer was attempting to bring them off: I could distinctly see a French soldier level his piece, fire, and bring him rolling to the ground. I saw his body on the spot next morning: he was an elegant young man, and even in death had a proud, aristocratic mien. He appeared as if asleep (such is the effect of gun-shot wounds), and had not then been stripped. He was sleeping in glory.[34]

Nemesis followed. French lancers swept in from the east to cut off and spear the scattered and exhausted British dragoons without mercy. Lieutenant Charles Wyndham of the Scots Greys perceived that the lancers were 'evidently going in pursuit of our wounded and dismounted men [and] did not attack the small main body of our regiment.'[35] 'I saw the lances rise and fall for a moment,' remembered Corporal Dickson, 'and Sam Tar, the leading man of ours, go down amid the flash of steel. I felt a sudden rage at this, for I knew the poor fellow well; he was a corporal in our troop. The crash as we met [the lancers] was terrible; the horses began to rear and bite and neigh loudly, and then some of our men got down among their feet, and I saw them trying to ward off the lances with their hands.'[36]

Troop Sergeant-Major Matthew Marshall of the Inniskilling Dragoons dealt a sword stroke to a cuirassier on his right only to receive a blow which broke his left arm. Further on he rode into a band of French horsemen and fell from his saddle as a lance pierced his side. He felt two other blows, one of which broke his right thigh. He came to only to find horses charging over him. Later he spotted a riderless horse and dragged himself towards it but just as he tried to mount a Frenchman cut him down. Marshall would spend the rest of the battle lying on the mud as French artillerymen fired their cannon over him; one gunner rested his foot on Marshall while reloading. Although suffering from nineteen wounds Marshall survived three nights on the battlefield and only died in 1825.[37]

Two brigades of Wellington's light cavalry under Major-Generals Sir John Vandeleur and Baron Charles-Etienne de Ghigny advanced from reserve to cover the retreat of the dazed survivors of the British heavy brigades. By 3.00 pm the valley was empty once more of troops but was strewn with hundreds of corpses. Wellington had beaten off an extremely serious attack and taken 3000 prisoners but had lost many of his best infantry. Moreover, his heavy cavalry was so badly mauled that it was practically a spent force. The commanders of both the Scots Greys and the 1st (King's) Dragoon Guards had been slain. The French, on the other hand, had 9000 splendid cavalrymen still in hand and at 4.00 pm these were unleashed on to the ridge.

# Notes

1. C. Hibbert ed., *The Wheatley diary* (1964), p.65
2. 'Operations of the Fifth or Picton's Division in the campaign of Waterloo', in *United Service Magazine* (June 1841), p.178
3. MacKenzie MacBride ed., *With Napoleon at Waterloo* (1911), p.159
4. 'Operations of the Fifth or Picton's Division in the campaign of Waterloo', in *United Service Magazine* (June 1841), p.178. Bijlandt's brigade, initially posted on the forward slope of the ridge, 100 metres south of the hedged track, withdrew to the ridge crest before Napoleon's Grand Battery opened fire.
5. Because of this staggering of the columns, the action on the crest of Wellington's ridge was far longer and slower and fragmented than is usually realised. The four columns consisted, from west to east, of the 28th and 105th Line infantry from Quiot's division; Donzelot's division; Marcognet's division; and Durutte's division. Durutte left one of his regiments in reserve and detached skirmishers to attack Papelotte, La Haye, Smohain and Frichermont. His column does not appear to have clashed with Wellington's infantry on the ridge crest as the other columns seem to have been repulsed before Durutte arrived. Colonel Best, commander of a Hanoverian landwehr brigade posted immediately east of Picton stated that only skirmishing occurred in his front, which indicates that Durutte's column was still on the march towards the ridge (BL Add MSS 34,704/279).
6. J. Kincaid, *Adventures in the Rifle Brigade and random shots from a rifleman* (1909), p.166; BL Add. MSS 34,707/212
7. Henry Houssaye asserted that the third column, Marcognet's division, went straight through the hedged track but it is clear that the first and second columns never crossed the track.
8. C. Terlinden, *Souvenirs d'un grognard belge* (n.d.)
9. BL Add. MSS 34,703/20; the testimony of Major-General Baron Jean-Victor de Constant-Rebecque, chief-of-staff of the Netherlands contingent, confirms that the bulk of Bijlandt's brigade broke and fled under the impact of the French columns: 'the first brigade ... received the first shock and was cut up. The enemy already penetrated beyond the hedged track on the plateau.' During the charge by the British Union Brigade, Rebecque was still trying 'to reform the battalions of General Bijlandt's brigade and to bring them forward again.' (Société des études historiques et folkloriques de Waterloo, Braine-l'Alleud et environs, *Mélanges historiques* [1970], p.146)
10. Letter of Lieutenant Alexander Forbes of the 79th Highlanders: BL Add. MSS 34,705/107; it is only fair to add that a NCO of Major Thomas Rogers's foot battery even spiked his gun at this stage of the action to render it useless should the French seize it, as he clearly expected them to do: H. Siborne ed., *The Waterloo letters* (1983), p.238
11. BL Add. MSS 34,707/136
12. 'Operations of the Fifth or Picton's Division in the campaign of Waterloo', in *United Service Magazine* (June 1841), p.177; this band was probably from the Belgian 7th Infantry.
13. E. Longford, *Wellington: the years of the sword* (1972), p.462
14. H. Siborne ed., *The Waterloo letters* (1983), p.21
15. G. Thomas, Earl of Albemarle, *Fifty years of my life* (1877), p.120
16. E. Longford, *Wellington: the years of the sword* (1972), p.355
17. Earl Stanhope, *Conversations with the Duke of Wellington* (1938), p.68
18. E. Longford, *Wellington: the years of the sword* (1972), p.400; Earl Stanhope, *Conversations with the Duke of Wellington* (1938), p.69
19. H. Maxwell, *Life of Wellington* (1900), v.2, p.70
20. Letter of Lieutenant Alexander Hope, 92nd Highlanders: BL Add MSS 34,703/20. Hope stated that the two units involved were the 1st and 44th but clearly muddled the 42nd and 44th. Later he states that the 42nd was posted on an important spot considerably to the left. Lieutenant Alexander Riddock of the 44th wrote that the 44th 'composed the left of the 5th or Scots Division and was on the Extreme left of the British front Line.' (BL Add MSS 34,704/123).
   The historian William Siborne wrongly assumed the 1st and 42nd Foot supported the 92nd in its successful counter-attack on the third French column. When Lieutenant Robert Winchester of

the Gordons read Siborne's history, he wrote to him in protest: 'now the fact is that the 92nd Highlanders and Scots Greys were the only Regiments which had any share whatever in the attack and defeat of the Column above alluded to, and, so far as I am aware the 42nd have never made the least claim as in any way participating in the affair.' (BL Add. MSS 34,708/212; see also BL Add. MSS 34,708/260)

21. BL Add MSS 34,703/20. According to Lieutenant James Kerr Ross, Pack told the 92nd's commander: 'every thing now depends on the 92nd, as all in front of yours have given way' (BL Add MSS 34,703/341). Lieutenant Robert Winchester gave the following version: '92nd, everything has given way on your right and left and you must charge this Column' (H. Siborne ed., *The Waterloo letters* [1983], p.383)

22. BL Add MSS 34,703/20. In contrast, accounts by British cavalry officers assert that the Highlanders were in confusion and that it was the cavalry which repulsed the French column: see, for instance, H. Siborne ed., *The Waterloo letters* (1983), p.81. See also BL Add MSS 34,704/279. Yet Picton's infantry officers insist that their units repulsed the French columns. For example, see 'Operations of the Fifth or Picton's Division in the campaign of Waterloo', in *United Service Magazine* (June 1841), p.179: 'with regard to any *"bayonet conflict,"* I saw none. We appeared to charge, and disperse, and *make a road through* the columns, – the usual result of the British charge.' The fact that the British battalions wheeled back from line into column to allow the cavalry through may have led the cavalrymen to conclude the infantry were in disorder: 'Operations of the Fifth or Picton's Division in the campaign of Waterloo', in *United Service Magazine* (June 1841), p.178. Nonetheless, the sudden appearance of the Scots Greys would certainly have hastened, if it did not actually provoke, the French column's flight.

23. H. Lot, *Les deux généraux Ordener* (1910), p.91

24. H. Siborne ed., *The Waterloo letters* (1983), p.79

25. 'Operations of the Fifth or Picton's Division in the campaign of Waterloo', in *United Service Magazine* (June 1841), pp.179–80

26. H. Siborne ed., *The Waterloo letters* (1983), pp.70–1

27. A Near Observer, *The Battle of Waterloo* (1816), pp.90, 72

28. H. Siborne ed., *The Waterloo letters* (1983), p.383

29. H. Maxwell ed., *The Creevey Papers* (1906), p.238

30. H. Siborne ed., *The Waterloo letters* (1983), pp.71–2

31. *Ibid*, p.84

32. W. Tomkinson, *The diary of a cavalry officer in the Peninsular and Waterloo campaigns, 1809–1815* (1894), p.300

33. A Near Observer, *The Battle of Waterloo* (1816), p.136. Research by Richard Moore has shown that in the confusion of this stage of the battle other standards were captured and then recaptured. The eagle of the 55th Line appears temporarily to have been in British hands (*The Journal of the Napoleonic Association*, nos. 10 and 11).

34. 'Operations of the Fifth or Picton's Division in the campaign of Waterloo', in *United Service Magazine* (June 1841), p.180

35. BL Add. MSS 34,707/24; we have corrected Wyndham's punctuation

36. MacKenzie MacBride ed., *With Napoleon at Waterloo* (1911), p.146

37. C. Dalton, *The Waterloo roll call* (1978), p.269

# 6

# THE PANORAMA: PREPARE TO
# RECEIVE CAVALRY!

Waterloo, like Gettysburg and Borodino, is one of those fortunate battlefields which has a giant panorama painting of the height of the fighting. The Waterloo panorama is on the top floor of the white circular building at the foot of the Lion Mound. It depicts the great French cavalry charges on Wellington's infantry, who formed up in defensive squares on the order 'prepare to receive cavalry!' Much of the actual ground on which the charges occurred was altered when the Lion Mound was built so it is best to follow this phase of the battle inside the panorama.

The panorama building was erected between 1910 and 1912 and initially gave rise to protests, as it hid a large part of the Lion Mound and seemed to signal the arrival of speculators keen to build tourist attractions over the battlefield.[1]

The main credit for the panorama lies with Louis Dumoulin who was ably helped by Desvreux, Robiquet, Malespina and Meir. All were French and had a variety of specialised painting talent from portraits to animals; a Belgian, Vinck, added the life-like terrain in front of the painting. Dumoulin and his colleagues benefitted from the advice of descendents of combatants from the three armies at Waterloo. Dumoulin disliked being distracted from his work so the door of the panorama building was always locked while he toiled at his masterpiece. One of the few to observe him painting the panorama was Lucien Pleunes, who in 1970 described what he saw:

Monsieur Dumoulin, whose volubility and French accent astonished me, carefully explained on location the creation of his immense plan and showed us a series of sketches which he himself and one of his French helpers had already drawn on the canvas. One of them portrayed Napoleon and his staff and left a strong impression on me. Next he showed us an extensive collection of small colour prints reproducing the uniforms of the various regiments which had participated in the battle and which he used as models in the execution of his work. After he had finished his explanations, the painter went to perch on a high, mobile platform and continued the work he had begun the previous day:

the painting showing the billows of fire and smoke bursting from the Château of Hougoumont. It is at this precise point that the artist started the stirring fresco which today still charms the mind and delights the eyes.[2]

The painting is twelve metres high and 110 metres long. A staircase ascends to the viewing gallery and immediately you find yourself in the middle of the battle. The panorama does not represent a single moment but compresses the two hours of the cavalry charges from 4.00 pm onwards into a frozen image of time.

The first charges were made by Lieutenant-General Count Edouard Milhaud's IV Cavalry Corps supported by Lieutenant-General Charles Lefebvre-Desnouëttes' Guard light cavalry. Shortly after 4.30 pm they were reinforced by Lieutenant-General François Kellermann's III Cavalry Corps and the Guard heavy cavalry under Lieutenant-General Baron Claude Guyot.

Marshal Ney had ordered the first charge after attacking La Haie Sainte with French infantry at 3.30 pm. He had noticed the foremost of Wellington's infantry along the ridge crest withdrawing under a fierce French artillery barrage. In fact, Wellington's units were moving back only a hundred metres or so to shelter on the reverse slopes. However, to the impetuous Ney it seemed to be the beginning of a general retreat. Ney was so elated that he called upon cavalry alone to overrun Wellington's lines. Modern military doctrine requires infantry to act in close support of armour which is attacking hostile infantry. Similarly, in the Napoleonic era it was vital to use infantry and artillery to support cavalry charging against infantry. In the absence of such close support by the other arms, Ney's cavalrymen were massacred by Wellington's firepower. Although they charged repeatedly they failed to break Wellington's infantry squares.

To follow the cavalry charges in detail on the panorama, face to the south and then rotate anti-clockwise. The central figure in the foreground is the fiery redhead, Marshal Ney himself, hatless and mounted on one of his luckless horses. He had at least five shot underneath him in the course of the battle. The officer in red hussar uniform and mounted on a grey horse is Ney's loyal ADC, Colonel Heymès. Behind follow massed squadrons of breastplated cuirassiers while in the background stands more cavalry in reserve.

Ensign Rees Gronow of the British 1st Guards was awestruck by the immense, powerful appearance of the massed ranks of armoured cuirassiers: 'not a man present who survived could have forgotten in after life the awful grandeur of that charge. You perceived at a distance what appeared to be an overwhelming, long moving line, which, ever advancing, glittered like a stormy wave of the sea when it catches the sunlight.'[3]

Further to the left, tall trees line the Brussels road, but this is a mistake as no trees were there in 1815. The trees were present, however, in 1912 when the

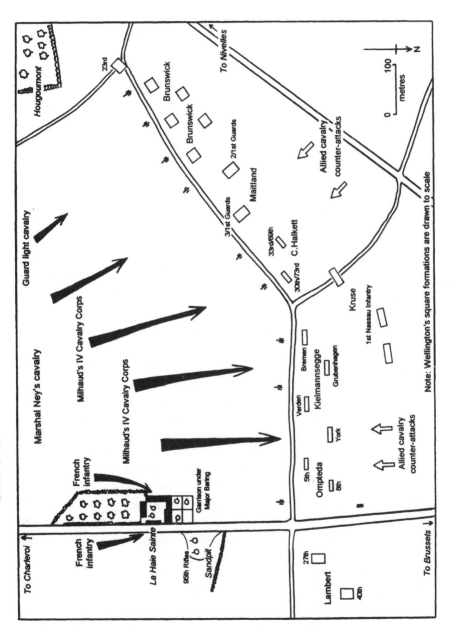

THE ONSET OF THE FRENCH CAVALRY CHARGES

To Charleroi

Houguomont

23rd

Brunswick

Brunswick

Brunswick

Maitland

2/1st Guards

3/1st Guards

To Nivelles

Allied cavalry
counter-attacks

0    100
metres

N

Guard light cavalry

Marshal Ney's cavalry

Milhaud's IV Cavalry Corps

Milhaud's IV Cavalry Corps

French infantry

French infantry

La Haie Sainte

Garrison under Major Baring

95th Rifles

Sandpit

33rd/69th

C. Halkett

30th/73rd

Kruse

1st Nassau Infantry

Bremen

Verden

Kielmannsegge

Grubenhagen

York

Ompteda

5th

8th

Allied cavalry
counter-attacks

Note: Wellington's square formations are drawn to scale

27th

Lambert

40th

To Brussels

panorama was painted. In the background you can see Napoleon on a white horse and followed by his staff. In fact, Napoleon only came as far north as this point in the evening, during the attack by his Middle Guard.

The farm of La Haie Sainte, still besieged by infantry, is easily distinguishable and in front are the Red Lancers of the Guard light cavalry. Behind the lancers follow the green-coated Guard Chasseurs à cheval. Preceeding the lancers are the 1st Cuirassiers, identified by the number on their horse furniture. They are advancing at a fast trot as the heavy ground and tired horses did not permit the horsemen to work up to a frenzied gallop. Even so, the earth reverberated under the heavy drumming of thousands of hooves as the cavalry advanced towards the steady infantry squares.

The 12th Cuirassiers are crossing the lane which marks the crest of Wellington's ridge. Near the crossroads, this lane was enclosed by steep, slippery banks ten or fifteen feet high.[4] According to the French novelist Victor Hugo, waves of cuirassiers tumbled into this sunken lane and crushed each other to death. Although Hugo exaggerated the scale of the catastrophe in order to explain the failure of the French cavalry charges, his account does have an element of truth. Colonel Count Michel Ordener, commander of the 1st Cuirassiers, described how he encountered the sunken lane, 'into which I rolled with our leading ranks and pulled myself out by hanging on to the tail of the horse of one of my cuirassiers.'[5] Nevertheless, the lane became progressively less deep further to the west and offered no obstacle to Ney's cavalry 175 metres from the crossroads.

Two squares of the 1st Nassau infantry in green coats and buff belts are assailed ferociously by French cuirassiers. Scenes such as these occurred all along the line. Lieutenant Wheatley of Ompteda's brigade wrote that 'the sharp-toothed bayonet bit many an adventurous fool, and on all sides we presented our bristly points like the peevish porcupines assailed by clamorous dogs.'[6] As the sharp musketry volleys ploughed into the cuirassiers, helmets fell to the ground, riders bounced convulsively from their saddles and horses reared in terror and anger from the pain of their wounds. Against a hail of fire distinctively clattering into their breastplates, the cuirassiers pushed forward with their heads tilted down as if fighting their way through a windy storm. Thus they appeared encased in armour from the top down: helmet crests like visors, breastplates like the armour of mediaeval knights.

Until 3.00 pm the 1st Nassau infantrymen had been wearing white protective covers over their shakos and cartridge pouches. However, their General August von Kruse found these served as such good targets for the French artillery that he ordered his troops to remove them.[7] A lieutenant in a nearby square saw a cannon-ball snatch a Nassau officer so cleanly from the saddle that his horse never stirred.[8] Major-General Baron Jean-Victor de Constant-Rebecque, chief-of-staff of the Netherlands contingent, described how:

I was often obliged to go to rally the three squares of the Nassau contingent, which were composed of young troops seeing action for the first time, and were often yielding ground. Several times I brought them back at a charge. At one moment, one of these battalions was totally routed by some explosions in the midst of its packed ranks. But by throwing myself in front of them, I succeeded in halting and bringing them back.[9]

The farm of Mont St Jean can be seen amidst the smoke immediately above the yellow Nassau flag. To the right of the Nassauers are Hanoverian infantrymen of Major-General Count Kielmannsegge's brigade.

Note the abandoned artillery piece on the track in front of the green-coated Nassauers. The front line batteries were positioned fifty metres or so in front of the track and fired directly at the approaching squadrons until the last moment.[10] Then the gunners would gather up their tools, such as ramrods and slowmatches, and dash back to shelter inside the infantry squares.

Sometimes they sheltered instead beneath the guns. A mounted cavalryman would find it almost impossible to reach down and kill a gunner who was sheltering beneath a cannon barrel and the wheels of a gun carriage. Instead, the French horsemen would pursue those gunners they had caught out in the open. According to Lieutenant-General Count Edouard Milhaud, commander of the French IV Cavalry Corps, his men sabred those 'gunners who had not had time to throw themselves into holes which had been prepared to shelter them.'[11] As soon as the rebuffed Frenchmen fell back from the squares, the gunners ran out again to fire into the retreating units. Each battery left its horses and ammunition waggons to the rear; waggons left at intervals to collect more ammunition from the depot in the Forest of Soignes. Captain Samuel Rudyard of Major William Lloyd's battery recalled that:

> The ground we occupied was much furrowed up by the recoil of our Guns and the grazing of the shot, and many holes from the bursting of shells buried in the ground. As horses were killed or rendered unserviceable, the harness was removed and placed on the waggons, or elsewhere. Our men's knapsacks were neatly packed on the front and rear of our limbers and waggons, that they might do their work more easily. Every *Gun*, every carriage, spokes carried from wheels, all were struck in many places.[12]

Wellington was well served by his artillery at Waterloo but did little to acknowledge it. Edward Cotton of the 7th Hussars, a perceptive eyewitness, commented that 'the fire of our artillery throughout the action surpassed anything of the kind ever before witnessed, frequently making wide roads through the enemy masses.'[13] Sergeant Morris of the 73rd Foot agreed that the well-sited allied artillery did great execution.[14]

Wellington's guns fired not only ordinary roundshot and shells at the French cavalry but also the deadly canister rounds, consisting of a tin can containing dozens of balls. When the gun was fired and the can burst, these balls razed the massed cavalry by bringing down men and horses in swathes. Corpses piled up like packs of cards, the men not even having been displaced from the saddle.[15] Often, the guns would be double loaded with both a roundshot and canister in order to wreak maximum destruction with a single discharge.

The French cavalry gave little thought towards neutralising the allied artillery fire. A few nails hammered into the touchholes could easily and effectively disable cannon. However, the cavalrymen were reluctant to dismount and put themselves at risk in the swirling *mêlée* of battle. Wellington's cavalry commander, Lord Uxbridge, was launching repeated mounted counter-attacks to sweep the French off the ridge.

Wellington's artillery moved in all directions about the field and not just laterally along the line to take up safer or more commanding positions. It also moved between the first and second line, either from reserve to reinforce the front line or to withdraw to refit and repair casualties. 'As the Artillery were shifted according to circumstances, it would (even if it were possible) create much confusion in detailing their situations on the ground,' noted Lieutenant-Colonel Sir John May, of the Royal Artillery staff.[16] However, batteries became more static as the battle progressed because of increasing casualties, especially among the teams of horses who pulled the guns.

To the left of the Nassauers are three squares of redcoats. In fact only two British squares stood in this section of the line: the 30th and 73rd Foot united in one square and the 33rd and 69th in the other. These units formed Major-General Sir Colin Halkett's British 5th Brigade. One of the squares is wrongly depicted as including Highlanders; the 73rd Foot was a Scottish regiment but wore trousers. Only the 42nd, 79th and 92nd wore kilts at Waterloo and they were all to the east of the crossroads.

Note how the squares in this sector are disposed in mutual support to set up a deadly crossfire. The bayonets of the squares' front two ranks presented a thick hedge of burnished steel while the rear two took aim with their muskets. The disciplined crashes of musketry volleys broke out along Wellington's line when the French had advanced to within thirty yards' distance from the squares. Several men and horses fell. Other chargers, terrified by the explosions and stabs of flashing fire, either halted and refused to go forward or swerved to sweep past the front face of the squares and through the intervals between the blocks of infantry.

Successive ranks of cavalry, their forward motion blocked by the barrier of dead and wounded horses, also swept past the flanks of the infantry formations, to be blasted by volleys from these faces too. Captain Alexander Cavalié Mercer, commander of 'G' Troop, Royal Horse Artillery, watched the extraordinary scene from reserve in Wellington's second line:

Suddenly a dark mass of cavalry appeared for an instant on the main ridge, and then came sweeping down the slope in swarms, reminding me of an enormous surf bursting over the prostrate hull of a stranded vessel, and then running, hissing and foaming, up the beach. The hollow space became in a twinkling covered with horsemen, crossing, turning, and riding about in all directions, apparently without any object.[17]

As they swirled around the small, beleaguered squares, the French cavalry were shattered. They became caught in the crossfire launched from the squares of both the first and second lines.

Although the musketry unhorsed many riders and intimidated the horses from approaching the squares, it was by no means as effective as artillery fire. Edward Cotton of the 7th Hussars wrote that 'the fire of the volleys from our squares did no serious damage, the individual file firing was the most destructive to the enemy's cavalry.'[18] He attributed this phenomenon to the tendency of infantry when loading in a hurry not to bother to ram the musketball down to the powder in the barrel. Thus the speed at which the ball was propelled out of the musket diminished significantly.[19] Ensign Rees Gronow provides another clue: 'our musketry did not at first seem to kill many men; though it brought down a large number of horses, and created indescribable confusion.'[20]

The infantry, obsessed with the belief that the armour of the cuirassiers was impenetrable by musketry, were aiming instead at the horses. The fallen cavalrymen then struggled, unhurt, to their feet, unfastened and abandoned their heavy breastplates before fleeing on foot to the French position. No wonder that Wellington's artillery, firing at men and horses alike, caused greater execution among the riders.

Note the cuirassier trying to back his terrified horse into the square of Highlanders. This was the only way the riders could make their mounts push into the bayonet-bristling squares. However, this method did not provide enough momentum to crush and break through the infantry ranks.

Sergeant Tom Morris was kneeling with bayonet fixed in the front ranks of one of Halkett's two squares. His neighbour had a slight defect of speech and used to call out to him each time the cavalry charged: 'Tom, Tom; here comes the *calvary*.'[21] Another redcoat was blinded by blood streaming down his face from a desperate head wound. Tom Morris watched as he rushed away in the belief he was heading for the hospitals in the rear: 'he was actually rushing into the thickest of the battle, calling out loudly and most piteously for relief. He met the cuirassiers who were again advancing, and the foremost of them cutting the poor fellow down with the sword, the rest of them rode over him.'[22]

One of the wounded cuirassiers lying on the ground could not bear his shame or agony. He tried to commit suicide with his sword but it was too long. Instead he found a bayonet nearby, placed it under his stomach and fell on it.[23]

The red-coated horsemen you can see exchanging sword strokes with the cuirassiers are British heavy cavalry launched by Lord Uxbridge to repel the now shattered and disordered French.[24] Sweat poured down the gallant earl's face as he galloped from unit to unit to urge them on. 'I've charged at the head of every cavalry regiment and they all want spurs', he commented after the battle.[25]

'The cavalry charges were continuous,' recalled Major-General Baron Jean-Victor de Constant-Rebecque, chief-of-staff of the Netherlands contingent. 'Those of the enemy rushed like torrents of lava between our squares, into which we repeatedly went to seek refuge. Then our cavalry charged in its turn. General Trip made a fine charge with our [Netherlands] carabiniers.'[26]

The cavalry clashes produced some terrific encounters. One British life-guardsman found himself fighting two cuirassiers and after killing one with his sword, he launched such a powerful backhanded cut to the neck of the other that the Frenchman's head, with the helmet still attached, flew off some distance. The terrified horse galloped off, with the headless rider staying in the saddle holding the reins as the blood spurted like a fountain from the neck. Then he gradually tottered, and slid into the mud.[27]

Usually, Uxbridge's cavalry won their encounters with the French horsemen as the later had already been disorganised by volleys from the infantry squares. On occasion, the superior discipline and manoeuvrability of the French cavalry gained the upper hand. Sergeant Roy of the 7th Cuirassiers remembered how Colonel Michel Ordener skilfully manoeuvred a cuirassier brigade so as to surround, as if in a circle of iron, a mass of English cavalry which was then almost entirely destroyed.[28]

Between the Nassauers and the redcoats is the Prince of Orange in a dark coat. He was the eldest son of the Dutch king and conducted himself with immense personal bravery even if his judgement in military matters was sometimes flawed. He was only twenty-two. To the right of the prince the 4th (Dutch) Light Dragoons and 8th (Belgian) Hussars are advancing to the charge.

To the left of the prince and above the second British square you can see the Duke of Wellington on his brown horse, Copenhagen. He later commented that the bravest action he had seen in battle was 'the repeated charges of the French Cavalry at Waterloo.'[29] On another occasion he was asked whether the French cavalry had not come up very well. 'Yes,' he replied with a laugh, 'and they went down very well too!' He was remembering the unhorsed cuirassiers sprawling helplessly on the ground in their heavy breastplates, like so many overturned turtles.[30]

Just below the Duke, Major-General Baron Jean-Baptiste van Merlen of the Netherlands cavalry collapses on his horse, having been mortally wounded by a cannon-shot. He died two hours later in a shed at Mont St Jean; his last words were that he died at peace, having never harmed anyone.[31] In former years he had served as second-in-command of Napoleon's Red (Dutch) Lancers of the Imperial Guard. When Napoleon fell in 1814, van Merlen entered the service of the United Netherlands for he could not have known that Napoleon would return from exile. In 1815, van Merlen remained loyal to his new allegiance even though it tragically opposed him both to his former Emperor and his old regiment, the Red Lancers. His own brother served at Waterloo in the French II Corps. Before being wounded, van Merlen is said to have encountered a French acquaintance whom he could have captured. Instead, he merely saluted and politely informed him: 'General, this is my side of the battlefield, yours is over there. Take care of yourself; farewell!'[32]

Note three gruesome episodes in the foreground. One dismounted cuirassier raises his sword to strike down an oblivious Highlander in front of him. To the left a trooper of the 8th Cuirassiers has just cut open a Scotsman's head. Below, a third Highlander, having no weapons but his teeth, bites a Frenchman's hand.

To the left of Colin Halkett's brigade are two squares of the British 1st Guards under Major-General Peregrine Maitland. Ensign Rees Gronow was in one of them. 'Our square was a perfect hospital, being full of dead, dying, and mutilated soldiers', he wrote. 'Inside we were nearly suffocated by the smoke and smell from burnt cartridges. It was impossible to move a yard without treading upon a wounded comrade, or upon the bodies of the dead; and the loud groans of the wounded and dying were most appalling.'[33]

Notice how a body of cuirassiers is sweeping round to avoid collision with one of Halkett's squares and is heading for the open ground between Halkett and Maitland. The French cavalry never charged home in massed formation on to the squares. 'I many times saw masses of horse advance to within thirty or forty yards of the squares, when, seeing the determined firmness of the latter, they invariably edged away and withdrew,' wrote Lieutenant Basil Jackson of the staff. 'Sometimes they would halt and gaze at the formidable triple [double] row of bayonets, when two or three individuals might be seen to leave their places in the ranks, striving by voice and gesture to urge them forward: placing their helmets on their swords, they waved them aloft, a bootless display of gallantry; for the fine fellows they addressed remained immoveable, knowing that certain death would be the consequence of any nearer approach.'[34]

Another eyewitness, an engineer officer sheltering in a square, wrote that:

> The first time a body of cuirassiers approached the square into which I had ridden, the men – all young soldiers – seemed to be alarmed. They fired high, and with little effect; in one of the angles there was just as much hesitation as made me feel exceedingly uncomfortable; but it did not last long. No actual dash was made upon us. Now and then an individual more daring than the rest would ride up to the bayonets, wave his sword about, and bully; but the mass held aloof, pulling up within five yards, as if, though afraid to go on, they were ashamed to retire.[35]

In the foreground, the Imperial Guard dragoons are overrunning a horse artillery battery whose gunners have not had time to run for shelter. The direction in which the guns are pointing is improbable. Brigadier-General Frédéric de Donop, commander of a cuirassier brigade, lies on the ground near the guns in a blue coat and white gloves. He had been wounded and unhorsed in an earlier charge.

Behind the Guard dragoons you can see Hougoumont, surrounded by trees, in flames. To the right of Hougoumont dense smoke conceals some Brunswick squares. One eyewitness described these black-coated Germans as revelling, like salamanders, in the fire of battle. They were certainly capable of bitter cruelty. Their Duke and commander had been killed at Quatre Bras. Ensign Rees Gronow of the nearby British Guards saw the Red Lancers charging a square of Brunswickers, to be deflected by the musketry. As they fell back, they left an officer trapped under his wounded horse. Two Brunswickers broke ranks, liberated the officer from his purse, watch and other valuables before putting his own pistols to his head and blowing his brains into the mud. Nearby British ranks jeered 'Shame! Shame!'

Gronow's comrade Ensign Robert Batty recalled how an Imperial Guard officer saw a gun in the vicinity about to be discharged at his men. Without hesitating, the officer rode straight at the gun and prevented it being fired until he was picked off by a Brunswicker. He had laid down his life for his friends.[36]

You have now completed a circuit of the panorama. It imparts a strong visual impact of the horror of the fighting. A recently installed sound system now indicates the deafening tumult but the panorama still fails to convey either the mingled smells of battle or the claustrophobic atmosphere of heat and smoke. Eyewitnesses affirm that along the contested ridge lay a zone of heavy smoke and to enter that zone was to enter an oven. The air had been heated by the ceaseless artillery fire, musketry and explosions of ammunition waggons. Sweat poured off man and beast so profusely that steam rose into the air. The aroma of the sweaty horses mingled with the acrid, suffocating smell of burnt powder.

Visibility was so poor that British staff officers, galloping across the fields, had to dash for the safety of the squares as swirls of smoke suddenly gave way to swirls of hostile horsemen. The smoke drifted gently over the corn for there was but little breeze. Wellington once sent his ADC, Colonel Sir Alexander Gordon, to ask Sir Colin Halkett what square of his was so far in advance. The Duke, peering through the smoke, had seen a red blob which in fact was no square but a mass of dead and wounded from the 30th and 73rd Foot.[37]

The noise was tremendous. Lieutenant Edmund Wheatley of Ompteda's brigade reflected on the field of battle: 'nothing could equal the splendour and terror of the scene. Charge after charge succeeded in constant succession. The clashing of swords, the clattering of musketry, the hissing of balls, and shouts and clamours produced a sound, jarring and confounding the senses, as if hell and the Devil were in evil contention.'[38]

The din made men deaf and hoarse. Besides the constant roar of artillery going off, men heard musket-balls and canister clattering on swords and breastplates, like a fierce hailstorm beating on a window pane. The unearthly humming of musket-balls and cannon-balls in flight bewildered many. One surgeon exclaimed: 'my God, what *is* that? What *is* all this noise? How curious! – how very curious!' Another cannonball whizzed past and the surgeon twisted round. '*There! – there!* What *is* it all?'[39] The cacophonous symphony of battle played on.

The killing intensified. Guns still roared over the desolate scene. Shattered muskets, abandoned swords, broken carts and heaped corpses littered the ravaged and trampled field. Shafts of sunlight occasionally broke through the heavy clouds to gleam off twisting swords and off breastplates.

Pillars of smoke from exploding ammunition waggons rose now and again and boiled up into the sky before opening into mushroom clouds. So great was the general noise of battle that no one, except in the immediate vicinity, heard these explosions. Frenzied horses dragged one blazing waggon along the rear of the allied lines. A British hussar fired his pistol at the panicking animals but missed. The waggon exploded seconds later killing or maiming the horses. Some of the mutilated beasts dashed around while others calmly began to eat grass until they finally collapsed and died. Another horribly mangled animal, sensing a safe haven, hovered about an infantry square.

Lieutenant Wheatley was horrified: 'I took a calm survey of the field around and felt shocked at the sight of broken armour, lifeless bodies, murdered horses, shattered wheels, caps, helmets, swords, muskets, pistols, still and silent. Here and there a frightened horse would rush scross the plain trampling on the dying and the dead.'[40] ADCs were also darting across, incredibly fast, taking messages from commander to commanded and back again.

Wellington's troops feared the destructive power of the French artillery far more than they did the cavalry charges. Ensign Rees Gronow decided that 'the charges of cavalry were in appearance very formidable, but in reality a great relief, as the artillery could no longer fire at us.'[41] The violence of the barrages was worse than anything the veterans had known.[42]

The squares afforded protection from sword and lance but were small and overcrowded, making them a perfect target for French gunners. Ensign Robert Batty asserted that the murderous intensity and deadly precision of the French artillery fire was never equalled. Whenever the French cavalry retired into the valley, their artillery opened up again. Batty and his comrades would lie down to shelter but every now and again a shell would bring death out of the sky.[43] Edward Cotton of the 7th Hussars remembered vividly how each charge was preceded 'by a tremendous fire of artillery, which played on every part of our right wing; the roundshot ploughing up the ground, or tearing open the files of the close and serried ranks; shells exploding in all directions: and at every moment the flashes of the guns, amidst expanding volumes of dense smoke challenging the attention of every man to the sources of destruction, the well-worked batteries.'[44]

Lieutenant Frederick Pattison of the 33rd Foot noted scores of cannon-balls bounding around the battlefield and making it seem like a giant cricket match. Yet such was their weight that even gently rolling cannon-balls could remove a man's foot. The 33rd were lying down in formation to shelter from the fire when a shell fragment suddenly killed one officer and tore an ear off Lieutenant Samuel Pagan. Lieutenant Pattison helped place the injured officer on a stretcher which two soldiers started to carry to the rear. They had hardly left the square when a cannon-ball struck one of the soldiers and carried off his leg.[45]

An howitzer shell blew Sergeant William Lawrence of the 40th Foot off his feet. The missile cut his deputy-sergeant-major in two, decapitated one of his company of grenadiers called William Hooper and burst just one yard behind him. The soggy soil soaked up much of the blast but even so Lawrence was blown two yards into the air. The side of his face was grazed and his nerves shaken. When he looked at his red sash he noticed its tail had been totally burnt off and the handle of his sword blackened.[46]

Later he was ordered to the regiment's colours, which were prime aiming points for the French guns. Already fourteen of Lawrence's fellow sergeants had been killed or wounded while in charge of them. The slaughter remained forever etched on his mind. 'Although I am now an old man, I remember it as if it had been yesterday. I had not been there more than a quarter of an hour when a cannon-shot came and took the captain's head clean off. This was again close to me, for my left side was touching the poor captain's right, and I was spattered all over with his blood.'

The decapitated officer was Captain William Fisher. 'Hullo, there goes my best friend,' shouted out one of his privates in jest, for Fisher had regularly punished him for misdemeanours.

'Never mind, I will be as good a friend to you as the captain', an innocent young subaltern reassured him. The private's reply, 'I hope not sir', puzzled the officer and raised a grim chuckle among the nearby men.

The same cannon-ball which had killed Captain Fisher also disabled twenty-five men; Captain Sempronius Stretton had never witnessed a more destructive shot during his long military career.[47]

Another moment of humour came when a musket-ball struck the shoulder of Major Donald Macdonald's horse. The command of the 92nd Highlanders had devolved upon Macdonald and for an awful moment it seemed the regiment would have yet another commander. For Macdonald's horse plunged violently and threw him on to the crown of his head. For several seconds he remained in

**Above:** Napoleon's headquarters of Le Caillou, at the edge of the Brussels road, in the early 1900s.

**Below:** The restored Le Caillou, as it is today.

The last review: Napoleon is acclaimed by his Guard and by a detachment of cuirassiers. In the foreground, gunners of the foot artillery struggle to bring their cannon forward into position across the muddy soil.

**Left:** On the morning of 18 June, Napoleon discusses Wellington's position with Lieutenant-General François Haxo, of the Imperial Guard engineers.

**Below:** Chantelet farm: Ney's headquarters on the eve of Waterloo.

**Above:** The British Guards close the North Gate of Hougoumont after a small band of French infantrymen burst in. Lieutenant-Colonel James Macdonell is leaning against the left gate, with a sword in his hand.

**Below:** The same place today.

**Above:** The North Gate today, looking from the outside of the farm towards the chapel. Note the Scots Guards plaque on the wall.

**Below:** The south face of the building block today. On the right is the garden wall, with a plaque to the French Brigadier-General Baron Pierre Bauduin.

**Opposite page:** Waves of French infantry unsuccessfully attack the gate of the Gardener's House, on the south side of Hougoumont.

**Above:** The garden of Hougoumont: the monument to the French soldiers who died assaulting the farm.

**Below:** Looking westwards from Hougoumont garden to the building block. Note the plaque to the 1st Guards on the wall of the chapel. In the background on the right is the Great Barn.

**Above:** Looking westwards along the road on the crest of Wellington's ridge. Sir Thomas Picton's 5th Division held this sector of the line. La Haie Sainte is in the middle distance on the left.

**Below:** Wellington's far eastern wing, from the French side of the valley. Papelotte farm stands on the right in the middle distance.

**Opposite page:** The Scots Greys and Inniskillings have destroyed the massive infantry columns of d'Erlon's I Corps and now attack Napoleon's great battery.

**Above:** The Waterloo re-enactment of 1995: French cavalry waiting to charge. In the foreground are two Red Lancers of the Guard.

**Below:** The 1995 re-enactment: grenadiers of Napoleon's Imperial Guard under fire.

**Above:** The Wounded Eagle monument to the last combatants of the Grand Army.

**Below:** The guardsmen lie dead in formation after their last stand.

**Above:** Wellington and Blücher meet by chance near La Belle Alliance at the end of the battle.

**Below:** La Belle Alliance today.

**Above:** The horrific sight of the battlefield after the fighting.

**Below:** The village of Waterloo after the battle. On the right is the Royal Chapel; opposite stands Wellington's headquarters.

**Above:** Wounded soldiers arrive at the Place Royale in Brussels.

**Below:** The same place today.

**Above:** The Grand' Place in Brussels; it served as an open-air hospital during the later stages of the campaign.

**Below:** The British Waterloo monument at Evere cemetery, Brussels.

this position between two ruts. Then the men exclaimed 'the major is killed.' Instantly, Macdonald rose, shook himself and replied: 'No! by God he is not.'[48]

The French cavalry squadrons were certainly overcrowded as they charged up the slippery mud slopes towards the squares. Yet the overcrowding was not as dire as sometimes represented. At the height of the charges, only 9000 horsemen were involved and not all the available squadrons charged at the same time. Some units would be reforming on the French side of the valley while others were milling around the squares. Some squadrons remained in one sector of the field undertaking repeated small scale attacks, like a column of Grenadiers à cheval, Gendarmerie d'élite and cuirassiers who charged Captain Alexander Cavalié Mercer's battery.[49] Edward Cotton noted how cavalry units 'frequently reformed in the valley just under our position, where the lances and the tops of their caps might be seen.'[50] Similarly, Captain the Hon. James Stanhope of the 1st Guards noted that the French cavalry 'charged with the most persevering gallantry, never retiring above 100 or 150 paces, and charging again.'[51]

After the first couple of charges, the entire French cavalry force did not sweep forwards and back as one wave. Indeed, it is unlikely that the French divisional or even brigade commanders would have been able fully to control and co-ordinate the movements of their various units. For Lieutenant Standish O'Grady of the British 7th Hussars wrote that 'the French Cavalry were in the first instance Cuirassiers and in Squadron but they soon became mixed with Cavalry of all arms and returned in masses of more or less size.'[52] For this reason, different squares faced different numbers of charges.

Further reduction of the overcrowding was caused by several units charging east of the Brussels road. The brunt of the charges certainly fell between Hougoumont and the crossroads but several British eyewitnesses stationed in the eastern sector of the field remember being charged too. Major-General Sir John Lambert's brigade had entered the front line immediately east of the crossroads and here came under cavalry attack. Captain Sempronius Stretton wrote that 'the field, immediately about the 40th, was thickly scattered with horses and men of the French Cavalry, who repeatedly charged our Squares (without making any impression), and who, passing and returning between the Squares of the 40th, 27th, and 4th Regiments, suffered severely from the fire of each.'[53]

Captain Stretton's account is confirmed by Lieutenant James Mill, also of the 40th Foot: 'whenever there was an intermission of this [artillery] fire,' Mill wrote, 'it was to find ourselves surrounded and beset by hordes of horsemen, who were slashing and cutting at our kneeling ranks. The file firing of our standing ranks, being concentrated and constant, was very effectual against their attacks, and both horse and rider were to be constantly discerned rolling over on to the plain, and the remainder flying back in disorder to their own lines.'[54]

Six hundred metres further east, Sergeant Duncan Robertson of the 92nd Highlanders remembered that 'about four o'clock the enemy made another attack on our part of the line, by a large body of lancers, who rode up to our squares with as much coolness as if subjecting us to a regimental inspection. We kept up a smart fire upon them, however, and put them to the right about. But before we had succeeded in turning them they did us considerable damage by throwing their lances into our columns [squares], which, being much longer than the firelock and bayonet, gave them a great advantage over us.'[55] Lieutenant Alexander Riddock of the 44th Foot recalled how several squadrons of cuirassiers swept round from the centre of the battlefield to menace the rear of the British 5th Division on the east wing. The cuirassiers were eventually cut to pieces by the British Life Guards.[56]

Historians have assumed Wellington's infantry remained solidly in square throughout the charges. In fact his troops distinguished themselves by their flexibility and excellent drill as much as by their robustness. Edward Cotton described how 'our squares often wheeled up into line, four deep, to make their fire more destructive on the French cavalry when retiring: on this, the Cuirassiers would suddenly wheel round to charge; but our infantry were instantly in square, and literally indulged in laughter at the disappointment and discomfiture of their gallant opponents.'[57] Lieutenant-Colonel William Harris claimed that the 30th and 73rd Foot, while still preserving their formation in square, charged the French cavalry and drove them away. This was not an isolated incident for Wellington wrote that he 'in fact attacked the Cuirassiers (who were in possession of the line of our cannon) with the squares of the infantry, and when once we moved them I poured in our Life Guards.'[58]

# Notes

1. *The Times*, 17 November 1911
2. Société des études historiques et folkloriques de Waterloo, Braine-l'Alleud et environs, *Mélanges historiques* (1970), p.162
3. R. Gronow, *The reminiscences and recollections of Captain Gronow 1810–1860* (1984), p.69
4. H. Siborne ed., *The Waterloo letters* (1983), p.32
5. H. Lot, *Les deux généraux Ordener* (1910), p.93; according to Georges Barral (*Itinéraire illustré de l'épopée de Waterloo* [1896], p.62) his grandfather, Captain Janot of the cuirassiers, was able to jump his horse over the chasm of the sunken lane without falling there.
6. C. Hibbert ed., *The Wheatley diary* (1964), p.65
7. O. von Pivka, *Napoleon's German allies 2: Nassau and Oldenburg* (1991), p.28; BL Add. MSS 34,706/121–2
8. C. Hibbert ed., *The Wheatley diary* (1964), p.66
9. Société des études historiques et folkloriques de Waterloo, Braine-l'Alleud et environs, *Mélanges historiques* (1970), p.147; several British eyewitnesses describe unsteadiness on the part of General Kruse's Nassauers but their accounts could in theory be motivated in part by national pride and xenophobia. However, Constant-Rebecque's testimony totally confirms the British accounts and the Netherlands chief-of-staff would be unlikely to exaggerate any failings on the part of his own troops.
10. One of the few exceptions was 'G' Troop, Royal Horse Artillery, which entered the front line

during the French cavalry charges and formed up immediately behind the track. On the eastern wing, the batteries supporting Picton's 5th Division also stood behind the hedged track, which served to protect both the gunners and guns from the French infantry columns.

11. L. Stouff, *Le Lieutenant-Général Delort* (1906), p.132; according to Lieutenant-General Sir Henry Clinton, commander of the 2nd (Anglo-Hanoverian) Division, 'about 11.00 am the Light Brigade and German Legion were ordered to furnish working parties to throw up breastworks to cover our guns; but when they arrived the officer with the entrenching tools was not present, and before these works were begun the enemy had commenced his attack. So the guns had no cover.' (quoted in C. Chesney, *The Waterloo lectures* [1907], p.207)

12. H. Siborne ed., *The Waterloo letters* (1983), pp.233–4

13. E. Cotton, *A voice from Waterloo* (1913), p.99

14. T. Morris, *Recollections of military service in 1813, 1814 and 1815* (1845), p.145

15. H. Siborne ed., *The Waterloo letters* (1983), p.234

16. BL Add MSS 34,704/100; H. Siborne ed., *The Waterloo letters* (1983), pp.187–8

17. C. Mercer, *Journal of the Waterloo campaign* (1985), p.168

18. E. Cotton, *A voice from Waterloo* (1913), pp.88–9; Jac Weller (*Wellington at Waterloo* [1967], p.209) doubted whether file firing was used by Wellington's infantry units at Waterloo but Cotton's testimony indicates file firing was used. This is confirmed by the account of Lieutenant James Mill (A regimental historical records committee, *The Royal Inniskilling Fusiliers* [1928], p.263) and W. Siborne, *History of the Waterloo Campaign* (1990), p.300. See also the letter of Lieutenant Aug. Kuckuck and Fred. Sohnath of the King's German Legion who describe how Du Plat's KGL infantry brigade was the target of several cuirassier charges 'which were however always failed by our well directed independent fire': BL Add. MSS 34,705/36

19. E. Cotton, *A voice from Waterloo* (1913), p.88

20. R. Gronow, *The reminiscences and recollections of Captain Gronow 1810–1860* (1984), p.191

21. T. Morris, *Recollections of military service in 1813, 1814 and 1815* (1845), p.148

22. *Ibid*, pp.149–50

23. *Ibid*, p.150

24. Letter of two King's German Legion officers of Colonel Du Plat's brigade: 'as soon as the Cuirassiers were driven back, our Cavalry came from behind our position and went in pursuit of them': BL Add. MSS 34,705/36

25. Marquess of Anglesey, *One-Leg* (1963), p.142

26. Société des études historiques et folkloriques de Waterloo, Braine-l'Alleud et environs, *Mélanges historiques* (1970), p.147

27. T. Morris, *Recollections of military service in 1813, 1814 and 1815* (1845), pp.151–2

28. H. Lot, *Les deux généraux Ordener* (1910), p.95

29. W. Fraser, *The Waterloo Ball* (1897), p.50

30. E. Longford, *Wellington: the years of the sword* (1972), p.432

31. Anon, *A propos du champ de bataille de Waterloo* (1912), pp.55–6; L. van Neck, *Waterloo illustré* (1903), pp.115–16

32. F. de Bas and J. de Wommerson, *La campagne de 1815 aux Pays-Bas* (1908), v.2, p.199; J. Coppin, 'Délicieux Brabant. Waterloo, le folklore de la bataille' in *Revue de folklore brabançon* (Sept. 1961)

33. R. Gronow, *The reminiscences and recollections of Captain Gronow 1810–1860* (1984), p.190; the suffocating smell Gronow mentioned resulted from the sulphur included in the powder used at Waterloo.

34. 'Recollections of Waterloo by a staff officer', in *United Service Magazine* (1847, Part III)

35. Quoted in D. Gardner, *Quatre Bras, Ligny and Waterloo* (1882), p.284; according to Sir Hussey Vivian, the French cavalry 'advanced close to our squares but never with that degree of determination or in such number as would have been requisite to penetrate': BL Add. MSS 34,706/95

36. A Near Observer, *The Battle of Waterloo* (1816), p.57

37. E. Cotton, *A voice from Waterloo* (1913), p.105

38. C. Hibbert ed., *The Wheatley diary* (1964), p.67

39. C. Mercer, *Journal of the Waterloo campaign* (1985), p.170

40. C. Hibbert ed., *The Wheatley diary* (1964), p.66

41. R. Gronow, *The reminiscences and recollections of Captain Gronow 1810–1860* (1984), p.190

42. J. Vansittart ed., *The journal of Surgeon James* (1964), p.47

43. A Near Observer, *The Battle of Waterloo* (1816), p.56

44. E. Cotton, *A voice from Waterloo* (1913), p.87

45. F. Pattison, *Personal recollections of the Waterloo campaign* (1870), pp.27–8

46. G. Bankes ed., *The autobiography of Sergeant William Lawrence* (1886), pp.206–7

47. H. Siborne ed., *The Waterloo letters* (1983), p.401

48. Letter of Lieutenant Robert Winchester: BL Add MSS 34,708/226

49. C. Mercer, *Journal of the Waterloo campaign* (1985), p.176

50. E. Cotton, *A voice from Waterloo* (1913), p.87; cf. Milhaud's report in L. Stouff, *Le Lieutenant-Général Delort* (1906), p.132

51. BL Add MSS 34,703/22

52. BL Add. MSS 34,705/73

53. H. Siborne ed., *The Waterloo letters* (1983), p.401 (see also p.398). Note that Sergeant William Lawrence of the 40th Foot also describes a French cavalry attack on his unit: A. Brett-James, *The hundred days* (1964), p.133

54. A regimental historical records committee, *The Royal Inniskilling Fusiliers* (1928), p.263

55. MacKenzie MacBride ed., *With Napoleon at Waterloo* (1911) p.162; however, Lieutenant James Kerr Ross did not recollect the 92nd being actually charged although the regiment more than once formed square: BL Add. MSS 34,706/254. According to Lieutenant James Hope of the 92nd, 'our centre was furiously assailed by a great body of cavalry, principally cuirassiers ... The enemy succeeded in penetrating to the crest of the eminence, but no further. There they were met by the 3rd division, and right of the 5th, who, in a few minutes, sent them reeling back on their reserves': Anon, *Letters from Portugal, Spain, and France, during the memorable campaigns of 1811, 1812 and 1813, and from Belgium and France in the year 1815* (1819), p.258

56. BL Add MSS 34,704/124

57. E. Cotton, *A voice from Waterloo* (1913), p.85

58. *Ibid*, pp.105, 254, 308

Mont St Jean farm

# 7

# THE CENTRE OF THE LINE: LA HAIE SAINTE FALLS

Now it is time to leave the panorama and return to the battlefield outside. First, walk south-westwards along the narrow road from the Panorama along the crest of Wellington's ridge. After 500 metres, you will find a memorial stone indicating the position of 'G' Troop, Royal Horse Artillery, under Captain Alexander Cavalié Mercer. Initially, 'G' Troop remained in reserve and only entered the front line towards 5.00 pm, at the point indicated by the monument. Captain Mercer was a gifted writer and in his journal he vividly described how he received a French cavalry charge as soon as he arrived in the front line. His account is so detailed that it is possible to follow the action on the ground:

> Our first gun had scarcely gained the interval between [two Brunswick infantry] squares, when I saw through the smoke the leading squadrons of the advancing column coming on at a brisk trot, and already not more than one hundred yards distant, if so much, for I don't think we could have been so far. I immediately ordered the line to be formed for action – *case shot!* and the leading gun was unlimbered and commenced firing almost as soon as the word was given: for activity and intelligence our men were unrivalled. The very first round, I saw, brought down several men and horses ... Still they persevered in approaching us (the first round had brought them to a walk), though slowly, and it did seem they would ride over us. We were a little below the level of the ground on which they moved – having in front of us a bank of about a foot and a half or two feet high, along the top of which ran a narrow road – and this gave more effect to our case-shot, all of which almost must have taken effect, for the carnage was frightful. I suppose this state of things occupied but a few seconds, when I observed symptoms of hesitation, and in a twinkling, at the instant I thought it was all over with us, they turned to either flank and filed away rapidly to the rear. Retreat of the mass, however, was not so easy. Many facing about and trying to force their way through the body of the column, that part next to us became a complete mob, into which we kept a steady fire of case-shot from our six pieces. The effect is hardly conceivable, and to paint this scene of slaughter and confusion impossible. Every discharge was followed by the fall of

numbers, whilst the survivors struggled with each other, and I actually saw them using the pommels of their swords to fight their way out of the *mêlée* ... At last the rear of the column, wheeling about, opened a passage, and the whole swept away at a much more rapid pace than they had advanced.[1]

The French cavalry were tiring. Casualties had been enormous. You will find a memorial stone to one of the dead horsemen, Lieutenant Augustin Demulder of the 5th Cuirassiers, on the ridge crest between Mercer's monument and the Panorama. Demulder was a Belgian in French service, having been born at Nivelles, only six miles away, in 1785. The inscription on the monument records that he was wounded in three battles before being killed at Waterloo. The stone is also in memory of all the horsemen who charged with Demulder.

Owing to these casualties and the blown condition of the horses, the pressure exerted by the French cavalry gradually slackened. The charges never came to a sudden end, they merely faded away. The burden of the battle began to return to Napoleon's infantry. At 5.30 pm Ney remembered the 6000 infantrymen of Lieutenant-General Count Honoré Reille's II Corps who had not been sucked

## MAJ-GEN ADAM'S BRIGADE ENTERS THE FRONT LINE

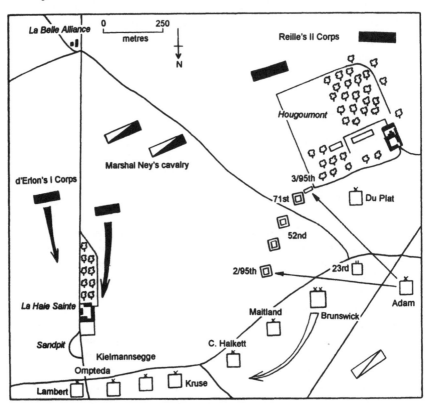

into the fight at Hougoumont. These troops struck Wellington's front line north of Hougoumont orchard. In the ensuing struggle Colonel du Plat fell at the head of his King's German Legion infantry brigade.[2] Wellington ordered up Major-General Frederick Adam's light infantry brigade from reserve and told it to 'drive those fellows away.' Adam did precisely that. He then halted his 2500 men and formed squares ahead of the original line on the forward slopes of the ridge. His new position north of Hougoumont orchard strengthened the hand of the troops there.

Today, you can follow a track from the ridge above Hougoumont towards La Belle Alliance to reach the position occupied by Adam's squares. Down here, the French artillery fire was ferocious. One shot killed or wounded seventeen men of the 71st (Highland) Light infantry; another whizzed past the head of an officer's horse causing the terrified animal to start and almost to unseat the rider. Young Ensign William Leeke of the 52nd Light infantry was standing inside one of the squares when he noticed something opposite:

> A gleam of sunshine particularly attracted my attention to some brass guns in our front which appeared to be placed lower down the French slope, and nearer to us, than the others; I distinctly saw the French artillerymen go through the process of spunging out one of the guns and reloading it; I could see that it was pointed at our square, and when it was discharged I caught sight of the ball, which appeared to be in a direct line for me. I thought, Shall I move? No! I gathered myself up, and stood firm, with the colour in my right hand ... It did not strike the four men in rear of whom I was standing, but the four poor fellows on their right. It was fired at some elevation, and struck the front man about the knees, and coming to the ground under the feet of the rear man of the four, whom it most severely wounded, it rose and, passing within an inch or two of the colour pole, went over the rear face of the square without doing further injury. The two men in the first and second rank fell outward, I fear they did not survive long; the two others fell within the square. The rear man made a considerable outcry on being wounded, but on one of the officers saying kindly to him, 'O man, don't make a noise,' he instantly recollected himself, and was quiet.[3]

Such was the intensity of the French fire that Major-General Adam shortly withdrew his brigade to the crest of the ridge. Even here losses were immense. Then, at 6.30 pm, disaster struck. Wellington's central outpost of La Haie Sainte finally fell to the French.

You can reach the farm of La Haie Sainte by walking 250 metres down the busy Brussels road from the crossroads to the eastern side of the farm. You will find that La Haie Sainte is almost unaltered in appearance. A few dormer windows have vanished from the farmer's house and the wall linking the entrance gate to the barn has been demolished. The barn, on the southern side of the courtyard, was extended slightly westwards in the nineteenth century so that its end is now flush with the outer wall of the stable block. The barn roof was destroyed by fire in 1936. Luckily the walls themselves survived but according to *The Times*, several beams bearing holes from rifle or musket-balls were burnt to cinders.[4]

You can easily follow the sequence of the epic fighting within the courtyard. The garrison commander was Major George Baring and his force consisted initially of the green-coated 2nd Light battalion, King's German Legion (KGL). This force had been detached from Colonel Christian von Ompteda's 2nd KGL brigade which stood immediately west of the crossroads.

The KGL was a crack unit with a remarkable fighting record. The formation of the KGL was a direct result of Napoleon's invasion of Hanover in 1803. Since George III was Elector of Hanover as well as King of Britain, it was natural for the defeated Hanoverian officers and soldiers to head for England. In December 1803, sufficient numbers had volunteered to form the King's German Legion, an integral part of the British Army. The KGL's main English base was the Sussex coastal town of Bexhill, four miles west of Hastings. KGL infantry arrived at Bexhill in August 1804 and maintained a depot here throughout the Napoleonic wars; nearly all of the KGL troops who fought so heroically at La Haie Sainte knew Bexhill well. One of them, Friedrich Lindau of the 2nd Light battalion, wrote that 'the time I spent in England – some eighteen months – was the best part of my life. Never again was I to lead such a carefree and merry life as in the barracks at Bexhill.'[5] Today, an exhibition at Bexhill museum is devoted to the KGL and the relics of their stay in the town.

The KGL soon proved itself to be a crack corps and brought added honour to the British flag under which it served. During the Peninsular war the KGL particularly distinguished itself at Garcia Hernandez on 23 July 1812, where unsupported KGL dragoons broke three French squares, and at the rearguard action of Venta del Pozo on 23 October 1812, where the two light infantry battalions coolly smashed powerful French cavalry attacks by their steady musketry. In no action did the KGL disgrace itself; the defence of La Haie Sainte farm at Waterloo was but the culmination of a long and brilliant record.

Major Baring held La Haie Sainte against repeated French attacks from 2.00 pm onwards but soon had to abandon the extensive orchard on the south side of the farm. Only a few trees exist in this orchard today but its extent is clearly demarcated by hedges. In spite of losing the orchard, Baring's men remained firmly in control of the building block itself and the small garden to the north.

Throughout the day, the sharp, accurate fire from Baring's garrison weakened the repeated French cavalry charges which passed La Haie Sainte to fall on Wellington's main line to the north. Major Baring recalled:

> It was clear to me that their intention was to attack the squares of our division in position, in order by destroying them to break the whole line. This was a critical moment, for what would be our fate if they succeeded? As they marched

upon the position by the farm, I brought all the fire possible to bear upon them; many men and horses were overthrown, but they were not discouraged. Without in the least troubling themselves about our fire, they advanced with the greatest intrepidity, and attacked the infantry. All this I could see, and confess freely that now and then I felt some apprehension.[6]

French infantry advanced again and again on the farm during the cavalry charges but were beaten off by accurate KGL rifle fire. Crack shots such as Corporals Diedrich Schlemm and Henry Müller picked off the officers and threw the men into disorder. Corporal Schlemm continued firing until shot in the lungs and forced to retire.[7]

Baring soon began to run out of ammunition. Yet in spite of his increasingly desperate pleas for more rifle rounds he received reinforcements of troops instead. The cart carrying the reserve rifle ammunition belonging to Colonel Ompteda's brigade was overturned in a ditch in the confusion behind Wellington's lines. Ompteda's brigade staff seem to have been in ignorance that the British 95th Rifles occupying the sandpit immediately north-east of La Haie Sainte possessed a plentiful supply of rifle rounds which they could have shared with the garrison.

By 6.00 pm La Haie Sainte contained the 2nd Light battalion and two companies of the 1st Light battalion, KGL. The light company of the 5th Line battalion was also in the farm, although during its march from the main position down the Brussels road to the entrance gate it lost fourteen men and its commander, Captain Ernest von Wurmb, to French cannon-fire. A company of 150 Nassau troops had also arrived from General August von Kruse's brigade.[8] This last contingent was particularly useful for the Nassauers carried large cooking pots. As the barn roof had gone up in flames, Baring led his men in filling the Nassauers' cooking pots with water from a pond to extinguish the flames, 'but alas!' he wrote, 'with the blood of many a brave man!'[9]

Still Baring had received no ammunition and although his devoted men swore that 'no man will desert you, – we will fight and die with you', they also demanded the means to defend themselves. Private Lindhorst of the 2nd Light battalion was reduced to defending a breach in the courtyard wall with his sword-bayonet, a large stick and a brick torn out of the wall.[10] Baring described the anguished mental turmoil which the loyalty of his men and their perilous situation caused him:

> No pen, not even that of one who has experienced such moments, can describe the feeling which this excited in me; nothing can be compared with it! – Never had I felt myself so elevated; – but never also placed in so painful a position, where honour contended with a feeling for the safety of the men who had given me such an unbounded proof of their confidence.[11]

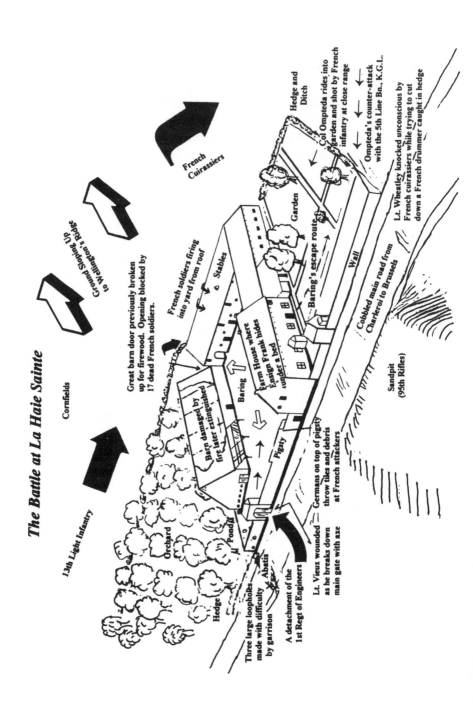

## The Battle at La Haie Sainte

French Cuirassiers

Ground Slopes up to Wellington's Ridge

Cornfields

13th Light Infantry

Great barn door previously broken up for firewood. Opening blocked by 17 dead French soldiers.

French soldiers firing into yard from roof

Stables

Garden

Hedge and Ditch

Col Ompteda rides into garden and shot by French infantry at close range

Ompteda's counter-attack with the 5th Line Bn., K.G.L.

Lt. Wheatley knocked unconscious by French cuirassiers while trying to cut down a French drummer caught in hedge

Baring's escape route

Wall

Cobbled main road from Charleroi to Brussels

Barn damaged by fire later extinguished

Farm House where Ensign Frank hides under a bed

Baring

Pigsty

Germans on top of pigsty throw tiles and debris at French attackers

Sandpit (95th Rifles)

Lt. Vieux wounded as he breaks down main gate with axe

Pond

Orchard

Hedge

Abatis

A detachment of the 1st Regt of Engineers

Three large loopholes made with difficulty by garrison

122

On the west of building block, the French 13th Light infantry scaled the roof of the stable block to pick off the ammunition-less Germans. The French also charged through the open barn gateway, whose wooden gates had been burnt as firewood the night before and which had soon been blocked by seventeen French corpses.[12] As the barn has since been extended ten metres or so westwards, the present gateway is not that existing in 1815.[13] On the eastern side of the farm, further French troops broke through the main gateway and surged into the courtyard.

This moment of the fighting is captured in Adolf Northern's epic painting, which depicts the buildings and uniforms remarkably accurately. You may wish to enter the farm courtyard and to compare the farm with the painting. The artist stood with his back to the stable block and looked towards the eastern side of the farm. Major Baring vividly described the vicious, hand-to-hand fighting depicted by the artist:

> Despising death, [the French] fought with a degree of courage which I had never before witnessed in Frenchmen. Favoured by their advancing in masses, every bullet of ours hit, and seldom were the effects limited to one assailant; this did not, however, prevent them from throwing themselves against the walls, and endeavouring to wrest the arms from the hands of my men, through the loopholes.[14]

Major Baring reluctantly gave the now inevitable order to abandon La Haie Sainte: 'inexpressibly painful as the decision was to me of giving up the place, my feeling of duty as a man overcame that of honour, and I gave the order to retire through the house into the garden. How much these words cost me, and by what feelings they were accompanied, he only can judge who has been placed in a similar situation!'[15] From the garden Baring's men retired to the main position on the ridge 200 metres to the north. Private Dahrendorf of the 2nd Light battalion had his leg shattered by a shot as he endeavoured to reach the ridge crest and was left senseless on the ground. He had already received three bayonet wounds but in spite of them he had defended La Haie Sainte to the end.[16]

Just over half the garrison escaped with Major Baring to the main position.[17] Among the prisoners was Private Friedrich Lindau of the 2nd Light battalion; he was bleeding profusely from two head wounds but on being ordered by Baring to fall out, had replied: 'he would be a scoundrel that deserted you, so long as his head is on his shoulders.' Lindau had looted a bag of gold from a French officer but lost it in turn to his captors.[18]

Another survivor was Ensign George Frank who had his arm broken by a musket-shot and then ran into a room of the farmer's house. He lay undetected under a bed until after the French evacuated the farm at the end of the battle. French troops ruthlessly shot two of Frank's wounded comrades lying on the floor of the same room, saying 'no mercy for these green rascals!' Frank's eighteen-year-old friend Lieutenant George Graeme also survived. Graeme was surrounded by five Frenchmen but they seemed so terrified he bolted into the garden and freedom, pursued by two ill-aimed musket-shots and a taunting cry of 'rascal!'[19]

On the eastern wall of La Haie Sainte you will find an iron plaque commemorating the heroic KGL defenders. The plaque was placed there by Prince George of Hanover in 1847. It replaced a marble memorial added in 1822 by the officers of the 2nd Light battalion.

Throughout the day the forward bastion of La Haie Sainte had weakened French onslaughts on Wellington's ridge. Napoleon's troops had been forced to give the farm a wide berth to escape the accurate rifle fire pouring from it. But after its capture, it served as a forward base for the French. Under the cover of its solid walls they mustered columns to assault the ridge. Guns opened fire from the vicinity of the farm on Wellington's front line at a range of just 200 metres.

All along the line, Marshal Ney was pushing forward an integrated force of infantry, cavalry and artillery acting in close co-operation. An appalling trial of strength by slaughter and attrition ensued. The French advanced towards Wellington's ridge crest and began to wear down the allied troops at point-blank range. The brave but rash young Prince of Orange insisted that Colonel Christian von Ompteda counter-attack towards the garden of La Haie Sainte with the 5th Line battalion, KGL. Ompteda was amazed, for nearby French cavalry would be sure to massacre the battalion. The Prince refused to listen.

Ompteda was an experienced veteran who knew that to obey the murderous order would cost him and his men their lives. But his honour left him no choice. 'I must still repeat my order to attack in line with the bayonet', the Prince of Orange told him, 'and I will listen to no further arguments.'[20]

Captain Berger of the 5th Line battalion described how he hastened to follow his colonel:

> I kept my eyes on him and on the enemy. I saw that the French had their muskets pointed at the colonel, but did not fire. The officers struck the men's barrels up with their swords. They seemed astonished at the extraordinary calm approach of the solitary horseman, whose white plume showed him to be an officer of high rank. He soon reached the enemy's line of infantry before the garden hedge. He jumped in, and I clearly saw how his sword-strokes smote the shakos off. The nearest French officer looked on in admiration without attempting to check the attack. When I looked round for my company I found I was alone. Turning my eyes again to the enemy, I saw Colonel Ompteda, in the midmost throng of the enemy's infantry and cavalry, sink from his horse and vanish . . .[21]

Ompteda's ADC, Lieutenant von Brandis, found his corpse by the garden hedge after the battle was over. He found a musket-ball hole in the collar of Ompteda's coat and the singed fabric around the hole showed that he had been shot at point blank range. The rest of the 5th Line battalion was cut to pieces by French cuirassiers as Ompteda had foreseen.[22] Lieutenant Johnny Kincaid of the 95th Rifles watched the disaster unfold from the eastern side of the Brussels highroad:

> I watched their movement with intense anxiety, for it had no reference to our side of the road but went direct towards the Farm house, which I thought it was their intention to retake, but they advanced rather loosely, which led me to dread the catastrophe which speedily overtook them, for when they reached the slope of the bank on which the Farm stands, the cuirassiers broke in among them, and so complete was the surprise that they were annihilated almost without firing a shot – a brigade of our light dragoons advanced when too late to their relief, but they made but a shabby charge – a few gallant fellows met at the head of each column and exchanged a cut or two, but in the mean while, our fellows who had been watching with their rifles pointed but afraid to open fire until the [KGL] redcoats were all down, now opened a terrific fire, which sent both parties to flight (and {as we were} not more than half pleased with the luke warm charge of our dragoons I very much doubt whether half the shots were not aimed at them – but this is *entre nous*) – The cuirassiers went off very sluggishly, stooping and stabbing at the wounded men as they lay on the ground.[23]

One of the lucky survivors was Lieutenant Edmund Wheatley who was knocked unconscious and came to only to find Ompteda dead a few feet away. French infantry soon made Wheatley prisoner and led him into the interior of La Haie Sainte, which he 'found completely destroyed, nothing but the rafters and props remaining. The floor, covered with mortar bricks and straw, was strewed with bodies of the German infantry and French.'[24] Wheatley's captors marched him miles on bare feet before he managed to escape.

Ompteda is supposed to lie in a mass grave north-east of La Haie Sainte beneath the Hanoverian monument which bears his name and those of twenty-seven other heroes of the KGL.[25] 'Whoever I asked after,' wept a depressed Major Baring, 'the answer was "killed", – "wounded"! I freely confess that tears came involuntarily into my eyes at this sad intelligence, and the many bitter feelings that seized upon me.'[26]

All along Wellington's line, the slaughter continued unabated. An entire face of a Hanoverian square was blown away by artillery. 'It was now to be seen,' thought young Ensign Edward Macready of the 30th Foot, 'which side had most bottom, and would stand killing longest.'[27]

The Prince of Orange, the gallant twenty-two year old commander of Wellington's I Corps, was now a casualty. He had been leading a charge by Nassau infantry when struck in the left shoulder by a musket-ball; a second shot hit his favourite horse, Vexy, in the chest. Captain Baron Jules de Constant-Rebecque de Villars, a Dutch-Belgian staff officer, witnessed the subsequent confusion which occurred where the Lion Mound now stands.[28] 'I saw His Royal Highness hurriedly dismount and move, tottering, in our direction,' wrote the captain. A Nassau officer spoke to the prince but seemed not to recognise him and returned to his post. Captain de Villars and a second officer rushed up and reached the prince simultaneously:

> His Royal Highness was pale, weakened by the large loss of blood and was standing on ground churned up by the rain and the cavalry charges. He leaned against the horse of this officer. As I noticed that the French cuirassiers were making a move a short distance away to attack us, and considering that the prince was on foot and that the danger of the position was becoming more imminent, I dismounted and urged His Royal Highness to take my horse. He made no reply for in this instant he had all but fainted in my arms, his head resting on my chest. After he had attempted several times to put his foot in the stirrup, while my horse became worried by the sound of a lively cannonade and by the continuous whistling of musket and cannon-balls, His Royal Highness, overcoming the pain which he felt, made an effort and placed himself in the saddle. In spite of his sufferings, the prince continued to turn all his thoughts to the battle, which he still wanted to direct. He was prevented in this by the effect of his great loss of blood.[29]

Fortunately the wound proved not to be mortal and in 1840 the prince became King William II of Holland. His nine-year reign saw the re-establishment of fiscal stability and was more tolerant and liberal than that of his autocratic father.

Another casualty was Captain the Hon. William Curzon, an officer of the 69th Foot employed on staff duties. He had been riding with Captain the Earl of March, an extra ADC to the Prince of Orange, when struck in the chest. 'Goodbye, dear March!' he called out as he fell. His friend did all he could, to no avail. Then March was forced to go over and encourage a nearby square of Nassau troops. The dying Curzon exclaimed faintly: 'that's right, well done, my dear March!' Now he lay dead, with his head resting on the neck of his horse. The horse itself was suffering from a shattered leg but hardly stirred as if not wishing to disturb its master. It merely neighed feebly until a soldier put it out of its misery. Horse and rider slept the eternal sleep together.[30]

Everywhere the scenes of horror numbed the mind. The worst spot was on a shallow mound immediately north-east of the crossroads. Major-General Sir John Lambert had brought his infantry brigade up from reserve at 3.30 pm and posted the 27th Inniskillings in square on this mound. It was imperative that they occupy this point, for the French threatened to thrust from La Haie Sainte up the Brussels road into Wellington's position. By standing in square the Inniskillings could, if necessary, pour a flanking fire into the Brussels road while simultaneously maintaining their frontal fire. French skirmishers concentrated their musketry at close range on the tempting target of the 27th's square exposed on the mound. Sixty-six per cent of the Inniskillings who entered battle became casualties.

On the 175th anniversary of the battle the Royal Irish Rangers, the unit descended from the 27th Foot, unveiled a memorial stone to the 27th's gallant stand. You will find the stone on the northern edge of the track to Papelotte, a little south-east of the mound on which the regiment was crucified. Lieutenant Johnny Kincaid of the 95th Rifles commanded skirmishers lining this track and when he looked back he saw that 'the twenty-seventh regiment were lying literally dead, in square, a few yards behind us.'[31] Eleven of the twelve most senior officers, including the commander Captain John Hare, were casualties. Major Fielding Browne of the neighbouring 40th Foot offered to lend the 27th some of his officers but this suggestion was declined; Inniskilling sergeants had the honour of commanding entire companies.[32]

Like all units, the 27th included one or two bad apples. Captain William Verner of the 7th Hussars met a solitary, unwounded Inniskilling sergeant who clearly had no right to be so far from his regiment.[33] The vast majority, however, did their duty heroically. An officer of the British 5th Division was in tears:

> I stood looking at an old gray-headed officer of the 27th, who lay on his face (if face it could be called, for half of it, with the upper half of the skull, had been carried away by a round shot): here was the cup of glory filled to the brim! ...
>
> The brave, the gallant 27th! – the ground was strewed with your dead. There is something peculiarly touching in lowly men sacrificing their lives for their country's glory – thus ennobling themselves! It is no less common than true that scenes of blood and carnage tend to sear the feelings and harden the heart. I had seen everything that morning nearly unmoved – but here I paused. At the sight of these poor fellows, of the humblest classes of society, who had opposed their bodies as a living rampart to the obstinate advance of the enemy – all now lying dead – I am not ashamed to say that a tear fell.[34]

From the crossroads to Papelotte, along a front of 1500 metres, Wellington's infantry blazed away at the swarms of skirmishers in front. The French were kneeling down to expose themselves as little as possible; occasionally their courageous officers, leading as always from the front, waved their swords and exhorted their troops to advance. The result was invariable. A brief, glorious surge dissolved in an impassible hail of musketry. The lucky survivors who scampered back to their original firing line left dozens of lifeless bodies slumped in the mud.

Lieutenant Johnny Kincaid found the smoke became so dense that he could distinguish the French barely forty metres away only by the flashes of their muskets. Towards 7.00 pm, he wrote, 'I walked a little way to each flank, to endeavour to get a glimpse of what was going on; but nothing met my eye except the mangled remains of men and horses, and I was obliged to return to my post as wise as I went. I had never yet heard of a battle in which everybody was killed; but this seemed likely to be an exception, as all were going by turns.'[35]

A fellow rifleman summed up the state of mind of Wellington's men by this stage: 'not a soldier thought of giving ground; but victory seemed hopeless, and they gave themselves up to death with perfect indifference.'[36] Exhaustion and shock were beginning to tell. Captain Mercer of 'G' Troop, Royal Horse Artillery, remembered young Brunswickers near his battery standing immobile like trees in formation. They were so battle-shocked that their NCOs had to thump and push them into position.

Assistant-Surgeon William Gibney was horrified when he rejoined his regiment in the firing line: 'to me, coming fresh on this part of the field, it seemed as if the French were getting the best of it slowly but surely, and I was not singular in this view, for a goodly number of experienced officers thought the same.'[37]

Two light cavalry brigades under Sir Hussey Vivian and Sir John Vandeleur arrived from the far east flank to bolster the centre but when they arrived Lieutenant-Colonel the Hon. Henry Murray of the 18th Hussars also found a seemingly hopeless situation: 'wounded or mutilated horses wandered around or turned in circles. The noise was so deafening, and the air of ruin and desolation that prevailed wherever the eye could reach gave no inspiration of victory.'[38]

Lieutenant-Colonel Joseph Muter of the Inniskilling Dragoons had taken over the command of the mauled Union Brigade. His helmet was beaten in and his arm in a sling. His men were in no better state; their heads and hands were bandaged and their horses exhausted.[39] The remains of the Union and Household Brigades were now formed up behind the infantry in a single rank to offer a show of strength. Nevertheless, they continued to suffer heavily from the French artillery.

In the front line, where the panorama now stands, Ensign Edward Macready of the 30th Foot watched as some French artillerymen drew up in front of his square to unlimber and fire several guns. The first blast of canister blew seven soldiers backwards into the square. The French quickly reloaded, as Macready related:

> It was noble to see our fellows fill up the gaps after each discharge. I was much distressed at this moment; having ordered up three of my light bobs, they had hardly taken their station when two of them fell horribly lacerated. One of them uttered a sort of reproachful groan, and I involuntarily exclaimed, 'I couldn't help it.' We would willingly have charged these guns, but, had we deployed, the cavalry that flanked them would have made an example of us.[40]

Macready was only seventeen but towards the end of the battle he found himself commanding the regiment's light company, so great had losses been. Casualties continued to mount. Sergeant Tom Morris of the 73rd was in the same square as Macready and watched helplessly as French guns fired canister at him at close range. This fire blew complete lanes through the living walls of the square and then cavalry dashed forward:

> But before they reached us, we had closed our files, throwing the dead outside and taking the wounded inside the square, when they were again forced to retire. They did not, however, go further than the pieces of cannon – waiting there to try the effect of some more grapeshot. We saw the match applied, and again it came as thick as hail upon us. On looking round, I saw my left-hand man falling backwards, the blood gushing from his left eye; my poor comrade on my right, by the same discharge, got a ball through his right thigh, of which he died a few days afterwards. Our situation now was truly awful; our men were falling by dozens every fire. About this time a large shell fell just in front of us, and whilst the fuze was burning out, we were wondering how many of us it would destroy. When it burst, about seventeen men were either killed or wounded by it.[41]

It is hard to imagine the sheer lethality of the atmosphere caused by the intensity of the firing. Tom Morris heard Captain John Garland, now in command of his regiment, call out for volunteers to follow him from the shelter of a bank to charge the French infantry. 'About a dozen of us responded to the call; and such was the destructive fire to which we were opposed, that we had not advanced more than six or seven paces before every one of the party, except me and my brother, was either killed or wounded. We carried our captain back to the shelter of the bank.'[42]

Wellington seemed to be wherever his men faced a crisis. He carefully shored up the centre of his front line with German troops from the reserve. At the sight of his famous hooked nose, the troops murmured, 'silence – stand to your front – here's the Duke!' The ranks were at once as steady as if on parade. 'Hard pounding this! let us see who will pound the longest,' he encouraged them. 'Stand fast, 95th!' he addressed the Rifles. 'We must not be beat: what would they say in England?'[43] Colin Halkett requested his shattered brigade be relieved. 'Impossible', replied the Duke. 'Very well, my Lord, we'll stand till the last man falls.'

So they did, or nearly so. A prisoner watching from French lines later described his pride 'at the sight of our little squares, enveloped in a slight mist, surrounded by innumerable Foes. The ground on which I had stood since the morning was bare and I felt a chill on supposing the whole of my Comrades had sunk under the French sword.'[44]

Held together by the Duke's leadership, by discipline, by regimental pride and by comradeship, the Anglo-Dutch-German army held out and in the end the French attackers fell back. Napoleon, preoccupied by the Prussian threat on his east flank, refused for the moment to release his Imperial Guard to clinch the victory over Wellington. Thus, unsupported, the French line units from Papelotte to Hougoumont started inching back from Wellington's ridge to reform in the valley below.

# Notes

1. C. Mercer, *Journal of the Waterloo campaign* (1985), pp.171–2; see also D. Hamilton-Williams, *Waterloo: new perspectives* (1993), pp.391–2. See also the letter Brevet-Major Mercer wrote to the historian William Siborne from Devonport on 26 November 1834: H. Siborne ed., *The Waterloo letters* (1983), pp.214–22 or BL Add MSS 34,703/347

2. BL Add. MSS 34,705/36

3. W. Leeke, *The history of Lord Seaton's regiment at the Battle of Waterloo* (1866), v.1, pp.32–3

4. *The Times*, 14 December 1936

5. Lecture by Manfred Bresemann of the Hanoverian-British Association at the Historical Museum, Hanover, December 1984: National Army Museum document 35694

6. N. Beamish, *History of the King's German Legion* (1837), v.2, pp.455–6

7. *Ibid*, v.2, p.512

8. This was the Flanquer, or light, company of the 2nd battalion, 1st Nassau Infantry. Its commander, Captain von Weiterhausen, was killed on the way to the farm: J. Pflugk-Harttung, *Belle Alliance* (1915), p.198; other sources argue that two Nassau companies joined the garrison (see, for instance, J. Pflugk-Harttung, *Belle Alliance* [1915], p.204)

9. N. Beamish, *History of the King's German Legion* (1837), v.2, p.457

10. *Ibid*, v.2, p.365

11. *Ibid*, v.2, pp.458–9

12. *Ibid*, v.2, p.455

13. H. Siborne ed., *The Waterloo Letters* (1983), p.403 (map); see also the painting in D. Howarth, *A Near Run Thing* (1968), p.41. See also the drawing and nineteenth century photograph in A. Griffiths, *Wellington and Waterloo* (1898), part 10, p.231

14. N. Beamish, *History of the King's German Legion* (1837), v.2, p.455

15. *Ibid*, v.2, p.459

16. Ibid, v.2, p.365

17. Most historians claim that only forty-two men escaped from La Haie Sainte. This resulted from a misreading of Major Baring's report. Baring stated that he had forty-two men left with him from his 2nd Light battalion at the close of the battle. However, other troops escaped from La Haie Sainte and then dispersed to the rear in search of ammunition. Furthermore, Baring was only referring to the forty-two men of his own battalion; the garrison comprised other units besides the 2nd Light battalion. For Baring's report, see N. Beamish, *History of the King's German Legion* (1837), v.2, p.462

18. N. Beamish, *History of the King's German Legion* (1837), v.2, p.457

19. H. Siborne ed., *The Waterloo Letters* (1983), pp.408–9

20. J. Pflugk-Harttung, *Belle Alliance* (1915), p.121; C. Hibbert ed., *The Wheatley diary* (1964), p.69

21. L. Ompteda, *A Hanoverian-English officer a hundred years ago* (1892), pp.312–13

22. See also: BL Add MSS 34,704/235 and 34,704/283

23. BL Add. MSS 34,707/219–20

24. C. Hibbert ed., *The Wheatley diary* (1964), p.71

25. L. Ompteda, *A Hanoverian-English officer a hundred years ago* (1892), p.313

26. N. Beamish, *History of the King's German Legion* (1837), v.2, p.462

27. E. Macready, 'On a Part of Captain Siborne's History of the Waterloo Campaign', in *United Service Magazine* (1845, Part I)

28. See also the letter of Lieutenant Henry Webster, extra ADC to the Prince of Orange: BL

Add. MSS 34,706/161; Captain de Villars was the nephew of the Netherlands chief-of-staff: Société des études historiques et folkloriques de Waterloo, Braine-l'Alleud et environs, *Mélanges historiques* (1970), p.148

29. F. de Bas and J. de Wommerson, *La campagne de 1815 aux Pays-Bas* (1908), v.2, pp.243–4

30. A Near Observer, *The Battle of Waterloo* (1816), p.277; R. Gronow, *The reminiscences and recollections of Captain Gronow 1810–1860* (1984), pp.194–5

31. J. Kincaid, *Adventures in the Rifle Brigade and random shots from a rifleman* (1909), p.170

32. A regimental historical records committee, *The Royal Inniskilling Fusiliers* (1928), pp.262–3

33. E. Richardson, *Long forgotten days (leading to Waterloo)* (1928), p.381

34. 'Operations of the Fifth or Picton's Division in the campaign of Waterloo', in *United Service Magazine* (June 1841), p.191

35. J. Kincaid, *Adventures in the Rifle Brigade and random shots from a rifleman* (1909), p.170

36. A Near Observer, *The Battle of Waterloo* (1816), p.50

37. R. Gibney ed., *Eighty years ago, or the recollections of an old army doctor* (1896), p.198

38. H. Siborne ed., *The Waterloo letters* (1983), p.179; see also BL Add. MSS 34,706/19

39. R. Gronow, *The reminiscences and recollections of Captain Gronow 1810–1860* (1984), p.198

40. E. Macready, 'On a Part of Captain Siborne's History of the Waterloo Campaign', in *United Service Magazine* (1845, Part I). Each British battalion had ten companies, one of which was a light company particularly suited for skirmishing tasks. Members of the light companies were known as light bobs.

41. T. Morris, *Recollections of military service in 1813, 1814 and 1815* (1845), p.149

42. *Ibid*, p.153; according to Captain Garland himself, he was wounded while the 73rd formed line: H. Siborne ed., *The Waterloo letters* (1983), p.343

43. E. Cotton, *A voice from Waterloo* (1913), p.311

44. C. Hibbert ed., *The Wheatley diary* (1964), p.72

La Haie Sainte

# 8

# EVENING 18 JUNE

A lull in the fighting ensued. But it was only the eye of the storm. Napoleon vigorously counter-attacked and contained the Prussian threat at Plancenoit with two Old Guard battalions and then prepared to throw six battalions of the Middle Guard against Wellington. Captain de Barail of the 2nd Carabiniers deserted the French lines and crossed the valley with his arms raised.[1] 'Long live the King!' this traitor exclaimed. Then he described how Napoleon was preparing to attack with his Guard within half an hour.[2]

Wellington was already making his final preparations. His last reserves had reinforced the crumbling centre. Lieutenant-General Baron David Chassé's Dutch-Belgian division had marched from Braine-l'Alleud 2000 metres away in the west and now stood along the Nivelles–Mont St Jean highroad ready to intervene immediately in the front line. All along the front, artillery batteries replenished their stocks of ammunition. Casualties had been immense and everywhere battalions had withered to mere bands. Yet morale remained firm; the survivors were grimly determined and Wellington's line was intact.

Shortly after 7.00 pm French guns redoubled their fire. Captain Harry Weyland Powell and his comrades of the British 1st Guards sheltered from this concentrated pre-assault barrage in a ditch and under a bank at the side of the track running along the ridge crest. 'Without the protection of this bank every creature must have perished', he wrote.[3]

Towards 7.30 pm the French bombardment ceased and six hollow infantry squares of the French Middle Guard marched across the blood-soaked valley from La Haie Sainte. Usually French infantry attacked in columns, but the Guard advanced in squares as if they expected to be counter-attacked by cavalry. Wellington's guns were firing now. Marshal Ney was at the head of this last assault. He led it diagonally across the field towards the spot now occupied by the Lion Mound. Fortunately for Wellington, Ney chose not to advance due north from La Haie Sainte and strike the shattered brigades of Ompteda and Kielmannsegge near the crossroads. French troops all along the front were advancing in support of the Middle Guard and some were already in action north of La Haie Sainte. Hence Ney inclined to the left.

So thick was the smoke of battle by this stage that the British could not see their approaching foe. Nevertheless, they could hear him. Seventeen-year-old Ensign William Leeke listened to the ominous drumbeats, 'the rumdum, the rumdum, the rummadum, dumadum, dum dum', followed by a hearty cheer of 'Vive l'Empereur!' Then the drums would restart, the whole sequence being repeated again and again.

Somewhere in the valley were thousands of Napoleon's crack troops. These tall, proud, redoubtable Imperial Guardsmen were veterans to a man. Time and time again they had punched through the opposing battle line to clinch Napoleon's victories. The painter, Benjamin Haydon, had studied these elite troops a year before: 'more dreadful looking fellows I never saw. They had the look of thoroughbred, veteran, disciplined banditti. Depravity, recklessness and blood-thirstiness were burnt in their faces. Black moustaches, gigantic bearskins and a ferocious expression were their characteristics.'[4]

At last the first battalions emerged from the smoke on the edge of the ridge, under 200 metres from Wellington's front line. Marshal Ney was leading six Middle Guard battalions accompanied by the eight guns of a Guard horse artillery battery.[5] The infantry, over 2500 strong, advanced in hollow squares on a front of 300 metres and struck Colin Halkett and Peregrine Maitland's brigades in succession, from east to west. Ensign Edward Macready was with the eastern half of Halkett's brigade at the present location of the panorama. Unfortunately, the Lion Mound now stands where the leading French unit, the 1st battalion of the 3rd Grenadiers, marched towards Macready and his comrades of the 30th and 73rd Foot. Macready watched in mounting trepidation:

> The Imperial Guard was seen ascending our position in as correct order as at a review. As they rose step by step before us, and crossed the ridge, their red epaulettes and cross-belts put on over their blue great-coats, gave them a gigantic appearance, which was increased by their high hairy caps and long red feathers, which waved with the nod of their heads as they kept time to a drum in the centre of their column. 'Now for a clawing,' I muttered, and I confess, when I saw the imposing advance of these men, and thought of the character they had gained, I looked for nothing but a bayonet in my body, and I half breathed a confident sort of wish that it might not touch my vitals.[6]

In a short while, Macready's formation recoiled in chaos. Fortunately, the dynamic Dutch Lieutenant-General Baron David-Hendrik Chassé, nicknamed 'General Bayonet', brought up one of his division's batteries under Captain Charles Krahmer de Bichin. These guns crashed out at close range and proved decisive in checking the 3rd Grenadiers. Macready was delighted: 'they were served most gloriously, and their grand metallic bang, bang, bang, bang, with the rushing showers of grape that followed, were the most welcome sounds that

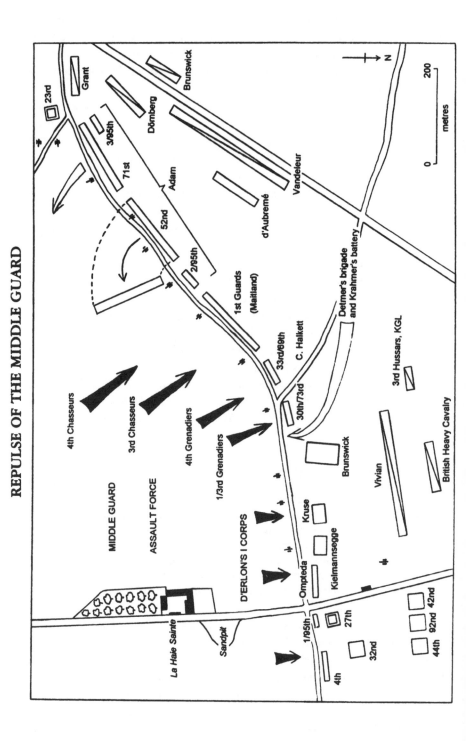

REPULSE OF THE MIDDLE GUARD

ever struck my ears – *until* I married.' The battery lost twenty-seven men killed and twenty-one wounded in this bitter confrontation.[7]

Chassé also launched Colonel Henri Detmer's Dutch-Belgian infantry brigade into the fray with a mighty cheer of 'long live the House of Orange! Long live the King!' Macready noticed this charge and described how 'a heavy column of Dutch infantry (the first we had seen) passed, drumming and shouting like mad, with their shakos on the top of their bayonets, near enough to our right for us to see and laugh at them.' A Belgian sergeant-major in Detmer's 35th (Belgian) Jägers later boasted to a Bruges newspaper about his unit's role:

> We commenced firing ... but that irritated us ... and we called out for an attack with cold steel. This order we were happy enough to obtain from our General [Chassé]. It was then that you should have seen how that fine Guard fled at full speed. Never in my life shall I see again such a carnage. Not one of that Guard, nor of the few cuirassiers who tried to help it, escaped. All perished by the bayonet. We only saw before and around us corpses of men and horses, guns, helmets and shakos ... We fought as if we were possessed. Our battalion had 150 killed and wounded. My captain, Guyot, was wounded in the side. Captain Dullart was slightly wounded.[8]

Soon it was over and the 3rd Grenadiers had broken. Macready was astonished. 'Our surprise was inexpressible', he wrote, 'when through the clearing smoke we saw the backs of the Imperials flying in a mass. We stared at each other as if mistrusting our eyesight. Some guns from the rear of our right poured in grape among them, and the slaughter was dreadful. Nowhere did I see carcasses so heaped upon each other.'

In the course of this bloody encounter, seventy-five metres to the west the French 4th Grenadiers had clashed with the 33rd and 69th Foot. An intense crossfire was now bringing down heaps of men on both sides. Lieutenant Frederick Pattison of the 33rd found himself surrounded by carnage:

> My right-hand man, a brave fellow, was at this instant shot right through the head. He leaned on me in falling: the ball entered his left temple, and I can never forget the expression on his countenance in the momentary transition from life to death. Directly after this my shako shook on my head. I took it off to ascertain the cause, when I found that a ball had gone right through it grazing my skull.[9]

The 4th Grenadiers refused to budge until compelled to do so by the repulse of neighbouring units either side. Even then they retired in good order.

In the meantime, the decisive clash of the Middle Guard attack occurred seventy-five metres from the panorama, along the track to Hougoumont. This spot is unspoiled by buildings and if you ignore the Lion Mound on your left, it is easy to imagine the scene. The bottom of the valley is hidden from view but La Belle Alliance is clearly distinguishable on the far side.

Two battalions of the 3rd Chasseurs progressed steadily over the brow of the ridge in front of you and into a devastating hail of canister. Lieutenant George Pringle remembered his battery inflicting huge casualties, 'the Column waving, at each successive discharge, like standing corn blown by the wind.'[10]

The chasseurs closed ranks and came on, their officers in front waving their swords. Like true guards, they were as regularly formed up as if on a field day. Along the track on which you are standing, Maitland's British 1st Footguards were lying down in line four deep. Wellington was on horseback behind them. As soon as the 3rd Chasseurs were fifty to sixty paces away, they saw a wall of redcoats rise from the golden cornfields in front. 'Whether', wrote Captain Harry Weyland Powell, 'it was from the sudden and unexpected appearance of a Corps so near them, which must have seemed as starting out of the ground, or the tremendously heavy fire we threw into them, *La Garde*, who had never before failed in an attack, *suddenly* stopped. Those who from a distance and more on the flank could see the affair, tell us that the effect of our fire seemed to force the head of the Column bodily back.'[11]

The scene was one of utter chaos. The French had halted, wrote Captain John Reeve, 'but from the warm reception they met with, instead of deploying they commenced firing several file deep evidently in confusion.' The chasseurs' indecision was obvious. 'Now's the time, my boys', roared Alexander, Lord Saltoun, as he led a triumphant charge which rolled the 3rd Chasseurs back in confusion. 'At that moment we charged them,' remembered Captain Reeve, 'they began to waver, went to the right about and fled in all directions – the rear of their Columns apparently first beginning to show disorder and run.'[12] For defeating the chasseurs, the 1st Guards would be awarded the title 'Grenadier Guards' on 29 July 1815, as at the time it was thought the French force had been grenadiers.

However, the final act of Waterloo's mighty climax was still to be played. The last unit of the Middle Guard's assault force, the 4th Chasseurs, arrived to check Maitland's advancing men and cause them to rush in disorder back to the ridge crest.

As Maitland rallied and traded fire with this new force of chasseurs, an extraordinary movement was occurring in Wellington's line to the south-west. Lieutenant-Colonel Sir John Colborne, the 'fire-eating' commander of the 52nd Light Infantry, swung his regiment in line four deep out of his position. Pivoting on his left hand company, he hurried the unit round till it was facing the western flank of the 4th Chasseurs. Slaughter ensued. Around 150 of Colborne's men were down while the rest were pouring an infernal fire into the French flank. Soon the cheering 52nd were pursuing the dazed survivors into the valley.

It was over and the entire French army sensed it. An incredible, ghastly cry of 'the Guard is falling back' – 'la garde recule' – spread like wildfire. Panic swiftly followed. Wellington waved his hat three times and his whole line charged forward. Some of his retinue advised caution but the Duke dismissed their warnings with the famous phrase: 'Oh, damn it! In for a penny, in for a pound.'[13]

In the evening light, fantastic scenes were occurring all over the field. 'I shall never forget some of the French Guards turning to look at their redoubtable enemies', wrote a British officer. 'Some lingering rays of the sun falling on their faces through the smoke now nearly cleared away, threw a lurid kind of glare upon their countenances, and gave them a fierce look, particularly when the gleam from the musketry assisted.'[14]

Lieutenant-Colonel Sir Augustus Frazer, commanding the Royal Horse Artillery, commented:

> I have seen nothing like that moment, the sky literally darkened with smoke, the sun just going down, and which till then has not for some hours broken through the gloom of a dull day, the indescribable shouts of thousands where it was impossible to distinguish between friend and foe. Every man's arm seemed to be raised against that of every other. Suddenly, after the mingled mass had ebbed and flowed, the enemy began to yield; and cheerings and English huzzas announced that the day must be ours.[15]

Ensign Robert Batty of the 1st Guards was stepping over the mounds of French corpses marking where the Middle Guard formations had taken such punishment on the ridge. He took the sunlight as a good omen: 'the sun, which had hitherto been veiled, at this instant shed upon us in departing rays, as if to smile upon the efforts we were making, and bless them with success.'[16]

For most, the general advance was a moment of exultation. Lieutenant Frederick Pattison of the 33rd Foot was so joyful that he felt as if he were walking on air. Yet anxiety still troubled Major-General Baron Jean-Victor de Constant-Rebecque, chief-of-staff of the Netherlands troops:

> At this moment a cannon-ball ricocheted under the belly of my horse, covering me with earth and stones and I was bruised on the flesh of my left leg. Immediately afterwards, while I still had my sword in my hand following the final cavalry charge, a canister shot struck the steel sheath of my sword against my leg. The scabbard was bent in such a way that I can sheath only half my sword in it. I was advancing with Lord Wellington in a hail of canister and my eyes were anxiously fixed on him but the happiness of victory shined in his. A canister shot passed through my horse's head; a fountain of blood came from its nostrils, covering me entirely, and it fell dead on the spot.[17]

Ensign William Leeke of the 52nd Light Infantry was nearing the bottom of the valley now, leaving Hougoumont to his right and heading for La Belle Alliance.

He had heard Wellington encouraging his commander: 'well done, Colborne! Well done! Go on, don't give them time to rally.'[18] Now he thought of what would happen to his soul if he were killed. Men were still falling around him and he needed both hands to carry the heavy flag he was bearing, leaving him unable to draw his sword in self-defence. 'I recollect I quieted the thought at once, by thinking that those who believed in the Saviour, the Lord Jesus Christ, would be saved; and that, as I believed in Him, all would be right if I should be killed that day.'[19]

Suddenly he found the flag pole was wet with blood. The buff cuff of his left sleeve was also stained red. The blood was not his own. Next morning he would find his thumb was black and swollen; he had probably been struck by a piece of the skull of a 52nd light infantryman advancing in front of him and killed by French canister.[20]

Wellington passed along his line, urging his units forward. Galloping ADCs were doing the same. Follow the Duke's route from the centre of the field to the crossroads, where Lieutenant Johnny Kincaid and the 95th Rifles had been awaiting the outcome of the Middle Guard attack. Kincaid vividly remembered how the sheer exhilaration of victory banished exhaustion:

> Presently a cheer, which we knew to be British, commenced far to the right, and made every one prick up his ears; – it was Lord Wellington's long-wished-for orders to advance; it gradually approached, growing louder as it grew near; – we took it up by instinct, charged through the hedge down upon the old knoll, sending our adversaries flying at the point of the bayonet. Lord Wellington galloped up to us at the instant, and our men began to cheer him; but he called out, 'No cheering, my lads, but forward, and complete your victory!'
>
> This movement had carried us clear of the smoke; and, to people who had been for so many hours enveloped in darkness, in the midst of destruction, and naturally anxious about the result of the day, the scene which now met the eye conveyed a feeling of more exquisite gratification than can be conceived. It was a fine summer's evening, just before sunset. The French were flying in one confused mass. British lines were seen in close pursuit, and in admirable order, as far as the eye could reach to the right, while the plain to the left was filled with Prussians.[21]

Baron Carl von Müffling, Wellington's Prussian liaison officer, noticed that the Duke's line consisted only of small, individual masses of men moving into the valley with large gaps between them. Back on the ridge crest an almost solid red line of dead and wounded redcoats marked the extent of the army's former positions.[22] Colonel Best, commander of a Hanoverian infantry brigade on the eastern wing, gazed at the scene with pride: 'all corps of infantry left their positions and formed in line and advanced, colours flying, drums beating and music playing, the cavalry following in second line. This was one of the finest military sights ever beheld, as the troops not only kept their proper distances but were also dressed in one uniform line as on a field day.'[23] Many of the soldiers lost their shoes as they struggled across the sticky, miry clay of the valley.[24]

Sir Hussey Vivian's hussars, supported by Sir John Vandeleur and William Dörnberg's light dragoons, passed the infantry to launch a decisive series of co-ordinated charges between La Haie Sainte and Hougoumont which overthrew the last of the French horsemen. Lieutenant-Colonel the Hon. Henry Murray remembered leading the 18th Hussars and being struck in the face and chest by earth thrown up by a cannon-ball falling under his horse. He charged diag-onally across the field and heard the brief clatter of hooves as his regiment galloped over the cobbled Brussels highroad south of La Haie Sainte. Then French artillery came dashing across the front of the 18th Hussars and in a moment the hussars were amongst them and seizing the guns. Next Murray led his men to overturn a cavalry formation.[25]

By sweeping away the French horsemen, Vivian, Vandeleur and Dörnberg enabled Wellington's advancing infantry to defeat the steady squares of Old Guard which were trying vainly to cover Napoleon's retreat. Nevertheless, tragedy did occur when a squadron of the 10th Hussars foolhardily launched an unsupported attack on one of these squares. The officers were the first casualties and although the furious hussars hacked at the bayonets they made no head-way.

Among the rampart of corpses before the square lay the squadron com-mander, Major the Hon. Frederick Howard. Shot through the mouth, he had fallen unconscious on the ground. A French guardsman stepped from the ranks and cold-bloodedly beat Howard's head in with his musket-butt. Captain Henry Grove of the 23rd Light Dragoons remembered nodding to Howard, 'within a few minutes of which he was killed – and a very fine, handsome fellow he was; but he evidently looked as if his time was come.'[26] Howard's father, the Earl of Carlisle, later had his remains removed from the battlefield to England; since 1879 they have rested in the family mausoleum at Castle Howard, Yorkshire. A brother officer recalled that 'I never knew Howard do or say a thing one could wish otherwise. He was an excellent officer too; and, I know, a sincerely attached husband.'[27]

Night had fallen now and Wellington's exhausted men halted while the Prussians took up the pursuit of the routed French and harried then away to the south. In years to come Waterloo would be celebrated in the British army as one of its most famous battles. But at the time, it was the terrible human cost that occupied the soldiers' thoughts. Lieutenant Johnny Kincaid commented that 'this was the last, the greatest, and the most uncomfortable heap of glory that I ever had a hand in.' After most actions, he added, officers would visit neighbouring units to ask, 'who's hit?' After Waterloo they inquired, 'who's alive?'[28]

To conclude your tour of Wellington's battlefield, stop at the inn of La Belle Alliance in the centre of the French position. Major Howard was killed in the fields one hundred metres or so west of La Belle Alliance.[29] The inn was also the scene of a chance encounter between Wellington and Blücher at 9.00 pm. Lieutenant Basil Jackson of the Royal Staff Corps recalled how Wellington had advanced with his army to Maison du Roi and then returned northwards:

> Just before he reached La Belle Alliance, the outlines of a numerous party on horseback, surrounded by crowds of infantry, could be made out, though it was dark, approaching the road from the direction of Papelotte and La Haye. When first observed, the party was about fifty yards from the road, and, on seeing it, the Duke, aware, perhaps, that it was Marshal Blücher and his Staff, turned aside to meet the brave old Prussian. I was very close to the two heroes during their short conference, which may have lasted about ten minutes; but it was too dark for me to distinguish old Blücher's features. It is a remarkable circumstance that this meeting should have taken place within two or three hundred yards of La Belle Alliance; and most probably Blücher did express a wish for the battle to bear that name ['the fine alliance'], as we have been told. It must have been quite half-past nine when these distinguished men shook hands and parted. The Duke then regained the chaussée, and proceeded, as before, at a walk. I think he was accompanied by only five persons, the rest of the Staff having got scattered in the confusion and darkness which prevailed during the last half-hour of the advance.[30]

North of La Belle Alliance, Wellington was forced to leave the road and to ride over the fields. Abandoned French guns and limbers entirely blocked the Brussels highroad itself. It is three and a half miles from La Belle Alliance to Waterloo and Wellington rode the whole way at a walk. Drained by his exertions and sickened by the slaughter, the Duke spoke to none of his suite. A month later he described to a friend his thoughts during that long, lonely ride: 'while in the thick of it, I am too occupied to feel anything; but it is wretched just after. It is impossible to think of glory. Both mind and feelings are exhausted.'[31]

At 10.00 pm he arrived back at his headquarters, dismounted from his horse, Copenhagen, and patted him on the hindquarters. Copenhagen was so surprised that he kicked out and nearly hit the Duke. It was the last but not the least of the many dangers Wellington had faced that day. It had also been his last battle for Providence granted him his wish: 'God grant that I may never see another! for I am overwhelmed with grief at the loss of my old friends and comrades.'[32]

# Notes

1. H. Lachouque, *Waterloo* (1975), p.180
2. H. Siborne ed., *The Waterloo letters* (1983), pp.280, 283
3. *Ibid*, p.254

4. E. Cotton, *A voice from Waterloo* (1913), p.307

5. H. de Mauduit, *Les derniers jours de la grande armée* (1848), v.2, p.417; Henri Houssaye incorrectly attributed only one battalion to the 4th Chasseurs.

6. E. Macready, 'On a Part of Captain Siborne's History of the Waterloo Campaign', in *United Service Magazine* (1845, Part I)

7. D. Boulger, *The Belgians at Waterloo* (1901), p.34

8. *Ibid*, p.35

9. F. Pattison, *Personal recollections of the Waterloo campaign* (1870), p.31

10. H. Siborne ed., *The Waterloo letters* (1983), pp.227–8

11. *Ibid*, p.255

12. BL Add. MSS 34,705/114

13. E. Longford, *Wellington: the years of the sword* (1972), p.479

14. 'Operations of the Fifth or Picton's Division in the campaign of Waterloo', in *United Service Magazine* (June 1841), p.187

15. E. Cotton, *A voice from Waterloo* (1913), pp.306–7

16. A Near Observer, *The Battle of Waterloo* (1816), pp.57–8

17. Société des études historiques et folkloriques de Waterloo, Braine-l'Alleud et environs, *Mélanges historiques* (1970), p.148

18. W. Leeke, *The history of Lord Seaton's regiment at the Battle of Waterloo* (1866), v.1, p.55

19. *Ibid*, v.1, p.54

20. *Ibid*, v.1, p.51

21. J. Kincaid, *Adventures in the Rifle Brigade and random shots from a rifleman* (1909), pp.170–1

22. C. Müffling, *Passages from my life* (1853), p.250

23. BL Add MSS 34,704/279–80. We have had to correct Colonel Best's punctuation and spelling in this particular extract.

24. BL Add. MSS 34,705/37

25. H. Siborne ed., *The Waterloo letters* (1983), pp.180–2

26. *Ibid*, p.102

27. W. Siborne, *History of the Waterloo campaign* (1990), p.366

28. J. Kincaid, *Adventures in the Rifle Brigade and random shots from a rifleman* (1909), p.171–3

29. BL Add MSS 34,703/302; see also Lord Chalfont, ed., *Waterloo: battle of three armies* (1979), pp.144–5, after Sergeant-Major Cotton's map.

30. 'Recollections of Waterloo by a staff officer', in *United Service Magazine* (1847, Part III); according to Major-General Baron Jean-Victor de Constant-Rebecque, who was also present, the meeting between Wellington and Blücher occurred between Le Caillou and Maison du Roi: Société des études historiques et folkloriques de Waterloo, Braine-l'Alleud et environs, *Mélanges historiques* (1970), p.149

31. E. Longford, *Wellington: the years of the sword* (1972), p.489

32. E. Cotton, *A voice from Waterloo* (1913), p.237; 'Recollections of Waterloo by a staff officer, in *United Service Magazine* (1847, Part III); Wellington's reaction to Waterloo is intriguingly similar to that of Britain's Duke of Marlborough to the slaughter of the Battle of Malplaquet in 1709. Marlborough wrote 'God Almighty be praised, it is now our power to have what peace we please, and I may be pretty well assured of never being in another battle' (C. Barnett, *Marlborough* [1974], p.239). One of Marlborough's British subordinates, Lord Orkney, prayed that 'I hope in God it may be the last battle I may ever see' (*English Historical Review* [1904], p.320). Wellington read widely in military history and may well have been remembering Marlborough's words when he hoped that Waterloo would be his last battle. Wellington always admired Marlborough: 'I can conceive nothing greater than Marlborough at the head of an English army' (E. Longford, *Pillar of State* [1972], p.412). It is noteworthy that during his advance from Waterloo to Paris, Wellington crossed the French frontier at Malplaquet.

# PART THREE: NAPOLEON'S SECTOR

# 9

# MORNING 18 JUNE:
## THE LAST REVIEW

To explore Napoleon's side of the battlefield, start at his headquarters of Le Caillou and then advance north up the Brussels road to the French front line.

The farm of Le Caillou is 3000 metres south of the shallow valley in which the fighting occurred. An eminent local historian, Lucien Laudy, converted it into an evocative museum in 1912 and as a result the visitor leaves Le Caillou with a vivid if strongly French-flavoured understanding of the battle. The museum is closed in January and on Mondays.

The building itself bears little resemblance to the farm occupied by Napoleon, as it was burnt by the Prussians immediately after the battle and has undergone extensive restoration and rebuilding since. One of the reasons the Prussians burnt the farm was their determination to destroy anything connected with Napoleon. Some wounded Frenchmen were trapped in an adjoining barn and five or six of them perished in the flames started by their vengeful foes.

Such was Napoleon's haste to escape the battlefield in the evening that he left two of his horses in the stables of Le Caillou. English officers sent one of these, Marengo, to England where it died a little later. You will find Marengo's skeleton on display at the National Army Museum in London. Napoleon rode on three horses at Waterloo: first Marie then Desirée and finally Marengo, an iron grey horse named after his victory of 14 June 1800 over the Austrians. After Napoleon's defeat, Marengo carried Napoleon back from the front line to Le Caillou where it was unsaddled. When the Prussian pursuit neared the farm, Napoleon mounted another horse and rode off.[1]

A particularly interesting relic in Le Caillou is a glass case containing the skeleton of a soldier, complete with the balls which killed him and the uniform buttons which enabled historians to identify him as a French hussar. He was found in 1910 at the site of the last stand of the Imperial Guard in the evening. He was clearly hit in the head by a ball and the gash in the skull was possibly made by a sabre cut. It is an absolute disgrace that, as a soldier who made the supreme sacrifice, he has not been reverently buried.

## NAPOLEON'S SECTOR OF THE BATTLEFIELD TODAY

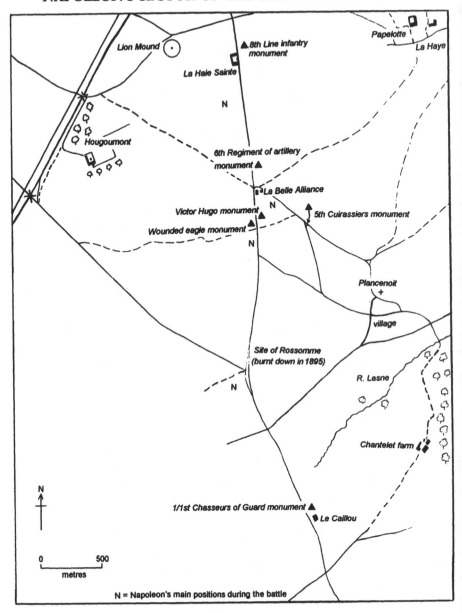

On the wall beside the skeleton hangs François Flameng's dramatic painting of the red-headed Marshal Michel Ney leading a frenzied host of French cavalry against a redoubtable square of Wellington's redcoats.

In the Salle des aides de camp, a bronze plaque records the names of the French generals and important members of Napoleon's suite who stayed at Le

Caillou with their Emperor. During the night of 17/18 June, Le Caillou was packed with officers sheltering from the torrential rain outside. They slept on straw in rooms, on the staircase and in the attic. The quarters Napoleon occupied on his campaigns were called the 'palace' and for the wretched rank and file forced to pass the night in the open, Le Caillou was a palace indeed. Napoleon's imperial green camp bed that you see in the Chambre de l'Empereur is not the one he used in 1815. He slept little on the eve of Waterloo in any case.[2]

Napoleon's servant, Mameluke Ali, described the Emperor's arrival on the evening of 17 June:

> It was night or nearly so when the Emperor reached the farm of Le Caillou; he set up his headquarters there. As his accommodation was not ready, a bivouac fire was lit near the buildings (which were on the right of the road) and there, lying on a bale of straw, he waited for his room to be made ready to receive him. When he had occupied the small hovel where he had to spend the night, he had his boots pulled off. It was troublesome to pull them off him as they had been soaked the whole day. Then, undressed, he went to bed where he had dinner. He slept little during the night, being disturbed constantly by people coming and going: some came to give him an account of a mission, others to receive orders.[3]

It rained all night and so soaked the ground that the commander of the Imperial Guard, Lieutenant-General Count Antoine Drouot, informed Napoleon that the ground must dry a little before the French artillery could deploy; the battle would have to be postponed for several hours.[4] Around dawn, the rain stopped and a light wind began to dry the water-logged terrain.[5]

At Le Caillou Napoleon's valet, Louis-Joseph-Narcisse Marchand, attended his master in a small, square room. This served as the Emperor's bedroom, study and dining room. Marchand remembered how for a long time Napoleon 'walked to and fro in this room, with his hands behind his back. He took some scissors and turned them around his fingernails. He seemed much more occupied by the battle which was going to be fought than by this detail of his toilette for he often went to the window and looked at the state of the sky.'[6] What was passing through the Emperor's mind? According to his memoirs, as he looked out of the window he saw rays of the morning sun peering through the clouds. 'France', he mused, 'was going to rise, that day, more glorious, more powerful and greater than ever!'[7]

It was approaching 5.00 am. Napoleon shaved and dressed and then dictated instructions for his army to be in position ready to attack at 9.00 am. The troops were to make soup and put their weapons in order. Nevertheless, the appalling weather had made even a 9.00 am attack doubtful. Sergeant Hippolyte de Mauduit of the 1st Grenadiers of the Guard related how even companies were disunited. Bands of troops had wandered off to seek shelter while some corps had bivouacked over three and a half miles south of Le Caillou.

At 8.00 am Napoleon held a pre-battle conference with his generals in Le Caillou. You can visit a reconstruction of the scene at the waxworks museum at the foot of the Lion Mound. Napoleon was wearing white breeches and his customary green undress uniform of a colonel of the Chasseurs à cheval of the Guard. On the battlefield he also wore his famous grey greatcoat and black cocked hat.

At his conference, Napoleon outlined his plan of battle and sought to boost his subordinates' confidence: 'The enemy army exceeds ours by nearly a quarter but the odds are nine to one in our favour' he announced.[8]

Napoleon's Chief-of-Staff, Marshal Nicolas Soult, voiced his fears that the British, whom he had fought against in Spain, were redoubtable foes to attack. Soult hence advised the recall of some of Marshal Grouchy's troops, from the pursuit of Blücher, to help in the battle against Wellington.

Napoleon's reply was caustic. 'Because you have been beaten by Wellington, you think him a great general. I tell you that Wellington is a bad general, that the English are bad troops and that this will be a picnic.' Nevertheless, Lieutenant-General Count Honoré Reille of II Corps, another veteran of the Peninsular war, concurred with Marshal Soult's opinion:

> Well posted as Wellington knows how to post them and attacked head-on, I consider the English infantry to be impregnable in view of its calm tenacity and superior firepower. Before we can reach them with the bayonet, half our attacking force would be shot down. But the English army is less agile, less supple, less manoeuvrable than ours. If we can not conquer it by a head-on attack, we could do so by manoeuvring.[9]

Napoleon uttered an exclamation of incredulity. The Emperor was too confident to consider any strategical finesse. Already the character of the coming battle was taking shape as an attritional pounding match.

Even when Prince Jérôme Bonaparte mentioned that a waiter at the Auberge du roi d'espagne at Genappe had told him an English ADC, at the town on 17 June during Wellington's retreat, had let slip that Blücher would be coming to link up with Wellington in front of Soignes forest, Napoleon dismissed it all:

'After a battle like Fleurus [Ligny] and being pursued by a substantial number of troops, it is impossible for the Prussians to join the English in less than two days. We should be delighted that the English are standing their ground. The coming battle will save France and be renowned in history.'

Then Napoleon uttered the words that finally set the nature of the battle: 'I shall bombard them with my numerous artillery, I shall charge them with my cavalry, so that they are forced to show themselves and, when I am quite sure where the English contingent is, I shall march straight at it with my Old Guard.'[10]

It was to be a head-on attack and the foundations for the blood-bath had been laid. Some artillery officers returned from scouring the fields, to announce that cannon could now be manoeuvred over the soaked ground, with some difficulty. In an hour's time the soil would be drier and the difficulties considerably lessened. Napoleon rose from the table: 'Gentlemen,' he said, 'if my orders are carried out well, we will sleep tonight at Brussels.'[11] With this parting remark the Emperor, stout, confident and forceful, left Le Caillou, mounted his horse, Marie, and rode north up the Brussels road.[12]

Before following in the wake of the Emperor up to the front line, visit the peaceful, walled orchard adjoining the farm. The 1st battalion of Brigadier-General Count Pierre Cambronne's 1st Chasseurs of the Guard bivouacked here on the eve of Waterloo. A monument inaugurated in 1965 records that: 'the 1st battalion of the 1st Regiment of Chasseurs à pied of the Imperial Guard, commanded by Major Duuring, bivouacked in this place on the night of 17 to 18 June. This battalion had distinguished itself at Marengo, Ulm, Austerlitz, Jena, Friedland, Essling, Wagram, Smolensk, La Moskowa, Hanau and Montmirail.'

The battalion's task was to guard Napoleon's headquarters and baggage from the looters who thrived on the lack of discipline in the French Army. Thus the battalion saw action only in the late evening when elements of it marched eastwards to repulse Prussian patrols which had swung round south of Plancenoit to bypass the fighting in the village in an attempt to cut the Brussels road.

Major Jean Duuring also placed two companies with fixed bayonets across the Brussels road outside Le Caillou in a vain effort to stem the steadily increasing stream of fugitives. In the end he abandoned all hope of rallying any but soldiers of the Guard. Napoleon's valet, Louis Marchand, was also at Le Caillou in the evening and related how 'night had still not fallen when we saw the road covered with artillery trains and wounded soldiers supported by unhurt men. This movement to the rear became alarming and I provisionally had the Emperor's bed put in its cases, I shut the necessities and held myself ready for any eventuality.'[13] Soon the imperial treasure and other baggage were sent to the south for safety. Unfortunately, they became stuck at Charleroi and were pillaged by French fugitives and Prussian pursuers.

The final duty of the 1st battalion, 1st Chasseurs, was to help escort the vanquished Napoleon to Genappe. Duuring related how 'we saw the Emperor arrive accompanied by some chasseurs à cheval and some generals including Counts Drouot and Lobau. His Majesty came to me, asked what I had done, my strength and my position and saying "I count on you," he gave me in person the order to close up and to follow him.'[14]

Pass from the orchard into the garden east of Le Caillou. Here, shaded by trees, is an ossuary built by Lucien Laudy and dedicated on 22 July 1912 to house the increasing quantity of bones discovered in recent years on the battlefield. The ossuary bears the Latin inscription 'for the Emperor often, for the Fatherland always', although it is more than likely that among the skulls and femurs of Napoleon's troops lie those of some of his enemies.

One of the striking aspects of Waterloo is the absence of cemeteries. Respect for dead soldiers did not extend to reverential burial in those days although senior officers fared better. Mass graves or cremation quickly disposed of the dead before infections could spread. In years immediately after the battle, bones discovered on the field were shipped to England to be ground down and used as fertiliser for farmers' fields. The ossuary at Le Caillou is one of the most haunting spots of the battlefield, just as the orchard is one of the most peaceful.

Two hundred and fifty metres south of Le Caillou a narrow road leads off to the east and the Farm of Chantelet, the quarters of Marshal Michel Ney before the battle. The farm witnessed minor skirmishing in the evening of 18 June when troops of the French 1st Chasseurs arrived from Le Caillou to drive off some Prussians. A plaque at Chantelet farm records Ney's stay. This is the sole memorial to Ney on the battlefield.

For most of the battle, Napoleon commanded from the rear of the front line in order to enjoy a view of, and control over, the entire battle. He relied on Ney to direct and inspire the troops in the thick of the fight. With the exception of the diversionary assault on Hougoumont, Ney personally led every French offensive against Wellington. His bravery and energy won the admiration even of his foes. In the evening he was heard bellowing at two depleted infantry regiments: 'Come, follow me, my comrades! I am going to show you how a Marshal of France dies, on the battlefield.'[15] Alas, he failed to find a soldier's death at Waterloo and was helped from the battlefield by Corporal Poulet of the 2nd Grenadiers until Major Schmidt of the Imperial Guard Lancers offered his horse.[16] Ney was shot in Paris by the restored Bourbon monarchy on 7 December 1815 and a stirring statue of the marshal on foot and brandishing a sword over his head marks the site of his execution. He deserves a similar monument on the field of Waterloo itself.

By returning from Chantelet to the Brussels road and following it northwards, you reach the farm of La Belle Alliance, which marks the front line of the French army. The farm dates from 1770 and served as a French field hospital during the battle. A plaque on the wall is dedicated 'to the memory of the French medical corps which on 18 June 1815 gave its most devoted care.' La Belle Alliance survived the fighting intact, apart from a few holes in the roof inflicted by gunfire.[17] The large barn adjoining the northern face of the farm was added after the battle. In the decades immediately following 1815, La Belle Alliance became one of the main tourist attractions and its visitor's books record scores of insults exchanged over the years by patriotic civilians. For instance: 'Irving Brock, of London, visited, for the third time, the fields of Waterloo and Planchenois, on the 26th July, 1826, he hopes with an increased feeling of gratitude to God for having delivered mankind, through the instrumentality of his countrymen, from the most detestable tyrant that ever wielded a sceptre.' Underneath, a French hand added: 'chien d'Anglais! Brute! Beast!'[18]

Napoleon reached La Belle Alliance from Le Caillou shortly after 9.00 am in order to examine the battlefield. A high bank on the southern edge of the road running south-east from La Belle Alliance to Plancenoit is signposted 'Napoleon's observation post'. Napoleon may have visited this point as he toured his outposts before battle began but it was not his main observation post.

It is known that Napoleon sent Lieutenant-General Baron Nicolas Haxo, the reliable commander of the Imperial Guard engineers, ahead of the French lines to reconnoitre Wellington's position. Napoleon wanted to know if Wellington had erected any earthworks or entrenchments but Haxo reported in the negative. In fact, Wellington had rejected the idea of entrenchments as that would show where he intended to fight and would only encourage Napoleon to manoeuvre around the position.[19]

Napoleon was still waiting for the whole of his army to arrive on the battlefield. Amidst the torrential rain of the previous evening only his leading formations had arrived from Quatre Bras before night fell. The II and VI Corps plus III Cavalry Corps and most of the Imperial Guard had halted along the Brussels road between Le Caillou and Genappe, over three and a half miles to the south.

The rest of the French army had spent a wretched night on the muddy slopes around Plancenoit and Rossomme with vedettes posted further north. Lieutenant J.L. Henckens of the 6th Chasseurs à cheval stated that:

> There was no way either we or our horses could lie down on the soaked ground so I spent the night of 17/18 June leaning against my horse which likewise preferred to sleep standing up. Furthermore, the rain resumed from time to time, the result of this being that the bivouac fires were quickly extinguished. On the morning of the 18th the plain was so soaked that, although the weather became superb, it was impossible to move. We awoke once dawn and the mist rising from the earth allowed us to see. After the men and horses had been provided for as well as possible and the mud more or less scraped off them, we had only to await what was required of us.[20]

Eighteen-year-old Louis Canler of the 28th Line infantry of I Corps remembered:

> We passed the night next to the campfire. Of course, it was no luxury for it rained continuously the whole night. Finally, dawn broke and each company

dismantled its muskets to grease them, to change the priming and to dry its greatcoats. After these preparations had been completed, we considered breakfast. The pot was put to boil on the fire and one of our corporals, being something of a butcher, killed, skinned and cut up our poor little sheep, which was cooked with some flour I had found on 16 June. After an hour, the company's captain and second lieutenant came to partake in our meal which, I hasten to say, tasted foul. Instead of salt, which we totally lacked, our cook had decided to throw a handful of powder into the pot.[21]

Only at 10.00 am was the French army massed south of the battlefield and ready to deploy. Napoleon decided to stage a massive display of might designed to overawe Wellington's watching army on the ridge opposite. It was to prove the last review of the Grand Army. 'The very earth seemed proud to support so many brave men,' thought Napoleon. 'I passed along the ranks; it would be difficult to express the enthusiasm which animated all the soldiers ... Victory seemed certain.'[22]

Louis Canler described how the 28th Line infantry picked up its muskets and marched to its position in the battle line. 'Then the Emperor passed in front of all the corps. With a spontaneous movement which resembled an electric current, helmets, shakos and bearskins were waved on the tips of sabres or bayonets to frenzied cheering of *Long live the Emperor!*'[23]

*Morituri te salutant!* had been the proud cry of doomed gladiators to the Emperors of Rome. 'We who are about to die salute you!'[24] Within twelve hours thousands of Napoleon's fine warriors would be broken, mangled corpses. For them, the future held only death and an unmarked common grave. But on that morning they revelled in their fleeting hour of glory as they paraded in gleaming breastplates or towering bearskins to the sound of their bands playing *Veillons au salut de l'Empire.*

'I am unable to recall this last review without intense emotion,' wrote Colonel Toussaint-Jean Trefçon, chief-of-staff to Lieutenant-General Baron Gilbert Bachelu of II Corps. 'I can compare the feeling which I experienced then with nothing better than that I had when I crossed the Niemen [into Russia] in 1812. The enthusiasm of the troops was intense, the bands were playing, the drummers beating and a quiver shook all these men – for many it was their last day. With all their strength they acclaimed the Emperor.'[25]

Lieutenant Jacques Martin of the 45th Line infantry was certain that never could Napoleon 'have heard "long live the Emperor!" shouted with more enthusiasm. Never was more absolute devotion written on the features, in the gestures and in the voices of his soldiers. It was like a frenzy. And what made this scene more imposing and solemn was that opposite us, at a thousand paces perhaps, we distinctly saw on the English ridge their long line marked in a sombre red.'[26]

According to Lieutenant-General Baron Jacques Delort, commander of a cuirassier division, 'the two armies, ready to come to blows, presented the most imposing sight. Their bearing presaged a bloody and stubborn battle. On both sides the spirit of the troops was stimulated to the highest degree for they were aware that the pre-eminence of nations hung on the terrible fight which was about to commence.'[27]

Towards 11.00 am the bulk of the French army was in position. Only a few formations and heavy artillery batteries had yet to deploy. 'As if by magic,' noted Sergeant Hippolyte de Mauduit of the 1st Grenadiers, 'the most profound silence and complete stillness had followed all these military deployments, all these fanfares and demonstrations.' From the church tower of Plancenoit village came the distinct sound of a bell chiming the hour.[28] It was the calm before the storm. By now, Napoleon had left the front line and retired 1500 metres southwards along the Brussels road. He occupied a mound near the farm of Rossomme and a short distance west of the main road. Rossomme was burnt down in 1895 but you can still see the high ground the Emperor occupied. At 11.00 am he dictated his order of battle to his chief-of-staff, Marshal Nicolas Soult. This order was addressed to each corps commander:

> Once the entire army has been drawn up in battle order, at around 1.00 pm, when the Emperor gives the order to Marshal Ney, the attack will begin to seize the village of Mont St Jean, where the roads unite. To this end, the 12-pounder batteries of II Corps and those of VI Corps will unite with those of I Corps. These twenty-four guns [later increased to eighty] will bombard the troops at Mont St Jean and Count d'Erlon will begin the attack by sending forward his left division and supporting it, as circumstances dictate, by the other divisions of I Corps.
> The II Corps will advance so as to keep level with Count d'Erlon. The engineer companies of I Corps will hold themselves in readiness to barricade themselves immediately at Mont St Jean.[29]

Napoleon's plan was clear: a massive frontal attack by d'Erlon's I Corps would punch through Wellington's east wing. But shortly after dictating this order, Napoleon modified his plan, for Marshal Ney added in pencil on a copy of the order: 'Count d'Erlon will understand that the attack will commence by the left instead of the right. Communicate this new disposition to General Reille.'[30]

Thus, while the main attack was being prepared, Reille's II Corps would launch a preliminary offensive in the west against Hougoumont. Reille's role was to contain Wellington's western flank by pinning it down at Hougoumont. Napoleon did not intend Reille to capture Hougoumont, merely to push a strong force of skirmishers into the wood. The entire French army was going to pivot on Hougoumont. The main attack would smash through Wellington's eastern flank before wheeling round and seizing Mont St Jean village. Then Napoleon's army would drive Wellington due west towards the Channel ports.

For this plan to succeed, Napoleon had to contain Wellington's western flank by pinning it down at Hougoumont. Major Jean-Baptiste Jolyet of Reille's 1st Light infantry asserted that his skirmishers had orders 'to limit themselves to preventing the enemy debouching on our left ... I had been clearly warned that the army had to pivot on us and that it was necessary at all costs to preserve our position [in the enclosures of Hougoumont].'[31]

Consequently, at around 11.30 am French skirmishers advanced towards Hougoumont wood and shortly afterwards the first gunfire broke out. Throughout the battle, Napoleon was accompanied by a local peasant, Jean-Baptiste Decoster, who served as a guide. Decoster had been taken prisoner at 5.00 am and to prevent him from escaping had his hands tied; he was then placed on a horse in the care of a Guard Chasseur à cheval of Napoleon's escort. Decoster was naturally terrified by the noise and carnage of the battle and Napoleon kindly reassured him: 'do not stir, my friend, a shot will kill you equally in the back as the front or wound you more disgracefully.'[32] Seeing Decoster duck at each passing shot, the Emperor joked, 'don't bow like that. You are not at the Tuileries!'[33]

Nevertheless, Decoster had reason to be afraid for enemy projectiles repeatedly fell in the vicinity of the Emperor; Lieutenant-General Baron Jean Desvaux de Saint-Maurice, commander of the Guard artillery, was cut in two by a cannon-ball nearby. Fortunately, Decoster survived and in the years immediately after the battle became a famous guide to the battlefield for the countless visitors. He used to describe how Napoleon asked him details of the features of the entire battlefield and would frequently take large pinches of snuff from a waistcoat pocket.

Napoleon was mainly to be found at either of two mounds along the Brussels road. One of these mounds was near Rossomme and the other was the rising ground you can see on the western side of the road immediately south of where the famous Wounded Eagle monument now stands. Lieutenant-General Baron Maximilien Foy watched him from afar: 'I saw him, with my telescope, walking up and down, dressed in his grey greatcoat, and often leaning on the small table bearing his map.'[34]

One of the most vivid recollections of Napoleon at Waterloo was left by Major Lemonnier-Delafosse. The major was waiting for an artillery battery to arrive along the Brussels road and found himself standing at the foot of Napoleon's mound near Rossomme. He thus enjoyed an opportunity of observing his Emperor at close range:

> Seated on a straw chair, in front of a coarse farm table, he was holding his map open on the table. His famous spyglass in his hand was often trained on the various points of the battle. When resting his eye, he used to pick up straws of wheat which he carried in his mouth as a toothpick. Stationed on his left, Marshal Soult alone waited for his orders and ten paces to the rear were grouped

all his staff on horseback. Sappers of the engineers were opening up ramps around the mound so that people could reach the Emperor more easily.

Never did one meet a greater or more perfect calm than that of Napoleon on the day of this battle, as he looked down over his army which for two hours already had attacked and pushed back the enemy on the whole line. Satisfaction could be seen written on his face, all was going well and there is no doubt that at this moment he thought his battle was won. I admired him for a long time, my eyes were unable to leave him. He was the genius of war.

I left at last, with our artillery and I never saw him again. I have this ever-present last memory.[35]

# Notes

1. L. Garros, *Le champ de bataille de Waterloo* (1952), p.84; *The Illustrated London News*, 1 October 1892

2. The authenticity of all the furniture on display at Le Caillou is suspect. Napoleon's valet, Louis Marchand, asserted that the furniture cluttering Napoleon's room in 1815 was thrown into the farmyard. Those pieces that survived their exposure to the rain were destroyed when Le Caillou was burnt on 19 June 1815. See J. Logie, *Waterloo: l'évitable défaite* (1989), p.89; T. Fleischman, *Histoire de la ferme du Caillou* (n.d.), p.76.

3. M. Ali, *Souvenirs du mameluck Ali sur l'empereur Napoléon* (1926), p.110

4. Drouot, like Napoleon, was an experienced and skilled gunner.

5. Napoleon claimed in his Memoirs that he toured the outposts during the night to try and see whether Wellington was continuing to retreat under cover of darkness or would stand and offer battle. Theo Fleischman and Jacques Logie doubt Napoleon's story (J. Logie, *Waterloo: l'évitable défaite* [1989], p.91; *Histoire de la ferme du Caillou* [n.d.], pp.62–3) whereas Henry Houssaye (*Waterloo 1815* [1987], p.277) believed it.

The evidence is insufficient to prove either argument. Although neither Mameluke Ali nor Louis Marchand mention Napoleon's nocturnal reconnaissance, this is not conclusive, as Napoleon stated that he took with him only the Grand Marshal of the Palace, Lieutenant-General Count Bertrand. Lieutenant-General Count d'Erlon recorded that Napoleon visited him and the outposts early in the morning but d'Erlon may be refering to Napoleon's visit of 9.00 am. It is certain that on the night before the Battle of Borodino on 7 September 1812, Napoleon constantly rose from his camp bed to reassure himself that the Russians had not left their defensive positions: D. Chandler, *On the Napoleonic wars* (1994), p.198

6. J. Bourguignon, *Mémoires de Marchand* (1952), v.1, p.163

7. S. de Chair ed., *Napoleon's memoirs* (1985), pp.520–1

8. *Ibid*, p.521

9. H. Houssaye, *Waterloo 1815* (1987), p.311

10. M. Foy, *Vie militaire* (1900), pp.278–9

11. J. Bourguignon, *Mémoires de Marchand* (1952), v.1, p.163

12. S. de Chair ed., *Napoleon's memoirs* (1985), p.522; L. Garros, *Le champ de bataille de Waterloo* (1952), p.84

13. J. Bourguignon, *Mémoires de Marchand* (1952), v.1, p.164

14. A. d'Avout, 'L'infanterie de la garde à Waterloo', in *Carnets de la Sabretache* (1905), p.20

15. J. Charras, *Histoire de la campagne de 1815* (1857), p.30

16. W. Aerts and L. Wilmet, *18 Juin 1815. Waterloo. L'attaque de la Garde. Les derniers carrés. La déroute* (1904), p.67

17. J. Logie, *Waterloo: l'évitable défaite* (1989), p.99

18. 'The Waterloo Albums', in *United Service Journal* (January 1839), pp.85–9

19. According to Lieutenant Alexander Riddock of the British 44th Foot, at 9.00 am a party of thirty French staff officers reconnoitred the whole of Wellington's front from west to east from a distance of only one hundred paces (about seventy-five metres). Not a shot was fired at them until

they arrived opposite Colonel Best's Hanoverian brigade stationed east of Sir Thomas Picton's British battalions. The fire of the Hanoverians wounded several of the French party and caused the remainder to retire. It is possible this party consisted of Baron Haxo and some of his officers; it may have included Captain Jean-Roch Coignet: J. Coignet, *The notebooks of Captain Coignet* (1986), p.278. See BL Add. MSS 34,704/123.

20. E. Henckens, *Mémoires* (1910), p.231. The 6th Chasseurs à cheval belonged to the light cavalry division of Lieutenant-General Count de Piré and therefore formed part of II Corps. However, while the infantry divisions of II Corps definitely passed the night at Genappe, Count de Piré's cavalry seems from Henckens' testimony to have advanced right up to the French front line. The weather on 18 June was never superb except at sunset; it remained cloudy during the day and showers occurred from time to time. Nevertheless, compared to the torrential rain of the previous night, 18 June saw calm and mostly dry weather.

21. L. Canler, *Mémoires de Canler, ancien chef de la police de sûreté* (1882), v.1

22. S. de Chair ed., *Napoleon's memoirs* (1985), pp.523–4

23. L. Canler, *Mémoires de Canler, ancien chef de la police de sûreté* (1882), v.1

24. Lady Longford, in M. Glover, *1815: the armies at Waterloo* (1973), p.10; V. Hugo, *Les Misérables* trans. by N. Denny (1985), p.308

25. A. Lévi, *Carnet de campagne du Colonel Trefçon* (1914), p.186

26. J. Martin, *Souvenirs d'un ex-officier* (1867), p.284

27. L. Stouff, *Le Lieutenant-Général Delort* (1906), p.147

28. H. de Mauduit, *Les derniers jours de la grande armée* (1848), v.2, pp.271–5

29. N. Bonaparte, *Correspondance de Napoléon 1er* (1869), v.28, pp.337–8; H. de Mauduit, *Les derniers jours de la grande armée* (1848), v.2, pp.275–6

30. See O. Levavasseur, *Souvenirs militaires* (1914), pp.296–7

31. 'Souvenirs de 1815' in *Revue de Paris* (Sept–Oct 1903), p.545

32. A Near Observer, *The Battle of Waterloo* (1816), p.136

33. G. Barral, *Itinéraire illustré de l'épopée de Waterloo* (1896), p.68; the Tuileries was Napoleon's palace in the centre of Paris.

34. M. Foy, *Vie militaire* (1900), pp.279–80; compare with A. Pétiet, *Souvenirs militaires* (1844), pp.213–14

35. M. Lemonnier-Delafosse, *Souvenirs militaires* (1850), pp.406–7

Napoleon at Waterloo

# 10

# THE ASSAULT ON HOUGOUMONT

N ow visit the front line of the French army, where you can follow the fierce fighting step by step. First, visit the Hougoumont sector on the western flank.

You can see Hougoumont farm from the French position, by walking along the dirt track which leaves the Brussels road 300 metres south of La Belle Alliance and runs westwards through the cornfields. This track is in the same condition it was in at the time of the battle.

Lieutenant-General Reille's II Corps extended all along this track. Prince Jérôme Bonaparte's division, which made the first assaults on Hougoumont, stood at the western end. Note the steep descent into the valley at this point and then the equally steep ascent to the building block and garden wall of the farm. In 1815 a wood occupied the slope immediately south of the buildings and garden.

Napoleon intended the attack on Hougoumont to be merely a secondary operation intended to pin down Wellington's western flank. It was not necessary actually to capture Hougoumont in order to fulfil this objective. So Reille ordered Prince Jérôme merely 'to occupy the low ground south of the wood, maintaining in front a strong line of skirmishers.'[1]

But an escalation of the French attack on Hougoumont was inevitable. The French troops were too fervent for anything but an all-out assault. They lacked the coolness and discipline of British troops. Furthermore, it soon became imperative to support the initial wave of skirmishers with further troops. Soon Brigadier-General Baron Pierre-François Bauduin's brigade, the 1st Light and 3rd Line infantry, was heavily engaged. The French infantrymen had to advance uphill through the wood, battling all the time against skilled, green-coated German light infantry. 'The fire of the enemy was so sharp and heavy,' noted Lieutenant-General Baron Maximilien Foy. 'For us the wood was a death trap.'[2] Bauduin himself was killed in the initial assaults.

So far, Jérôme had sent only one brigade into the wood, keeping the second, under Brigadier-General Baron Jean-Louis Soye, in reserve. But soon the first brigade was so embattled that reinforcements became necessary. Colonel

# THE ASSAULT ON HOUGOUMONT

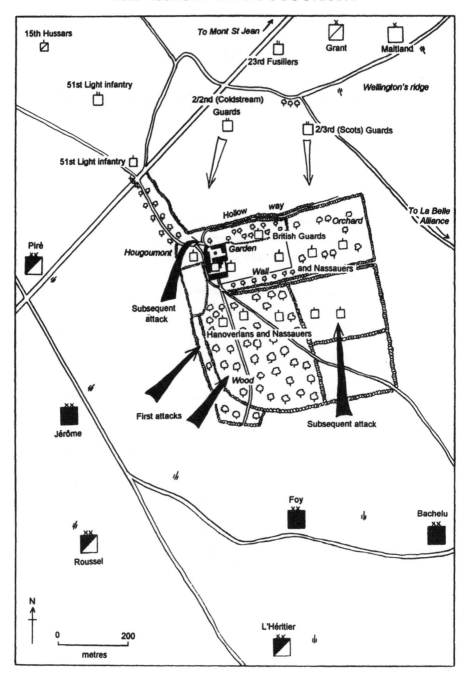

15th Hussars

To Mont St Jean

Grant

Maitland

23rd Fusiliers

51st Light infantry

Wellington's ridge

2/2nd (Coldstream)
Guards

2/3rd (Scots) Guards

51st Light infantry

Hollow     way

To La Belle
Alliance

Orchard

Piré

British Guards

Hougoumont

Garden

and Nassauers

Wall

Subsequent
attack

Hanoverians and Nassauers

First attacks

Wood

Subsequent attack

Jérôme

Foy

Bachelu

Roussel

N

0          200

metres

L'Héritier

Octave Levavasseur, ADC to Marshal Ney, rode towards the wood of Hougoumont to see how the fight was faring:

> In spite of the musket-balls whistling past my ears, I approached the wood which our infantry were holding and I found all the troops standing behind the trees, begging for help. Their colonel asked me earnestly to bring up troops to extricate him. Jérôme had sent only two regiments to take this wood ... These two regiments had crossed the open ground and had reached the wood but could not go further because the enemy was pinning them down.
>
> I returned as fast as possible to Prince Jérôme and I hotly remonstrated to him that this wood could be captured by brute strength only with his entire division and that to send just two regiments was to massacre them. This wood, attacked again by Prince Jérôme and Count Reille, was taken and retaken several times during the day.[3]

Colonel Levavasseur clearly did not know that Reille had ordered Jérôme only to make a limited diversionary attack. Jérôme must have assumed that Levavasseur was acting on higher authority in demanding an escalation of the assault. Jérôme, in any case, needed no encouragement to send in more troops.

The thirty-one-year-old Jérôme Bonaparte had always been overshadowed by the brilliance of his elder brother, Napoleon. Although Napoleon had made him King of Westphalia, Jérôme never had many military skills and, indeed, had spent the early years of his career as a naval officer. Jérôme had frequently exasperated Napoleon. For instance, in 1812 during the invasion of Russia, Jérôme's tardiness had allowed the Russian General Bagration to escape a trap. Napoleon raged: 'Tell him [Jérôme] that it would be impossible to manoeuvre in worse fashion ... Tell him that he has robbed me of the fruit of my manoeuvres and of the best opportunity ever presented in war – all on account of his failure to appreciate the first notions about warfare.'[4]

In 1813, Napoleon condemned the easy-going, 'merry monarch' of Westphalia with the harsh words: 'you are hateful to me. Your conduct disgusts me. I know no one so base, so stupid, so cowardly; you are destitute of virtue, talents and resources.'[5]

Now in 1815 Jérôme wished to prove his valour and worth to the great elder brother who had called him a 'scamp.' At Quatre Bras on 16 June, he had fought furiously. A ball had struck the gold scabbard of his sword leaving him with a severe bruise on the thigh but, overcoming the pain, he had stayed at the head of his troops. At Waterloo, Jérôme now had the honour of opening the battle and sought glorious success in his attack on Hougoumont.

So, although Napoleon had intended the Hougoumont attack to draw in Wellington's reserves, in fact it was sucking in more and more French troops. Nineteen-year-old Larreguy de Civrieux disobeyed orders to remain in reserve and instead advanced with his regiment bearing its precious eagle standard. He recalled in later years how around Hougoumont 'thousands of dead, dying and wounded were piled in heaps. We soon doubled their number.' Larreguy's feet waded through blood. 'Each soldier stoically awaited death or horrible wounds. We were covered with splashes of blood yet our spirit had climbed to the highest degree of exultation.'[6]

Soon dozens of wounded were drifting back out of the wood towards the spot where you are standing. Captain Bourdon de Vatry, a nineteen-year-old hussar attached to Prince Jérôme's staff, was horrified:

> Soon, from where we were standing, we saw the men who had carried their wounded comrades to the ambulances return with downcast faces saying, 'it is dreadful, we have no more ambulances. Only the carriages remain, without teams of horses.'
> This is what had happened. The Emperor, pressed to organise transport at the moment of opening the campaign, had issued a decree that a postillon and horses from each relay post were to be put at the disposal of the War Administration to provide the teams and drivers of ambulance carriages. These makeshift drivers, most of whom had never heard gunfire, became nervous under the fire of the English batteries, unharnessed their horses or cut the traces and galloped off leaving the carriages without their horse teams. This heartbreaking sight had a dismal effect on the troops.[7]

However, soldiers of Lieutenant-General Baron Maximilien Foy's infantry division, to the east of Jérôme, witnessed the fierce fanaticism that still animated many of the wounded. One soldier with both legs shattered by a cannonball called out as he was stretchered past Foy's regiments: 'This is nothing, comrades! Long live the Emperor! Glory to France!'[8]

The French surgeons did all they could for the wounded but were soon swamped by the enormity of their task. Napoleon's remarkable Surgeon-General, Baron Dominique Larrey, had in the course of the Napoleonic wars introduced fast, well-sprung, horse-drawn carriages to ensure the prompt evacuation of stretcher cases and had set high standards for the speed of operations. At Waterloo, he faced more difficulties than usual owing to Napoleon's defeat. 'The disorder progressively increased,' he remembered, 'and the wounded were coming to us from every direction. But in spite of our zeal and spirit, our efforts became useless, either because the [enemy] cavalry charges were coming up to our ambulances or because we were deprived of daylight.'[9] Larrey was taken prisoner by some Prussians, who mistook him for Napoleon and nearly shot him. Fortunately, a Prussian surgeon recognised and saved him just in time.

While Prince Jérôme was engaged in Hougoumont wood, the divisions of Lieutenant-Generals Maximilien Foy and Gilbert Bachelu came under heavy artillery fire as they waited in reserve. As you can see, they enjoyed no protection whatsoever from the terrain: you are standing on the open crest of a shallow ridge. By contrast, Wellington tried to shelter his troops on the reverse slopes of his ridge on the opposite side of the valley. Colonel Toussaint-Jean Trefçon, General Bachelu's chief-of-staff, described how 'the English artillery fire was so violent that their cannon-balls and canister fell even on our division, although it was unengaged and was a quite respectable cannon-shot away.'[10] Major Lemonnier-Delafosse, General Foy's ADC, recalled that:

> Behind us and in reserve was the brigade of carabiniers [of Lieutenant-General François Kellermann's III Cavalry Corps], on which the cannon-balls which passed us went to fall. To get out of their range, this brigade moved to the left, which provoked General Foy to laugh: 'Ha! ha! the big boots don't like the rough stuff.' We received the cannon-balls standing firm. They covered us with mud and the soaked ground, by conserving the marks of their paths, looked like a field ploughed by the wheels of carts. This was lucky for our line, for many of the projectiles buried or muffled themselves while rolling along this muddy soil.[11]

Before reinforcing the skirmishers in Hougoumont wood, Jérôme's 1st Light infantry had also suffered heavily from this artillery fire. The second battalion had been particularly exposed and soon lost twenty-odd men. Cannon-balls followed so rapidly that the battalion was forced to retire into the shelter of the sunken lane you are standing in.

After Jérôme's troops had descended into the valley at the southern edge of Hougoumont wood they were less exposed to the gunfire. Yet even there Major Jean-Baptiste Jolyet of the 1st Light infantry had a narrow escape: 'while I was sitting at the foot of a bank at the edge of the wood, I heard something rolling behind me. I turned round and saw a shell descending the slope on my right. I had just time to fling myself down before it burst without harming me.'[12]

Eventually one of Foy's brigades was sucked in to support Jérôme. Foy's brigade tried to seize the Château of Hougoumont by taking the orchard east of the garden and then swirling round to the north of the garden, hence cutting the garrison off from the main ridge. At around the same time, Jérôme sent the 1st Light and 3rd Line infantry to storm round the west of the building block. Although a handful of Jérôme's men did burst through the North Gate on the far side of the building block, this success was short-lived and the Gate was closed once more. Meanwhile, Foy's brigade repeatedly seized then lost the orchard. The trees of the orchard have long since vanished; they used to occupy the field immediately east of the garden, whose loopholed wall is easily iden-tifiable.

Fighting at Hougoumont raged continuously for the rest of the battle, but apart from a howitzer battery assembled around 2.30 pm to shell the building block, no new French forces entered the conflict. Already, 9000 Frenchmen were tied up in it; 'it was a battle of giants!' averred Colonel Toussaint-Jean Trefçon.[13]

# Notes

1. J. Ney, *Documents inédits sur la campagne de 1815* (1840), p.61
2. M. Foy, *Vie militaire* (1900), pp.282–3
3. O. Levavasseur, *Souvenirs militaires* (1914), p.301
4. D. Chandler, *The campaigns of Napoleon* (1966), p.776
5. P. Haythornthwaite, *The Napoleonic Source Book* (1990), p.330
6. L. de Civrieux, *Souvenirs d'un cadet* (1912), pp.167–70
7. G. Grouchy, *Mémoires du maréchal de Grouchy* (1873), v.4, p.106
8. M. Lemonnier-Delafosse, *Souvenirs militaires* (1850), pp.387–8
9. D. Larrey, *Relation médicale de campagnes et voyages de 1815 à 1840* (1841), p.10
10. A. Lévi, *Carnet de campagne du Colonel Trefçon* (1914), pp.187–8
11. M. Lemonnier-Delafosse, *Souvenirs militaires* (1850), p.380
12. 'Souvenirs de 1815' in *Revue de Paris* (Sept–Oct 1903), pp.544–5
13. A. Lévi, *Carnet de campagne du Colonel Trefçon* (1914), p.187

Hougoumont: the ruins of the château adjoining the chapel. Behind, and to the right of the chapel, is the Gardener's House.

# 11

# THE MAIN ATTACK:
# TRIUMPH THEN DISASTER

Now look to the east. As you can see, none of the French soldiers stationed around Hougoumont were able to see the repulse of Napoleon's second attack east of the Brussels road. So to follow the progress of this phase of the battle, you need to pass over to the eastern sector of the field. First, walk the 1000 metres to La Belle Alliance.

Napoleon's second attack opened at 1.30 pm with a tremendous barrage by a massed battery of eighty guns: thirty-six 12-pounders, twenty-four 8-pounders and twenty 6-inch howitzers. The left flank of this battery rested on the Brussels road 600 metres north of La Belle Alliance. The long line of guns then extended north-eastwards along a shallow rise in the ground.[1]

From the battery's firing position, Wellington's ridge lay at a range of between 600 and 800 metres: the guns towards the north-eastern end of the battery were nearer their target. Napoleon's 6-inch howitzers could land a shell 1200 metres away and his cannon had an even longer range. The powerful 12-pounders, Napoleon's 'beautiful daughters' as he called them, had a maximum range of 1800 metres and thus could hit Mont St Jean village.[2] However, the most efficient range for Napoleon's guns was between 700 and 900 metres. Thus, except for a 6-inch howitzer placed on the western end of the massed battery, Wellington's ridge was well within effective range.

In theory, the French guns could fire one or two rounds a minute; in practice, the rate slowed as the action continued. Guns of the Napoleonic era had no mechanism to absorb the recoil and a 12-pounder could recoil as much as twelve feet over dry ground. After each shot the weary gunners had to man-handle the piece back into its original firing position. A 12-pounder cannon and its carriage together weighed 3400 pounds and at Waterloo would have sunk into the muddy soil.

From time to time, the barrels of the guns had to be allowed to cool after repeated firing lest the heat cause a premature explosion of the powder during loading. All guns were muzzle-loaders and a lengthy procedure had to be followed with each round. First the inside of the barrel had to be sponged out to

163

extinguish lingering sparks which might ignite the next round as it was inserted into the barrel. Then the round, consisting of a powder charge and a projectile, was rammed down the barrel. During this operation, the vent at the lower end of the barrel was covered to prevent air fanning any smouldering old powder not extinguished by the wet sponge. Then the cartridge would be punctured through the vent and a paper tube of gunpowder or impregnated cotton inserted. The gun would be fired by applying a lighted slowmatch to the vent.

Accuracy was difficult as the guns were all smooth-bores and threw out clouds of smoke which rapidly obscured the target. The artillery pieces had to be repositioned and aimed after each recoil. Nevertheless, a massed battery would compensate for the inaccuracy of individual guns; the thunderous roar and constant deluge of projectiles often had a devastating effect on opposing troops. The massed battery was a psychological as much as a physical weapon; it incapacitated men by shattering their nerves as well as by killing them. Napoleon, who had trained as an artillery officer, knew this as well as any. 'Great battles are won by artillery,' he declared.

A host of ammunition caissons was required to supply the eighty guns pounding Wellington's ridge at Waterloo. Fifty metres behind the guns stood a first line of caissons, from which ammunition could be carried forward to the gun line. A second line of caissons was a further fifty metres to the south and these vehicles would be driven forward when necessary to replace empty caissons of the first line. One hundred metres to the south of the second line stood other vehicles, which carried spare or specialised equipment and a mobile forge. These vital supporting vehicles were thus sheltered behind the shallow ridge on which the guns were stationed.

A 12-pounder gun needed eight specialist and seven non-specialist crew. To serve the massed battery at Waterloo and to keep it supplied with ammunition and spare parts there were approximately 2000 men. This was the numerical equivalent of an entire infantry brigade.

On the eastern border of the Brussels road, one hundred metres north of La Belle Alliance, stands a memorial stone with the inscription: 'on 18 June 1815, from La Belle Alliance to Papelotte, units of the 6th Regiment of Foot Artillery under Colonel Hulot supported the attacks of the French I Corps with their effective fire.'

The 6th Regiment provided half of the guns comprising the massed battery. The remaining pieces were 12-pounders and 6-inch howitzers from the Guard, the II and the VI Corps. The battery's thunderous fire was certainly impressive and boosted French morale but the soaked ground swallowed many of the projectiles and prevented them from ricocheting. Wellington had ordered his infantry to lie down on the reverse slopes of his ridge, where they were slightly more sheltered from cannon-balls. Nevertheless, the ridge provided no shelter from the high trajectory howitzer shells, although the muddy soil muffled the shell bursts. In short, although Napoleon's massed battery failed to annihilate Wellington's troops it caused heavy casualties. Wellington's men justifiably feared the French artillery far more than the other two arms.

Retrace your steps south to La Belle Alliance and walk along the dirt track leading to Papelotte farm. From this track you can see the whitewashed walls and dull, grey roofs of La Haie Sainte to the north-west, beyond the massed battery's position. Still further north is Wellington's crossroads and, immediately opposite you, the ridge defended by the British 5th Division and Major-General Count van Bijlandt's Dutch-Belgian infantry brigade. This ridge is just over 1000 metres away and was the target of Napoleon's second attack.

Napoleon entrusted the attack to the four infantry divisions of Lieutenant-General Count Drouet d'Erlon's I Corps. At the commemcement of the battle, these troops were lined up along the track on which you are standing. To assault Wellington's ridge, d'Erlon formed his infantrymen into four massive columns. These columns comprised battalions arrayed in line one behind the other. Each column was around 180 men wide and up to twenty-four ranks deep. These columns set off in succession, from west to east; the intention was that the leading column in the west would distract enemy fire from the others.

A brigade of cuirassiers from Count Edouard Milhaud's IV Cavalry Corps rode in support on d'Erlon's western flank. D'Erlon also detached an infantry brigade from his 1st Division to assault the farm of La Haie Sainte. On the eastern flank, skirmishers from d'Erlon's 4th Division probed the enemy defences around the houses of Papelotte, La Haye and Smohain. In between these two flanks, the four massed infantry columns marched across the shallow valley.

You can follow the progress of d'Erlon's advance by eye from where you stand. Louis Canler, an eighteen-year-old in the ranks of the 28th Line infantry, described vividly his experiences as he crossed the valley under fire. Canler's regiment belonged to d'Erlon's 1st Division, which formed the left wing of I Corps. The division detached the 54th and 55th Line infantry to attack La Haie Sainte but its other brigade, comprising the 28th and 105th Line, continued to advance in column against the ridge crest. Canler begins his narrative with a description of the awesome barrage by Napoleon's massed battery and of the English counter-fire:

> Cannon-balls and shells whistled past over our heads. After a half hour wait, Marshal Ney ordered us to attack and to carry the English guns by assault ... At last the columns had been formed and General Drouet d'Erlon stationed himself in the middle of his corps. In a strong and deliberate voice he uttered these words alone:
> 'Today you must conquer or die!'
> The cry of 'Long live the Emperor!' came from every mouth in reply to this short speech and ... with the drummers beating the charge, the columns moved off and headed for the English guns without firing a musket-shot.

## THE ATTACK BY D'ERLON'S I CORPS

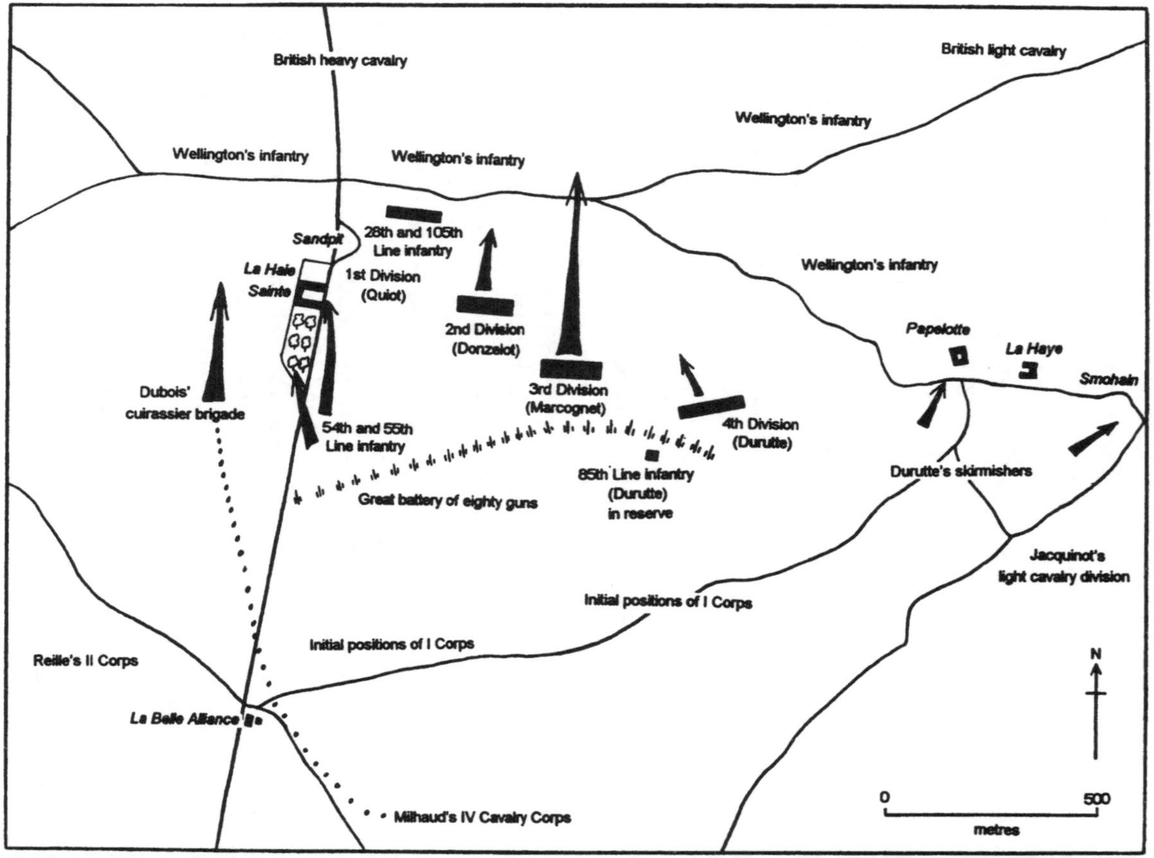

British light cavalry

British heavy cavalry

Wellington's infantry

Wellington's infantry

Wellington's infantry

Wellington's infantry

Wellington's infantry

Smohain

La Haye

Papelotte

Durutte's skirmishers

Jacquinot's light cavalry division

4th Division (Durutte)

85th Line Infantry (Durutte) in reserve

3rd Division (Marcognet)

2nd Division (Donzelot)

28th and 105th Line Infantry

1st Division (Quiot)

Sandpit

La Haie Sainte

54th and 55th Line Infantry

Great battery of eighty guns

Initial positions of I Corps

Initial positions of I Corps

Initial positions of I Corps

Dubois' cuirassier brigade

Le Belle Alliance

Reille's II Corps

Milhaud's IV Cavalry Corps

N

0    500
metres

At that point the enemy batteries which until then had sent only cannon-balls and shells were aimed at our columns and decimated them with canister. We had hardly gone one hundred paces when the commander of our second battalion, Marins, was mortally wounded. The captain of my company, Duzer, was hit by two balls. Adjudant Hubaut and eagle bearer Crosse were killed.

In the midst of everything the calm, serious voices of our officers gave just one order: 'Close ranks!'

At the second discharge of the English guns the grenadiers' drummer, Lecointre, lost his right arm ... but the courageous man continued to march at our head beating the charge with his left hand until loss of blood caused him to lose consciousness. In 1828 I saw him again at Paris, where he had entered the Invalides {military hospital}.

The third discharge reduced the frontage of our battalion to that of a company. The terrible command of 'close ranks!' was heard again. This command, far from bringing dread or despair into our hearts, produced a totally opposite effect. It boosted our courage and inspired in us not only the idea of winning but also that of avenging our unfortunate comrades who were dying before our eyes.

After marching for twenty minutes we arrived near the earthwork [ridge] where the English guns stood and we began to ascend it. The rain which had fallen all night had drenched the naturally slimy soil so that while I was ascending, the foot strap of my right gaiter broke and my heel came out of my shoe. I hurriedly bent down to put my shoe back on but at that very moment I felt a violent shock which threw my shako back. The shako would very probably have fallen off had it not been for the chin strap which held it to my chin.

I had just received a ball which had left a 0 from the number 28 on my shako plate and had exited the other side grazing my head.[3]

At this point, Louis Canler's column halted and tried to deploy into line to increase its firepower as it grappled with the British and Netherlands infantry on the ridge crest. From the French side of the valley, everything seemed to be going marvellously. Marshal Soult sent a letter to Marshal Davout in Paris indicating that the battle was very well engaged and gave hope of a great success.[4] Lieutenant Jacques Martin of the 45th Line infantry was 400 metres east of Louis Canler, in the column formed by Lieutenant-General Pierre Binet de Marcognet's 3rd Division. Martin described how:

English battalions, lying in wait in a hollow way, suddenly rose and fired at us at a range of a few paces. We chased them with the bayonet, ascended further and crossed the stretches of thick hedge which screened their guns. We were on the plateau and shouted victory.

But our very elan caused our ranks to fall into confusion and in our turn we were assailed with the bayonet by new enemies. The struggle recommenced and a dreadful *mêlée* followed. In this bloody confusion the officers did their duty by seeking to restore some order and to reform the platoons, for troops in disorder can do nothing and go nowhere. Just as I was pushing one of our soldiers into the ranks, I saw him fall at my feet to a sabre cut. I swirled round ... English cavalry were penetrating into our midst from all directions and were cutting us to pieces.

In vain did our poor soldiers tip-toe and stretch out their arms: they could not pierce these horsemen mounted on powerful horses with their bayonets. The few musket-shots which were fired in this confused crowd turned out to be lethal to our men as often as to the English. Thus we remained defenceless against a relentless enemy who, in the intoxication of combat, sabred even the drummers and fifers without pity. Our eagle was taken at that time and I saw death very close for my best friends were falling around me and I awaited the same fate. All the while I was mechanically brandishing my sword.[5]

Lieutenant Martin's men had been overrun by the Scots Greys. Further to the west, the 1st and 2nd Divisions met a similar fate at the hands of English and Irish dragoons. The precious eagle standards of the 45th and 105th Line regiments were lost and Colonel Pierre Heymès, ADC to Marshal Ney, was in awe as he beheld these dragoons of the British Union Brigade 'laying waste to everything like a cloud of grasshoppers.'[6] Louis Canler described this terrible onrush of powerful, hostile cavalry from the midst of the struggle within the 1st Division:

Hardly did we reach the summit of the plateau than we were met by the Royal Dragoons who fell on us with wild cheering. The 1st Division not having time to form square, was unable to withstand this charge and was broken.

A real carnage then ensued. Everyone saw he was separated from his comrades and fought for his own life. Sabres and bayonets slashed at the quivering flesh for we were too close to each other to use firearms.

But the position was untenable for footsoldiers fighting isolated in the midst of horsemen. Thus I soon found myself alone, a prisoner and disarmed. Suddenly I heard the order 'At the trot!' French lancers and cuirassiers were arriving to help us. The English dragoons were obliged to abandon us to repulse this charge. I took advantage of this moment of freedom to hide myself in a wheatfield nearby. The French cavalry attacked the English dragoons furiously, sabering and lancing them in such a wild manner that the English ended by retreating and leaving a good number of their men on the battlefield.

This allowed me to cross the field to rejoin my corps. When making a detour to the left, I found myself near an English dragoon officer who had been killed in the mêlée. A sabre cut had split his head open and the brains had burst out of the skull. From his fob hung a superb golden chain and in spite of the hurry of my flight I stopped a moment to loot this chain and a beautiful watch also in gold... The English had taken my knapsack and my weapons...

A little later I met my colonel accompanied by some officers. He was galloping like a madman to the left and the right as fast as his horse could go, shouting 'To me, 28th! To me!' His shouts, stamped with the deepest despair, clearly showed that the disaster which had befallen his regiment was a blow to his own honour. I was going to join him when I heard some piteous cries to my

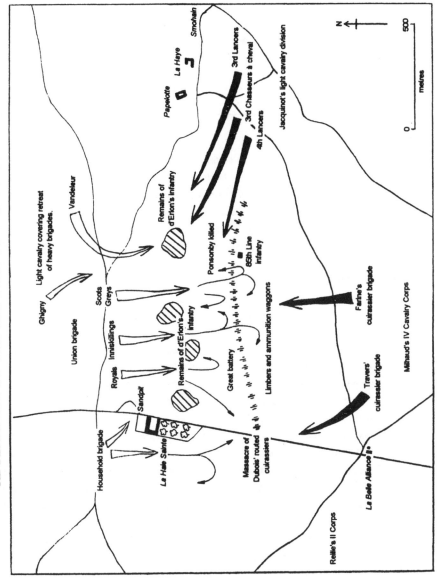

AFTERMATH OF THE REPULSE OF D'ERLON'S I CORPS

right. I made my way there and I noticed, stretched out on the ground, a young soldier of the 105th Line.

This wretched man, whose right tibia had been broken by a ball, was suffering horribly from his wound which had been neither dressed nor even bandaged.

'Comrade', he appealed to me. 'I beg you please not to abandon me! I cannot drag myself to the ambulance and if the cavalry comes to pass by here, I will assuredly be trampled underfoot.' While uttering these words, he stretched out begging hands to me. I could not resist this appeal and rushed to him.

Immediately kneeling down, I took a shirt from a knapsack I had just found and bandaged his wound. Then I took him on my back and I carried him like that, with much trouble and exhaustion, across the battlefield to the first ambulance in which I managed with difficulty to place him. I then went to join some of my comrades.[7]

As Louis Canler described, French cavalry had decisively counter-attacked the disorganised British dragoons. The Britons had charged out of control. Lieutenant-General Baron Pierre Durutte, commander of the 4th Division of d'Erlon's corps, witnessed the débâcle from the eastern end of the French battleline. Durutte had left his 85th Line infantry in reserve and detached skirmishers to attack Papelotte, La Haye and Smohain. Then he had advanced with the remainder of his division in the wake of d'Erlon's other columns towards Wellington's ridge.[8] But Durutte's column met the same fate as the others. As he watched British dragoons break his column and then ride triumphantly on, he decided that they 'were either drunk or did not know how to rein in their horses.'[9]

The leading Britons traversed the valley, sabred the gunners of Napoleon's massed battery and put about fifteen guns out of action. Nevertheless, the British horsemen had rapidly lost both their energy and cohesion. Towards the eastern end of the Great Battery the 85th Line infantry, left by Durutte in reserve, was formed in a single square two ranks deep. Captain Chapuis remembered how his men fired as if on the parade ground, bringing down scores of red-coated dragoons.[10] Further retribution ensued. Napoleon had sent an ADC, Lieutenant-General Count Pierre Dejean, to order a cuirassier brigade of Count Edouard Milhaud's IV Cavalry Corps to counter-attack. Lieutenant-General Baron Jacques Delort instantly advanced with Brigadier-General Count Pierre Farine's 6th and 9th Cuirassiers; Dejean joined the charge. The cuirassiers charged forward across the dirt track on which you stand and into the disorganised and exhausted Britons.

'In a moment,' Delort proudly related, 'this brigade dashed on to the English cavalry, overwhelmed them and strewed the battlefield with their dead ... In spite of their numerical inferiority and their disadvantage in attacking an enemy who was encouraged by a brilliant success [against d'Erlon's infantry], the cuirassiers did not lose a single man and included barely some wounded. The cannon were retaken and the infantry promptly rallied.'[11] According to Count Milhaud, the cuirassier brigade rescued twenty guns and several thousand of d'Erlon's foot-soldiers, as well as capturing 150 horses.[12]

Furthermore, Lieutenant-General Baron Charles Jacquinot, commander of the light cavalry division of I Corps stationed south of Frichermont, launched the Marquis de la Woestine's 3rd Chasseurs à cheval, Colonel Martigue's 3rd Lancers and Colonel Bro's 4th Lancers into the eastern flank of the beleaguered British Union Brigade. 'On no occasion' averred the veteran General Durutte, 'did I appreciate as well as in this encounter the superiority of the lance over the sabre.'[13] The 4th Lancers speared trooper after trooper as they chased the scattered Britons to the north. Although two allied light cavalry brigades charged to support their retreat, the heavy dragoons were badly mauled as they fell back.

The commander of the Union Brigade, Major-General the Hon. Sir William Ponsonby, was killed near the eastern end of the massed battery. The Belgian whom Ponsonby had placed in charge of his two fine chargers had bolted with them to Brussels leaving the general to ride a small hack. But for this, he might have escaped. As it was, the exhausted hack became stuck in a muddy, ploughed field. Ponsonby handed his watch and snuff box, which contained a portrait of his wife, to his ADC. Although this ADC managed to ride out of danger, Ponsonby's body was later found with seven lance wounds. The fatal thrust was delivered by Sergeant Urban of the élite company of the 4th Lancers and a recipient of the coveted medal of the Legion of Honour. Urban kept Ponsonby's sabre as a trophy of war. In 1815, Urban was thirty years old and he died twenty-seven years later without issue. Ponsonby's sword was hence sold, acquired by collectors and after the Great War finally discovered in the collection of a French officer, Monsieur Barbet de Vaux, in Paris. The generous Frenchman immediately gave the sword to Ponsonby's descendants. In a letter to the family, he described how in 1918, Field Marshal Sir Douglas Haig had visited him and, deep in thought, had held the sword in his hands for several minutes without saying a word.[14]

By walking 1500 metres along the track from La Belle Alliance towards Papelotte, you will arrive at the location of a desperate *mêlée* recalled by Colonel Bro de Commères, commander of the 4th Lancers. Bro launched his counter-attack from the undulating fields south of Frichermont and charged due west:

> Our infantry, cut into sections, disbanded. Drouet d'Erlon sent an order for the cavalry to charge. Soaked ground prevented us from manoeuvring at ease. I took my 4th Lancers off to the charge. To the right of a small wood we noticed the English cavalry which had swiftly reformed and threatened to outflank the 3rd Chasseurs à cheval. I took the head of the squadrons shouting 'Come on, children, we must overturn this rabble!' The soldiers replied to me: 'Forwards! Long live the Emperor!'

Two minutes later the shock occurred. Three enemy ranks were bowled over. We struck into the others terribly! The *mêlée* became dreadful. Our horses crushed corpses and screams rose from the wounded on all sides. I found myself lost for a moment in the powder smoke. When I came out of it, I noticed some English officers surrounding Second Lieutenant Verrand, eagle-bearer.

Rallying some horsemen, I rushed to help him. Sergeant Orban killed General Ponsonby with a lance thrust. My sabre cut down three of his captains. Two others were able to flee.

I returned to the front to save my adjudant-major. I had emptied my second pistol when suddenly I felt my right arm paralysed. With my left hand, I felled the attacker who was braving me ... A dizzy spell compelled me to seize the mane of my horse. I was strong enough to say to Major Perrot 'Take command of the regiment!' General [Charles] Jacquinot came up and, seeing the blood flooding my clothes, supported me and said 'Withdraw!' He left to join the charge. Major Motet cut my dolman and applied a bandage over some shredded linen, saying 'it is not mortal but you must not remain here.' Having to leave my squadrons made me weep with anger.[15]

The British evacuated the valley, covered by two light cavalry brigades under Sir John Vandeleur and Major-General Charles de Ghigny. The withdrawal was also covered by fire from Wellington's rocket battery which provided, if not a deterrent, at least a distraction. Marshal Ney's ADC, Colonel Pierre Heymès, estimated that the battery 'fired more than 300 rockets at us, which first astonished and then amused us without doing us the least harm.' Indeed, Ensign William Mountsteven of the British 28th Foot noted indignantly how 'the Rocket Troop fired from behind the 28th after our charge, when we were down on the slope of the hill. I recollect this well, because the first rocket which I saw thrown, made a slight mistake, and came nearly into the centre of our ranks instead of those of the enemy.'[16]

The battery commander, Captain Edward Whinyates, was equipped with both 6-pounder cannon and with rockets. These rockets had been designed by Sir William Congreve and consisted of a warhead – a roundshot, a shell or canister – a propellant charge and an eight- to ten-foot stabilising stick. Used only by the British and Austrians, the rockets could be fired along the ground or at an elevation into the air. Their main disadvantage was their inaccuracy; they adopted erratic flight paths and on occasion even soared vertically into the air before turning round and chasing the firer. When fitted with a carcass, they were effective in setting fire to besieged towns but otherwise Wellington's distrust of them was as pronounced as Whinyates' enthusiasm.

Whinyates had left his cannon behind and advanced with his cherished rockets in the wake of the British Union Brigade to the forward slope of Wellington's ridge. There he fired salvoes of rockets which ricocheted along the ground through tall, standing crops. Whinyates himself admitted that salvoes were more impressive than rockets fired individually for the erratic flight path of a single rocket was readily apparent. Facing a salvo of rockets could be a daunting experience, particularly for cavalrymen, whose horses were terrified of the furious, fiery missiles. A Russian general who had seen British rockets in action at Leipzig in 1813 had commented that 'they look as if they were made in hell, and surely are the devil's own artillery.'[17] In 1815, Major-General Baron Jean-Victor de Constant-Rebecque, chief-of-staff of Wellington's Netherlands contingent, compared the rockets to flaming dragons.[18] Two decades after Waterloo, Whinyates learnt to his satisfaction how a British dragoon officer left wounded on the French position had heard the rockets passing and French soldiers cursing the English for wanting to burn them alive.[19]

Meanwhile, to the west of La Haie Sainte the British Household Brigade had charged slightly earlier than the Union Brigade and had overwhelmed Brigadier-General Baron Jacques Dubois' 1st and 4th Cuirassiers whom Ney had sent to protect d'Erlon's left flank.[20]

The routed French cuirassiers poured along the western hedge of the orchard of La Haie Sainte on to the Brussels road and then dashed towards La Belle Alliance. If you stand at the edge of the Brussels road between La Belle Alliance and the orchard of La Haie Sainte you will be at the scene of a murderous massacre. The French cuirassiers' line of retreat was blocked by other French horsemen advancing north to the rescue. In 1815, this section of the road was enclosed by steep banks which trapped the cuirassiers when the British 1st Life Guards fell on their rear. Crushed together, the French were unable to raise a single arm in self-defence. Colonel Octave Levavasseur, a witness, was horrified: 'I heard only the clinking of sabres which penetrated beneath the breastplates of the horsemen. The enemy inflicted a dreadful carnage.'[21]

Scores of cuirassiers were slain before French infantry lined the banks above the road and fired down on to the 1st Life Guards. A great many British corpses now cluttered the road and Colonel Levavasseur had no difficulty in appropriating an English officer's fine horse.[22] Brigadier-General Baron Etienne Travers de Jever's 7th and 12th Cuirassiers then counter-attacked the remainder of the British heavy cavalry in this sector.[23]

# Notes

1. It is not clear precisely when this great battery opened fire. According to H. de Mauduit, *Les derniers jours de la grande armée* (1848), v.2, p.292, light batteries and skirmishers were in action while Jérôme attacked Hougoumont. The great battery as a whole probably opened fire towards 1.30 pm. For the position of the battery see BL Add. MSS 34,705/153–4: map showing the extent of the British Union Brigade's charge which ended amidst the guns of the Great Battery. See also BL Add. MSS 34,706/378.

2. Additional range could be achieved by ricochet fire but the muddy soil at Waterloo made this difficult.

3. L. Canler, *Mémoires de Canler, ancien chef de la police de sûreté* (1882), v.1

4. H. Parker, *Three Napoleonic battles* (1983), p.157

5. J. Martin, *Souvenirs d'un ex-officier* (1867), pp.287–9

6. J. Ney, *Documents inédits sur la campagne de 1815* (1840), p.15

7. L. Canler, *Mémoires de Canler, ancien chef de la police de sûreté* (1882), v.1

8. H. de Mauduit, *Les derniers jours de la grande armée* (1848), v.2, pp.306–7

9. L. Garros, *Le champ de bataille de Waterloo* (1952), p.32; E. Gallo, 'Le "Waterloo" de Henry Houssaye' in *Revue des Etudes Napoléoniennes* (Jan–June 1915)

10. 'Notice sur le 85e de ligne' in *Journal des sciences militaires* (July–Sept 1863), pp.77–8; the 85th's square consisted only of two ranks as the regiment was numerically weak.

11. L. Stouff, *Le Lieutenant-Général Delort* (1906), p.153; S. de Chair, *Napoleon's memoirs* (1985), p.529

12. L. Stouff, *Le Lieutenant-Général Delort* (1906), p.131

13. E. Gallo, 'Le "Waterloo" de Henry Houssaye' in *Revue des Etudes Napoléoniennes* (Jan–June 1915)

14. J. Ponsonby, *The Ponsonby family* (1926), pp.221–2; H. de Mauduit, *Les derniers jours de la grande armée* (1848), v.2, p.300

15. H. Bro, *Mémoires du général Bro* (1914), pp.148–9

16. BL Add. MSS 34,707/135; J. Ney, *Documents inédits sur la campagne de 1815* (1840), p.15

17. P. Haythornthwaite, *The Napoleonic Source Book* (1990), p.92

18. Société des études historiques et folkloriques de Waterloo, Braine-l'Alleud et environs, *Mélanges historiques* (1970), p.146

19. H. Siborne ed., *The Waterloo letters* (1983), p.205

20. Previously, these two cuirassier regiments had cut up the Hanoverian Lüneburg Light battalion which had been despatched to the support of the garrison of La Haie Sainte. The battalion's flag was captured: H. Lot, *Les deux généraux Ordener* (1910), p.91

21. O. Levavasseur, *Souvenirs militaires* (1914), p.299

22. H. Siborne ed., *The Waterloo letters* (1983), p.45

23. H. Lot, *Les deux généraux Ordener* (1910), p.91; L. Garros, *Le champ de bataille de Waterloo* (1952); see also Lieutenant George Graeme's letter in which he states that 'in the first attack, I perceived *no* French Cavalry on the British left of the farm of La Haye Sainte.' (H. Siborne ed., *The Waterloo letters* [1983], p.406)

French infantry attack

# 12

# MARSHAL NEY'S MASSED
# CAVALRY ONSLAUGHT

The next phase of the battle, Marshal Ney's grand cavalry charges, saw fighting almost exclusively on Wellington's side of the valley. You will find no relics of the charges in the French sector of the field except a memorial stone to Colonel Baron Gobert's 5th Cuirassiers, one of the regiments in Lieutenant-General Count Edouard Milhaud's IV Cavalry Corps. The stone stands amidst a colourful bed of pink roses on a traffic island halfway along the road between La Belle Alliance and Plancenoit. At the start of the battle, Napoleon's cavalry stood in reserve on both wings of the army behind the infantry. The 5th Cuirassiers were drawn up around 500 metres north-east of their monument.

On the crest of Wellington's ridge another memorial stone commemorates Lieutenant Augustin Demulder of the 5th Cuirassiers who was killed in action. On 18 June, the regiment lost two officers killed and twelve wounded out of the thirty-nine who had marched at its head into Belgium on 15 June. Another lieutenant had been mortally wounded at Ligny.[1]

Marshal Ney first summoned Milhaud's cuirassiers to charge when he detected signs of what he interpreted as Wellington retreating. At the time Ney was leading an infantry assault on La Haie Sainte in the shocked aftermath of the destruction of Napoleon's second attack. From the farm Ney saw some of Wellington's battalions withdrawing to shelter behind the ridge from French artillery fire.

Immediately, the impetuous Ney ordered up one of Count Edouard Milhaud's cuirassier brigades. But Lieutenant-General Baron Jacques Delort, one of Milhaud's experienced divisional commanders, intervened:

> I halted Brigadier-General Farine's brigade which was heading for the great plateau on the direct order of Marshal Ney and without my involvement. I enjoined Farine not to leave the division and pointed out to him that I only received orders from the general [Milhaud] who commanded the corps to which my division belonged. During this dispute, which suspended the movement of this brigade, Marshal Ney came in person, bubbling over with impatience. Not

only did he persist in the execution of his first order but he demanded the two divisions [of Milhaud's corps] in the name of the Emperor. Still I hesitated ... I pointed out that heavy cavalry should not attack infantry which was posted on heights, had not been shaken and was well placed to defend itself. The marshal shouted 'Forwards, the salvation of France is at stake!' I obeyed reluctantly.[2]

As his corps trotted off, Count Milhaud shook hands with Lieutenant-General Charles Lefebvre-Desnoüettes, commander of the Guard light cavalry standing behind his corps. 'I am going to charge; support me', Milhaud urged, which his headstrong colleague did only too eagerly by joining the charge.

Soon these approximately 4500 colourful horsemen had filled the valley between Hougoumont and La Haie Sainte. Colonel Count Michel Ordener commanded the 1st Cuirassiers and recalled how the serried ranks of cavalry moved off cheering 'Long live the Emperor!':[3]

> I do not know if military history contains other examples of such a mass of horsemen charging simultaneously into action. I myself had participated in the famous charges of Austerlitz, Jena, Eylau, Friedland and Wagram but I never saw such a mingled mass. We numbered nearly five thousand. Marshal Ney placed himself at our head; it was 4.00 pm. At first, our impact was irresistible. In spite of a hail of iron which beat on our helmets and breastplates, in spite of a sunken lane above which were sited the English batteries, we crowned the crest of the heights, passed like lightning through the guns.'[4]

The French squadrons surged towards Wellington's infantry who had formed into defensive square formations. The intrepid Lieutenant-General Baron Jacques Delort is said to have saluted his foes as he led his cuirassier division down on them.[5] Baffled by volleys of musketry, Marshal Ney's horsemen swarmed vainly between the squares before falling back to rally. Dismounted horsemen floundered about, weighed down by breastplates and helmets. Their enormous boots stuck in the mud as effectively as if they had been glued down.[6]

The tide of cavalry soon swept back up to the crest of Wellington's ridge. Colonel Michel Ordener remembered:

> To give himself a moment of respite, the English commander summoned all the remnants of his cavalry to help him. But the Dutch cavalry brigade opposed to us was overthrown and its debris retreated, spreading terror everywhere. Already we noticed distinctly the enemy baggage and massed fugitives rushing in disorder along the road to Brussels ... Nevertheless, the infantry squares still held and the volleys from their faces inflicted dreadful havoc in our ranks.[7]

The pattern had been set for the next one and a half hours. In between each charge, French artillery bombarded Wellington's men and caused immense losses. 'The battlefield resembled a real furnace,' remembered Colonel

Toussaint-Jean Trefçon of II Corps. 'The gunfire, the musketry, the screams of the combatants, all that added to the blazing sun, made the battlefield seem like the hell of the damned.'[8] The crude but brutal French tactics were beginning to tear the guts out of Wellington's army. But it was a slow process and the Prussians were now penetrating on to the battlefield from the east. Napoleon sent some of his precious reserve troops to hold Blücher in check. 'To know whether we were victorious or in danger the soldiers, even the officers, sought to divine the answer from the expression on my face,' the fallen Emperor reminisced at St Helena. 'But it radiated only confidence. It was the fiftieth pitched battle that I had conducted in twenty years.'[9]

Soon after 4.30 pm, on Napoleon's order, Lieutenant-General François Kellermann's III Cavalry Corps joined the charges from the left wing. Lieutenant-General Baron Claude Guyot's Guard heavy cavalry followed Kellermann into action.[10] Napoleon had been surprised that Ney had engaged the reserve cavalry so early but had recognised that he now had little choice but to support the units already engaged.[11] Colonel Michel Ordener agreed: 'it was absolutely necessary either to resign ourselves to retreat or to triumph over the British tenacity by a supreme effort.'[12]

In contrast, the experienced Kellermann considered it madness to reinforce the French cavalry already assailing Wellington's line. However, one of Kellermann's divisional generals, Baron Samuel L'Héritier, had already moved off and Kellermann had no choice but to follow with one brigade of his other division. He left his other brigade, Brigadier-General Baron Amable Blancard's elite carabiniers, in a hollow near Hougoumont. This was the sole unit of French heavy cavalry still unengaged and Kellermann had ordered it not to move without his personal authorisation.

Kellermann soon found it impossible to withdraw L'Héritier's men from the charges without causing a débâcle. Further tragedy ensued as Marshal Ney, ignoring Blancard's protests, swept even the carabiniers into his charges. Kellermann seethed with anger:

> I might be tempted to believe the wretched fate of France led Marshal Ney to the point where he found this still intact brigade. He had spotted it in the plain, he galloped over to it and lost his temper over its inaction. He ordered it to hurl itself on seven or eight English squares, placed in a chequered pattern on the slope of the hill near the wood [orchard] of Hougoumont and flanked by numerous artillery batteries. The carabiniers were forced to obey but their charge met with no success and half of this brigade was left lying on the ground.[13]

Around 9000 French horsemen were now storming again and again over and about the slippery, congested slopes of Wellington's ridge under a hail of fire. From his vantage point south of Hougoumont, General Maximilien Foy of II Corps watched in amazement: 'in a few moments, the plateau between

Hougoumont and the main roads of Charleroi and Nivelles were covered and flooded by the equestrian mass. The Imperial Guard cavalry were there, the carabiniers and the cuirassiers too: the best of all that France possesses . . . I have never seen anything like it in my life.'[14] Colonel Toussaint-Jean Trefçon, also of II Corps, echoed Foy's words:

> From the spot I occupied, at the edge of Hougoumont wood, I could see the battlefield very well. The charges of our fine cavalry were certainly the most admirable thing I have ever seen. They rushed at the English and, in spite of the musketry, got to the bayonets. They came to reform around the small wood where we were and then they charged again. I was moved more than I can express and despite the perils which I myself was running, I had tears in my eyes and shouted my admiration to the cavalrymen. The carabiniers in particular struck me. I saw their golden breastplates and their helmets shining in the sunlight; they passed by me and I saw them no more.[15]

Colonel Léopold's green-coated 7th Dragoons charged with its squadrons formed in line one behind the other. One of its officers, Major Letang, noted the resolute bearing of Wellington's infantry squares as he charged towards them. They were clearly going to reserve their fire until the very last minute. A concentrated volley at point-blank range would destroy scores of men and horses. The leading squadron of the dragoons swerved to the right to avoid it. Successive squadrons followed this movement and the charge was not carried through on to the bayonets. The 7th Dragoons rallied near La Haie Sainte.[16] This was a typical experience; no unit pressed home its attack at speed on to Wellington's bayonets. Nevertheless, the French swarmed around the beleaguered infantry squares, hacking and jabbing at the foot-soldiers with swords and lances.

The fight raged with intense bitterness: one French eyewitness described how 'the smallest hillock, the most trivial embankment was frequently taken and retaken several times. Repeated charges of cavalry took place; the field of battle was heaped with dead, and the firing, instead of slackening, became more and more violent. Both sides contended with equal fury and the defence was as obstinate as the attack was impetuous.'[17]

Frenchmen who participated in these massed cavalry charges later claimed to have broken several infantry squares and captured six or seven flags but this is contradicted by evidence from Wellington's army. Nevertheless, it is undisputed that the 1st Cuirassiers captured the flag of the Lüneburg Light battalion of Major-General Count Kielmannsegge's Hanoverian brigade during d'Erlon's attack at 2.00 pm. It is also agreed that the King's Colour of the 8th Line battalion, King's German Legion, was lost when the battalion formed into line and counter-attacked some French infantry near La Haie Sainte during Ney's cavalry charges.[18] The other flags the French claim to have captured were certainly not British but may have been German or Netherlands standards. Ney's cavalry certainly failed to penetrate and disperse any of Wellington's infantry squares.

At one stage Ney was on foot in the midst of an abandoned battery, madly beating one of the hostile cannon barrels with the flat of his sword. But none of the cavalrymen ventured to put the murderous guns out of action by hammering a spike into the vent. The successive waves of fine cavalry continued to rush on to Wellington's ridge, past the temporarily abandoned and ignored artillery pieces, to flow around the rock-like squares. Colonel Count Michel Ordener of Milhaud's cuirassiers described how the charges followed each other without interruption. It seemed the French were almost masters of the plateau but Wellington's mauled units held out. They seemed, like trees, to be rooted in the earth: 'we would have had to kill them to the last man.'

Exhausted by fatigue, the French cavalry halted on the ridge crest. Colonel Ordener described how the ranks of horsemen stood exposed to a hail of musketry and artillery fire. They were too tired to advance again; too proud to retire. 'Disaster ensued,' Ordener remembered. 'My brigade took enormous losses there. It was then that my unfortunate brother, who had already been wounded by one of Ponsonby's dragoons earlier, was mortally wounded. A ricocheting cannonball struck his helmet and bruised his head.' Lieutenant Gaston Ordener died from the effects of the blow on 10 July; he was only twenty-two.[19]

Casualties among the French senior officers were equally horrific: General Jean-Baptiste Jamin, marquis de Bermuy, the commander of the Guard Grenadiers à cheval, had fallen dead over the barrel of a gun.[20]

In Ney's array of cavalry formations, four out of six divisional commanders and six out of eight brigade commanders were wounded. A seventh brigade commander, Brigadier-General Frédéric de Donop, had fallen wounded to the ground and was never seen again. One of the divisional commanders, Lieutenant-General Baron Jacques Delort, had three horses killed and two seriously wounded beneath him; he himself received several sword cuts and a serious wound from a shot. His hat, his uniform and the great black coat which enveloped him were all torn to pieces by musket-balls.[21] Scores of other officers were struck. Count Milhaud's chief of staff, Baron Chasseriau, was mortally wounded and General Baron François Lallemand, commander of the Guard Chasseurs à cheval, was also injured.

One of the worst hit regiments, the 6th Cuirassiers, had lost eighty per cent of its officers while Sergeant Reynier of the 4th Cuirassiers and his mount received thirty-six wounds between them in the course of the battle.[22] Colonel Lacroix had received a mortal injury at the head of the 3rd Cuirassiers and both Colonels Léopold of the 7th Dragoons and Gobert of the 5th Cuirassiers were wounded.[23] Count Fleury de Chaboulon, Napoleon's secretary, saw a cuirassier with both his arms mutilated by sabre cuts. 'I am going to have my wounds dressed,' the man raged. 'If I cannot use my arms, I will use my teeth – I will eat them.'[24]

A handful of French cuirassiers passed through the intervals between Wellington's infantry squares and, unable to return the same way, surrendered to British dragoons. But these captured cuirassiers then broke away and galloped down the main road leading from Mont St Jean towards Nivelles in an attempt to escape. North-west of Hougoumont they were halted by a road block, an abatis, manned by the 51st Light infantry, and were massacred by musketry. Just over a dozen broke through to rally south of Hougoumont; they had charged right round the farm anti-clockwise. Major Lemonnier-Delafosse witnessed their return to French lines:

> Suddenly we saw smoke rising, like that which a burning stack of hay or straw could have produced. We ran to the spot and saw there fifteen to eighteen cuirassiers ... Men and horses were disfigured, covered in blood, black with mud. It was no more than a shapeless mass. One second-lieutenant alone had gathered these men from that perilous, fatal passage across half of an army! The horses were covered in sweat and the smoke we had noticed was nothing other than the emanations of the vapour from their bodies ... The officer, when questioned, said that his squadron commander, too committed to execute the about turn, offering as it did as many dangers as charging forward, had shouted 'Conquer or die!' ... Eighty cuirassiers, three officers and the squadron commander were left dead on the battlefield! What a terrible charge![25]

By 5.30 pm, Ney's cavalry was almost exhausted by casualties and fatigue. The marshal now called on the 6000 men of Count Honoré Reille's II Corps who had not been sucked into the holocaust at Hougoumont. These infantrymen consisted of Lieutenant-General Baron Gilbert Bachelu's division and one of Baron Maximilien Foy's two brigades. The hot-blooded Ney would have done better to have launched a combined arms attack earlier in the afternoon, with these 6000 infantrymen following in the wake of the massed cavalry on to the ridge crest to pour a devastating musketry into Wellington's infantry squares at close range. According to Wellington, 'Buonaparte gained some of his battles by the use of his Cuirassiers as a sort of accelerated infantry, with which, supported by masses of cannon, he was in the habit of seizing important parts in the centre or flanks of his enemy's position, and of occupying such points till his infantry could arrive and relieve them.'[26] Now it was too late. The cavalry were too tired to support the infantry who advanced in columns north-westwards from La Belle Alliance towards Wellington's ridge. These columns marched along, and parallel to, a dirt track you can still follow today. General Foy recalled how his troops skirted Hougoumont orchard, the north-east corner of which extended to within 100 metres of the track on which you are walking:

## THE ATTACK BY LT-GENS FOY AND BACHELU

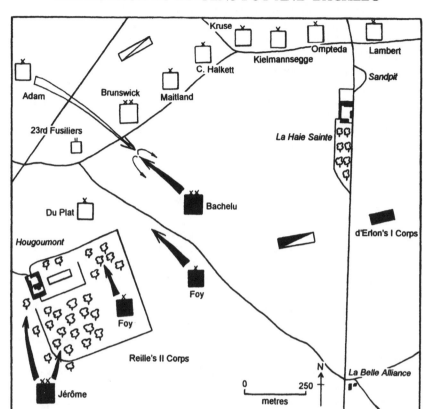

I kept my left flank at the hedge [of the orchard]. In front of me I had a battalion deployed as skirmishers. When we were about to meet the English, we received a very lively fire of canister and musketry. It was a hail of death. The enemy squares had the front rank kneeling and presenting a hedge of bayonets. The columns of Bachelu's division fled first and their flight precipitated the flight of my columns.[27] At this moment I was wounded. A ball passed through the top of my right arm; the bone was not touched. After being hit, I thought that I had only a contusion and stayed on the battlefield. Everyone was fleeing. I rallied the debris of my division in the valley adjacent to the wood of Hougoumont. We were not followed.[28]

Foy's ADC, Major Lemonnier-Delafosse, was beside his general during this time and offers another account of the attack:

Bachelu and Foy, formed in squares which stood in a chequered pattern, moved off and courageously ascended the slopes of the plateau under the redoubled fire of the enemy artillery and infantry who ... vigorously defended the approach of the plateau. The square formed by Bachelu's division was on our

181

right and was further forward than that of Foy's division. When we were a musket shot away, General Foy tapped me on the shoulder and said, so optimistic was he still: 'tomorrow you will be at Brussels and promoted colonel by the Emperor! I smiled at this and, by way of reply, indicated to him Bachelu's square. One of its faces had yielded and the division collapsed into a triangle, whose base was beginning to sway. 'Let's go on', said General Foy, 'and let us do better.' At this moment we had arrived at close range and the fire of the infantry joined to that of the artillery totally shattered our squares ... Everyone ran for his life. All was finished! This was the last effort of the [II Corps] infantry who, employed too late, was no longer strong enough to take the plateau and the sixty cannon which defended it.[29]

Colonel Toussaint-Jean Trefçon was chief-of-staff to Lieutenant-General Baron Gilbert Bachelu and described the attack as Bachelu's men experienced it:

> Hardly had we left the wood [of Hougoumont] and formed in divisional column than musketballs and canister came raining down on us. I was next to General Bachelu when he was hit by several projectiles and had his horse killed under him. The brigade commander was wounded at the same moment and I provisionally assumed command of the division.
>
> Our élan carried us along and in spite of their fire, we were going to reach the English when a sizeable reinforcement[30] reached them. Had it not been for that, they would undoubtedly have been forced to fall back. Just as we were touching the English with our bayonets, we were greeted by a fire of incredible violence. Our soldiers fell in hundreds; the others had to retreat hurriedly or not one of them would have come back.
>
> I received two heavy bruises on my chest and had my horse killed under me by a blast of canister. In falling, I sprained my left wrist. The violence of the shock and the pain I suffered made me lose consciousness but very luckily for me, my unconsciousness was short-lived and I quickly regained all my awareness. Sheltered behind the body of my horse, I let a charge of English dragoons pass in pursuit of our unfortunate division. Once the English had moved far enough away, I sought to find my bearings so as to rejoin a French unit, or else I would have been captured by the Allies, who were passing over the plain in all directions.
>
> A short distance away I saw troops rallying in the shallow gully near the wood of Hougoumont. I made for them as quickly as possible and with infinite precautions. They were the remnants of Bachelu and Foy's divisions which were reforming.[31]

Note the sweeping field of fire Wellington's guns had from the crest of the ridge above you. Throughout their approach march, Foy and Bachelu's men were exposed to a murderous fire. The fire of Wellington's gunners was accurate and deadly and was a major reason for Napoleon's defeat. 'The English artillery made dreadful havoc in our ranks,' wrote a French eyewitness:

We were so completely exposed, that their ricochets passed easily through all the lines, and fell in the midst of our equipage, which was placed behind on the road, and its environs. A number of shells too burst amongst them, and rendered it indispensable for the train to retire to a greater distance. This was not done without considerable disorder, which the English clearly perceived ...

The continuous detonation of ... artillery; the fire of the battalions and light troops; the frequent explosions of caissons, blown up by shells which reached them; the hissing of balls and [canister]; the clash of arms; the tumultuous roar of the charges, and shouts of the soldiery – all created an effect of sound [which] the pen is impotent to describe; and all this within a narrow space, the two armies being close to each other, and their respective lines contracted into the shortest length possible.[32]

Towards 6.30 pm, the French at last scored their first tangible success of the day: the capture of La Haie Sainte farm in the centre of the battlefield. Troops from the battered I Corps had been repeatedly assaulting this strong-point ever since 2.00 pm. Now, on the east side of the farm, the gigantic Lieutenant Vieux of the French engineers hacked at the main gates on the Brussels road with an axe. A shot smashed his left hand but he fought on until hit again in the shoulder. He left to have his wound dressed but comrades took his axe and eventually broke through the gateway and stormed into the courtyard.[33] On the west of the building block, the French 13th Light infantry scaled the roof of the stable block to pick off the ammunition-less Germans.

Outside the farm, Colonel Count Michel Ordener of the French 1st Cuirassiers was watching the progress of the struggle: 'suddenly, a lively fusillade came from La Haie Sainte where Marshal Ney's voice was rekindling the ardour of d'Erlon's infantry regiments. Some of our cavalrymen dismounted and acted as skirmishers in support of this attack.'[34] Colonel Octave Leva-vasseur, a French ADC, was also in the vicinity:

I rode down towards the [Brussels] highroad where I found two companies of engineers.... Their captain came up to me and giving me his card exclaimed 'Aide-de-camp, look! There is my name.' Then he had the charge beaten on the drums and his engineers ran towards the farm shouting 'Forwards!' ... The sappers seized the garden hedges and ferreted out the enemy, who retreated. This all happened before the eyes of the [French] infantry, who marched to support the attack. La Haie Sainte was occupied by our troops.[35]

Today, you will find a tribute at La Haie Sainte to the French soldiers who died so gallantly beneath the whitewashed walls. A plaque on the wall of the farm just north of the main gate reads: '18 June 1815. Towards 6.30 pm the farm of La Haie Sainte was taken by Marshal Ney thanks to the heroic assaults of the sappers of the 1st regiment of engineers of Colonel Lamare (2nd company of the

2nd battalion) and of the 13th Light infantry regiment of [Lieutenant-General Baron François] Donzelot's division.'[36]

It is easy to appreciate the significance of the seizure of La Haie Sainte. If you advance up the Brussels road past the farmhouse, you will see a fifty metre long wall extending along the Brussels road from the north of the farmhouse. On the other side of the wall is a garden which the French filled with skirmishers who sniped at Wellington's front line, which stood just 200 metres away. All afternoon, the defenders of La Haie Sainte had hampered French attacks by constricting their width and making them run a gauntlet of flanking fire.

But now the French held this bastion and they exploited it. Ney brought up a horse artillery battery to the vicinity of the farm and began pounding Wellington's front line at point blank range. All along Wellington's line French infantry, cavalry and artillery were finally acting in close mutual support. The heavy, close-range firing devastated the Duke's centre. Particularly hard-hit was Colonel Christian von Ompteda's bereaved and already ravaged 2nd King's German Legion infantry brigade. To the east of the Brussels road and just south of the Hanoverian monument, you will find a memorial stone which indicates that: 'in this location on 18 June 1815 the 8th Line infantry regiment of General Durutte's division successfully attacked Colonel Ompteda's 2nd German Legion.'

Lieutenant-General Count Pierre Durutte's division was originally at the extreme eastern flank of d'Erlon's I Corps and contended with Wellington's Nassau troops for possession of Papelotte, La Haye and Smohain. But at 4.30 pm Marshal Ney commanded Durutte to detach Brigadier-General Jean Pégot's brigade, consisting of the 8th and 29th Line infantry. Pégot's men moved to the west to help fill gaps caused by losses in the other divisions of I Corps.[37] The 8th Regiment, under Colonel Ruelle, did cause Colonel von Ompteda's KGL and Major-General Count Kielmansegge's Hanoverian brigades to waver but failed to break through.

This was representative of scenes along the whole line. Wellington's skilful reinforcing of his front prevented the French attaining any lasting success. The French were as exhausted as Wellington's men. Lieutenant Jacques Martin of the 45th Infantry wrote that:

> Our division, General Marcognet's, was the most maltreated of the four [belonging to I Corps] and numbered no more than a few hundred men. However, towards 4.00 pm it descended once more into the valley to attempt to seize again this plateau from where we had been so roughly hurled. We met there again these English divisions with which we had already fought, and which were as depleted as us. The fight degenerated into skirmishing and lengthened without result on either side; the issue had to be decided elsewhere.[38]

So Ney requested use of Napoleon's precious Guard but, under increased

Prussian pressure at Plancenoit village, Napoleon refused. 'Troops!' he snapped at Colonel Pierre Heymès, the marshal's ADC. 'Where does he expect me to get them? Does he expect me to make them?'

A lull occurred in which the unsupported French troops fell back from Wellington's ridge crest to regroup. By 7.30 pm the Guard was freed from its earlier paralysis by a brilliant French counter-attack at Plancenoit against the Prussian menace. Napoleon left Rossomme and led six crack battalions of his Middle Guard, just under 3000 men, up the Brussels road for his last assault on Wellington's line.

# Notes

1. C. Oman, 'The French losses in the Waterloo campaign', in *English Historical Review* (Oct 1904 and Jan 1906); A. Martinien, *Tableaux par corps et par batailles des officiers tués et blessés pendant les guerres de l'empire (1805–1815)* (n.d.), p.526

2. L. Stouff, *Le Lieutenant-Général Delort* (1906), p.156

3. After Brigadier-General Baron Etienne Travers de Jever was wounded during the charges, Colonel Ordener assumed command of a brigade formed by the 1st and 7th Cuirassiers.

4. H. Lot, *Les deux généraux Ordener* (1910), p.93; at Eylau over 10,000 French cavalrymen charged under Marshal Joachim Murat but they were not concentrated in such a small sector as Ney's cavalry were at Waterloo.

5. L. Stouff, *Le Lieutenant-Général Delort* (1906), p.98

6. M. Lemonnier-Delafosse, *Souvenirs militaires* (1850), p.394

7. H. Lot, *Les deux généraux Ordener* (1910), p.94

8. A. Lévi, *Carnet de campagne du Colonel Trefçon* (1914), pp.187–8; most eyewitnesses state, however, that for most of the day the sky was overcast.

9. S. de Chair, *Napoleon's memoirs* (1985), p.531

10. Henry Houssaye (*Waterloo 1815* [1987], p.365) concluded that Guyot followed Kellermann on Napoleon's order, although Napoleon denied this in his memoirs. It is perfectly possible, given Napoleon's vague orders during the campaign to Marshal Grouchy, that Napoleon sent an ADC with an imprecise order which was taken to apply to both Kellermann and Guyot but which Napoleon intended only for the former.

11. H. Houssaye, *Waterloo 1815* (1987), p.364

12. H. Lot, *Les deux généraux Ordener* (1910), p.94. Just as the limited French attack on Hougoumont escalated into a full-scale assault, so too did Ney's cavalry charges escalate out of control. More and more troops became engaged to support those already in action and the original, limited, objectives were lost sight of. The Americans were to experience the same unhappy process during the Vietnam war in the 1960s.

13. H. de Mauduit, *Les derniers jours de la grande armée* (1848), v.2, p.345

14. M. Foy, *Vie militaire du général Foy* (1900), p.281

15. A. Lévi, *Carnet de campagne du Colonel Trefçon* (1914), pp.188–9

16. J. Logie, *Waterloo: l'évitable défaite* (1989), p.130

17. A Near Observer, *The Battle of Waterloo* (1816), p.115

18. L. Stouff, *Le Lieutenant-Général Delort* (1906), pp. 131–2, 154; H. Lot, *Les deux généraux Ordener* (1910), p.91

19. H. Lot, *Les deux généraux Ordener* (1910), p.94

20. H. Houssaye, *Waterloo 1815* (1987), p.373

21. L. Stouff, *Le Lieutenant-Général Delort* (1906), p.99

22. D. Johnson, *The French cavalry, 1792–1815* (1989), p.160

23. H. de Mauduit, *Les derniers jours de la grande armée* (1848), v.2, p.349; A. Martinien, *Tableaux par corps et par batailles des officiers tués et blessés pendant les guerres de l'empire (1805– 1815)* (n.d.)

24. F. de Chaboulon, *Mémoires de Fleury de Chaboulon* (1901), p.152

25. M. Lemonnier-Delafosse, *Souvenirs militaires* (1850), pp.395–6

26. E. Cotton, *A voice from Waterloo* (1913), pp.307–8

27. In fact, it would appear from other sources that Bachelu and Foy formed only one column each.

28. M. Foy, *Vie militaire* (1900), p.282

29. M. Lemonnier-Delafosse, *Souvenirs militaires* (1850), pp.383–4; the French formations were in fact columns, although Lemonnier-Delafosse calls them squares.

30. Major-General Frederick Adam's brigade of 2500 infantrymen.

31. A. Lévi, *Carnet de campagne du Colonel Trefçon* (1914), pp.190–2

32. A Near Observer, *The Battle of Waterloo* (1816), pp.115–16

33. H. de Mauduit, *Les derniers jours de la grande armée* (1848), v.2, p.334; H. Houssaye, *Waterloo 1815* (1987), p.378

34. H. Lot, *Les deux généraux Ordener* (1910), p.94

35. O. Levavasseur, *Souvenirs militaires* (1914), p.302

36. Colonel J. Lamare was one of the numerous Belgians serving in the French army in 1815. He had been born in Brussels and later became a general: J. Delhaize and W. Aerts, *Waterloo: études relatives à la campagne de 1815 en Belgique* (1915), p.227.

37. F. de Bas and J. de Wommerson, *La campagne de 1815 aux Pays-Bas* (1908), v.2, p.209

38. J. Martin, *Souvenirs d'un ex-officier* (1867), p.293

A square of Brunswick infantry repelling French cuirassiers

# 13

# THE GUARD GOES INTO ACTION

The six magnificent battalions of the Middle Guard marched proudly
through the smoke and carnage of battle, as if on an immaculate parade
ground. Renowned Guard generals led the advance: veterans such as
Lieutenant-General Count Louis Friant, commander of the Grenadiers, and
Count Claude Michel, second-in-command of the Chasseurs. Baron Paul Poret
de Morvan was present at the head of the 3rd Grenadiers, Baron Louis Harlet
with the 4th Grenadiers, and Baron Christophe Henrion with the 4th Chasseurs. Colonel Octave Levavasseur, one of Ney's ADCs, later remembered the
dramatic procession of formidable troops:

> Then I saw the Emperor, followed by his staff, pass by close to me. When he
> arrived opposite his Guard, which was drawn up on the other side of the road, he
> said: 'Let everyone follow me!' He rode forward along the road which was swept
> by one hundred enemy guns.
>
> One hundred and fifty bandsmen now marched down at the head of the
> Guard, playing the triumphant marches of the Carroussel. Soon the road was
> covered by the Guard marching by platoons in the Emperor's wake. The
> cannonballs and canister which struck them left the road strewn with dead and
> wounded.[1]

If you stand on the edge of the Brussels road immediately south of the orchard
of La Haie Sainte, you will be at the spot to which Napoleon led his guardsmen
before handing over command of them to Marshal Ney. This was the most
advanced position occupied by Napoleon at Waterloo. You should visit this
spot at sunset, for it was at dusk on 18 June that Napoleon watched his Middle
Guard strike Wellington's line where the Lion Mound now stands. Count Louis
Friant returned, wounded in the hand, to announce the advance was going well.
But soon it foundered. Count Claude Michel's ADC recalled how the
guardsmen 'arrived on the plateau and half a musket shot from the motionless,
waiting English. We were received by a dreadful discharge. General Michel fell
from his horse crying "My God, my arm is broken again!" I hurriedly dismounted and unbuttoned his tail coat to find his wound. My general was dead.
A musketball had struck above the left breast and gone through his body.'[2]

Lieutenant-General Baron Jacques Delort of the cuirassiers watched the Middle Guard coming under a murderous discharge of musketry and canister. To him, the terrible firing on the ridge crest seemed like a violent storm with flashes of lightning ceaselessly cutting across the sky and thunderclaps creating a ferocious din.[3]

In a short while, the guardsmen were repulsed and their Emperor had met his final, irrevocable defeat. The French army had not just been physically beaten; it had been psychologically destroyed. 'We are betrayed!' the fleeing troops cried. 'Everyone for himself!' The sun had set on the Napoleonic era. Prince Jérôme Bonaparte was at the side of his brother and described the end in a letter to his wife, Catherine:

> By some fateful chance, the Guard attack failed! The Guard was brought back ... we had to beat a retreat, but there was no longer time. The Emperor wanted to get himself killed. We were in the midst of balls and of enemies. Wellington had a totally fresh cavalry force which he released into the plain at 8.00 pm. At 9.00 pm a terrifying panic seized the army; at 10.00 pm it was a rout ... The Emperor was carried away. No one gave orders and we ran until south of the River Sambre.[4]

But the last agony of the French army had yet to be undergone. The Old Guard battalions who had remained in reserve in the bottom of the valley and further south prepared a desperate rearguard action to cover the rout of the rest of the army. On the west side of the Brussels road, 240 metres south of La Belle Alliance, you will find the Wounded Eagle monument. This commemorates the last combatants of the French Grand Army, who by their heroic self-sacrifice saved many of their fleeing comrades from Prussian sabres.

The monument was the work of Jean-Léon Gérôme and was dedicated on 28 June 1904, under a radiant sun. The driving force behind the erection of the memorial was the dynamic Count Albert de Mauroy, who chose the location after walking over the battlefield and speaking with lawyers and local inhabitants. He then joined with Gustave Larroumet and the great French historian Henry Houssaye to buy the ground. Some French journalists objected that the monument should be sited not at Waterloo but at Ligny, where Napoleon gained his last military victory two days earlier. Houssaye, who enjoyed immense prestige as the celebrated author of *Waterloo 1815*, easily dismissed such narrow-minded objections: 'we do not want to commemorate the Battle of Waterloo, which was a defeat; we want only to honour the French soldiers who, in this battle of giants, died for their country.'[5]

The ceremonies of 28 June 1904 commenced at 9.00 am with a Requiem mass at Plancenoit church in memory of the French soldiers who died at Waterloo. Shortly before 2.00 pm, a special train left Brussels for Braine-l'Alleud, bearing many dignitaries, scores of French and Belgian officers, deputations from every French society in Belgium, the French Minister in Brussels and Lieutenant-General Bruylant, a representative of the Belgian King Leopold II. The houses of Braine-l'Alleud were decked with French and Belgian flags; the battlefield of Waterloo lies in Wallonia, the French-speaking southern half of Belgium. The people of this area have always looked to France for inspiration and protection and the unveiling of the French monument in 1904 provoked an immense swell of popular emotion. A band played the two national anthems, the *Marseillaise* and then the *Brabançonne*.

The official party boarded a tram which until a few decades ago ran to the battlefield and then south along the Brussels road to La Belle Alliance. There, the procession formed up and, preceded by Belgian gendarmes resplendent in full dress uniform with bearskins and dark blue tunics, made its way to the monument, which was veiled by a large French flag.

From the nearby villages teachers had brought 400 or 500 children who waved little tricolour flags as they sang an *Ode to the French soldiers who fell in Belgium during the 1815 campaign*. The Belgian gendarmes formed a guard of honour around the monument, which was also encircled by the flags of local French societies and of Belgian military veterans. From a band drifted those familiar tunes Napoleon's troops had played on countless battlefields across Europe and finally, for the last time, at Waterloo on the morning of the battle.

A succession of speeches followed and Edouard Détaille, the great French military artist, spoke from his heart:

> It is with a deep emotion and a feeling of patriotic piety that we tread upon this soil, this impassive witness of so much heroism, where the combatants of Waterloo rest for eternity. As in a cemetery, where we come to visit the tomb of a relative but can not refrain from a respectful emotion before the other tombs, we salute as we pass the remains of all the brave men who rest side by side united in death. But we go straight to our dead, our soldiers, our grenadiers whose whitened bones, still in formation, indicate the location of the last square of the Old Guard and bring to them the tender remembrance of the country of France.

As Détaille finished speaking, the tricolour flag fell from the eagle. Then Henry Houssaye, with his long, black beard, paid tribute to the sculptor Gérôme, who had died in January after completing his masterpiece; Gérôme's daughters were present at the ceremony. Houssaye then dwelt on the realisation of the wish that, 'next to the Belgian monument[6], the English monument, the Prussian monument and the Hanoverian monument, there should be a French stone in this cemetery of glory.' Ever afterwards, Houssaye considered this to be the finest day of his life.[7]

Numerous descendants of French combatants had come to pay respect not just to the French dead but to their own ancestors. Among the most prominent was Baron de Grandmaison, the grandson of Lieutenant-General Georges

Mouton, Count of Lobau. The baron placed on the base of the Wounded Eagle monument the sword carried by the commander of VI Corps during the battle. Baron Durutte was present to remember his grandfather, who had commanded an infantry division of I Corps and had been disfigured for life by the wounds he received in the battle. Two descendants of Lieutenant-General Count Philippe Duhesme, the commander of Napoleon's Young Guard, made a pilgrimage to his grave at the Church of St Martin at Ways, four miles south of the battlefield near Genappe.

A special guest was also present. Madame Thérèse Dupuis was 103 years old and was one of the last eyewitnesses of the campaign. All her life she had lived at the village of Chapelle-lez-Herlaimont eight miles north-west of Charleroi. In 1815 she had been Thérèse Roland, a thirteen-year-old girl. A few weeks before the ceremony she had told a journalist how she listened to the battle of Waterloo raging fifteen miles north-east of her home:

> In the evening we heard the booming of great cannon, and from the windows I could see the clouds of smoke rising into the air like trees. I was in the mill, and the windows rattled. All night long we heard the tramp of silent men and the creaking, stumbling guns passing our doors. When I looked out next morning I could hear a sound like a rough sea breaking against the rocks. There were clouds of smoke, and I saw men galloping, and masses of my brave soldiers moving hurriedly across the fields. Then the doctors came, and took out the bullets from the wounds of the soldiers.[8]

Now she was greeted by Monsieur Gérard, the French Minister at Brussels. She saw the Wounded Eagle, heard part of the speeches and retired overcome by emotion, with tears in her eyes.

In the evening, after the ceremony, the Society of English Pilgrims of Waterloo chivalrously placed a wreath of English roses and French violets in front of the eagle. In a spirit of peace and reconciliation, the inscription read: 'to the immortal memory of the French heroes who died on the battlefield of Waterloo on 18 June 1815.'

*The Times* estimated the spectators to have numbered 50,000.[9] The Lion Mound was black with spectators and so heavy was the congestion at Braine-l'Alleud station that the dignitaries returned to Brussels by taking the tram eastwards to Rixensart station. In fact, reliable sources indicate that the crowd was probably even greater than *The Times* realised. The railway stations at Brussels issued 57,000 tickets to the battlefield and many more people travelled from elsewhere in Belgium and from France. Possibly as many as 100,000 people attended the ceremonies. Never since the battle itself had so many been on the battlefield simultaneously. Their numbers equalled those of the troops Napoleon commanded there. Such was the awesome power exerted by a battlefield which has come to haunt the soul of the French nation.[10]

For the French, the last moments of Waterloo are shrouded in mystery. The last battalions of the Old Guard which Napoleon still had in reserve rallied the survivors of the Middle Guard just repulsed by Wellington. These units, formed in squares, resisted the tide of hostile troops until they were driven back. They beat a fighting retreat out of the valley towards La Belle Alliance. On the way they were mostly broken up, overwhelmed and destroyed. The commander of the 3rd Chasseurs, Colonel Mallet, and countless others were dead or dying. The survivors made their way in small, defiant bands to Rossomme where the 'oldest of the old', the 1st Grenadiers, stood as the last reserve.

One general, the gallant, loyal and acerbic Pierre Cambronne, reputedly rejected a demand from the English for his 2nd battalion, 1st Chasseurs, to surrender with a single expletive: 'merde!' Other accounts give his reply as 'the Guard dies but does not surrender.' Whatever the response the guardsmen made, Cambronne's battalion was shortly crushed by point-blank musketry and gunfire. The survivors fell back with the eagle of the Guard Chasseurs. Cambronne found himself alone with no choice but to surrender himself to Lieutenant-Colonel Hugh Halkett and a Hanoverian *landwehr* battalion from the town of Osnabrück. Hugh Halkett had galloped up to strike Cambronne down but the Frenchman called out he would surrender. Shortly afterwards a shot wounded Halkett's horse and made it collapse. 'In a few seconds,' remembered Halkett, 'I got him on his feet again, and found my friend, Cambronne, had taken French leave in the direction from where he came. I instantly overtook him, laid hold of him by the aiguillette, and brought him in safety and gave him in charge to a sergeant of the Osnabrückers to deliver to the Duke.'[11]

Nevertheless, Cambronne has come to symbolise the defiance of the French Guard. A metro station in Paris is named after him while a statue of him is located at Verdun. Another statue, showing the general resolutely holding an eagle standard in one hand and a sword in the other, is at Nantes, where Cambronne died in 1842; his tomb is in the Cimitière de la Miséricorde.

Napoleon himself sheltered with General Baron Jean-Martin Petit's two imperturbable squares of the 1st Grenadiers near Rossomme. The drums of the regiment sounded to rally dispersed guardsmen whose battalions had already been crushed. When the tide of fugitives and foes became too strong, Napoleon ordered the 1st Grenadiers to retreat steadily down the Brussels road to Genappe, Charleroi and France.

One Guard unit, Major Belcourt's 2nd battalion, 3rd Grenadiers, was nearly wiped out. Napoleon had posted it in the valley between Hougoumont and La Haie Sainte. Decimated by close-range gunfire and struck by a succession of infantry and cavalry onslaughts, the battalion's square beat a fighting retreat through a boiling sea of foes. Mounting casualties caused it to collapse into a triangle. Then it fired a last volley, cheered 'Long live the Emperor!' and dis-

## LAST STAND OF THE OLD GUARD

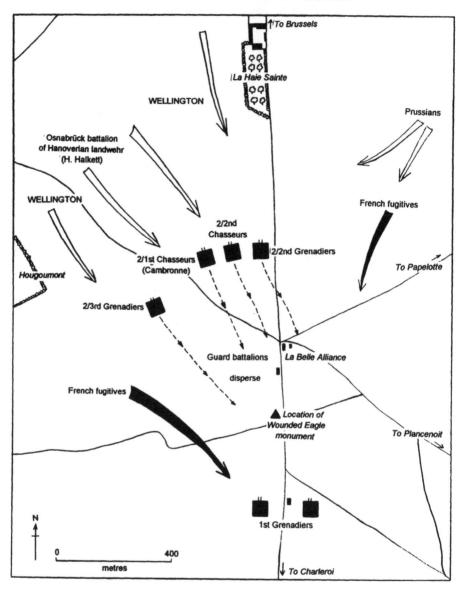

integrated. The surviving grenadiers fought their way south to Rossomme. It is the epic defiance of this unit especially that is commemorated in the Wounded Eagle monument. One of the bronze eagle's wings is perforated by musket-balls and canister. One claw grasps a standard while the other still menaces the foe.

In 1990 a stone memorial was laid on the earth at the foot of the Wounded Eagle. The memorial commemorates the crack, blue-coated squadron of Polish

Lancers who served with the Imperial Guard light cavalry under Lieutenant-General Charles Lefebvre-Desnouëttes. Poles had served loyally in the French Revolutionary armies and then under Napoleon as they saw in France an opportunity to gain independence. Their country had been divided in 1795 between Prussia, Russia and Austria. In the Treaty of Tilsit of 1807 Napoleon set up the Duchy of Warsaw, a French satellite state, but this did not survive his fall.

Nevertheless, the Poles added to their already glorious martial history. Their most gallant exploit was the action of Somosierra in Spain on 30 November 1808, in which the Polish light horse of the Guard (later renamed the Polish Lancers) captured a Spanish battery by charging along a pass under a murderous fire. Sixty of the eighty-eight Poles who charged were killed or wounded but they opened the pass. When Napoleon departed for exile on the island of Elba in 1814, he took with him a battalion of Guard grenadiers and also a squadron of 120 volunteers of the Polish Lancers. In March 1815, this squadron of lancers escorted Napoleon on his return to Paris and then charged for him at Waterloo. Their commander, Major Baron Jean-Paul Jerzmanowski, was wounded in the battle at the head of his men.

The Poles won a brief period of freedom after World War One, only to lose it in 1939 to Hitler and Stalin. As their ancestors had served with Napoleon, so the Poles now served under the British flag with great distinction. Major-General Stanislaw Maczek's 1st Polish Armoured Division fought with exceptional gallantry in Normandy in August 1944.[12] But Soviet Russia still maintained her evil spider's web of tyranny and Poland did not recover true independence until 1989. Nevertheless, it was for that noble end that the Polish Lancers fought and died so gallantly at Waterloo. The leaders of the modern world owe it to their memory never to let Poland be trampled on again.

One of the ironies of the French sector of the battlefield is that whereas neither Napoleon nor Marshal Ney have a monument dedicated to their memory, a French novelist does. He was Victor Hugo, one of the greatest figures of nineteenth century French literature.

Hugo's monument is the tall, stone column on the eastern edge of the Brussels road, 140 metres south of La Belle Alliance. The first stone was laid on 22 September 1912 and the monument attained its present condition in 1956. Work was interrupted by two world wars and a lack of funds and has never been fully completed. Originally a Gallic cock was intended to surmount the column. The monument bears a large bronze medallion of Hugo and several lines from one of his poems: 'Waterloo, Waterloo, Waterloo, mournful plain!'

Victor Hugo was a writer of genius and a vigorous campaigner on behalf of the oppressed. His greatest work, *Les Misérables*, was published in 1862 and is an uncompromising indictment of the French social order. 'Dante tried to make a hell with poetry,' Hugo commented. 'I have tried to make one with reality.'

The heroes and heroines include such underdogs as an escaped prisoner, a street urchin and an orphan.

Hugo was a genius whose enthusiasms were as sudden and unaccountable as a whirlwind. One of his enthusiasms was the epic battle of Waterloo, so Hugo included nineteen chapters about it in Les Misérables, a novel intended to challenge French social oppression. Only the final Waterloo chapter, which includes some of the book's main characters, has any relevance to the plot of the novel.

Hugo had refused to visit the battlefield when in Belgium in 1837. 'Waterloo is more odious to me than is Crécy [the triumph of English archers over French knights in 1346]', he informed his wife. 'It is not only the victory of Europe over France, it is the complete, absolute, shattering, incontestable, final, supreme triumph of mediocrity over genius. I have not been to see the battlefield of Waterloo. I am well aware that the great downfall which occurred there was perhaps necessary so that the spirit of the new age could dawn. It was necessary that Napoleon made way for it.'[13]

Yet Hugo's father had been a Napoleonic general and Hugo shared France's nostalgia for the glorious days of Napoleonic martial grandeur. So when exiled from France, Hugo made an intensive exploration of the battlefield between May and July 1861.[14] He stayed at Mont St Jean village, north of the battlefield, in the Hôtel des Colonnes. In spite of fierce protests, the hotel was demolished in 1962. However, the balcony was preserved and you can see it in the collection of relics at Le Caillou. 'I have spent two months at Waterloo', Hugo wrote. 'There, I made the autopsy of the catastrophe. For two months, I have been on this corpse.' To a fellow exile, Hugo wrote that the 'sombre battle' of Waterloo, far from being more odious than Crécy, was 'one of my permanent emotions.'[15]

Hugo's account of Waterloo in Les Misérables has justly been criticised for its historical inaccuracies. Yet Hugo himself honestly admitted to being an amateur: 'we need hardly say here,' he noted in Les Misérables, 'that we do not pretend to write a history of Waterloo ... For our part, we leave the historians to contend; we are only a distant witness, a passer-by across the plain and perhaps taking appearance for reality. We possess neither the military nor the strategic competence to assess the mass of facts professionally.'[16] Hugo read widely about the battle and in his account mentions some of the standard histories, including those of William Siborne, Jean-Baptiste Charras and Antoine Jomini. 'I have studied Waterloo profoundly,' he wrote. 'I am the only historian who has passed two months on the field of battle.' He carefully considered the battlefield and artefact evidence:

Almost at the spot where [Napoleon's] horse stood, cannon-balls, old sabre blades, and shapeless rust-eaten projectiles have been picked up. A few years ago, a live shell was dug up, the fuse of which had broken off . . . The writer of these lines himself found, while digging in the dusty earth of that hillock, the remains of a shell rotted by the oxyde of forty-six years, and pieces of iron which broke like sticks of barley-sugar between his fingers.

Nevertheless, Hugo also listened to the tales of local peasants and his own tempestuous nature led him to take the legends they told him on trust. At the end of his description of Hougoumont farm he writes: 'all this so that a yokel today may say to the traveller[17], for three francs, Monsieur, I shall tell you the story of Waterloo.' It seems hardly to have occurred to Hugo that such yokels were likely to exaggerate in order to call forth the listener's attention and francs more readily.

Hugo's most famous mistake was to describe waves of French cavalry tumbling into an unforeseen sunken lane on the crest of Wellington's ridge. Historians agree that although a small part of the track running along the ridge was enclosed by steep banks in 1815, the major part of it was easily traversed by the French cavalry. Nevertheless, Hugo certainly did not invent the legend of the sunken lane; indeed it is clear from *Les Misérables* that local peasants were the origin of the myth and Hugo even expressed some scepticism: 'according to local tradition, which clearly exaggerates, two thousand horses and fifteen hundred men perished in the sunken lane of Ohain. The figure probably includes bodies which were thrown into it later, on the day after the battle.'

Hugo seized on the myth of the sunken lane as it so suited his purpose. He interpreted the episode as being the major cause of Napoleon's defeat. For Hugo, Napoleon lost Waterloo not because of Wellington but because of destiny: 'to the question, was it possible for Napoleon to win this battle, our answer is, No. Because of Wellington? Because of Blücher? No. Because of God . . . It was time for that great man to fall . . . Napoleon had been impeached in Heaven and his fall decreed; he was troublesome to God.'

In Hugo's eyes, the sunken lane was the means by which God ended the Napoleonic era.

Victor Hugo was not an historian. But he was the finest writer to describe Waterloo. He conveys the reality of the battle in a manner unattained by all literary figures. 'You will marvel,' one commentator insists, 'at the power and grace of all this prose . . ., at the courage . . . of the writer, at his mastery over the language, and at the wide sweep of his imagination.'[18]

In Victor Hugo, the great battle of Waterloo found a narrator of equal stature. Hugo's style is powerful. He contrasts the sun which rose at the Battle of Austerlitz in 1805 during the first years of Napoleon's glory with the sun which set on the ruins of the First Empire in 1815: 'the sky had been overcast all day, but at eight o'clock it cleared to allow the sinister red light of the setting sun to flood through the elms on the Nivelles road – the same sun that had risen at Austerlitz.'

For Hugo, light and dark were supreme opposites with no shades in between. Struggle between the two was never ending, a struggle between good and evil, life and death. This struggle met in Napoleon, 'a creature of light and dark ... the darkness of the despot counteracts the majesty of the leader.'

Hugo excels at describing souls buffeted by the storms of the great events of destiny. On the morning of Waterloo, Napoléon is the 'titanic coachman of destiny,' jesting and laughing. But Napoleon is also the victim of destiny and Hugo stresses the tragic irony and hubris of the great conqueror who by nightfall is reduced to 'the giant somnambulist of a shattered dream.' For Hugo, Napoleon's rise and fall was merely indicative of life in general, though on a grander scale.

Hugo likens the French army dissolving into rout to the 'thawing of a glacier.' Indeed, the metaphysical alliance between water and defeat is a prominent one: 'a few drops of water, more or less, were what decided Napoleon's fate,' stated Hugo. The 'immobile waves' of the battlefield's ridges reflect the waves of the French attacks surging forward to break like surf on Wellington's rock-hard line. The battle ebbs and flows. At the end, the torrent of fugitives swirls and eddies around the solid rocks of the last squares of the Imperial Guard. It was watery Waterloo that bogged Napoleon down and ended his reign.

Few passages on Waterloo are as evocative as this one from *Les Misérables*:

> The field of Waterloo today resembles any other plain ... But at night a sort of visionary mist rises from it and the traveller who chooses to look and listen enters the hallucination of catastrophe. That monumental hillock with its nondescript lion vanishes and the fearful event comes back to life. The battlefield resumes its identity, the lines of infantry undulate across the plain, furiously galloping horses cross the horizon. The startled dreamer catches the gleam of sabres, the sparkle of bayonets, the flame and thunder of cannon fire. Like a groan emerging from the depths of a tomb the listener may hear the clamour of a ghostly conflict and see the shadowy forms of grenadiers and cuirassiers and the images of men departed – here Napoleon, there Wellington. All this is nonexistent yet still locked in combat, while the ditches run with blood, the trees rustle, the sound of fury rises to the sky and over those stern heights, the spectral hosts whirl in mutual extermination.

# Notes

1. O. Levavasseur, *Souvenirs militaires* (1914), p.304
2. J. Logie, *Waterloo: l'évitable défaite* (1989), p.144
3. L. Stouff, *Le Lieutenant-Général Delort* (1906), p.157
4. A. du Casse, *Mémoires et correspondance du Roi Jérôme et de la Reine Cathérine* (1866), v.7, p.24
5. L. van Neck, *Waterloo illustré* (1903), p.204

6. Houssaye is referring to the Lion Mound, as the Belgian monument at Wellington's crossroads was erected only in 1914.

7. L. Sonolet, *Henry Houssaye* (1905), p.48; Houssaye was born on 24 February 1848 and died on 23 September 1911. He was a hero of the Franco-Prussian war of 1870–1.

8. C. Dalton, *The Waterloo roll call* (1978), p.278

9. *The Times*, 29 June 1904

10. E. Martin, *L'inauguration du monument français de Waterloo* (1904): an extract from the *Carnet du Sabretache* (July 1904)

11. H. Siborne ed., *The Waterloo letters* (1983), pp.308–10; BL Add. MSS 34,706/402

12. J. Keegan, *Six armies in Normandy* (1982)

13. H. Fleischmann, *Victor Hugo. Waterloo. Napoléon* (n.d.), p.65

14. Some commentators consider that Hugo also visited the battlefield in 1852, while in exile following Napoleon III's coup d'état of 2 December 1851. However, there is some doubt that this visit occurred; certainly, Hugo has left no notes about a visit in 1852, whereas he minutely detailed his 1861 stay and recorded excursions he made in 1852 to Louvain and Hal. (See J. Massin, *Victor Hugo. Oeuvres complètes* (1968), v.8, pp.1162–6). L. Daudet's *La tragique existence de Victor Hugo* (1937), describes a visit by Hugo to Waterloo in 1852 but his book is clearly romanticised and not a strictly factual work. We are most grateful to Lucien Gerke for this information.

15. H. Fleischmann, *Victor Hugo. Waterloo. Napoléon* (n.d.), pp.72–3.

16. The translation is our own from the original French of *Les Misérables*. For the most accessible, though slightly edited, English version of the book, see the Penguin Classics translation by N. Denny.

17. As Hugo makes clear earlier, 'the traveller' is a reference to himself.

18. A. Wilson-Green, *Victor Hugo. Prose et poésies*, p.viii

Marshal Ney at the head of the Guard

# PART FOUR: BLÜCHER'S SECTOR

# 14

# THE PRUSSIAN MARCH TO
# THE BATTLEFIELD

Following the operations of the Prussian army on 18 June is not simply a matter of walking over Blücher's battle sector at Waterloo. The Prussians were in action for less than half of the battle, from 4.30 to 9.00 pm. Therefore you need first to follow the Prussian march to the battlefield from the town of Wavre, which is nine miles east of Waterloo.

Following his defeat at Ligny on 16 June, Blücher rallied his mauled but resilient army around Wavre during the 17th. Two rearguards protected his southern flank against the 33,000 French troops Napoleon had detached under Marshal Grouchy on the 17th to pursue the Prussians. Commanding the defile at Mont St Guibert, five miles south of Wavre, was a detachment under Lieutenant-Colonel von Lebedur, consisting of the 10th Hussars, two battalions and two guns. Meanwhile, three miles south-east of Wavre at Vieux-Sart, stood 14th brigade of Bülow's IV Corps.

Patrols maintained communications between these rearguards and the army headquarters in Wavre. East of Wavre, scouts covered the countryside north of the Dyle to protect Blücher's flank and communications with Prussia. To the west, reconnaissances were finding no hostile troops in the River Lasne sector.[1] Furthermore, Gneisenau had ordered Lieutenant-General von Ziethen 'to ensure that the area on the left [west] bank of the Dyle is under constant observation for all enemy movements and that communications are maintained with the Duke of Wellington.'

Communications between the two allies had temporarily broken down in the evening of 16 June following Blücher's defeat at Ligny. But once re-established on 17 June, these communications never failed again. By 6.00 am on 18 June Wellington had received not just assurances of support but details of the Prussian march with at least two corps to his aid: 'Bülow's [IV] Corps will set off marching tomorrow at daybreak in your direction. It will be immediately followed by the [II] Corps of Pirch. The I and III Corps will also hold themselves in readiness to proceed towards you.'

Towards midnight on 17/18 June, Prussian headquarters in Wavre issued orders

## BLÜCHER'S ARMY LEAVES ITS BIVOUACS AROUND WAVRE:
## 18 JUNE

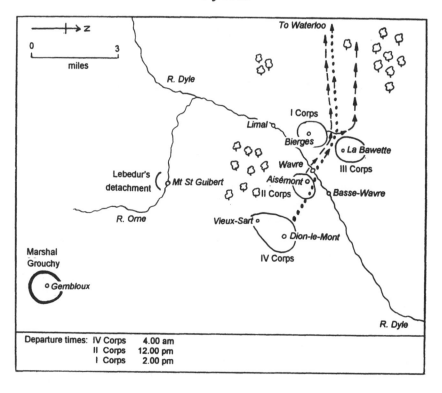

to each of its four army corps. Lieutenant-General von Bülow was instructed: 'you will march with the IV Corps from Dion-le-Mont at dawn, traverse Wavre and head for Chapelle St Lambert where you will conceal your forces as much as possible if the enemy is not seriously engaged with the Duke of Wellington. Otherwise you will vigorously attack the enemy's right flank. II Corps will support you. I and III Corps will be ready to move in the same direction.'[2]

Prussian headquarters had decided that IV Corps should lead the march since it was the strongest and freshest corps. It did contain a large proportion of Silesian landwehr but even these were all experienced troops who had fought the French in the 1813 and 1814 campaigns. Yet IV Corps was also the easternmost formation. It would have been quicker to send I Corps first. This corps was not fresh but would not have as far to march to Wellington's aid. Blücher and his chief-of-staff, Gneisenau, did not appreciate that speed of reinforcement was more vital than its freshness or strength. This was a serious error and the consequent delay nearly resulted in a French victory.

The Prussians may have lacked judgement; they certainly did not lack energy. The first troops were awake and on the march even before dawn.

Patrols had observed the region between Wavre and Wellington on 17 June. Now a detachment of the 6th Hussars set out to reconnoitre the Lasne defile in detail. A cavalry detachment under Major von Falkenhausen which had been scouting towards Genappe the day before was now ordered to shift its attention further north and help the hussars examine the valley of the Lasne.

The results were most encouraging: the Lasne valley, a formidable defensive position, was totally free of the foe. The contrast between the Prussian activity and French lethargy was striking; only late in the morning did Napoleon dispatch his 7th Hussars to reconnoitre on his eastern flank and to establish direct communications with Grouchy.

Bülow's IV Corps set off at 4.00 am as dawn was breaking. The congestion at Wavre delayed Bülow's men, who had to cross the bivouac area of II Corps to reach the town before filing through the streets. Only Bülow's advanced guard – the 6th Hussars, one battery and 15th brigade – made it out of the town before a fire broke out towards 6.00 am; the fire appears to have been caused by a careless baker lighting his oven.[3] Monsieur Debienne, a local justice of the peace, later reported how he immediately hastened to the spot with the town's two fire engines and the few citizens he encountered. Prussian infantrymen were running down the road. Monsieur Debienne passed between the troops and tackled the flames. The 1st battalion, 14th Infantry and the 7th engineer company of II Corps joined the fire fighting operations which eventually extinguished the blaze. Monsieur Debienne claimed that the Prussian formations were able to continue marching past in front of the fire but other accounts indicate that the proximity of ammunition waggons meant the bulk of Bülow's column had to wait for two hours.[4]

The march resumed, with a shepherd from Wavre acting as a guide for IV Corps.[5] Bülow reported after the battle that 'pouring rain had spoiled the tracks and baggage from the different army corps, directed to Wavre, obstructed the routes. These hitches delayed the march and lengthened my column.'[6] Nevertheless, his troops were keen to avenge the Prussian defeat at Ligny. Such was the morale and thirst for revenge that permeated the entire Prussian army, that enquiries made after the campaign discovered that no house more than fifty paces either side of the routes Blücher used had been visited or pillaged.[7] Tradition has it that while on the march the 3rd battalion, 18th Infantry of 15th brigade, tore off their stiff, uncomfortable collars. After the campaign the regiment wore pink collars in commemoration of this incident.[8]

For the first stage of Blücher's march, from Wavre to the Lasne valley, the routes of the Prussian columns are difficult to trace. Modern roads and housing development obscure what was once soggy countryside traversed by narrow, muddy tracks. From Wavre, IV Corps passed Bierges and headed south-west towards Chapelle St Lambert. One thousand seven hundred and fifty metres east of Chapelle St Lambert, you will find a small chapel on the bank of a dusty track. This is the Chapelle St Robert which Bülow's men passed on 18 June. Note the date 1756 inscribed on the chapel, which stands on a high, exposed plateau.

Between 7.00 and 8.00 am Major Gröben of the staff returned to Wavre after reconnoitring to the south. He reported that the French forces following the Prussian retreat on Wavre were at Gembloux, ten miles away. Gröben under-estimated their strength at around 15,000; in fact Marshal Grouchy had double that number under his command. Nevertheless, Gröben rightly claimed that a single corps would suffice to hold the River Dyle as a rearguard while the rest of Blücher's army marched to join Wellington.[9]

At 11.00 am Blücher left Wavre with his entourage. 'In spite of all my sufferings from my fall [at Ligny],' he declared later, 'I would rather have been tied to my horse than miss the battle.'[10] At 9.30 am, he had written a characteristic note to Baron Carl von Müffling, the Prussian liaison officer at Wellington's headquarters. 'I request Your Lordship to tell the Duke of Wellington, in my name, that, ill as I am, I intend to put myself at the head of my troops.' If Wellington found himself under French attack, he could expect Prussian forces to bear down on Napóleon's right flank. 'If, however, today should pass without any enemy action, then I believe that we should make a combined attack on the French army tomorrow.'

To this ebullient despatch, Blücher's cautious and suspicious chief-of-staff, Lieutenant-General Count August von Gneisenau, added an anxious note asking Müffling whether Wellington intended to fight a real battle or instead to put up a show of resistance and then to use the arriving Prussians as a diversion to cover his retreat.

At noon, Pirch's II Corps followed in the wake of Bülow. The corps had been under arms since the early morning but was forced to wait for Bülow's delayed men to pass by. At 2.00 pm, Ziethen's I Corps set off by a more northerly route, via Froidmont and Genval. While IV and II Corps directly assailed Napoleon's right flank, I Corps would reinforce Wellington's left wing.

Unfortunately, to reach Froidmont from Bierges, I Corps had to cross the route of II Corps from Wavre to Chapelle St Lambert. Ziethen used the intervals between II Corps units to send the first of his units off. This incident illustrated another flaw in the Prussian headquarters' planned order of march.

Lieutenant-Colonel von Reiche, Ziethen's chief-of-staff, graphically described the state of the countryside Blücher's army had to traverse:

> Our march to the battlefield was very difficult. Hollow tracks cut into deep defiles had to be negotiated. On each side grew almost impenetrable woods, so that we had no chance of avoiding the track. Progress was very slow, particularly as at many points men and horses could pass through only in single file and artillery could be brought up only with very great trouble. Consequently, the columns became extremely extended and wherever the ground allowed it, the

# THE PRUSSIAN MARCH TO THE BATTLEFIELD OF WATERLOO

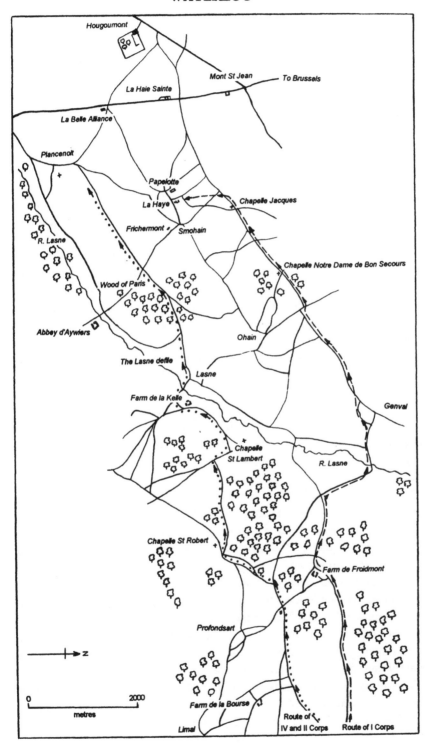

Hougoumont

Mont St Jean

To Brussels

La Haie Sainte

La Belle Alliance

Plancenoit

Papelotte

Chapelle Jacques

La Haye

Frichermont

Smohain

R. Lasne

Chapelle Notre Dame de Bon Secours

Wood of Paris

Abbey d'Aywiers

Ohain

The Lasne defile

Lasne

Farm de la Kelle

Genval

Chapelle St Lambert

R. Lasne

Chapelle St Robert

Farm de Froidmont

Profondsart

Farm de la Bourse

Limal

Route of IV and II Corps

Route of I Corps

0        2000
metres

z

heads of the columns had to halt to give the rearmost units time to close up again.[11]

By tradition, the infantry left the tracks to make way for the artillery. As the guns rumbled past, the infantry marched on the banks either side with their bands playing. Their spirits were high and when Captain von Reuter's battery passed by, they cheered: 'Hurrah! here come our gallant 12-pounders!'

Thielmann's III Corps was commanded to follow the rest of the army if no French forces appeared south of Wavre. However, Marshal Grouchy arrived at Wavre after 3.00 pm as Thielmann was making preparations to leave. Thielmann accordingly placed his troops in Wavre and behind the River Dyle to protect the rear of Blücher's march to Waterloo. The subsequent clashes between Grouchy and Thielmann on 18–19 June constituted the Battle of Wavre.

Blücher joined Bülow's leading units at Chapelle St Lambert towards 1.00 pm. Bülow's men were so strung out that his last formation, 14th brigade, arrived only at 3.00 pm. Nevertheless, Blücher decided at 2.00 pm that sufficient troops were at Chapelle St Lambert to begin crossing the Lasne defile.

An hour earlier, at 1.00 pm, Napoleon at Rossomme had swept the horizon with his telescope before ordering Marshal Ney to launch the main attack against Wellington's left wing. To the north-east Napoleon noticed what seemed to be a mass of troops in the direction of Chapelle St Lambert, about five miles away.

'All the glasses of the general-staff were fixed on this point,' related Napoleon later. 'The weather was rather misty. Some maintained, as often happens on such occasions, that they were not troops, but trees; others that they were columns in position; some others that they were troops on the march.'[12]

In fact, Chapelle St Lambert is too low-lying to be visible from Rossomme. Napoleon's eagle eye had spotted troops at Chapelle St Robert, where the ground was sufficiently high to appear over the intervening contours;[13] he was seeing the second half of Bülow's corps advancing. The first units had already passed the spot unnoticed.

Napoleon ordered two light cavalry divisions from reserve, under Lieutenant-Generals Baron Jean-Simon Domon and Baron Jacques Subervie, to swing east and reconnoitre. General Baron Simon Bernard, one of Napoleon's ADCs, rode on ahead with a small escort. Bernard dismounted and approached the Lasne brook on foot under the cover of woods and hedges. He distinguished Prussian infantry and rode rapidly back to Napoleon.[14]

The Emperor had already received further intelligence. Colonel Baron Marcellin de Marbot's 7th Hussars of I Corps had been scouting to the east since late morning and towards 1.15 pm some of Marbot's men brought in a

Prussian hussar they had captured. Interrogated by Napoleon, the prisoner readily informed him that Bülow's 30,000 men were bearing down on the French army.

Napoleon therefore ordered Lobau's VI Corps to support Domon and Subervie. Lobau's corps contained three infantry divisions. However, one of these, under Lieutenant-General Baron François Teste, was serving on detachment with Marshal Grouchy's force. This left Lobau with just two divisions, or a total of 6000 infantrymen. Napoleon ordered Lobau to choose a good position where he could delay a superior foe. Napoleon vainly hoped that Marshal Grouchy's detachment was hard on the heels of the Prussians. Hence he commanded Lobau to wait until he heard the first of Grouchy's cannon in Bülow's rear before launching a vigorous frontal attack on the Prussians.[15]

Meanwhile Marshal Soult, Napoleon's chief-of-staff, sent an order to Grouchy: '... a letter just intercepted says that General Bülow is going to attack our right flank. We think that we can perceive this corps on the heights of St Lambert. Do not lose one moment, therefore, in coming closer to us, in joining us and in crushing Bülow who will be absolutely destroyed.'

Bülow's march to Waterloo occurred in two distinct phases. The first stage was the approach to the Lasne valley. For the Prussians, the Lasne was a psychological barrier as much as a physical obstacle. They were not just crossing the Lasne but the Rubicon, the point of no return.[16] Once on the western bank, the Prussians had to win or be annihilated. Retreat with the Lasne defile in their rear was out of the question.

One of the main reasons for the Prussians' late arrival at Waterloo was the need to wait until sufficient numbers of Bülow's troops had massed at Chapelle St Lambert ready to cross the Lasne in strength. Otherwise the individual Prussian formations ran the risk of being crushed in succession on the far bank. Towards 11.00 am a Prussian patrol had informed a piquet of the British 10th Hussars, stationed on Wellington's far left flank, that Bülow was advancing to join the Duke's army.[17] The news was taken to Wellington, who naturally expected early support. Wellington seems not to have been aware that only Bülow's advanced guard had so far reached Chapelle St Lambert. Only at 2.00 pm, when most of the corps had come up, could Blücher order his units to begin crossing the Lasne.

From Chapelle St Lambert onwards, the route of Bülow's march is readily apparent. Narrow roads pass south of the village church and begin the descent to the Lasne. After 1250 metres, the Prussians arrived opposite the village of Lasne, where they crossed the river.

Today, the Lasne runs gently through the meadows at the foot of the valley. On 18 June, it was swollen by the torrential rains of the previous day. The steep valley sides were a slippery nightmare for the Prussian gunners in particular; even in dry weather local carts found the descent difficult. Inhabitants had

207

# THE ROUTE OF THE PRUSSIAN IV AND II CORPS TODAY

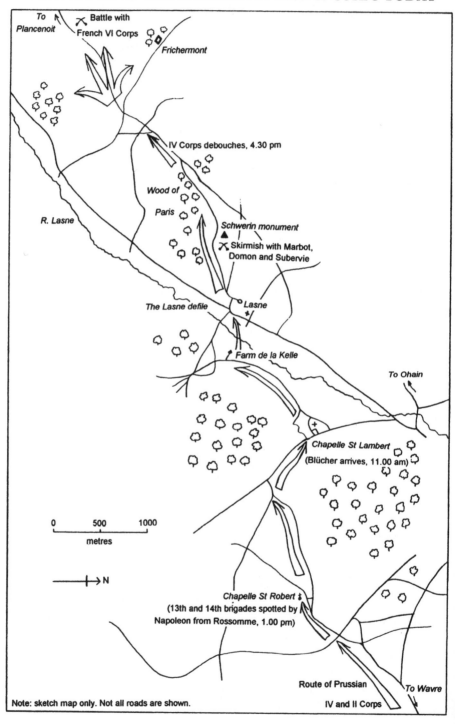

To Plancenoit

Battle with French VI Corps

Frichermont

IV Corps debouches, 4.30 pm

Wood of Paris

R. Lasne

Schwerin monument

Skirmish with Marbot, Domon and Subervie

The Lasne defile

Lasne

Farm de la Kelle

To Ohain

Chapelle St Lambert
(Blücher arrives, 11.00 am)

0    500    1000
metres

→N

Chapelle St Robert
(13th and 14th brigades spotted by
Napoleon from Rossomme, 1.00 pm)

Route of Prussian
IV and II Corps

To Wavre

Note: sketch map only. Not all roads are shown.

placed tree trunks across the tracks here and there to form points where the horses could rest.[18]

Blücher's men used a track running past the Ferme de la Kelle; as you can see, the more gentle gradient here offers the easiest means of access to the river. A narrow brick bridge has replaced the one the Prussians used to cross the Lasne at the bottom of the valley.[19] Some Prussians were in despair at the difficulties posed by the defile but Blücher put fire into them all. 'Forwards!' he urged. 'I hear some say it is impossible, but it has to be possible. I have given my word to Wellington and you surely do not want me to break it. Exert yourselves a little longer, children, and victory will be ours.'[20]

Some commentators have heavily criticised Napoleon for not pushing Lobau's VI Corps as far east as the Lasne defile. The presence of his 6000 infantry would have imposed a lengthy delay on the Prussian crossing. Blücher may eventually have managed to cross the river by sheer weight of numbers or by finding another bridge but probably would have arrived too late to save Wellington from defeat. However, Napoleon had learnt of the Prussian presence at Chapelle St Lambert less than one hour before Blücher commenced crossing the Lasne valley. Lobau's VI Corps would have had insufficient time to march the three miles from the battlefield to the valley and adopt defensive positions. Furthermore, it is clear from his orders to Marshal Grouchy that at this stage Napoleon underestimated the Prussian threat. He assumed only Bülow's IV Corps was descending on his eastern flank and that Grouchy was in a position to join him at Waterloo and crush Bülow.

As a result the only French opposition in the Lasne valley was provided by Colonel Baron Marcellin de Marbot's 7th Hussars. Marbot himself recalled the ensuing skirmishes:

> The head of the Prussian column approached, though very slowly. Two times I threw back into the valley the hussars and lancers which preceded it. I strove to win time by holding the enemy at bay as much as possible. The enemy could only debouch with great difficulty from the muddy, sunken tracks in which he was engaged.[21]

Marbot's outnumbered hussars fell back up the valley slopes to the west. There they joined Domon and Subervie's light cavalry divisions who were apparently waiting at the eastern edge of the Wood of Paris.[22] A fierce clash awaited the leading Prussians; it is possible to follow this fight in detail.

One hundred metres south-west of Lasne church is a crossroads, at which you take the road heading north-west. Fifty metres on, turn left and after another fifty metres, left again on to a narrow tarmacked road. Ignore the 'forbidden to pedestrians' sign and walk along this road, which ascends the steep valley slopes. The first Prussians to climb up here were Count Wilhelm von Schwerin, one of Bülow's cavalry brigade commanders, and the 6th Hussars. Immediately after reaching the plateau, Schwerin was killed. A five-metre high stone column to his memory stands surrounded by hawthorn hedges and trees in the fields north of the track you are on. A path leads across the fields to permit closer inspection. The German inscription reads: 'William, Count von Schwerin, knight and superior officer of the king, fallen in a foreign country for the Fatherland, during the victory of 18 June 1815.'

Schwerin was hurriedly buried and when a couple of years later his family searched for his remains they found them only thanks to a local woman. The remains were reburied with due reverence beneath the monument. In gratitude, Schwerin's widow gave two bells to the commune of Lasne as well as 100 Prussian florins each year to the local priest until she died, for the poor.

A German researcher, Colonel Hans Möser, has suggested that Schwerin was buried where he fell as he was probably killed by a cannon-shot. His mutilated body would have been in no state to transport to a church cemetery.[23] This would indicate that Domon and Subervie brought their two attached horse artillery batteries with them to the eastern edge of the Wood of Paris. If you stand at the border of this wood and look eastwards, you will see that the monument stands on the very edge of the plateau. Schwerin seems to have been killed by artillery fire just as he appeared over the horizon.

Domon, Subervie and Marbot's 7th Hussars retreated westwards soon afterwards to unite with Lobau's infantry and await the renewed Prussian advance. The Wood of Paris was abandoned to Bülow. It is still thickly wooded but it no longer extends as far south or east as it once did. The dirt track running through the wood is in its 1815 condition. Prussian soldiers formed up all around where you are standing. The atmosphere was tense and hushed, the troops nervous and keen to go into action. Lieutenant-General von Bülow reported how he deployed his units:

> First two battalions and the regiment of Silesian hussars were placed under cover in this thick wood. Behind this detachment came the 15th and 16th brigades together with the reserve artillery and cavalry. These troops were deployed on a wide front on both sides of the track through the wood, with the artillery on the track itself and the whole force ready to debouch at the right moment towards the open heights of Frichermont situated in front of the wood. The reserve cavalry was posted in the rear of, and very close to, the wood so as to be in time to follow the infantry immediately.[24]

Bülow's remaining two units, 13th and 14th brigades, were still moving up from the Lasne valley. Bülow commented that during this time the French 'showed an incomprehensible negligence and seemed to pay no attention to our existence.'[25] In fact, Lobau had good reason to leave the Prussians alone for the moment. He would have incurred immense losses in attacking the heavily defended Wood of Paris and might have provoked the Prussians into an early offensive. Lobau's sole task was to delay Blücher's advance when it resumed; he was too experienced a general to attempt more when so outnumbered. Napoleon had ordered him to attack Bülow vigorously only when he heard Grouchy's guns in action against the Prussians' rear.[26]

According to Blücher's ADC, Lieutenant-Colonel Count von Nostitz, the Prussian commander watched the progress of the battle from the edge of the Wood of Paris. Today modern houses block the view. It is certain that Prussian observers west of the wood near Frichermont could see clearly how Napoleon's cavalry charges were sweeping over Wellington's ridge crest, past his batteries and around his squares. They could also distinguish powerful French reserves.

Frequent reports from Baron von Müffling, the Prussian liaison officer attached to Wellington's army, indicated how fiercely the Duke was being assailed. Müffling was stationed to the north of Papelotte and from here, he related, 'I despatched officers in continual succession to Field-Marshal Blücher, to keep him accurately informed of the events of the battle. After 3 o'clock the Duke's situation became critical, unless the succour of the Prussian army arrived soon. On the receipt of my reports, it was resolved not to await the arrival of the whole of Bülow's corps on the plateau, but to advance out of the wood.'[27]

# Notes

1. K. Damitz, *Histoire de la campagne de 1815* (1840), v.1, p.231
2. W. Aerts, *Waterloo. Opérations de l'armée prussienne du Bas-Rhin* (1908), p.193
3. *Ibid*, p.207
4. Société des études historiques et folkloriques de Waterloo, Braine-l'Alleud et environs, *Mélanges historiques* (1970), p.19
5. G. Barral, *Itinéraire illustré de l'épopée de Waterloo* (1896), pp.114–15
6. F. de Bas and J. de Wommerson, *La campagne de 1815 aux Pays-Bas* (1908), v.3, p.523
7. L. Navez, *Les Quatre Bras, Ligny, Waterloo et Wavre* (1903), p.46
8. P. Haythornthwaite, *Uniforms of Waterloo* (1979), p.159
9. K. Damitz, *Histoire de la campagne de 1815* (1840), v.1, p.232
10. C. Ollech, *Geschichte des Feldzuges von 1815 nach archivalischen Quellen* (1876), p.190
11. L. Reiche, *Memoiren des königlich preussischen Generals der Infanterie Ludwig von Reiche* (1857), v.2, pp.209–10
12. S. de Chair, *Napoleon's memoirs* (1985), p.526
13. J. Logie, *Waterloo: l'évitable défaite* (1989), p.165
14. J. Charras, *Histoire de la campagne de 1815* (1857), pp.258–60
15. S. de Chair, *Napoleon's memoirs* (1985), p.527
16. J. Weller, *Wellington at Waterloo* (1967), p.129
17. H. Siborne ed., *The Waterloo letters* (1983), p.169
18. W. Aerts, *Waterloo. Opérations de l'armée prussienne du Bas-Rhin* (1908), p.210
19. *Idem*
20. *Ibid*, p.211
21. M. Marbot, *Mémoires du Général Baron de Marbot* (1891), v.3, p.406
22. The 'Bois de Paris' is the French for 'Wood of Paris.'
23. C. Ollech (*Geschichte des Feldzuges von 1815 nach archivalischen Quellen* [1876], p.243) stated that Schwerin was killed by artillery near Plancenoit. But it is unlikely that his mutilated body would have been carried all the way to the fields west of Lasne if this had been so. According to C.

Schepers, *Waterloo: a guidebook to the battlefield* (1892), p.16, Schwerin was killed by a grapeshot (or rather, a canister shot) in his forehead. Unfortunately he does not give any authority for this statement but, if true, it would indicate that Schwerin's gruesome corpse would indeed have been in no fit state to transport a long distance.

24. F. de Bas and J. de Wommerson, *La campagne de 1815 aux Pays-Bas* (1908), v.3, p.525

25. *Ibid*, v.3, p.525

26. S. de Chair, *Napoleon's memoirs* (1985), p.527

27. C. Müffling, *Passages from my life* (1853), pp.246–7

Napoleon interrogates a Prussian prisoner, who announces the approach of Blücher's IV Corps

# 15

# IV CORPS AND II CORPS UNDER FIRE

It was 4.30 pm. In Bülow's words, Blücher ordered that, 'to give the English army an immediate breathing space, the available troops would advance without delay to the attack.'[1] Count Nostitz for one had voiced fears that Napoleon would wheel round with all his reserves and overwhelm Bülow's incomplete corps. Gneisenau, though, was certain that Napoleon would fight a mere delaying action against the Prussians while continuing to rain blows at Wellington. Napoleon was single-minded in attack and would concentrate on knocking out his main enemy.

What the Prussians lacked in numbers they more than compensated for by their dramatic entry on to the battlefield. At 4.30 pm 15th brigade emerged from the Wood of Paris, threw out skirmishers and deployed rapidly into battalion columns. The 6th Hussars covered this deployment and soon Bülow had cleared sufficient ground to enable his 16th brigade to advance and form up south of the 15th. Prussian batteries came swiftly into action, as much to herald Blücher's arrival and boost Wellington's morale as to kill Frenchmen. Indeed, Wellington's troops were overjoyed that their Prussian allies were now in action. Captain Thomas Dyneley, of 'E' Troop, Royal Horse Artillery, stood on the eastern end of Wellington's line. He watched as the Prussians 'advanced with a very heavy body of cavalry in front, with which they charged the moment they came on the ground. This was a remarkably fine sight and our army gave them three cheers.'[2]

You can follow the Prussian advance on foot along the track leading to Plancenoit village. This track became the axis of the Prussian attack. At first it is tarmacked and bordered by modern houses. Soon these give way to open farmland. Nine hundred metres after debouching from the Wood of Paris you find the track is crossed by a diagonal path running south-east from Frichermont to the Abbey of Aywiers. Now the top of the Lion Mound emerges into view. The track is no longer totally tarmacked and dirt stretches occur. Five hundred metres further on, you enjoy a spectacular view. Ahead is the steeple of Plancenoit church. The whole of the Lion Mound is now in sight and before it, the whitewashed walls and grey roofs of La Haie Sainte are particularly noticeable. At the time the Prussians reached this point, the last of the massed

## THE PRUSSIAN ENTRY ON TO THE BATTLEFIELD: 4.30 PM

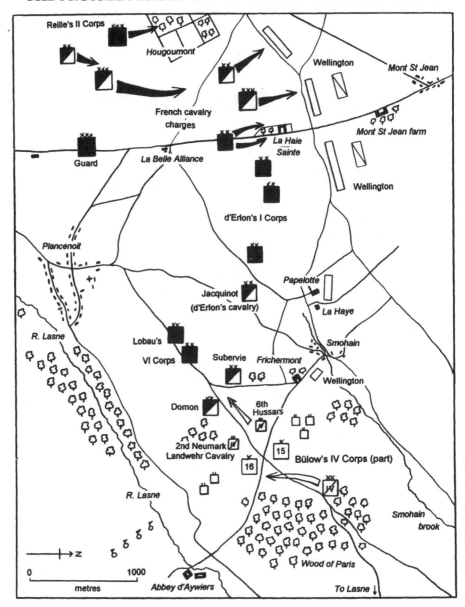

cavalry charges were still in progress. 'The English army fought with a valour which it is impossible to surpass' recalled Gneisenau, but the strong reserves Napoleon had in hand worried him.[3]

Blücher needed to establish reliable links with Wellington's left wing and also to secure his own right flank. Hence he detached three battalions of 15th brigade to the château of Frichermont and hamlet of Smohain. To protect the left flank, 16th brigade sent two battalions to observe the terrain up to the River Lasne. South of the river Major von Falkenhausen was scouting with 100 horsemen of the Silesian landwehr.

French light cavalry trotted forward to menace the centre of Bülow's front line. The Prussian 6th Hussars and 2nd Neumark Landwehr Cavalry advanced to meet them but the French horsemen were merely covering the approach of Lobau's infantry skirmishers. A lively firefight soon developed.

On the western horizon you can clearly distinguish cars driving along the Brussels road. Particularly visible on high ground is the inn of La Belle Alliance with its red roofs and white walls. Gneisenau reported how 'in the middle of the position occupied by the French army, and exactly upon the height, is a farm, called La Belle Alliance. The march of all the Prussian columns was directed towards this farm, which was visible from every side.'[4]

Thus 15th and 16th brigades now commenced a general advance against Lobau's VI Corps. The two Prussian brigades had detached five battalions to cover their flanks, leaving just over 8500 men. Lobau had just 6000 infantry but these Frenchmen belonged to old, tough regiments. Even the 10th Line, which had participated in the Duke of Angoulême's brief royalist resistance to Napoleon's return to power in March 1815, defied the Prussians to the bitter end at Waterloo. Napoleon had dismissed the regiment's royalist colonel and packed the unit with veterans recalled to the eagles.[5] Lieutenant-General von Bülow described the relentless advance of his men against Lobau's fine troops:

> From this moment on, everyone advanced ... in a continuous and well-ordered movement. The able manner with which all the arms were led, the calm and the order which reigned in all the formations truly deserve to be mentioned with the highest praise. Our artillery fire and that of our skirmishers chased the enemy from one undulation to another. Where our skirmishers had obtained a solid foothold, the artillery advanced with the rapidity the situation demanded and passed them to direct its fire at short range against the enemy. The line of massed battalions followed and behind came the supporting cavalry, watching the advancing line of skirmishers ceaselessly.
>
> Several times the enemy cavalry menaced our chain of skirmishers without however undertaking anything serious. Thus our cavalry only had the chance of demonstrating its endurance, coolness and good countenance under gunfire and musketry. Only once an enemy cavalry regiment charged our skirmishers, in front of the junction of the 15th and 16th brigades. Major von Colomb dashed forward at the head of the 8th Hussars, cut up the enemy and pursued him up to his line of infantry. The considerable losses suffered by our cavalry will perpetuate for a long time the glory it acquired this day.[6]

A deafening artillery duel had steadily increased in intensity; three guns of a Prussian battery were soon disabled.[7] Bülow's batteries were galloping successively up to the front line. As you can see, the terrain slightly favoured the Prussian guns, which were established on higher ground. Note how little cover is offered by the gently rolling, open terrain in this sector. The ridges are perpendicular to the front lines, denying troops the shelter Wellington's enjoyed. Between Plancenoit and Frichermont not a single building existed to offer protection and concealment. Both Prussian and French formations suffered severely. Colonel Auguste Pétiet of the French staff recalled the effect of the Prussian fire:

> Bülow turned his gunfire on the French light cavalry stationed in support of General Lobau's infantry. Lieutenant-General [Baron Charles] Jacquinot, commander of the light cavalry division of d'Erlon's I Corps, saw a cannonball smash into the flank of the neighbouring cavalry division, of Lieutenant-General Subervie. The ball beheaded one squadron commander, took two legs off the horse of another and killed the mount of Colonel Jacquinot, commander of the 1st Lancers and brother of the divisional general. At a stroke, the three senior officers of the 1st Lancers were down. Lieutenant-General Jacquinot rushed to the scene and such was his moral toughness and self-discipline that he re-established order before satisfying himself that his brother was unhurt.[8]

Bülow's corps was acting in two distinct wings, each with a different set of objectives. In the north, 15th brigade sought to hold Lobau, Domon, Subervie and Jacquinot in check and to secure Blücher's link up with Wellington's left flank at Frichermont and Smohain. In the south, 16th brigade attacked towards Plancenoit. This village was to obsess Blücher. If it could be captured, the Prussians would have a base from which to push 1000 metres further west to cut the Brussels road and surround Napoleon's army.

To such an extent did the big push on Plancenoit absorb Blücher's attention and resources that his battle line became unbalanced. Only two cavalry regiments, the 1st Uhlans and the 1st Pommeranian Landwehr Cavalry, supported 15th brigade. The remainder of Bülow's reserve cavalry under Prince William of Prussia (destined to be crowned Kaiser Wilhelm I of Germany in 1871) backed up 16th brigade's push. The consequences were obvious to Captain Thomas Taylor of the British 10th Hussars as he watched from Wellington's far eastern flank to the north. 'The Prussians kept their right stationary,' he remembered, 'but pushed on their left getting round the Enemy, so that ... their right formed an acute angle [with Wellington's front line].'[9] The situation on IV Corps' right wing, opposite Lobau's men, became critical. Bülow himself admitted that:

> The skirmishers of 15th brigade, who were continuously the target of the enemy musketry, had to be relieved several times and our fire began to slacken slightly on this part of the line. The foe seemed therefore to have obtained a momentary advantage there and his intention was perhaps to act offensively

against our right wing, while the fight increased in violence at Plancenoit, so as to penetrate between our right wing and the English left. Indeed, strong masses of his infantry and cavalry could be seen opposite 15th brigade.[10]

Fortunately, reinforcements arrived on the battlefield from 5.00 pm to pre-empt a French onslaught in this sector. 13th brigade deployed behind the 15th and pushed its first units into action. Shortly thereafter, 14th brigade joined the 16th on the left wing.[11]

At around 5.30 pm the entire Prussian IV Corps was on the battlefield. Bülow hence exploited his numerical superiority and broke the stalemate Lobau had managed to impose since 4.30 pm. While 15th and 13th brigades held the northern sector, the 16th and 14th manoeuvred round Lobau's open southern flank, thus avoiding the heavy casualties that would have resulted from a head-on attack. Lobau fell back step by step and garrisoned the village of Plancenoit on his southern flank with Brigadier-General Baron Antoine de Bellair's brigade: the 5th and 11th Line infantry regiments.

At about this moment a desperate plea for help reached Blücher from Lieutenant-General von Thielmann. The terribly outnumbered III Corps, left behind as a rearguard, was being attacked at Wavre by Marshal Grouchy. Gneisenau had the moral courage to dictate a tough reply: 'you will dispute with the enemy every step he wishes to take forward with all the strength at your disposal. However big the losses suffered by your corps, they will be compensated for by victory over Napoleon.'[12]

It was shortly before 6.00 pm when the Prussians launched their first attack on Plancenoit. Six batteries pounded Lobau's men in the village and then six battalions of 16th brigade advanced in three columns with the 14th brigade acting in support. For the next two and a half hours fighting was to rage in Plancenoit almost without respite.

The village lies in low ground 1000 metres east of the Brussels road and in 1815 contained 520 inhabitants.[13] Unfortunately, the village is not included in the terrain covered by the 1914 Protection of the Battlefield Law. Conse-quently, numerous modern houses have been built, particularly north of the village. Nevertheless, it is still possible to follow the action in the village centre, aided by the numerous memorial stones that have been erected in recent years.

Four hundred metres south-east of the church, a monument commemorates the defence of the village against the first Prussian attack. The inscription reads: 'in this place on 18 June 1815 the 5th Line infantry regiment of Colonel Roussille, [Lieutenant-General Baron François] Simmer's division, heroically opposed General von Bülow's Prussian corps.'

Colonel Roussille was among those killed in action before Plancenoit. His death was one of the most tragic, for he had no wish to fight in Napoleon's cause. When Napoleon had returned from exile in March 1815, Roussille, faithful to the restored Bourbon monarchy, had refused to open the gates of Grenoble to him. But the soldiers of Roussille's 5th Line had forced him to give way and he had then begged Napoleon to leave him in command of his unit by saying, 'my regiment abandoned me, but I will not abandon it.' Three months later at Plancenoit, Roussille fell at its head, faithful to his men even unto death. He made the supreme sacrifice, not for the Emperor but out of a personal sense of duty and honour.[14]

The Prussians soon seized the church and surrounding cemetery, which together formed the principal strongpoint of Plancenoit. Lobau's men held on in the houses nearby but were desperately outnumbered and unless Napoleon launched a vigorous counter-attack, he risked a Prussian infantry thrust from Plancenoit cutting the Brussels road and surrounding his army. Already Prussian gunfire was striking the Brussels highroad. At this time Mameluke Ali was at Le Caillou to collect some refreshments for Napoleon and his suite. On his way to Le Caillou, he had noticed the first few Prussian cannon-balls landing near the road. As he returned north to Napoleon, he saw they had much increased in number.[15] Fierce old Blücher had carried the fight into the heart of the French position. The situation became so critical that even canister began to sweep the Brussels road.[16]

At 6.00 pm, Napoleon was forced to deplete his last reserve by sending the Young Guard division under Lieutenant-General Count Philippe Duhesme, a total of 4000 men, with three foot batteries, to drive Bülow out of Plancenoit.[17] Duhesme accomplished his task to the letter and the Prussians had to rally and prepare another assault. Frustrated old Blücher is said to have sworn grimly, 'if only we had the damned village!'

The Young Guardsmen were mostly volunteers from Paris and Lyons and fought magnificently. At the church, a plaque beside the main entrance commemorates their heroic struggle against the odds. The inscription reads: 'in this village of Plancenoit, the Emperor Napoleon's Young Guard distinguished itself under the command of General Count Duhesme who was mortally wounded.'

On the opposite side of the entrance, a second plaque pays tribute to one of the Young Guard officers, Lieutenant M. Louis of the 3rd Tirailleurs. He was a Belgian by birth and died at the age of twenty-eight during the struggle for Plancenoit. Inside the church a white marble tablet is dedicated to Lieutenant Jacques Tattet of the Guard artillery who fell aged only twenty-two early in the battle. Another French memorial stands 280 metres north of the church. It records that the Young Guard gloriously opposed Bülow's troops at this point but mistakenly asserts that the guardsmen were in action as early as 5.00 pm.

Barely fifty metres north-east of this stone, at the side of the track leading to Lasne, is a black Gothic monument to the Prussian fallen. It was erected in 1819 and is the only memorial on the battlefield to Blücher's troops. In 1832

Plancenoit Church in 1815

resentful French troops damaged it while marching to help the Belgian Revolution against Netherlands rule by expelling Dutch forces from Antwerp. The French commander was Marshal Maurice Gérard, who had commanded Napoleon's IV Corps in 1815. He immediately had the monument restored. The inscription reads: 'to the dead heroes, their grateful King and country. May they rest in peace. Belle-Alliance, 18 June 1815.' One thousand two hundred and twenty-five Prussians died at Waterloo. A further 5773 were wounded or missing.

The Prussian monument stands on a mound once occupied by a French battery which inflicted heavy losses on Bülow's men. Thanks to the lofty elevation of this mound, you can see the iron cross atop the monument glittering in the sunlight from afar.

Towards 6.30 pm the Young Guard faced the second Prussian assault on Plancenoit. Colonel Hiller von Gärtringen, commander of 16th brigade, advanced in three infantry columns, each two battalions strong. The northern column was composed of the 15th Infantry, the central one of the 1st Silesian Landwehr and the southern column of the 2nd Silesian Landwehr. 14th brigade followed as a reserve and pushed forward the 1st battalions of the 11th Infantry and 1st Pommeranian Landwehr in support. Hiller described vividly the progress of his onslaught:

> Overcoming all difficulties and with heavy losses from canister and musketry, the troops of the 15th Infantry and of the 1st Silesian Landwehr penetrated to the high wall around the churchyard held by the French Young Guard. These two columns succeeded in capturing a howitzer, two cannon, several ammuni-

tion waggons and two staff officers along with several hundred men. The open square around the churchyard was surrounded by houses, from which the enemy could not be dislodged in spite of our brave attempt. A firefight continued at fifteen to thirty paces range which ultimately decimated the Prussian battalions. Had I, at this moment, the support of only one fresh battalion at hand, this attack would indeed have been successful.[18]

Colonel von Hiller was forced to retreat but rallied his men. French cavalry pursued but retired after coming under artillery fire.[19] Meanwhile, to the north of Plancenoit, Lobau's VI Corps was still holding out and offering a robust defence. One of Lobau's soldiers, Fusilier Verdurel of the 2nd battalion, 47th Line, was lying dead in the mud. Later someone would pick up his *livret*, or military record book, from the ground near his body.[20]

Prince William of Prussia had now placed his reserve cavalry in the front line. The fight at Plancenoit was absorbing so many infantry that the cavalry had to stand in the open in order to fill the gap south of 15th and 13th brigades. The cavalrymen came under not only gunfire but even musketry, to which they had little defence. Among the many casualties was a brigadier, Lieutenant-Colonel von Watzdorff, a brave and distinguished officer who refused to leave the field when wounded and was then killed by a cannon-ball.[21] Another of Prince William's three brigadiers, Count von Schwerin, had already been killed at Lasne.

A further attack on Plancenoit, spearheaded by two fresh battalions from 14th brigade, failed. Colonel von Hiller noticed that Prussian morale remained high. Gneisenau was at hand to help the officers rally their men. Assault columns went in yet again. This time 14th brigade comprised the bulk of the attack force with the battle-hit 16th brigade contributing just two battalions from the 15th Infantry. Dramatic success ensued.

Napoleon was forced to send further reinforcements from his Guard. He ordered Brigadier-General Baron Jean Pelet, commander of the 2nd Chasseurs of the Old Guard: 'go with your 1st battalion to Plancenoit where the Young Guard is entirely overthrown. Support it. Keep your troops closed up and under control. If you clash with the enemy, let it be with the bayonet.'

Pelet ran to the village and passed the dying General Duhesme who was being held on his horse by his men. Then some Young Guard voltigeurs came running in full flight; Brigadier-General Chartrand told Pelet that he could do nothing with them. Pelet promised to check the Prussians and urged the voltigeurs to rally behind his battalion. Pelet hurled his first company into a bayonet charge on the leading Prussians who were descending the street opposite. The Prussians fled but the company began to shoot and hence lost the momentum of its charge. Pelet brought up fresh troops to repel more hostile infantry. Again his men started firing. Soon Pelet's last companies had entered the firefight and were dispersed in skirmishing order. He could no longer rally a formed body of men with which to continue his charge.

He hurried some men into the churchyard and from there exchanged point-blank musketry with the Prussians. 'At each interval between the gardens,' he wrote, 'I saw muskets aiming at me forty paces away. I can not imagine how they did not shoot me twenty times.' To appreciate Pelet's peril fully, you should note that in 1815 houses stood much nearer the church than they do today. Plancenoit church now stands in the middle of a large open square.[22] A stream of howitzer shells were bursting in the village. The Prussians hanged or slit the throats of some of their prisoners. Pelet rushed over to prevent some of his chasseurs doing the same to some disarmed Prussians. He was revolted to see one perish before his very eyes and had the survivors guarded by his bearded sappers. One of these prisoners, a terrified officer, grovelled and started talking about his French friends and those of his family.[23]

At last, the hard pressed Pelet saw the 1st battalion, 2nd Grenadiers, arrive under Lieutenant-Colonel Golzio.[24] The grenadiers swept irresistibly down the streets and overturned Bülow's men with a bayonet charge. Captain Cretté cut open the right shoulder of a Prussian sergeant with his sword but the Prussian coolly shifted the muzzle of his musket to Cretté's heart and shot him dead at point blank range. The Prussian sergeant was instantly killed by one of Cretté's men. Two other grenadiers attacked a muscular Prussian officer who grasped their bayonets and appealed to Lieutenant Faré: 'officer, prevent your grena-diers from killing me!' The Prussian was rescued just in time from his ferocious assailants. Nearby, Drum Major Stubert was fighting like a furious lion, stunning anyone in his path with his heavy baton.[25] An attack by a battalion composed of men like this was irresistible. In their exuberance some of the victorious grenadiers pushed eastwards out of Plancenoit up to the Prussian batteries only to be cut down by a squadron of the Prussian 6th Hussars under Captain von Wolff. The 1st Grenadiers stationed on the Brussels road detached some skirmishers to check the Prussians between Plancenoit and the River Lasne. South of the river, a detachment of the 1st battalion, 1st Chasseurs, advanced from reserve at Napoleon's quarters of Le Caillou to the farm of Chantelet to check some of Bülow's cavalry patrols.

Napoleon's counter-attack on Bülow had been as dramatic and decisive as that by the British heavy cavalry on d'Erlon's massed assault of 2.00 pm. The French had won a badly-needed breathing space.[26]

'It was half an hour past seven,' reported Gneisenau, 'and the issue of the battle was still uncertain.'[27] Bülow's corps had been contained. Its left wing had been absorbed by the street fighting at Plancenoit; 16th and 14th brigades had suffered immense losses there. So far Blücher's intervention had failed to turn the tide of battle. Yet it had depleted Napoleon's reserves to such an extent that only six Middle Guard battalions undertook the last assault on Wellington.

Bülow's intervention had also boosted Wellington's morale; Major-General Baron Jean-Victor de Constant-Rebecque, chief-of-staff of the Duke's Netherlands contingent, noted that 'in the distance to our left we saw the flashes of the Prussian cannon.' Lieutenant Edmund Wheatley of the King's German Legion remembered how the news that the Prussians had arrived was passed down Wellington's line and received with cheers.[28] Furthermore, Bülow's onslaughts had worn down the French troops opposing him and one last attack would win a decisive success, the fruit of the labours of IV Corps over the past three hours. Fresh troops for just such an assault had arrived.

For at 6.00 pm the head of Pirch's II Corps had reached the Wood of Paris. Pirch advised Blücher of his arrival and was ordered to detach one of his infantry brigades to cover the army's southern flank. Originally, III Corps had been earmarked to form a southern column but was now tied up in battle at Wavre. Accordingly, Pirch commanded 7th brigade and the 4th Kurmark Landwehr Cavalry to march from Chapelle St Lambert along the south bank of the River Lasne via Couture to Maransart.

Pirch then pushed forward his reserve cavalry to reinforce that of IV Corps which was taking such punishment from artillery fire. 'At the request of General Count Bülow von Dennewitz,' reported Pirch, 'all the reserve cavalry advanced to reinforce the left wing.'[29]

At this moment, Pirch's leading infantry unit, 5th brigade, also reached the battlefield. Pirch himself claimed that 'the 5th brigade could not have arrived at a more opportune moment.'[30] The brigade appeared dramatically on the heights east of Plancenoit as the shattered units of IV Corps were regrouping after their repulse by the two Old Guard battalions. It fell to the 5th brigade to spearhead the final Prussian onslaught on Plancenoit and the brigade did so at the charge, with drums beating. In the centre, two battalions of the 2nd Infantry thrust directly towards the church while the 5th Westphalian Landwehr sought to encircle the village from the north. The 25th Infantry stormed along to the south. In support marched the battle-hit 11th and 15th Infantry, the 1st Silesian and 2nd Pommeranian Landwehr from IV Corps.

The artillery duel was vicious. The two leading batteries of Pirch's II Corps had just entered the fray. One Prussian officer was awestruck at the scene:

> The firing became so violent, that the Enemy's cannon-balls flew by us without ceasing, not to mention our own fire; I could scarcely hear the notices that were brought, and give the necessary orders; and, though my voice is very powerful, I was obliged to exert it to the utmost, in order to be heard. As our troops continued to be reinforced, we advanced cautiously, but incessantly: it was a grand sight to see our battalions ... descend from the heights, which rise like terraces, preceded by their ... sharpshooters.[31]

Inside Plancenoit, the Prussians were forced to advance step by step against a

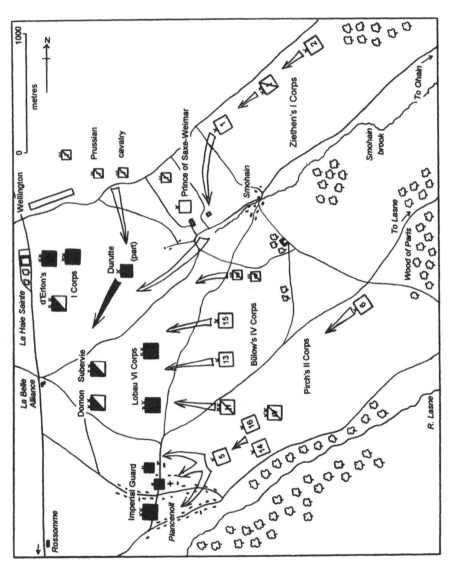

THE PRUSSIAN DISPOSITIONS TOWARDS 8.00 PM

tenacious foe. It was a hand-to-hand fight to the death, reminiscent of the Battle of Ligny on 16 June. The mighty struggle continued in houses, gardens and orchards. The fiercest fighting raged at the Church of Saint Catherine, the toughest strong point in Plancenoit. The church was rebuilt in 1857 but you can still appreciate the strength of the position. The cemetery surrounding the church is today horizontal but used to be on a slope and was surrounded by a wall built with rubble.[32] The Prussian 2nd Infantry desperately sought to force its way down lanes either side of the cemetery but the intense crossfire poured into it checked its assault.

## PLANCENOIT TODAY, SHOWING THE DISPOSITIONS DURING THE FINAL PRUSSIAN ASSAULT

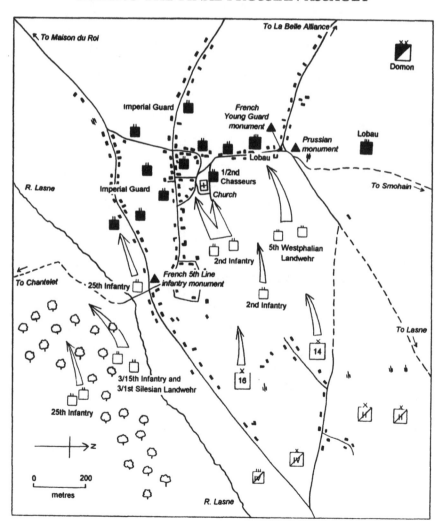

General Pelet was inside the churchyard with men of his 1st battalion, 2nd Chasseurs, and epically described the Prussian onslaught: 'I persisted in the midst of a hail of howitzer shells, in the midst of fires which were beginning to flare up in various houses and in the midst of a terrible, continuous musketry. I held on like a demon; I could not gather my men but they were all under cover and were pouring on the enemy a murderous fire which contained him.'

Plancenoit was crammed with troops. Five thousand French guardsmen held the village. Twenty thousand Prussian infantry were either advancing through the shattered streets or following the assault battalions in support. No part of the battlefield equalléd the intense horror and slaughter here except for the Château of Hougoumont. As Hougoumont became the centre of attention for Wellington's line, so the terrific, protracted combat at Plancenoit eclipsed other points of the Prussian sector. The burning houses of the village could be seen far off. Lieutenant-Colonel Sir John Colborne of the British 52nd Light Infantry remarked on the flames as he descended from the north with Wellington's general advance at 8.15 pm.[33]

A voltigeur battalion of the Young Guard was wiped out in Plancenoit cemetery, 'but still more wild and awful,' wrote the English historian William Siborne, 'must have been the scene within the Church, as the red flood of light which ... poured through the windows of the aisles, fell upon the agonised and distorted features of the wounded and dying with which that sacred edifice was at that moment filled.'[34]

Only when other Prussian units threatened to surround the village did the French resistance crumble. 'The French troops fought with desperate fury,' wrote Gneisenau. 'However, some uncertainty was perceived in their movements, and it was observed that some pieces of cannon were retreating.'[35]

Lobau's VI Corps north of the village also gave way at last. Bülow's 13th and 15th brigades had combined to launch a powerful offensive by fourteen battalion columns advancing in four assault waves. 'As if he had been struck by a thunderbolt, the enemy suddenly ceased fire,' reported Pirch. 'Our guns alone continued to break up his ranks which were fleeing in disorder. All our men marched forwards. The cavalry rapidly traversed the village and followed the enemy ... on the *chaussée*.'[36]

General Pelet and his Old Guard chasseurs fell back under fire: 'outside the village I found myself in a terrible confusion of men who ran for their lives while shouting "Stop! Stop! Halt! Halt!" Those who shouted most loudly ran the fastest. These noises were accompanied by cannon shots and musketry, which gave legs to the laziest. The enemy also sniped at us, especially from the wood of Maransart, by which these rogues had outflanked me.' Pelet rallied a band of his men to repel a mixed force of Prussian infantry and cavalry before slipping away into the darkness of the night.

The conduct of the Guard units at Plancenoit and of Lobau's men further north had been most noble. Their heroic self-sacrifice enabled countless comrades from other sectors of the field, and Napoleon himself, to escape encirclement by the Prussian army. Blücher managed to cut the Brussels road, the French line of retreat, too late to trap and annihilate Napoleon's entire army.

As you emerge from Plancenoit, walk north-east along the road to La Belle Alliance. This inn had been the target of Bülow's attacks throughout the combat. Towards the end of the road you will spot the curiously shaped spire of the Church of St Etienne at Braine-l'Alleud on the western horizon. Legend has it that on the morning of 18 June, Prussian troops asked their officers when they would know the battle was won. The reply was, 'when you perceive a church tower surmounted by a helmet.' This myth probably arose in the second half of the nineteenth century when most German troops wore a spiked helmet, the *pickelhaube*, whose appearance was exactly like that of Braine-l'Alleud church spire. In 1815, however, the Prussians were still wearing shakos and soft caps.[37]

## Notes

1. F. de Bas and J. de Wommerson, *La campagne de 1815 aux Pays-Bas* (1908), v.2, p.222
2. F. Whinyates ed., *Letters written by Lieut.-General Thomas Dyneley C.B., R.A., while on active service between the years 1806 and 1815* (1984), p.65
3. A Near Observer, *The Battle of Waterloo* (1816), p.178
4. *Ibid*, p.180
5. H. Houssaye, *1815* (1893), v.1, pp.411–17; H. Lachouque, *Waterloo* (1975), p.122
6. F. de Bas and J. de Wommerson, *La campagne de 1815 aux Pays-Bas* (1908), v.3, pp.529–31
7. W. Siborne, *History of the Waterloo campaign* (1990), p.320
8. A. Pétiet, *Souvenirs militaires* (1844), p.219
9. H. Siborne ed., *The Waterloo letters* (1983), p.171
10. F. de Bas and J. de Wommerson, *La campagne de 1815 aux Pays-Bas* (1908), v.3, p.533
11. 14th brigade was only 5500 men strong as it had detached the 3rd battalion, 11th Infantry, and the 3rd battalion, 1st Pommeranian Landwehr, to help Lieutenant-Colonel von Lebedur to guard the Mont St Guibert defile south of Wavre. Lebedur's detachment also included the 10th Hussars and two guns.
12. F. de Bas and J. de Wommerson, *La campagne de 1815 aux Pays-Bas* (1908), v.2, p.226
13. W. Aerts, *Waterloo. Opérations de l'armée prussienne du Bas-Rhin* (1908), p.242
14. H. Houssaye, *1815* (1893), v.1, p.256
15. M. Ali, *Souvenirs du mameluck Ali sur l'empereur Napoléon* (1926), p.111
16. S. de Chair, *Napoleon's memoirs* (1985), p.530
17. J. Charras, *Histoire de la campagne de 1815* (1857), p.290
18. C. Ollech, *Geschichte des Feldzuges von 1815 nach archivalischen Quellen* (1876), p.248
19. K. Damitz, *Histoire de la campagne de 1815* (1840), v.1, p.281
20. See the photograph of this *livret* in H. Lachouque, *Napoléon à Waterloo* (1965), p.224
21. K. Damitz, *Histoire de la campagne de 1815* (1840), v.1, p.282
22. Anon, *A propos du champ de bataille de Waterloo* (1912), p.45
23. A. d'Avout, 'L'infanterie de la Garde à Waterloo', in *Carnets de la Sabretache* (1905), pp.7–11; W. Aerts, *Waterloo. Opérations de l'armée prussienne du Bas-Rhin* (1908), pp.262–3
24. Several sources assert the 2nd battalion, 2nd Grenadiers, went to Plancenoit. This is unlikely; Hippolyte de Mauduit, who fought at Waterloo in the Guard, states that the 1st battalion went there.
25. H. de Mauduit, *Les derniers jours de la grande armée* (1848), v.2, p.401

26. Compare the Old Guard's counter-attack at Plancenoit with that by the 2nd battalion, Worcesters, at Gheluvelt during the Battle of First Ypres on 31 October 1914. A handul of crack regulars can produce an effect out of all proportion to their numbers: M. Glover, *A new guide to the battlefields of northern France and the Low Countries* (1987), p.211

27. A Near Observer, *The Battle of Waterloo* (1816), p.179

28. C. Hibbert ed., *The Wheatley diary* (1964), p.68

29. F. de Bas and J. de Wommerson, *La campagne de 1815 aux Pays-Bas* (1908), v.3, p.507

30. *Ibid*, v.3, p.509

31. A Near Observer, *The Battle of Waterloo* (1816), p.81

32. Anon, *A propos du champ de bataille de Waterloo* (1912), p.45

33. H. Siborne ed., *The Waterloo letters* (1983), p.286

34. W. Siborne, *History of the Waterloo campaign* (1990), p.380; W. Aerts and L. Wilmet, *18 Juin 1815. Waterloo. L'attaque de la Garde. Les derniers carrés. La déroute* (1904), p.48

35. A Near Observer, *The Battle of Waterloo* (1816), p.179

36. F. de Bas and J. de Wommerson, *La campagne de 1815 aux Pays-Bas* (1908), v.3, p.509

37. Société des études historiques et folkloriques de Waterloo, Braine-l'Alleud et environs, *Mélanges historiques* (1970), p.193

Field Marshal Prince Gebhard Leberecht von Blücher

# 16

# I CORPS IN ACTION

Meanwhile a fresh Prussian force, the head of Ziethen's I Corps, had stormed on to the north-east of the battlefield. This area is one of the least visited yet most evocative. From the start of the battle it had been occupied by a brigade of Germans from the Duchy of Nassau. The task of the brigade commander, Prince Bernhard of Saxe-Weimar, was to guard Wellington's far left flank by occupying the farms of Papelotte, La Haye and Frichermont and the hamlet of Smohain.[1]

The French never assailed this sector in strength for the heavily wooded and undulating terrain offered serious obstacles. At 2.00 pm, when the French I Corps attacked Wellington's left flank, a line of French skirmishers moved towards Papelotte farm. These French troops were from Lieutenant-General Count Pierre Durutte's division of I Corps. The Prince of Saxe-Weimar instantly ordered Captain von Rettberg to counter-attack with the light company of the 3rd battalion, 2nd Nassau Infantry, and the French fell back across the valley. Skirmishing had also flared up further east at La Haye farm and the hamlet of Smohain, which were held by the Orange-Nassau Regiment.

Towards 4.00 pm the French skirmishers advanced on Papelotte again, this time supported by an infantry column. Captain von Rettberg recognised that Papelotte, built around a courtyard and surrounded by sunken lanes and hedges, was highly suitable for a vigorous defence and had prepared it as a redoubt. He now withdrew his company of Nassauers inside and pinned down the French column with his fire. He requested reinforcements from his battalion commander, who promptly sent four companies from reserve. These launched a brisk bayonet attack and threw the French back across the valley.[2]

In the evening French skirmishers again renewed the attack but suddenly pulled back, for three Prussian battalions from 15th brigade had reached Frichermont and Smohain. About an hour later two battalions from 13th brigade would also arrive. The Prussian generals had detached these battalions to protect their right flank and to link up with Wellington's left wing.

Sadly, the Prussians mistook some of the Nassauers for Frenchmen owing to the similarity of their style of uniform. Tragedy ensued near Papelotte as Captain von Rettberg found himself attacked by skirmishers and infantry

# THE SCENE OF THE PRUSSIAN–NASSAU CLASH:
## THE AREA AROUND PAPELOTTE

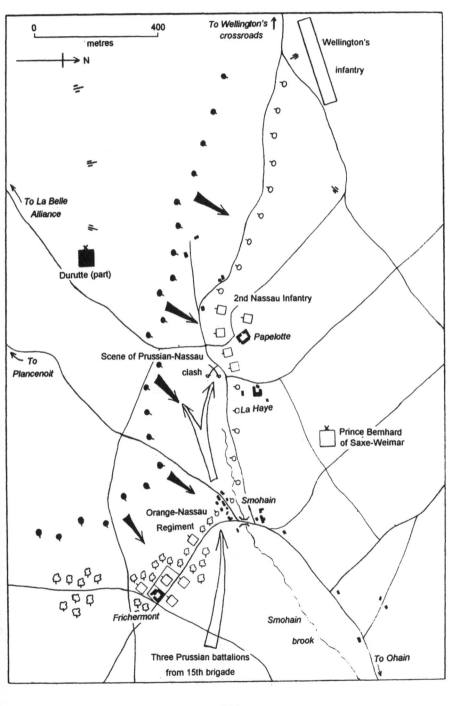

229

columns. He counter-attacked briskly only to realise he was facing Prussian troops. Nassau officers later described how 'our companies, which knew nothing of the arrival of the Prussian troops, replied to their fire until they realised their mistake. Captain von Rettberg, taking some men with him, went to the Prussians and disabused them of their error. The fire ceased on both sides and was then continued jointly against the enemy into the evening.' Nevertheless, both sides lost many men during this clash which lasted for ten minutes.[3]

You may want to visit this sector of the battlefield. The château of Frichermont dated from the sixteenth century and served as the Duke of Marlborough's headquarters in 1705 but was destroyed in 1857. It was a formidable stronghold.[4] Another building erected on the same spot was demolished around 1960. You will find only a few walls, some gate posts and a small wood. In 1815, the château's owner, Count Jean-Charles Le Hardy de Beaulieu, refused to leave his home and seek refuge in the Forest of Soignes like his neighbours. Instead, suffering from old age and rheumatism, he stuck to his bed while the fighting raged around him. When the Prussians arrived they treated him roughly, as they habitually behaved to anyone speaking French. According to tradition, this brutality cured the count of his infirmity and certainly he lived until 1831.[5]

Smohain is today called La Marache and although modern houses have replaced old ones, the hamlet has not increased much in size. La Haye farm, 400 metres to the west, was destroyed by fire in around 1910. It was rebuilt with brick walls and tile roofs and looks much easier to defend today than it was in 1815. During the battle, the farm buildings were only one storey high and the walls were made from cob, a composition of clay, gravel and straw. The roofs were made of thatch.[6] Papelotte farm, 100 metres west of La Haye, was rebuilt after being devastated by fire during the battle. In 1860 a belvedere was added over the main gateway.[7]

In spite of the temporary confusion caused by the 'friendly fire' incident, at least some Prussians were now directly supporting Wellington's troops in this sector. The French still threatened Smohain but already the head of Ziethen's column was approaching this area from the north-east to provide powerful reinforcements. Already two of Wellington's light cavalry brigades under Sir Hussey Vivian and Sir John Vandeleur had been able to leave the east flank and reinforce the Duke's mauled centre, where the situation was critical.[8]

Ziethen's advanced guard had passed the village of Ohain around 6.00 pm. Ohain lay only 3000 metres north-east of the battlefield and Ziethen's chief-of-staff, Lieutenant-Colonel Ludwig von Reiche, rode on ahead to see where I Corps could intervene most effectively. 'As I came out of the wood on to the plateau of Ohain,' Reiche wrote, 'I could see the battle in full swing before me.' You can still follow Reiche's route from a roundabout on the northern outskirts of Ohain past first the Chapelle Notre-Dame de Bon Secours and then the Chapelle Jacques. The Chapelle Notre-Dame de Bon Secours originates from 1673 but was rebuilt in 1859. The Chapelle Jacques is not the same chapel which existed in 1815; the original edifice was smaller and local legend contends that it was transferred to La Haye farm.[9]

On the battlefield, Reiche found Baron Carl von Müffling, Wellington's Prussian liaison officer. The Duke had posted Müffling in this sector of the field to supervise the arrival of I Corps. Müffling warned that Wellington was anxiously awaiting Ziethen. Time was running out. Unless Ziethen came up soon and reinforced the Anglo-Dutch-German left flank, Wellington might have to retreat.

Reiche went to give Ziethen's advanced guard directions before returning to the battlefield. Here he repeatedly assured Prince Bernhard of Saxe-Weimar's exhausted Nassau troops that the Prussian I Corps would arrive at any minute. As Reiche dashed once more back to the head of Ziethen's column, one of Blücher's staff officers came up. It was Captain von Scharnhorst. Bülow's IV Corps was facing tough resistance around Plancenoit and Napoleon's Old Guard counter-attack had caused Blücher to look for reinforcements. He had sent Scharnhorst to order Ziethen to turn south off the track leading to Wellington's left wing. Instead, Ziethen was to bring his men into action south of Frichermont.

Blücher's order was sheer military madness. Obsessed by Plancenoit, tantalised by the hope of surrounding Napoleon's army, Blücher failed to see the wider picture. His single-minded drive towards La Belle Alliance from the east blinded him to Wellington's peril if left unsupported in the north. A Prussian breakthrough in the north-eastern corner of the battlefield, at Smohain, would benefit Bülow's IV Corps further south. Nevertheless, Blücher obstinately insisted on packing formation after formation into the battleline between Frichermont and Plancenoit instead of maximising his numerical superiority by attacking at several points.

If Blücher was obsessive, Captain von Scharnhorst was the worst type of Prussian: an inflexible staff officer concerned only that the orders he carried be obeyed to the letter irrespective of the situation. Lieutenant-Colonel von Reiche remonstrated in vain:

> I pointed out to him that everything had been arranged with Müffling, that Wellington counted on our intervention close to him but von Scharnhorst did not want to listen to anything. He declared that such were Blücher's orders and that if I did not obey, I would be held responsible. Never had I found myself in a similar predicament in any moment of my career. On one hand, our troops were in peril in the direction of Plancenoit; on the other, Wellington counted on our help. I was in despair at this dilemma. General Ziethen was nowhere to be found. Moreover, this was the moment at which the head of the column of I Corps had

to know what it should do. It had even passed the point where it ought to turn off towards Blücher when General Steinmetz, who commanded the advanced guard of I Corps, seeing me conferring with the head of the column, charged at me, shouted at me, as was his custom, and without wanting to hear my explanation, ordered his advanced guard to retrace its steps to the fork and to head towards Plancenoit. Fortunately, at that very moment General Ziethen appeared and after having listened to me, he corrected the march of his troops towards Wellington's left flank.[10]

Ziethen's decision to disobey Blücher could not have been easy. He was helped by Müffling who, seeing the head of I Corps recoiling, had galloped over to discover the cause. 'The battle is lost,' warned Müffling, 'if the corps does not keep on the move and immediately support the English army.'[11] The incident had wasted thirty minutes. Nevertheless, the moral courage of Ziethen and Reiche had at least ensured that the advanced guard of I Corps saw action somewhere. If I Corps had headed for the south of Frichermont, it would have had almost twice as far to cover to the front line. Furthermore, it would have caused immense congestion as it competed with the arriving II Corps for space. In Ziethen, Blücher had, if not a brilliant subordinate, at least one he could rely on to exercise initiative and common sense. Ziethen would rightly become a Field Marshal in 1835.

By 7.30 pm, Ziethen's advanced guard, four and a half battalions of 1st brigade, four regiments of cavalry and four batteries, deployed north of Smohain. Two thousand five hundred metres to the south-west, Napoleon's Middle Guard was marching through the smoke-filled valley on Wellington's centre. The Nassau troops defying the French in the Papelotte–Smohain sector were at the end of their tether after their long, heroic defence. It was high time for Ziethen to intervene. Soon his batteries opened up. Ziethen himself reported that:

> Thanks to the intelligent and courageous leadership of Lieutenant-Colonel von Reiche, the action of the artillery was directed in such a manner that two batteries directed their fire against the left flank of the enemy troops opposed to the II and IV Corps, and two against the right flank of those advancing against the English. This fire soon became so effective that, on the two points, the foe was forced into a disorganised retreat, which obtained the greatest advantages as much for the English army as for the Prussian.[12]

Ziethen's 1st brigade hurried into action. Led by skirmishers and two companies of Silesian jägers, the battalions descended the slopes to chase the French away from Smohain, La Haye and Papelotte. After a bitter struggle the Prussians overcame the French and linked up with Bülow's right flank at Frichermont. The soldiers of d'Erlon's I Corps who were in the vicinity of this new, sudden onrush of Prussians fled in panic. It was nearly 8.00 pm; to the west the French Middle Guard was assaulting Wellington's centre.

Ziethen was justifiably proud of the impact of his entry on to the field. I Corps, he wrote, 'arrived at the most decisive moment.'[13] Nevertheless, his success owed much to events occurring outside his sector, for the French troops he attacked had already been worn down by Bülow.

Ziethen's eruption on to the battlefield was important not just for its physical but also its moral effect. In order to create a surge of fervour in support of the Guard attack on Wellington, Napoleon had spread false rumours among his men that Marshal Grouchy was about to join them. When Ziethen arrived instead, the shock of disillusionment shattered French morale. Lieutenant-General von Bülow noted that where his right flank adjoined Ziethen's men, 'the enemy retired from this side with visible hurry, so much so that our battalions could advance continuously at the quick march.'[14] Colonel Michel Ordener of the French cuirassiers testified that the sight of Ziethen's arrival caused turmoil to rage in Napoleon's army.[15]

Ziethen's 1st brigade pressed on from La Haye and Smohain to seize the heights to the south. Major von Osten charged Lieutenant-General Durutte's disintegrating battalions with the 5th Dragoons and seized three guns. The Prussian infantry had punched a hole through the north-eastern angle of the French battle line and Ziethen's cavalry swarmed through it.[16] Durutte himself, his forehead sliced open and his right wrist cut, was borne out of the fray by his galloping horse. You can see his blood-stained shabraque today at the Brussels Army Museum. A kind-hearted cuirassier sergeant guided Durutte out of the battle and safely into France.[17]

The Prussian artillerymen did their best to support their comrades but their ignorance of the pace of Wellington's general advance to the west caused some of their shot tragically to hit allied troops. Nevertheless, they had done far more good than harm.

Only Ziethen's leading units saw action at Waterloo but as the subsequent troops swung round off the track and over the fields, they gazed upon an awesome spectacle. Henri Nieman of the 6th Uhlans found himself lost for words:

> After a long and dreadfully hard march the whole day ... we arrived at last in full trot at the field of battle ... Our brigade of four regiments of cavalry was commanded by the brave Major-General von Folgersberg, Lützow having been taken prisoner on the 16th. Hard work for the Prussian army again. Wellington was almost beaten when we arrived, and we decided that great day ... At about nine o'clock in the evening the battlefield was almost cleared of the French army. It was an evening no pen is able to picture: the surrounding villages yet in flames, the lamentations of the wounded of both armies, the singing for joy; no one is able to describe nor find a name to give to those horrible scenes.[18]

Captain Reuter, one of Ziethen's battery commanders, dwelt upon 'the beautiful, soft summer evening, as lovely a one as I ever remember.' Thousands of bloody bodies lay strewn over the field. 'The wounded, as we came rushing on, set up a dreadful crying, and in holding up their hands entreated us, some in French and some in English, not to crush their already mangled bodies beneath our wheels. It was a terrible sight to see those faces with the mark of death upon them, rising from the ground and the arms outstretched towards us. Reluctant though I was, I felt compelled to halt, and then enjoined my men to advance with great care and circumspection.' Soon darkness had fallen and moonlight lent the battlefield a ghostly aura, with 'here and there, a burning homestead.'[19]

All serious French resistance had ceased. Gneisenau later described how:

> The retreat became a rout, which soon spread through the whole French army and ... assumed the appearance of the flight of an army of barbarians. It was half-past nine. The Field Marshal [Blücher] assembled all the superior officers, and gave orders to send the last horse and the last man in pursuit of the enemy. The van of the army accelerated its march. The French [army] being pursued without intermission, was absolutely disorganized. The causeway presented the appearance of an immense shipwreck; it was covered with an innumerable quantity of cannon, caissons, carriages, baggage, arms, and wrecks of every kind.[20]

The Prussian cavalry was at the forefront of the pursuit. As soon as the French battleline broke, the Prussian horsemen passed through the infantry to the fore. Ziethen's cavalry cut diagonally across the battlefield from Smohain to La Belle Alliance before being all but halted by the packed masses of struggling fugitives. Bülow's horsemen under Prince William of Prussia passed through and past Plancenoit and soon reached the Brussels highroad. Captain the Hon. James Stanhope of the British 1st Guards was lost in admiration: 'the arrival of the Prussian cavalry sweeping round the right flank of the enemy, in masses with columns as far as the eye could reach, was a magnificent spectacle.'[21]

The 3rd battalions of the 15th and 25th Infantry, which had outflanked Plancenoit to the south via Chantelet, were with the leading pursuers but the bulk of IV Corps infantry followed the cavalry. Ziethen's infantry halted at Maison du Roi on the Brussels road while II Corps, except 5th brigade which had become caught up in the pursuit, immediately marched back to the east throughout the night in an attempt to cut Grouchy's line of retreat to the south. Pirch reached the village of Mellery, three and three-quarter miles north of the battlefield of Ligny, at 11.00 am on 19 June. However, his men were so exhausted by their continuous twenty-four hour march he had to rest there until the next morning. This enabled Grouchy to escape.

Immense quantities of baggage and guns fell into Blücher's hands. Indescribable chaos reigned. Not only had the French army dissolved into a terrified mob of fugitives, but Prussian discipline had broken down too in the ecstasy of triumph. The pursuit soon became a bloodthirsty hunt. Lieutenant Basil Jackson, a British staff officer, described the chaos with the detachment of the outsider:

> After passing La Belle Alliance some of our people became mingled with the Prussians, and the latter were firing in a very disorderly manner; I was also amongst them, and really thought myself in considerable danger of being shot. As to the unhappy Frenchmen who lay about wounded, they met with no mercy. I got clear of the Prussians as soon as I could, and was glad to find myself with a whole skin among the 52nd, which was one of the most forward [British] regiments.[22]

Wellington himself had ridden south before returning towards his headquarters in the village of Waterloo. As he neared La Belle Alliance, he happened to meet Blücher who exclaimed: 'mein lieber Kamerad, quelle affaire!' My dear comrade, what a battle. Wellington later joked that the last two words of Blücher's greeting formed his entire French vocabulary. It was an emotional moment. The two commanders congratulated each other knowing that together they had won the decisive battle of the age. This was the first time the two friends had met since their conference at Bussy mill on 16 June just before the Battle of Ligny and so much had happened in the fifty-five hours since. One of the witnesses of this meeting was Colonel Count Francis von Blücher, the Prussian marshal's son and commander of the 4th Hussars. He wrote home to his mother that 'Father Blücher embraced Wellington in so hearty a manner, that every one present said it was the most touching scene that could be imagined.'[23]

Truly this victory was won by a 'fine alliance'. It had been the immovable Wellington and the irresistible Blücher who had triumphed together; for the Prussians, Waterloo was always known as the Battle of La Belle Alliance.

Wellington had by now ordered his units to keep to the west of the Brussels highroad and to halt in the positions occupied by the French that morning.[24] The pursuit would be left to the Prussians. This wise decision avoided the two allied armies mingling in confusion and obstructing each other. It also prevented numerous instances of friendly troops clashing. As it was, several men had already been killed when the British 18th Hussars mistakenly exchanged sabre cuts with Prussian cavalrymen. Such tragic errors were inevitable in the darkness; fortunately they were relatively few.

Each ally held the other in immense respect and gratitude. Wellington's men stood by the side of the Brussels road as Prussian columns passed by in slow time and with bands playing 'God save the King' in salute. A Prussian officer stopped and asked young Ensign William Leeke of the 52nd Light Infantry if the flag he was carrying were an English one. When Leeke replied in the affirmative, the Prussian embraced it and, patting Leeke on the back, exclaimed: 'Brave Anglais!'

To the south, the Prussian pursuit pressed along the Brussels road. 'To the sound of bugles and drums, of cheering and songs of victory, we advanced without respite,' recalled Major-General von Pirch. 'The enemy were chased from bivouac to bivouac. Mere detachments pushed before them whole battalions ... Our dead of the battle of 16 June demanded victims.'[25]

At Genappe some Frenchmen attempted to halt the pursuit by barricading the Brussels road through the town with overturned waggons. The attempt only made the situation worse. The torrent of fugitives was caught at the entrance of Genappe unable to pass the barricades except at a trickle. Colonel Octave Levavasseur was astounded: 'how surprised I was, when I arrived at Genappe, to see this town so cluttered with carriages that it was impossible to walk along the streets. The infantrymen had to crawl under the teams of horses in order to make their way through. The cavalry rode around the town.'[26] The bridge bearing the Brussels road over the River Dyle was only two metres and ten centimetres wide and created a further bottle-neck.[27]

Napoleon himself, having ridden off his stricken battlefield, took over an hour to pass through Genappe and soon the Prussians descended on those luckless Frenchmen still to the north. Gneisenau reported how 'the enemy had entrenched himself with cannon, and overturned carriages: at our approach, we suddenly heard in the town a great noise and a motion of carriages; at the entrance we were exposed to a brisk fire of musketry; we replied by some cannon shot, followed by a *hurrah*, and, an instant after, the town was ours.'[28]

French morale had been shattered beyond repair and the troops thought of nothing but flight. Among the many trapped and abandoned carriages the Prussians seized at Genappe was Napoleon's post-chaise, in which he had not ridden since he was at Avesnes, before his invasion of Belgium.[29] The 3rd battalion, 15th Infantry, found the Emperor's sword, uniform and boxes of diamonds. The battalion chose the finest diamond to give to the Prussian king while the subaltern officers later dined upon Napoleon's silverware.[30]

The storm passed over Genappe and away to the south as the Prussian advanced guard pressed on. Blücher reached Genappe at 11.30 pm and halted there with the bulk of IV Corps for the night. He entered the Auberge du roi d'espagne where Wellington had stayed two nights before, after the Battle of Quatre Bras. You can still see this inn today, on the east side of the Brussels road in the northern part of Genappe. Note the plaque on the exterior wall to the memory of Lieutenant-General Count Philippe Duhesme.

Duhesme had been mortally wounded in the head by a shell burst near Plancenoit. Accompanied by his two ADCs, one of whom was his nephew Captain Marquiaud, he arrived at the inn on a stretcher. In spite of care by Blücher's own surgeon, Dr Brieske, Duhesme died on the night of 19/20 June in the arms of his nephew. You will find Duhesme's tomb at the Church of St Martin at Ways, a small village 875 metres east of Genappe. Note his family's inscription on the tomb, calling him an 'intrepid warrior who was also a model husband and father.'

Lieutenant-General Baron Maximilien Foy, commander of a French infantry division south of Hougoumont, had wisely avoided the Brussels highroad. With his ADC, Major Lemonnier-Delafosse, and a handful of men he retreated across country throughout the night. Lemonnier-Delafosse later recalled seeing three fires blazing on the horizon like lighthouses. The first seemed to be at Genappe, the second at Quatre Bras and the third at Gosselies. These flames marked the progress of the rout along the Brussels road.

In stark contrast to the uproar on the road, the countryside itself was oppressively silent. 'After all the agitation and ceaseless tumult of a long day of battle, how imposing the silence of night became! Only our march disturbed it,' mused Lemonnier-Delafosse. Plunged into despair, General Foy and his men trudged gloomily, as if they were a funeral procession.

Lemonnier-Delafosse galloped over to the east to see what was happening at Genappe:

It was then that I could form an idea of the disorder of a routed army. What a hideous sight! A torrent of water descending mountains and uprooting every momentary obstacle, is a weak image of this heap of men, horses and waggons. They were tumbling over each other, gathering before the slightest obstacle to form a mass to knock over everything on the road it was opening for itself. Woe to he who fell in this whirlwind: he was crushed, lost!

Lemonnier-Delafosse returned to General Foy. The general had been wounded in the shoulder at 5.30 pm but his wound was still undressed. However, the physical pain was less than the emotional ache caused by defeat. Foy was wrapped up in himself, preoccupied by the gloomy prospects offered by the future and made no reply to Lemonnier-Delafosse's observations. The small band followed a path parallel to the Brussels road in the moonlight. After a while they noticed the noise to the east was dying away; their path had begun to diverge to the west.[31]

Colonel Toussaint-Jean Trefçon, of the French II Corps, considered that 'the disorder was at its height. It exceeded in horror that which I had seen during the return from Russia and the retreat from Leipzig. Enveloped in this mass of men, having lost my companion in misfortune {a wounded cuirassier previously met in Spain] I would certainly have perished if the idea had not occurred to me of leaving this road and reaching the countryside.'[32]

'It was the finest night of my life,' Gneisenau later admitted. Indeed, he was avenging not just Ligny but also the disastrous Battle of Jena back in 1806. For nine years he had observed and learnt from Napoleon's system of war, had helped remodel and rebuild the defeated Prussian army and now was pursuing the French with the relentless ferocity they had employed after Jena. It was the climax of Gneisenau's military career.

'It was moonlight,' he later reported, 'which greatly favoured the pursuit, for the whole march was but a continued chase, either in the cornfields or the houses.' The French made a few desultory stands, 'but as soon as they heard the beating of our drums, or the sound of the trumpet, they either fled or threw themselves into the houses, where they were cut down or made prisoners.'[33]

Gneisenau mounted one of his exhausted infantry drummers on a horse and wherever the French heard those ominous drumbeats approach, they fled in renewed terror. In the darkness, the drumming seemed to presage hosts of bloodthirsty infantry with fixed bayonets. In fact, Gneisenau had barely some squadrons and a detachment of the 3rd battalion, 15th Infantry, when he halted in the early hours of 19 June near Frasnes, at an inn ironically called 'A l'Empereur'. The rest of his men had become so exhausted that they had dropped behind. Before Gneisenau's puny advanced guard an entire army had fled.

The Prussian contribution to the victory of Waterloo had been immense. It was the achievement of the entire Prussian army: a triumph of inspiring leadership but also of supreme will-power on the part of the rank and file.

Bülow's IV Corps had set off from Dion-le-Mont at 4.00 am on 18 June and its leading detachments halted at Frasnes in the early hours of 19 June. Hence some Prussians had been on the march or in battle unceasingly for over twenty hours and, taking into account the movements on the battlefield, had covered at least thirty miles.

Although the Prussians arrived at Waterloo later than Wellington expected, the troops were not to blame. They achieved Herculean feats in their cross-country march over terrible muddy terrain before engaging in a ferocious four and a half hour battle. After following on foot their long march you will have nothing but admiration for the accomplishment of the Prussian soldiers.

Whatever the Prussians lacked in discipline and sophistication they compensated for with their faultless perseverance and enthusiasm. 'Never will Prussia cease to exist,' proclaimed old Blücher, 'while your sons and your grandsons resemble you.'[34]

British historians have over-emphasised Blücher's unexpectedly late arrival on the battlefield. The Prussian army began to have a powerful effect on the course of the battle as early as 1.30 pm, before it had even crossed the River Lasne. For according to Napoleon, he originally intended d'Erlon's attack on Wellington's eastern wing to be made by both I and VI Corps, supported by Lieutenant-Generals Domon and Subervie's light cavalry divisions. The appearance of the Prussians on the heights of Chapelle St Robert compelled Napoleon to weaken his main attack on Wellington by diverting VI Corps to meet Blücher.[35]

Some commentators have criticised Blücher heavily for his tactics during the Battle of Waterloo. In particular, they condemn him for aiming his main thrust at Plancenoit. The low-lying village simply absorbed Bülow's units and enabled numerically inferior French forces to check the momentum of the Prussian army. The German historian Oscar von Lettow-Vorbeck argued that Blücher would have saved many Prussian lives and made his impact felt sooner by avoiding the murderous street fighting at Plancenoit. This could have been done by thrusting from the north-east with a powerful right wing.[36]

Although superficially attractive, Lettow-Vorbeck's theory is flawed. Fighting in a built-up area invariably produces high casualties. Yet among Bülow's foot-soldiers, the worst-hit regiment was the 18th Infantry, which lost 815 men and belonged to 15th brigade on the right wing. Another unit of the same brigade, the 3rd Silesian Landwehr, suffered 625 casualties. By contrast, the 15th Infantry, which bore the brunt of the action at Plancenoit and was part of 16th brigade, lost 622 men. Bülow's 13th and 15th brigades, fighting on the murderously exposed terrain north of Plancenoit, together lost only 600 fewer men than did 14th and 16th brigades inside the deadly village.

Nor was Lettow-Vorbeck justified in assuming a powerful Prussian right wing would have won a quick, dramatic success. Bülow's troops were up against tough French regiments of the line and elite guardsmen. Major-General von Losthin, commander of 15th brigade, stated bluntly that 'for several hours the enemy defended his position with stubbornness.'[37] The Prussians would have taken heavy losses and progressed slowly wherever they had thrust. Consequently, it mattered not so much where they attacked as that they assaulted the French as soon as possible with all the might at their disposal. Blücher's battle-cry was 'forwards!' With this slogan he could not, in the circumstances of Waterloo, go seriously wrong.

The assault on Plancenoit, in the right rear of Napoleon's army, won no immediate physical gains but immense moral ones. The thrust by Bülow's left wing took the battle to the enemy. The French troops continued striking Wellington's front line but were constantly anxious about the Prussian threat to their line of retreat. A French ADC recalled how 'the eyes of the entire army turned towards the right.'[38] At the height of the French massed cavalry charges on Wellington's ridge, Colonel Michel Ordener of the 1st Cuirassiers noted that 'already in the distance sounded this sinister gunfire which none of us yet comprehended.'[39] The fighting at Plancenoit, just 1000 metres from Napoleon's command post, fatally distracted the Emperor at 6.30 pm from the best opportunity of breaking through Wellington's line, right after the capture of the farm of La Haie Sainte. Even when Napoleon did hurl his Middle Guard against Wellington an hour later, the Prussian menace at Plancenoit induced him to retain his Old Guard on the French side of the valley.

Thus Blücher's thrust on Plancenoit was a sound military decision. Some commentators might argue that Blücher's obvious obsession with Plancenoit caused him to neglect other sectors. Blücher might have broken the stalemate imposed by Napoleon's Guard at Plancenoit sooner by using more flexible tactics: by punching alternately with the left and right wings. However, IV Corps was too weak to attack everywhere. 13th and 15th brigades had detached five battalions to help Wellington's Nassauers hold Smohain and Frichermont. Even after 13th brigade deployed in the front line south of the 15th, the reserve cavalry of IV Corps had to occupy a gap in the line north of 16th and 14th brigades. Only after the reserve cavalry of II Corps arrived were 15th and 13th brigades free to undertake a powerful offensive of their own. Hitherto they had done well to check and keep up the pressure on Lobau's VI Corps.

Nevertheless, Blücher does deserve heavy criticism for ordering I Corps to join Bülow south of Frichermont. The first breakthrough the Prussians gained at Waterloo came not at Plancenoit but in the north-east when Ziethen's I Corps eventually arrived. Ironically, the momentary confusion caused by Blücher's order for Ziethen to march on Plancenoit delayed this breakthrough by at least half an hour. This incident sadly marred Blücher's otherwise magnificent generalship throughout 18 June.

## Notes

1. Various spellings of Frichermont exist; the modern version is Fichermont.
2. J. Pflugk-Harttung, *Belle Alliance* (1915), pp.211–12
3. F. de Bas and J. de Wommerson, *La campagne de 1815 aux Pays-Bas* (1908), v.3, p.570; Most historians assign this 'friendly fire' incident to the period when Ziethen's I Corps arrived towards dusk. However, D. Boulger, *The Belgians at Waterloo* (1901), p.63, quoting the chief-of-staff of the Dutch-Belgian 2nd Division (to which the Nassauers belonged), makes clear that the Prussians in question were from IV Corps not I Corps: it was Bülow who debouched from 'the wood [Wood of Paris] lying between Jean Loo and Aywiers.' Captain von Rettberg asserted that after the clash he joined the Prussian skirmishers, who were from the 18th Infantry. The 18th formed part of IV Corps, not I Corps; of the three battalions sent by 15th brigade to link up with Wellington's left flank, two were of the 18th Infantry: J. Pflugk-Harttung, *Belle Alliance* (1915), p.212. The link up with Nassau forces at Frichermont and Smohain seems to have proceeded without incident.
4. Anon, *A propos du champ de bataille de Waterloo* (1912), pp.40–1; J. Weller, *Wellington at Waterloo* (1967), p.134
5. F. de Bas and J. de Wommerson, *La campagne de 1815 aux Pays-Bas* (1908), v.2, p.223
6. Anon, *A propos du champ de bataille de Waterloo* (1912), p.41
7. H. de Mauduit, *Les derniers jours de la grande armée* (1848), v.2, p.340; Major-General Baron Jean-Victor de Constant-Rebecque, chief-of-staff of the Netherlands contingent, wrote that 'we saw the farm of Papelotte in flames': Société des études historiques et folkloriques de Waterloo, Braine-l'Alleud et environs, *Mélanges historiques* (1970), p.149
8. Carl von Müffling (*Passages from my life* [1853], p.247) claimed that he ordered Vivian and Vandeleur to transfer their brigades to the centre. However, Colonel Sir Horace Seymour, ADC to Lord Uxbridge, asserted that he brought the order for Vivian to move towards the centre: H. Siborne ed., *The Waterloo Letters* (1983), p.20. This is apparently another instance of Müffling exaggerating the importance of the role he played.
9. Anon, *A propos du champs de bataille de Waterloo* (1912), p.43

10. L. Reiche, *Memoiren des königlich preussischen Generals der Infanterie Ludwig von Reiche* (1857), v.2, pp.210–13

11. Müffling's account of this incident is inaccurate and shows clearly how he consciously or unconsciously exaggerated his own role. Müffling wrongly calls Reiche 'an inexperienced young man' who mistook Wellington's wounded for fugitives and told Ziethen that the English were retreating. According to Müffling, this was why Ziethen's leading units regressed to the track leading off to the south of Frichermont. Müffling contends that only his intervention caused Ziethen to join Wellington and save the battle. Müffling appears to have been ignorant of Blücher's order conveyed by Scharnhorst.

12. F. de Bas and J. de Wommerson, *La campagne de 1815 aux Pays-Bas* (1908), v.3, p.501. Carl von Müffling, *Passages from my life* (1853), p.249, claimed that he brought two of Ziethen's batteries into action to enfilade the French. If true, it is surprising that Ziethen does not mention Müffling as well as Reiche.

13. F. de Bas and J. de Wommerson, *La campagne de 1815 aux Pays-Bas* (1908), v.3, p.501

14. *Ibid*, v.3, p.537

15. H. Lot, *Les deux généraux Ordener* (1910), p.95

16. S. de Chair, *Napoleon's memoirs* (1985), p.535

17. J. Charras, *Histoire de la campagne de 1815* (1857), p.311

18. F. Thorpe ed., 'The journal of Henri Nieman', in *English Historical Review* (July 1888)

19. E. May ed., 'A Prussian gunner's adventures in 1815', in *United Service Magazine* (Oct 1891)

20. A Near Observer, *The Battle of Waterloo* (1816), p.180

21. BL Add MSS 34,703/23; we have corrected the punctuation in this particular extract.

22. 'Recollections of Waterloo by a staff officer' in *United Service Magazine* (1847, Part III)

23. J. Marston, *The life and campaigns of Field-Marshal Prince Blücher of Wahlstatt* (1815), p.421; W. Aerts and L. Wilmet, *18 Juin 1815. L'attaque de la Garde. Les derniers carrés. La déroute* (1904), p.51

24. E. Cotton, *A voice from Waterloo* (1913), p.147; 'Recollections of Waterloo by a staff officer', in *United Service Magazine* (1847, Part III), p.188

25. F. de Bas and J. de Wommerson, *La campagne de 1815 aux Pays-Bas* (1908), v.3, pp.509–11

26. O. Levavasseur, *Souvenirs militaires* (1914), p.305

27. W. Aerts and L. Wilmet, *18 Juin 1815. Waterloo. L'attaque de la Garde. Les derniers carrés. La déroute* (1904), p.58

28. A Near Observer, *The Battle of Waterloo* (1816), p.180

29. S. de Chair, *Napoleon's memoirs* (1985), p.538

30. A Near Observer, *The Battle of Waterloo* (1816), p.81

31. M. Lemonnier-Delafosse, *Souvenirs militaires* (1850), pp.389–90

32. A. Lévi, *Carnet de campagne du Colonel Trefçon* (1914), p.193

33. A Near Observer, *The Battle of Waterloo* (1816), p.180

34. G. Jones, *The Battle of Waterloo* (1852), p.327

35. S. de Chair, *Napoleon's memoirs* (1985), p.525

36. O. Lettow-Vorbeck, *Napoleons Untergang 1815* (1904), v.1, p.448

37. *Ibid*, v.1, p.431

38. M. Lemonnier-Delafosse, *Souvenirs militaires* (1850), p.383

39. H. Lot, *Les deux généraux Ordener* (1910), p.94

# PART FIVE: BRUSSELS

# 17

# BRUSSELS IN JUNE 1815

Since Brussels is just twelve miles north of the battlefield of Waterloo, many tourists will use the city as a base for their explorations. Brussels has plenty of modern hotels and good restaurants but also much historic charm. It is an ideal place to stay while visiting the battlefields of the 1815 campaign.

Moreover, Brussels has its own place in the history of the campaign. The city was Napoleon's objective and tumultuous scenes occurred as the French steadily approached until checked at Waterloo. Brussels also served as a vast hospital for the wounded. Inevitably, the city has changed much since 1815 and today it serves not just as the capital of Belgium but the centre of Europe. In 1815, the population of Brussels was just 80,000; today it is around one million. Nonetheless, it is still possible in the old quarters of the city to follow the dramatic events that occurred there in June 1815.

Until Napoleon's first abdication in 1814, British high society had been shut out of Europe by the long years of war. Then they had flocked to the continent, particularly to Brussels where the cost of living was cheap. Even after Napoleon's return to the throne of France in 1815 Brussels still teemed with these Britons, most of whom resided in a fashionable quarter near the Park.[1] They little expected that Brussels would become the target of a French invasion. Indeed, they thought of Brussels as a social centre for entertaining Wellington's glittering officers and as a launch pad for an allied invasion of France in July. 'Balls are going on here as if we had had none for a year,' commented Caroline Capel.[2] Wellington himself planned to give a ball on 21 June, the anniversary of his Peninsular victory of Vittoria, as a farewell to Brussels.

Much of the old Brussels Wellington knew has now vanished. The city ramparts have gone. However, you can still see the house Wellington occupied in the rue Royale, which runs along the western side of the park. Wellington arrived in Brussels on 4 April 1815 to assume command of the Anglo-Dutch-German army. He occupied the ground floor of the large house of Monsieur van den Cruyce, a gentleman of Ghent.[3] The house is at 54 and 56, rue Royale and is occupied today by a Belgian company and the Ministère de la fonction publique.

From April until Napoleon invaded, Wellington was hard at work. He toured Belgium to inspect defences and ports and wrote hundreds of letters and orders to bring his army up to optimum strength and efficiency. He also strove to ensure he had the right officers to lead it but was not always successful. 'I have got an infamous army', he complained, 'very weak and ill-equipped, and a very inexperienced staff. In my opinion they are doing nothing in England. They have not raised a man; they have not called out the militia either in England or Ireland; are unable to send me any thing; and they have not sent a message to Parliament about the money.'[4] Much of Wellington's later success on the battlefield was due to his long, hard weeks of preparation in this house at Brussels.

As a break from his arduous duties, the Duke liked to stroll in the park just across the street. On one of these strolls, just two or three weeks before the Battle of Waterloo, he was accompanied by an English friend, Thomas Creevey. After discussing the latest political news from London, Creevey asked the Duke what he thought he would make of the coming campaign:

> He stopt, and said in the most natural manner:– 'By God! I think Blücher and myself can do the thing.' – 'Do you calculate,' I asked, 'upon any desertion in Buonaparte's army?' – 'Not upon a man,' he said, 'from the colonel to the private in a regiment – both inclusive. We may pick up a marshal or two perhaps; but not worth a damn.' – 'Do you reckon,' I asked, 'upon any support from the French King's troops at Alost?' – 'Oh!' said he, 'don't mention such fellows! No: I think Blücher and I can do the business.' – Then, seeing a private soldier of one of our infantry regiments enter the park, gaping about at the statues and images:– 'There,' he said, pointing at the soldier, 'it all depends upon that article whether we do the business or not. Give me enough of it, and I am sure.'[5]

War burst upon the English society's blissful existence at Brussels on 15 June when Wellington received a series of intelligence reports showing that Napoleon had commenced hostilities against the Prussians at Charleroi. The Duke coolly attended a Ball given that night by the Duchess of Richmond to keep the atmosphere in Brussels calm. Some sergeants of the 92nd (Gordons) were also there, to give a display of Highland dancing.[6] Lord Byron movingly described the emotional scenes in his most famous lines:

> There was a sound of revelry by night,
> And Belgium's capital had gather'd then
> Her Beauty and her Chivalry, and bright
> The lamps shone o'er fair women and brave men;
> A thousand hearts beat happily; and when
> Music arose with its voluptuous swell,
> Soft eyes look'd love to eyes which spake again,
> And all went merry as a marriage bell.

Residence of the Duke and Duchess of Richmond

Sadly, all traces of the residence in which this historic ball occurred have now vanished. It used to stand 800 metres north-west of the Park, in the rue de la Blanchisserie; in the nineteenth century a new road, the rue des Cendres, was built through the Richmonds' residence and obliterated the ballroom.[7]

In the midst of the revelry, an ADC galloped up with an urgent report for the Duke: French forces had pushed northwards along the Brussels road as far as Quatre Bras, just twenty miles away. The shock of this news was intense. 'The room was in the greatest confusion and had the appearance of anything but a ball-room,' remembered Captain William Verner of the 7th Hussars. 'The officers were hurrying away as fast as possible, in order that nothing might prevent their joining their regiments.'[8]

Ah! then and there was hurrying to and fro,
And gathering tears, and tremblings of distress,
And cheeks all pale, which but an hour ago
Blush'd at the praise of their own loveliness;
And there were sudden partings, such as press
The life from out young hearts, and choking sighs.

Soon the night sky over Brussels filled with the blaring of bugles and other martial clamour. Wellington's Reserve Corps, quartered in and around the city, was mustering ready to march south against Napoleon. To Lieutenant Alexander Riddock of the 44th Foot, the mingled sounds of bugles and drums seemed to be calling sinners to their Judgement. In response to the summons, the soldiers arrived bearing blazing torches or with lighted candles stuck in the muzzles of their muskets.[9]

Lieutenant Johnny Kincaid of the 95th Rifles tried to snatch some sleep on the pavement as he waited for the last troops of Lieutenant-General Sir Thomas Picton's 5th Division to arrive from their scattered billets: 'we were every instant disturbed, by ladies as well as gentlemen; some stumbling over us in the dark – some shaking us out of our sleep, to be told the news – and not a few, conceiving their immediate safety depending upon our standing in place of lying.'[10]

A fourteen-year-old servant, Edward Healey, judged that the confusion stemmed mostly from an irrational fear that the French were nearly at the gates of Brussels. Calm suddenly reasserted itself as if by magic and by the time the sun rose above the horizon shortly before 4.00 am, Brussels was quiet.[11] Lieutenant Basil Jackson of the Royal Staff Corps returned from delivering a despatch:

> I re-entered Brussels, and found stillness reigning in all the lower streets through which I had to pass. Ascending by the Rue de la Madeleine, I traversed the beautiful Place Royale, leading into the Park, where all the available space, without the railings, was filled with infantry; yet not a sound was audible save a slight clatter of horses' shoes upon the pavement. Seeing a long line of kilted men, I recognised Picton's division standing at attention, while its redoubtable Commander, attended by his Staff, was riding along the line, making his inspection, thereby causing the sounds alluded to, which alone interfered with the general stillness.[12]

Several days' provisions were issued to each man prior to his departure from the city.[13] In the ranks of the 92nd Highlanders, Pipe-Major Alexander Cameron was preparing to make the streets of Brussels resound with 'Hey, Johnny Cope, are ye waukin' yet?'

Miss Charlotte Ann Waldie was staying in a hotel in the Place Royale. The Place adjoins the south-west corner of the Park and the houses around it retain their old character, although trams and a statue of the crusader Godefroy of Bouillon were added later. Miss Waldie wrote movingly of the tumultuous, grand, historic scenes she saw beneath her on 16 June as she watched from the windows of her hotel:

> As the dawn broke, the soldiers were seen assembling from all parts of the town, in marching order, with their knapsacks on their backs, loaded with three

days' provision ... Unconcerned in the midst of the din of war, many a soldier laid himself down on a truss of straw, and soundly slept, with his hands still grasping his firelock; others were sitting contentedly on the pavement, waiting the arrival of their comrades. Numbers were taking leave of their wives and children, perhaps for the last time, and many a veteran's rough cheek was wet with the tears of sorrow. One poor fellow, immediately under our windows, turned back again and again, to bid his wife farewell, and take his baby once more in his arms; and I saw him hastily brush away a tear with the sleeve of his coat, as he gave her back the child for the last time, wrung her hand, and ran off to join his company, which was drawn up on the other side of the Place Royale.

Many of the soldiers' wives marched out with their husbands to the field, and I saw one young English lady mounted on horseback, slowly riding out of town along with an officer, who, no doubt, was her husband. But even at this interesting moment, when thousands were parting with their nearest and dearest to their hearts ... my sorrow [was] turned into mirth, by the unexpected appearance of a long train of market carts, loaded with cabbages, green peas, cauliflowers, early potatoes, old women and strawberries, peaceably jogging along, one after another, to market. These good people, who had never heard of battles, and who were perfectly at a loss to comprehend what could be the meaning of all this uproar, stared with astonishment at the spectacle before them, and actually gaped with wonder, as they slowly made their way in their long carts through the crowds of soldiers which filled the Place Royale ...

Soon afterwards the 42nd and 92nd Highland regiments marched through the Place Royale and the Parc, with their bagpipes playing before them, while the bright beams of the morning sun shone full on their polished muskets, and on the dark waving plumes of their tartan bonnets ... We could not restrain a tear at the reflection, how few of that warlike band who now marched out so proudly to battle might ever live to return. Alas! we little thought that even before the fall of night these brave men, whom we now gazed at with so much interest and admiration, would be laid low.

During the whole night, or rather morning, we stood at the open window, unable to leave these sights and sounds of war, or to desist for a moment from contemplating a scene so new, so affecting and so deeply interesting to us. Regiment after regiment formed and marched out of Brussels; we heard the last word of command – March! the heavy measured uniform tread of the soldiers' feet upon the pavement, and the last expiring note of the bugles, as they sounded from afar ...

Before seven in the morning, the streets, which had been so lately thronged with armed men and with busy crowds, were empty and silent. The great square of the Place Royale no longer resounded with the tumult and preparation for war. The army was gone, and Brussels seemed a perfect desert. The mourners they had left behind were shut up in their solitary chambers, and the faces of the few who were slowly wandering about the streets were marked with the deepest anxiety and melancholy.[14]

Fanny Burney, Madame d'Arblay, must have been the only Briton in Brussels to have passed the tumultuous night unaware of anything unusual. After breakfast at 8.00 am she set out to post a letter and was just in time to see Duke Frederick William of Brunswick's contingent leaving the city. The Brunswickers wore black uniforms to mourn the Duke's father who had been killed by the French at the Battle of Auerstädt in 1806. 'This gloomy hue gave an air so mournful to the procession,' remembered Fanny Burney, 'that I contemplated it with an aching heart.'[15] Her heart would have ached more if she had known that by sunset the gallant Duke Frederick William and many of his devoted band were destined to fall in the Battle of Quatre Bras. The Brunswickers, part of Wellington's Reserve Corps, were based at Laeken two miles north of Brussels, and now followed Picton's 5th Division through the centre of Brussels and south to Quatre Bras.[16]

By afternoon on 16 June, the city ramparts were crowded with people listening to the distant, muffled rumble of gunfire from the Battles of Quatre Bras and Ligny twenty miles to the south. Nerves became increasingly strained. Charlotte Waldie recalled that:

> Unable to rest, we wandered about, and lingered till a late hour in the Parc. The Parc! what a different scene did its green alleys present this evening from that which they exhibited at the same hour last night! Then it was crowded with the young and the gay, and the gallant of the British army, with the very men who were now engaged in deadly strife, and perhaps bleeding on the ground. Then it was filled with female faces, sparkling with mirth and gaiety; now terror, and anxiety, and grief, were marked upon every countenance we met.[17]

In 1916, in southern England, Prime Minister Herbert Asquith would take his mind off the distant thunder of the barrage heralding the Somme offensive by playing game after game of bridge. The British residents in Brussels in 1815 were in a similar state. Caroline Capel listened with hushed breath.[18] Suspense played tricks with the imagination, or perhaps the wind changed, or the thunderstorm over Ligny added to the distant roar, for listeners in Brussels thought the noise was drawing closer. Charlotte Waldie was convinced of it:

> Heard through the density and stillness of the evening air, the cannonade did, in fact, seem to approach nearer, and become more tremendous. During the whole evening we wandered about the Parc, or stood in silence on the ramparts, listening to the dreadful thunder of the battle. At length it became less frequent. How often did we hope it had ceased, and vainly flatter ourselves that each peal was the last! when, again, after an awful pause, a louder, a longer roar burst on our ears, and it raged more tremendously than ever. To our great relief, about half-past nine, it became fainter and fainter, and at last entirely died away.[19]

The mood in the city during the campaign was unstable and veered between shaky optimism and blind panic. The inhabitants were less uneasy on the morning and afternoon of 17 June as they heard little gunfire. Stories of British heroism at Quatre Bras the previous day were arriving and inspired confidence.[20]

On 17 June, the Secretary of State, Baron de Capellen, started to issue successive bulletins which were attached to the walls of Brussels. These bulletins contained up-to-date news of the situation at the front; some copies are on display today at Le Caillou museum on the battlefield of Waterloo. The first bulletin, which appeared shortly after 7.30 am, was reassuring: 'an officer, who returned from the advanced posts this morning, brings the news that everything is going well ... Our armies will recommence their attack on the enemy today.' A second bulletin at 10.00 am informed its readers that the Battle of Quatre Bras had been bloody but the outcome glorious. The Prince of Orange was in the best of health and while battle was going to begin again that morning, everything gave reason to hope for happy results.[21]

The first wounded soldiers had reached Brussels on the evening of 16 June.[22] On 17 June, the Mayor of Brussels, Baron Vanderlinden d'Hooghvorst, appealed to his citizens to bring mattresses, sheets, blankets and pillows to the Town Hall in the Grand'Place: 'the pressing circumstances in which we find ourselves makes it imperative that people should come to the aid of the army.'[23] Old linen and lint for bandages were to be deposited with priests. Faced with an influx of thousands of wounded troops, the generous people of Brussels did more than their duty. Multitudes of inhabitants went out to meet the injured. Families had become attached to the troops billeted on them before hostilities commenced and now they looked anxiously to see if their soldiers were among the bloodied and exhausted casualties streaming in. Many of the regiments previously stationed at Brussels were Scottish and the Highlanders were great favourites, especially with the children. Some weeks earlier, a woman who had Highlanders quartered in her house had told a British tourist that 'they are such good people, they are as gentle as lambs.' The tourist had assured her that in battle they would be lions.[24]

Soon injured troops filled the city. Many fainted in the streets, drained by their exertions and loss of blood. Practically every house would contain some wounded while barracks and even churches served as temporary hospitals.[25] To help the doctors, chalked words on doors would indicate the numbers and nationalities of the wounded inside.

One of the main casualty stations was the cobbled Grand'Place. Today it contains tourists laughing and dining at restaurants. Sometimes festivities are held in front of the Town Hall. In June 1815, it teemed with mangled humanity. Friend and foe lay indiscriminately side by side on straw. Only hours before they had been hacking at each other with swords and bayonets. Waggons continually drew up to unload more wretches. Paths of empty ground enabled surgeons to reach the sufferers but the tragic scale of their task swamped the professional medics. The ladies of Brussels set to work with the dedication that would characterise Florence Nightingale in the Crimean war forty years later. What they lacked in experience they made up for in beauty and gentleness. 'One lady I noticed particularly', recalled Sergeant Edward Costello of the 95th Rifles. 'She was attended by a servant bearing on his shoulder a kind of pannier, containing warm and cold refreshments: her age I guessed about eighteen, and the peculiarity of the moment made her appear beyond the common order of humanity. She moved along with an eye of lightning, glancing about for those whom she thought most in need of her assistance.'[26]

However, the evening of 17 June brought one of the worst moments for the inhabitants of Brussels. News came of Blücher's defeat at Ligny and of Wellington's retreat to Waterloo, only twelve miles to the south. Baron de Capellen vainly issued his third bulletin at 7.00 pm in an effort to reassure the people:

> According to news which arrived from Headquarters at 6.00 pm, His Serene Highness Prince Blücher, with a view to uniting his army corps with that of General Bülow, has brought his headquarters at Wavre. This movement of the Prussian army corps has determined Field Marshal the Duke of Wellington to concentrate his forces and to establish his headquarters at Waterloo, so as to be constantly ready to carry out his junction with the Prussian armies.
>
> The enemy has made no move since yesterday and his positions are the same. Our troops, only a part of which has been engaged up to now, are in the best dispositions. His Royal Highness the Prince of Orange and His Royal Highness Prince Frederick enjoy the best of health.[27]

Baron de Capellen's attempt to conceal the gravity of the situation failed utterly. He studiously avoided all mention of the serious defeat of the Prussians in battle at Ligny but a swift glance at a map would have shown to anyone that Wellington and Blücher had fallen back to within twelve miles of Brussels.[28] The shock of this retreat was all the greater in that the first two bulletins had stated that the Allies were going to attack the French. Those residents of Brussels who were able to leave, such as Charlotte Waldie, now did so and headed for the port of Antwerp by road or canal. Others were frustrated by the shortage of horses and barges which had been commandeered for the military.[29] Such conveyances as were available were expensive, yet all the banks were closed.[30]

The result of the panic was catastrophic. All the fugitives were single-mindedly intent on self-preservation and the road to Antwerp was clogged. Riders whose horses slipped on the wet cobbles were thrown into the path of merciless waggon wheels and were crushed to death. Peasants looted baggage, made off with valuables and scattered unwanted debris.[31]

At Antwerp, a measure of calm reasserted itself for the fugitives were now over thirty-six miles from Napoleon, the 'Corsican ogre' as he was known. If

Napoleon did defeat the Allies, English ships could easily rescue the British civilians from Antwerp harbour. Nevertheless, eyewitnesses spoke of some scenes of horror at Antwerp as well. An officer's wife was told her husband had been slain at Quatre Bras. She ran hysterically around the market place followed by a small, crying boy and screaming 'my husband is not dead, he is just coming; his head is not shot off.'[32]

Caroline Capel was one of those who had remained at Brussels. She never forgot the horrors of the night of 17/18 June. The rain poured down and wretched, drenched, wounded Brunswick soldiers filled the courtyard of her château in the countryside near Laeken Palace, two and a half miles north of Brussels.

Lieutenant William Ingilby of 'E' Troop, Royal Horse Artillery, left the battlefield of Waterloo towards 4.00 am, at the crack of dawn, with orders to find a route through the Forest of Soignes in case Wellington was beaten in battle and forced to continue his retreat. 'I went into Brussels,' Ingilby remembered. 'The streets were wholly deserted, except by the wounded that were straggling in from the Cavalry affair of yesterday and at Quatre Bras the day before; many of them were lying and seated about the steps of the houses as if unable to proceed further in search of a hospital. I managed to get a hasty breakfast in the Hotel d'Angleterre with a gentleman anxious for news, and who proved to be Admiral Malcolm.'[33]

Ingilby then set off to return to the battlefield and make his report. He took with him a cold fowl for his comrades, whom he knew had nothing. It was 8.00 am.

Fourth Bulletin
According to the latest news, the position of the armies is as follows: the Duke of Wellington has his headquarters at Waterloo. His right wing extends from Braine-l'Alleud along the Forest of Soignes. The left extends towards Wavre, where two Prussian army corps are situated. Marshal Prince Blücher is at Gembloux with the considerable reinforcements he has received. The enemy appears so to fear being attacked that he is entrenched on the Namur chaussée, having made ditches and breastworks in the chaussée.[34]

18 June was a Sunday and in the morning church bells rang all over the city to summon the faithful to mass. But the congregations were preoccupied by their worldly peril. At the Church of St Nicolas the preacher suddenly noticed his flock was beginning to fidget; panic set in and soon the people were rushing out of the church.

Towards noon the long, heavy cannonade, silent since the end of Quatre Bras, began again. Some firing had been heard during Wellington's retreat of 17 June but not the ceaseless roar that was heard now. Inhabitants of Brussels described the sound of the Battle of Waterloo as 'one uninterrupted peal of thunder in their ears for ten hours.'[35] Miss Elizabeth Ord wrote that the day 'was passed in a sort of stupid state of despair.'

Except for sudden, short-lived moments of panic the people in Brussels seemed totally self-controlled. In fact they were desperately frightened and their apparent calm resulted only from their being paralysed by anxiety. Fanny Burney remembered that:

> All the people lived in the streets. Doors seemed of no use, for they were never shut. The individuals, when they re-entered their houses, only resided at the windows: so that the whole population of the city seemed constantly in public view. Not only business as well as society was annihilated, but even every species of occupation. All of which we seemed capable was, to inquire or to relate, to speak or to hear.

Fanny spent the whole campaign visiting the houses of her friends to learn the latest intelligence.[36] Most of it was depressing. Every hour brought news of a British officer killed or wounded.[37] A steady procession of ammunition carts rolled southwards and returned laden with wounded.[38]

Baron de Capellen's bulletins were failing to satisfy the inhabitants, who eagerly believed every rumour. Indeed, de Capellen had so far failed to issue a bulletin since 8.00 am. A British tourist, Captain William Frye, remarked that 'the proclamation of the Baron de Capellen to the inhabitants, wherein he exhorts them to be tranquil and assures them that the Bureaux of Government have not yet quitted Bruxelles, only serves to increase the confusion and consternation.'[39] At 3.00 pm Thomas Creevey decided to walk two miles out of Brussels towards the battle. If he had expected to find much indication of how it was faring, he was soon disappointed. In the suburbs he found people 'sitting about tables drinking beer and smoking and making merry, as if races or other sports were going on, instead of the great pitched battle which was then fighting.'[40]

As the afternoon wore on, reports worsened. Wellington's line was being worn down in a terrible battle of attrition and news of the immense casualties were now reaching Brussels. William Frye was writing a letter:

> The grand conflict has begun with us. It is now four o'clock pm. The issue is not known. The roar of the cannon continues unabated. All is bustle, confusion and uncertainty in this city. Car[t]s with wounded are coming in continually. The general opinion is that our army will be compelled to retreat to Antwerp, and it is even expected that the French will be in Bruxelles to-night. All the townspeople are on the ramparts listening to the sound of the cannon ...
>
> All the caricatures and satires against Napoleon have disappeared from the windows and stalls. The shops are all shut, the English families flying to Antwerp ... The inhabitants in general wish well to the arms of Napoleon, but they know that the retreat of the English Army must necessarily take place

through their town; that our troops will perhaps endeavour to make a stand, and that the consequences will be terrible to the inhabitants, from the houses being liable to be burned or pillaged by friend or foe. All the baggage of our Army and all the military Bureaux have received orders to repair and are now on their march to Antwerp, and the road thither is so covered and blocked up by waggons that the retreat of our Army will be much impeded thereby. Probably my next letter may be dated from a French prison.[41]

A cowardly Hanoverian regiment, the Cumberland Hussars, caused brief but intense terror in the city. The hussars had fled from the second line at Waterloo and now galloped through the Place Royale in Brussels shouting that the French were at their heels. Their cowardice must have been more obvious than the French for Brussels was quiet again 'in an instant', according to Thomas Creevey.[42]

Later, shouting broke out to herald the arrival of French prisoners and two captured eagle standards. Although these captives were escorted by a strong contingent of British heavy cavalry, their French uniforms caused a brief panic. In the Grand'Place inhabitants dashed indoors while a wounded rifleman imperturbably loaded his rifle. Wellington had left the British 81st Foot and some *landwehr* infantry regiments of the Hanoverian reserve in Brussels but their presence seems to have inspired little confidence. The French prisoners were taken to the barracks of Petit-Château, one mile north-west of the Park. Some were then transported by canal to Antwerp. 'The poor fellows cut a sorry figure,' thought Edward Healey. 'They must have fought gallantly for scarcely one of them had a hat or cap on, and nearly all of them were more or less wounded, principally sabre wounds. They were all drenched to the skin with rain and covered with mud. A few thoughtless people insulted them, with "Where's Boney now?" and such like, but speaking generally they were more pitied than anything else.'[43]

Brussels remained without news of the outcome well after nightfall. Women went to sleep in their clothes in case they were suddenly woken with news of the arrival of French troops in the city.[44] Some Belgian inhabitants were praying for a French victory to free them from their union with Holland in the Kingdom of the United Netherlands. The Bonapartist family of Tresigny had prepared a great supper to welcome Napoleon.[45]

At 4.00 am on 19 June Thomas Creevey peered out of his window and noted troops and baggage marching south up the rue de Namur from the Place Royale, towards the battlefield. This seemed a favourable sign and, indeed, two hours later he learnt of Napoleon's defeat.[46] Creevey insisted that the first news reached Brussels around 3.00 am but Lady Georgiana Lennox and Edward Healey both asserted that the news of the victory reached Brussels, if not Creevey, in the late evening of 18 June.[47] The inquisitive Creevey, who moved in the most prestigious circles and usually was well informed of the latest developments, seems to have been one of the last Britons in Brussels to learn of the victory.

Soon copies of Baron de Capellen's fifth bulletin were appearing on the walls. De Capellen had proved no less nervous than those he sought to reassure. At 8.00 pm on 18 June he had left Brussels and ridden fourteen miles northwards to the comparative safety of Malines, where he arrived in the early hours of 19 June and learned of the victory at Waterloo. De Capellen promptly had his fifth bulletin printed at the works of P.J. Hanicq and fraudulently addressed 'Brussels 19 June 1815 at 3.00 am.' He then returned to Brussels. It is only fair to state that de Capellen's move had been urged by Wellington's Austrian liaison officer, Baron de Vincent, who had returned from the battlefield of Waterloo wounded in the hand. Nevertheless, the departure of someone of de Capellen's position can hardly have calmed the situation in Brussels.[48]

### Fifth Bulletin

His Royal Highness the Prince of Orange has arrived in Brussels. The precious life of this hero, who contributed so much in the course of yesterday and who has just acquired so many new claims to our affection, to our gratitude, has been preserved in spite of the continuous danger to which it has been exposed. However, towards 8.00 pm, His Royal Highness was struck by a musket-ball which passed through his left arm at the shoulder. The wound is not dangerous and His Royal Highness' health has not suffered. Yesterday's battle has been bloody and the result outstanding. The army of Field Marshal the Duke of Wellington has covered itself with glory. Our armies have won a complete victory. The enemy has been totally beaten and routed. He has lost more than one hundred cannon. Marshal Prince Blücher has joined the Duke of Wellington and their armies are pursuing the enemy beyond Genappe.[49]

At 11.00 am Creevey was outside Wellington's house in the rue Royale, hoping to catch a glimpse of the victor. The Duke had ridden in from Waterloo to finish his victory despatch. Now he noticed Creevey in the street outside and beckoned to him. In a short while Creevey was enjoying the privilege of hearing about the great victory from Wellington himself. 'It has been a damned serious business', declared the Duke. 'Blücher and I have lost 30,000 men. It has been a damned nice thing – the nearest run thing you ever saw in your life.'

'By God!' he added as a thought suddenly struck him. 'I don't think it would have done if I had not been there.'[50] Later he joined the Duke of Richmond and Lady Georgiana Lennox in the park outside. 'He looked sad,' thought Georgiana, 'and when we shook hands and congratulated him, he said, "It is a dearly bought victory. We have lost so many fine fellows."'[51]

At noon, Baron de Capellen issued his sixth bulletin to announce the arrival of Wellington in Brussels, to confirm that the victory of Waterloo was complete and decisive and to urge the inhabitants to continue their care for the wounded.[52]

Victory brought welcome relief to Brussels from the tensions of the past three days. The inhabitants had not suffered physically but their psychological plight had been acute. Even so, wrote Miss Elizabeth Ord, 'I think it was not till it was all over that the consciousness of what we had escaped came upon us in its full force.'[53] On 20 June, inhabitants sang 'Te Deum Laudamus' to thank God for the deliverance of Brussels and the victory of Waterloo.[54] Later, a requiem mass was said at the Cathedral of Saints Michael and Gudule for those of all nationalities who had lost their lives in the short campaign.

Brussels remained a vast hospital station and morgue for weeks after the battle. The authorities had requisitioned all the carriages in Brussels to remove the injured from the battlefield and the influx of casualties continued unabated.[55] Hundreds of dead horses lay in the streets and three thousand human corpses on the ramparts. There was simply no time or space to bury them. Ladies were constantly busy making lint for the wounded while civilian and military surgeons had rushed from England to assist by carrying out amputations. One of these new arrivals, Charles Bell, described how 'it was a strange thing to feel my clothes stiff with blood, and my arms powerless with the exertion of using the knife! and more extraordinary still, to find my mind calm amidst such variety of suffering; but to give one of these objects access to your feelings was to allow yourself to be unmanned for the performance of a duty.'[56]

The surgeons cared for the casualties regardless of nationality but those responsible for collecting the wounded from the battlefields and transporting them to the hospitals sought the allied casualties first. Consequently wounded Frenchmen were still being collected a week after the battle. Let one of those wretched Frenchmen tell of the care he received from the inhabitants of Brussels. He was Major Jean-Baptiste Jolyet of the 1st Light infantry and had been wounded at Waterloo by a musket-ball in the stomach. Eventually he received preliminary treatment at the Auberge du roi d'espagne at Genappe, a village four miles south of the battlefield. Then his Prussian captors loaded him on to a cart and sent him along the main road to Brussels:

As we left the Forest of Soignes we were greeted by the delegates of the Corporation of Hatters of Brussels, who offered us bread and wine and commiserated with us. This meeting gave us a pleasant surprise. Soon the cart arrived in Brussels and passed through the streets in the midst of the curious people. Some insulted us but most were very friendly and gave us shredded linen, tobacco and refreshments. Hardly were we settled in the attics of Petit-Château {barracks} than the ladies of Brussels in great number brought us provisions, wine, cordials, stock, linen etc. All day came a procession of these good and charitable ladies, who added encouragements and consolations to their gifts. It was the same the following day but the English felt some jealousy at this and the ladies could not visit us more than some moments each day. Certainly all those who, like myself, were wounded and dispirited by seven days' suffering and were comforted by these visits and affections, will retain forever a cordial and sincere gratitude for the ladies of Brussels.[57]

Only in mid-July did the pestilential air of Brussels clear; many of the wounded were now encamped outside the city or evacuated to other locations, particularly Antwerp. On the evening of 29 June, Major Jolyet left Brussels for Antwerp and from there sailed as a prisoner-of-war to England. On 29 December 1815, following the Treaty of Paris on 20 November which formally concluded peace, he finally returned to France and landed at Le Havre.

For months after Waterloo, Brussels remained a ghost of its former self, for Wellington's officers had marched with the army on Paris. The park where they had once strolled with the ladies was deserted. English society, fearful of diseases which might follow the influx of casualties to Brussels, had fled to the healthier resorts of Spa and Paris.[58]

# Notes

1. T. Fleischman and W. Aerts, *Bruxelles pendant la bataille de Waterloo* (1956), p.155
2. Marquess of Anglesey ed., *The Capel letters 1814–17* (1955), p.102
3. G. Barral, *Itinéraire illustré de l'épopée de Waterloo* (1896), p.117
4. J. Gurwood ed., *The dispatches of the Duke of Wellington* (1838), v.12, p.358
5. H. Maxwell ed., *The Creevey papers* (1904), v.1, p.228
6. C. Gardyne, *The life of a regiment* (1901), p.424
7. See W. Fraser, *The Waterloo Ball* (1897); *The Times*, 22 August 1890, 26 August 1890, 19 September 1890, 1 October 1890; T. Fleischman and W. Aerts, *Bruxelles pendant la bataille de Waterloo* (1956), p.224
8. E. Richardson ed., *Long forgotten days (leading to Waterloo)* (1928), p.374
9. BL Add. MSS 34,706/293
10. J. Kincaid, *Adventures in the Rifle Brigade and random shots from a rifleman* (1909), p.154
11. D. Chandler, *On the Napoleonic Wars* (1994), p.219
12. 'Recollections of Waterloo by a staff officer', in *United Service Magazine* (1847, Part III)
13. J. Anton, *Retrospect of a military life* (1841), p.186; Lieutenant Robert Winchester of the 92nd Highlanders asserted the troops received several days' rations of biscuit: BL Add. MSS 34,706/244; Lieutenant Alexander Riddock of the 44th stated that the troops received three days' bread plus an allowance of spirits: BL Add. MSS 34,706/293
14. C. Eaton, *Waterloo days* (1888), pp.21–4
15. F. d'Arblay, *Diary and letters of Madame d'Arblay* (1854), v.7, p.119; Fanny Burney stated in her diary at this point that she knew the Brunswickers were destined for a battle yet on page 120 she asserted that she did not yet know the campaign had begun.
16. BL Add. MSS 34,706/29
17. C. Eaton, *Waterloo days* (1888), p.26
18. Marquess of Anglesey ed., *The Capel letters* (1955), p.112
19. C. Eaton, *Waterloo days* (1888), p.29
20. J. Gore ed., *Creevey's life and times* (1937), p.87
21. T. Fleischman and W. Aerts, *Bruxelles pendant la bataille de Waterloo* (1956), pp.143–4
22. D. Chandler, *On the Napoleonic wars* (1994), p.220
23. A. Brett-James, *The hundred days* (1964), p.196; T. Fleischman and W. Aerts, *Bruxelles pendant la bataille de Waterloo* (1956), p.144
24. W. Frye, *After Waterloo. Reminiscences of European travel 1815–1819* (1908), p.9
25. W. Aerts and L. Wilmet, *18 Juin 1815. Waterloo. L'attaque de la Garde. Les derniers carrés. La déroute* (1904), p.89

26. E. Costello, *Adventures of a soldier, written by himself* (1852), pp.195–6

27. T. Fleischman and W. Aerts, *Bruxelles pendant la bataille de Waterloo* (1956), p.147

28. The people of Brussels were certainly aware from other sources that the Prussians had been beaten: Marquess of Anglesey ed., *The Capel letters* (1955), p.114; de Capellen's closing sentence about the health of the two Dutch princes is reminiscent of Napoleon's notorious bulletin after the catastrophic retreat from Moscow in 1812: 'His Majesty's health has never been better'.

29. F. d'Arblay, *Diary and letters of Madame d'Arblay* (1854), v.7, p.122–8

30. Marquess of Anglesey ed., *The Capel letters* (1955), pp.114–15

31. J. Simpson, *Paris after Waterloo* (1853), p.20

32. *Idem*

33. H. Siborne ed., *The Waterloo letters* (1983), p.197

34. T. Fleischman and W. Aerts, *Bruxelles pendant la bataille de Waterloo* (1956), p.154; the position of Wellington's army is correctly described but the rest of the bulletin is inaccurate. At this stage the whole of Blücher's army was around Wavre or on the march to Waterloo, and Gembloux was in French hands. The French on the Nivelles–Namur chaussée were certainly not in fear of being attacked.

35. J. Simpson, *Paris after Waterloo* (1853), p.19

36. F. d'Arblay, *Diary and letters of Madame d'Arblay* (1854), v.7, pp.121, 124–5, 128

37. J. Gore ed., *Creevey's life and times* (1937), pp.87–8

38. D. Chandler, *On the Napoleonic wars* (1994), p.222

39. W. Frye, *After Waterloo. Reminiscences of European travel 1815–1819* (1908), p.25; de Capellen made his reference to having made no preparation to depart in his First Bulletin, issued at 7.00 am on 17 June.

40. H. Maxwell ed., *The Creevey papers* (1904), v.1, p.232

41. W. Frye, *After Waterloo. Reminiscences of European travel 1815–1819* (1908), pp.24–5

42. H. Maxwell ed., *The Creevey papers* (1904), p.232–3

43. W. Aerts and L. Wilmet, *18 Juin 1815. Waterloo. L'attaque de la Garde. Les derniers carrés. La déroute* (1904), p.89; letter of Lieutenant John Linton of the 6th (Inniskilling) Dragoons: BL Add. MSS 34,705/239; BL Add. MSS 34,707/61; D. Chandler, *On the Napoleonic wars* (1994), p.224

44. J. Gore, *Creevey's life and times* (1937), p.88

45. G. de Ros, 'Personal recollections of the great Duke of Wellington', in *Murray's Magazine* (1889), v.5, no.25, p.43

46. H. Maxwell ed., *The Creevey papers* (1904), v.1, p.235

47. *Murray's Magazine* (1889), v.5, no.25, p.44; D. Chandler, *On the Napoleonic wars* (1994), p.224. T. Fleischman and W. Aerts, the two authorities on Brussels during the campaign, stated that the news arrived at 10.00 pm: *Bruxelles pendant la bataille de Waterloo* (1956), p.160. According to Captain William Frye, the news of the victory circulated through Brussels early in the morning of 19 June: W. Frye, *After Waterloo. Reminiscences of European travel 1815–1819* (1908), p.26.

48. In later years the baron would deny he had ever left the city, in spite of his fifth bulletin bearing the words 'the printing works of P.J. Hanicq at Malines'. It is noteworthy that in his first bulletin, of 7.00 am on 17 June, de Capellen wrote, 'I declare that up to now I am making no preparation to leave.' See Bibliotheque Royale, *Waterloo 1815*, p.65; T. Fleischman and W. Aerts, *Bruxelles pendant la bataille de Waterloo* (1956), pp.158–9

49. T. Fleischman and W. Aerts, *Bruxelles pendant la bataille de Waterloo* (1956), p.166; it is interesting to note Baron de Capellen dwells so long at the beginning of his bulletin on the Prince of Orange before announcing the victory. Perhaps like Winston Churchill announcing the D-Day landings to the House of Commons on 6 June 1944 he wished, mischievously, to keep his audience in suspense. Churchill achieved this by describing the news from Normandy only after dwelling at length on the importance of the capture of Rome on 4 June. Alternatively, de Capellen was merely being loyal to the House of Orange; furthermore, laudatory statements such as these would help distract attention from his flight to Malines on 18 June.

50. H. Maxwell ed., *The Creevey papers* (1904), v.1, pp.236–7

51. *Murray's Magazine*, (1889), v.5, no.25, p.45

52. T. Fleischman and W. Aerts, *Bruxelles pendant la bataille de Waterloo* (1956), pp.167–8

53. J. Gore ed., *Creevey's life and times* (1937), p.86

54. W. Aerts and L. Wilmet, *18 Juin 1815. Waterloo. L'attaque de la Garde. Les derniers carrés. La déroute* (1904), p.91

55. W. Frye, *After Waterloo. Reminiscences of European travel 1815–1819* (1908), p.28

56. A. Brett-James, *The hundred days* (1964), p.203

57. 'Souvenirs de 1815' in *Revue de Paris* (Sept–Oct 1903), p.549

58. Marquess of Anglesey ed., *The Capel letters* (1955), pp.119–28; the best examination of the care of the wounded after the 1815 campaign is Edgar Evrard's fine chapter in J. Logie et al., *Waterloo 1815: l'Europe face à Napoléon* (1990).

Wellington's residence in the rue Royale, Brussels

# 18

# THE BRITISH MONUMENT AT EVERE CEMETERY

Apart from a memorial tablet of 1858 in the Royal Chapel at Waterloo, the only monument in Belgium to all those of the British Army who fell in the 1815 campaign is at the Evere cemetery in the north-eastern suburbs of Brussels. You can reach Evere from the city centre by bus 63 from the Place du Congrès. The cemetery is open from 8.30 am to 4.30 pm but is usually closed on Mondays. You reach the monument from the entrance gates at the south-west corner of the cemetery by walking along the 8th avenue beneath the tall red brick wall which forms the southern boundary of the burial plots.

The monument is hallowed ground for within its vault lie the remains of British soldiers. The monument, of red Treves sandstone, is nine metres long and four wide. Britannia, surrounded by three bronze lions, by helmets and flags, kneels at an altar, mourning her sons and holding her helmet with one hand while lowering her trident in salute with the other. Beneath the statue of Britannia is the Latin inscription *mortuorum patria memor*: the country mindful of its dead.

You descend to the vault by one of two flights of stone steps. On either side of the entrance are affixed bronze shields listing the British regiments who fought at Waterloo. Above the entrance you read the dedication:

IN MEMORY
of the British officers non-commissioned officers
& men who fell during the WATERLOO CAMPAIGN in 1815
& whose remains were transferred to this cemetery in 1889.
This Monument is erected by Her Britannic Majesty
Queen Victoria, Empress of India, & by their Countrymen
on a site generously presented by the City of Brussels.

The monument was unveiled by the Duke of Cambridge, Commander-in-Chief of the British Army, on 26 August 1890. In spite of poor weather, all the British residents in Brussels attended, together with the Lord Mayor of London, the Burgomaster of Brussels, General Baron de Rennette representing King

Leopold II of the Belgians and Captain Robin representing the Belgian Ministry of War. Six sergeants whose fathers or grandfathers had fought at Waterloo also attended as representatives of the British rank and file.[1] Such was the emotion evoked in Britain by the memorial that the Belgian Mail Steam Packet Company had announced that it was offering special facilities on the Dover to Ostend route for travellers wishing to attend the imminent inauguration.[2]

After a solemn religious service, Lord Vivian, chairman of the English Committee in Belgium for the erection of the monument, read an address to the Duke of Cambridge. Lord Vivian was the grandson of Lieutenant-General Sir Hussey Vivian, commander of a light cavalry brigade at Waterloo. In his address, Lord Vivian described the genesis of the idea of the monument:

Your Royal Highness, – In the year 1887 the Municipal Council of Brussels decreed the immediate closing of all the old cemeteries, and the transfer of the remains interred therein to the new cemetery at Evere.

In these cemeteries lay the remains of many British officers and men who had either fallen on the field of Waterloo or died from wounds received in the battle, and we, British residents in Belgium, considered that it would be unworthy of all the traditions of our country to allow the ashes of its soldiers, who had died for it, to be scattered abroad without thought or care for their memory.

The year 1887 was the anniversary of the 50th year of the reign of our gracious Queen, and we felt that our loyal sympathy with this auspicious event could not be better marked than by the erection of a monument to the memory of men who had fought and died for their Sovereign and their country.

Committees were accordingly formed at Brussels and Antwerp, and subsequently at London, for the collection of subscriptions, and appeals were made to the British Government and nation in favour of the scheme.

These appeals received a generous response both in England and Belgium.

The Queen, his Royal Highness the Prince of Wales, and your Royal Highness were the first to come forward, her Majesty heading the list with a large subscription. At the instance of her Majesty's Government, Parliament voted a grant of £500 out of public funds in aid of the project; the Army, the City of London, the British communities in Belgium, and several private persons subscribed liberally, and in the end a sum amounting to £2,467 was collected, which has almost sufficed to defray the cost of the construction and erection of the monument, there being only a small deficit to be made good.

This cost would have been much heavier but for the munificence of the Municipality of Brussels, who have not only made us a free gift of the site, but have also undertaken the preservation of the monument, and for the generosity of Count de Lalaing, who has declined any remuneration for the great pains and labour he has devoted to a work which has enlisted all his sympathy.

The net cost has been further considerably reduced by the substitution of the galvano-plastic process for that of casting, by which a large saving has been effected, and by employment of Kylberg stone instead of granite for the base of the monument. Before deciding to adopt these economies the committee were careful to satisify themselves that they would in no way impair the excellence or durability of the work.

The remains of 15 British officers and one non-commissioned officer have been transferred from their former resting-places in the old Brussels cemeteries, at Hougoumont and at Quatre Bras to the vaults under the monument, where tablets record their names and the regiments to which they belonged. We are deeply indebted to the municipal authorities for the reverent care with which they effected the removal and re-interment of these remains, under the super-intendence of our committee.

The monument which your Royal Highness is about to unveil is intended as a national memorial to our soldiers of all ranks who fell in the Waterloo campaign, and as a lasting record of their country's grateful recollection of their gallant conduct; no other feeling would be in harmony with the repose of this sanctuary, where human passions are hushed in the presence of death, or with our cordial feeling towards the great nation with which 75 years of peaceful and friendly intercourse have effaced all bitter recollections of former strife.

On behalf of the General Committee,

VIVIAN, Chairman.

The Duke of Cambridge expressed his gratitude to those who had made the monument possible, after which the Burgomaster of Brussels promised that his municipality would faithfully preserve the monument.[3] The municipality has fulfilled its promise. If the monument has been neglected then it is by the British themselves. You are likely to find no wreaths or flowers. In the days after the monument's inauguration, the art critics of the great Brussels journals unanimously agreed that the monument was an original work of artistic genius. *The Times* was also enthusiastic and averred that 'the site could not have been better selected.'[4]

The Waterloo heroes transferred to the vault were:

Colonel Sir William Howe de Lancey, *Deputy Quartermaster-General*

Lieutenant-Colonel the Hon. Sir Alexander Gordon, *ADC to the Duke of Well-ington*

Lieutenant-Colonel William Henry Milnes, *1st Foot Guards*

Major William John Lloyd, *Royal Artillery*

Major Archibald John Maclean, *73rd Foot*

Captain Thomas Brown, *1st Foot Guards*

Captain Edward Grose, *1st Foot Guards*

Captain William Stothert, *3rd Foot Guards*

Captain the Hon. Hastings Forbes, *3rd Foot Guards*

Captain John Lucie Blackman, *2nd Foot Guards*

Lieutenant Michael T. Cromie, *Royal Artillery*

Lieutenant Charles Spearman, *Royal Artillery*

Lieutenant the Hon. Samuel Shute Barrington, *1st Foot Guards*

Lieutenant John Clyde, *23rd Royal Welsh Fusiliers*
Ensign James Lord Hay, *1st Foot Guards, ADC*
Sergeant-Major Cotton, *7th Hussars*

In 1895, the remains of Lieutenant-Colonel Edward Stables of the 1st Guards joined those of his valiant comrades at Evere. He had been disinterred from his old tomb in the garden of a house at Joli-Bois, a small hamlet between the battlefield and the town of Waterloo. In 1992 his empty and dismantled tomb was restored by Belgian paratroopers.

When the old graves of these men were opened, their skeletons were found well preserved and these were placed in zinc coffins bearing the names of the heroes. The coffins were buried provisionally at Evere until they could be moved into the vault on completion of the monument. Three of the old tombstones were also brought to Evere. Two are now on the bank opposite the entrance of the vault and the third, de Lancey's, is on the north side of the monument.

*The Times* reported with satisfaction that 'these operations were carried out with much reverent care.' It also remarked upon the surprising height of the skeletons. On 28 May 1890, its correspondent reported: 'Sir A. Gordon, I observed, had suffered amputation of the thigh, and Captain Forbes had been shot through the head. Both must have been very tall men.'

While you are in the vault, you may care to reflect on the lives of three of the gallant men buried within its walls: Sergeant-Major Edward Cotton, Ensign James Lord Hay and Colonel Sir William Howe de Lancey. They represent the honourable conduct of the British soldier and the terrible tragedy of war.

Cotton was born on the Isle of Wight around 1792 and served at Waterloo in the ranks of the 7th Hussars. He particularly distinguished himself by saving Hussar Gilmore of his regiment who lay trapped under his wounded horse in front of the main line. Cotton could see the French cuirassiers coming on again and, knowing that they rarely spared a foe outside the protection of the infantry squares, he sprang from his saddle and ran forward. He managed to extricate Gilmore and to bring him back to safety just as the tide of French horsemen rushed up to Wellington's line.

After leaving the army, Cotton lived at Mont St Jean village where he soon gained a reputation as a fine battlefield guide. In 1845, the *Naval and Military Gazette* described him as 'an intelligent, active, good-looking man of fifty-three years of age, and the very cut of a hussar.' From the many fellow Waterloo veterans who visited the field, Cotton built up a formidable knowledge of the battle and published an excellent book called *A Voice from Waterloo*. His collection of relics occupied a building at the foot of the Lion Mound but has now been dispersed.

'I sincerely hope' wrote one veteran, Lieutenant-General Sir Hussey Vivian, to Cotton in 1839, 'that from the occupation which you have undertaken, you will derive the means of passing the remainder of your days in competence and comfort; and thus reap the reward of your intelligence, on a field where you had previously proved your courage.' Cotton died on 24 June 1849. He had been ill for some time but had soldiered on and only two days before his death he had shown an English family round the battlefield.[5]

Cotton was buried in the garden of Hougoumont, and rested there until 18 August 1890 when he was disinterred for reburial at Evere. Sister Stanislas, superior of *Soeurs de Marie* convent at Braine-l'Alleud and daughter of the sergeant-major, was present at the ceremony.[6]

Now move over to the tablet inscribed with the name of James Lord Hay, who died three weeks short of his eighteenth birthday. He was a fine, spirited officer serving as ADC to Major-General Peregrine Maitland, the commander of the 1st brigade of Guards. Caroline Capel remembered Lord Hay as 'one of the finest young men I ever saw.'[7] Ensign George Keppel of the 14th Foot recalled seeing him win a horse race at Grammont on 13 June:

> I was standing close to Lord Uxbridge, when a cheer from the neighbourhood of the judge's stand announced the winner of the sweepstakes. I thought I had hardly ever seen so handsome a lad. He was beaming with health and spirits, as he took his places in the scales in his gay jockey dress. It was Lord Hay, an ensign in the First Regiment of Guards, and aide-de-camp to General P. Maitland. The races were on a Tuesday; on the Friday young Hay was killed at Quatre Bras.[8]

History records one other image of Hay's last days – at the Duchess of Richmond's Ball on the eve of his death. Lady Georgiana Lennox, one of the duchess' daughters, lamented that 'it was a dreadful evening, taking leave of friends and acquaintances, many never to be seen again ... I remember being quite provoked with poor Lord Hay, a dashing, merry youth, full of military ardour, for his delight at the idea of going into action, and of all the honours he was to gain.'[9]

The first news to reach Lady Georgiana from the front on 16 June was that Lord Hay was dead. He had been picked off soon after entering the Battle of Quatre Bras by a French skirmisher who in turn was killed by one of Maitland's guardsmen. Lord Hay was acting as adjutant to Lord Saltoun, a distinguished officer of the 1st Guards. It was upon the neck of Saltoun's horse that Hay's body toppled before falling to the ground.

Some time before the opening of hostilities, Hay had spoken with Caroline Capel's daughter, Maria, who was the same age as himself. Maria's nickname was Muzzy and Hay had named his favourite mare after her. 'Remember,' he told her laughingly, 'I shall fall in the first action and I shall fall on Miss Muzzy; if I have time to speak I shall send her to you, and you must always keep her.'[10]

Besides Lord Hay, three other officers of the 1st Guards laid down their lives for their country at Quatre Bras. They were Captains Edward Grose and

Thomas Brown and Ensign the Hon. Samuel Barrington. The remains of all three also repose in the Evere monument's vault. Ensign Robert Batty witnessed their burial at Quatre Bras on the morning of 17 June 1815:

> We succeeded in finding the bodies of our four officers ... and had the satisfaction of paying the last tribute of respect to their remains. They were buried near the wood [of Bossu], and one of our officers read the service over them. Never did I witness a scene more imposing: those breasts which had, a few hours back, boldly encountered the greatest perils, did not now disdain to be subdued by pity and affection; and if the ceremony wanted the real clerical solemnity due to its sacred character, it received an ample equivalent in this mark of genuine regard, and the sincerity with which we wished them a more immortal halo than that which honour will confer.[11]

Finally, find the tablet to Colonel Sir William Howe de Lancey. He was Wellington's Deputy Quartermaster-General and had married the beautiful Lady Magdalene only a short while before Waterloo, on 4 April 1815. Their brief time together forms the greatest love story of the campaign. 'How active and how well I was!' wrote Magdalene. 'I scarcely knew what to do with all my health and spirits. Now and then a pang would cross my mind at the prospect of the approaching campaign, but I chased away the thought, resolved not to lose the present bliss by dwelling on the chance of future pain.'[12]

The start of hostilities took the de Lanceys by surprise and shattered their happiness forever. On 15 June Magdalene watched silently as her husband laboriously wrote out all the orders for Wellington's units to march to meet Napoleon. Early next morning they leaned together out of the window of their Brussels house in the fresh air as the troops marched by in the street below. Then they parted, William to go with the army and Magdalene to the relative safety of Antwerp, ready to escape by sea to England if Napoleon should win.

A succession of terrors assailed Magdalene as different rumours arrived from the front. She could do nothing except wait and pray for her husband's preservation.

At 4.00 pm on 18 June, William was riding beside Wellington when a cannon-ball whizzed past. Although the ball did not strike William, it passed so close that the rush of air knocked him from his horse and separated all the ribs on his left side from the backbone. He was still alive, much to Wellington's amazement, and was carried back to the village of Waterloo.

When Magdalene heard that William was lying grievously wounded she set out for Brussels only to be told on the way that William was dead. Magdalene returned in grief to Antwerp and at first refused to believe subsequent news that in fact William was still alive and might recover. After many tribulations, but also much help from kind, well-placed friends, Magdalene finally regained William's side in a cottage.

She cared for him as best she could, helping to apply leeches to drain blood from his terrible injuries but soon she saw he was not to recover. Even a visit by Wellington failed to rouse William. 'Poor fellow!' the Duke later reminisced. 'We knew each other ever since we were boys. But I had no time to be sorry. I went on with the army and never saw him again.'[13]

'He grew more uneasy,' recalled Magdalene, 'he was restless and uncomfortable; his breathing was like choking, and as I sat gazing at him I could distinctly hear the water rattling in his throat.' Later he gave a little gulp and a doctor murmured 'he is gone.'[14] It was the evening of 26 June; the de Lanceys had been married for just three months.

'There was such perfect peace and placid calm sweetness in his countenance, that I envied him not a little,' sighed Magdalene. 'He was released; I was left to suffer.'[15] William was buried in the Protestant cemetery of St Josse Ten Noode in Brussels, from where he was moved to Evere three-quarters of a century later. 'I had a stone placed,' wrote Magdalene, 'with simply his name and the circumstances of his death.' This stone you can see today in front of the statue of Britannia on the Evere monument.

Magdalene retired to England, 'in a violence of grief ... more like delerium than the sorrow of a Christian.' She remarried in 1817 but died just five years later. She had written an account of her experiences which came to the notice of the novelist Charles Dickens. Like all readers of her narrative, he was profoundly affected. 'If I live for fifty years,' he wrote, 'I shall dream of it every now and then, from this hour to the day of my death, with the most frightful reality.'[16]

It is a pity Magdalene's remains could not be brought to rest with William's at Evere.

## Notes

1. *The Times*, 27 August 1890
2. *The Times*, 22 August 1890
3. *The Times*, 27 August 1890
4. *The Times*, 29 August 1890, 27 August 1890
5. C. Dalton, *The Waterloo roll call* (1978), p.269 and *The Times*, 3 July 1849
6. *The Times*, 20 August 1890
7. Marquess of Anglesey ed., *The Capel letters* (1955), p.113
8. G. Thomas, Earl of Albemarle, *Fifty years of my life* (1877), p.136
9. *Murray's Magazine*, (1889), v.5, no.25, p.43
10. Marquess of Anglesey ed., *The Capel letters* (1955), p.113
11. G. Jones, *The Battle of Waterloo* (1852), p.39
12. B. Ward ed., *A week at Waterloo in 1815* (1906), pp.40–1
13. E. Longford, *Wellington: pillar of state* (1972), p.5
14. B. Ward ed., *A week at Waterloo in 1815* (1906), p.97
15. *Ibid*, p.99
16. *Ibid*, p.125

# PART SIX: THE LAST SHOTS OF THE 1815 CAMPAIGN

# 19

# THE BATTLE OF WAVRE

W hile Blücher assaulted Napoleon's flank at Waterloo, the Prussian III
Corps had been fighting a tough rearguard action at Wavre. The corps
commander, Lieutenant-General Baron Johann von Thielmann, had established a defence line along the River Dyle to protect the rear of Blücher's army
as it marched to Waterloo. On 17 June Napoleon had ordered Marshal
Grouchy to pursue the defeated Prussians from the battlefield of Ligny. At first
Grouchy assumed the Prussians were recoiling north-eastwards. Only in the
night of 17/18 June did he discover that a host of them were at Wavre.
Grouchy reckoned these troops had halted at Wavre before continuing their
retreat on Brussels and did not imagine that they might attempt a cross-
country march over very difficult terrain to unite with Wellington at Waterloo.
Thus on the morning of 18 June Grouchy directed his march to Wavre. His
leading troops appeared south of Wavre towards 3.00 pm.

Thielmann had just 15,000 men and 35 guns with which to hold at bay
Grouchy's 33,000 troops and 96 guns. He retained the bulk of his III Corps in
reserve, north of the Dyle valley. His headquarters were at the Château of La
Bawette, 1400 metres north of Wavre. Near the château stood Thielmann's
Reserve Cavalry under Major-General von Hobe. Further forward were the
infantry brigades, each of which had two cavalry squadrons and an artillery
battery attached to it. Behind Wavre were 10th and 11th brigades while 12th
brigade was at the village of Bierges.

Only advanced posts and skirmishers lined the Dyle itself. The river was
swollen after the heavy storms of the previous night and was impassable except
by several bridges. The Prussian eastern flank rested on the village of Basse-
Wavre. This post was held by sharpshooters, who destroyed the wooden bridge
here. On the Prussian west wing lay the mill of Bierges, which guarded a
wooden bridge. A company of the 31st Infantry garrisoned this mill, which
stood on the north bank of the Dyle.

In between these two wings was Wavre, which rested mainly on the north
bank. A suburb stood on the south side. The main bridge at Wavre was the
stone Bridge of Christ, which was barricaded with three waggons and a dozen
big barrels. These obstacles were found with difficulty, for the inhabitants of

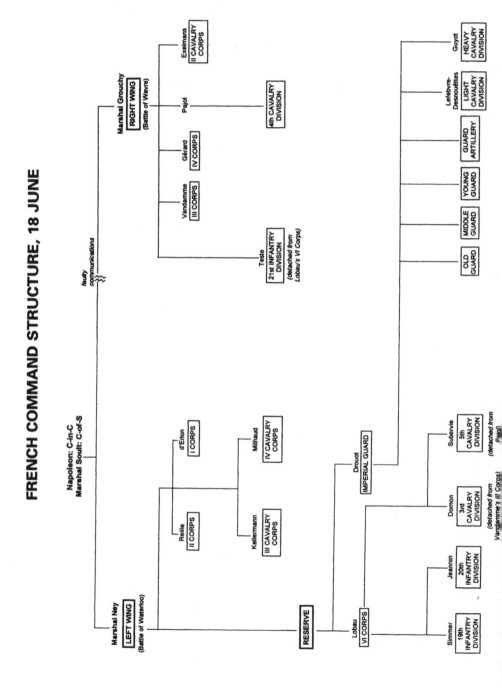

FRENCH COMMAND STRUCTURE, 18 JUNE

Napoleon: C-in-C
Marshal Soult: C-of-S

*faulty communications*

Marshal Ney
LEFT WING
(Battle of Waterloo)

Reille
II CORPS

d'Erlon
I CORPS

Kellermann
III CAVALRY CORPS

Milhaud
IV CAVALRY CORPS

Marshal Grouchy
RIGHT WING
(Battle of Wavre)

Vandamme
III CORPS

Gérard
IV CORPS

Pajol

Exelmans
II CAVALRY CORPS

4th CAVALRY DIVISION

Teste
21st INFANTRY DIVISION
*(detached from Lobau's VI Corps)*

RESERVE

Lobau
VI CORPS

Simmer
19th INFANTRY DIVISION

Jeannin
20th INFANTRY DIVISION

Domon
3rd CAVALRY DIVISION
*(detached from Vandamme's III Corps)*

Subervie
5th CAVALRY DIVISION
*(detached from Pajol)*

Drouot
IMPERIAL GUARD

OLD GUARD

MIDDLE GUARD

YOUNG GUARD

GUARD ARTILLERY

Lefebvre-Desnouëttes
LIGHT CAVALRY DIVISION

Guyot
HEAVY CAVALRY DIVISION

**Above:** The Chapelle St Robert, in front of which the Prussian IV and II Corps marched on their way to the Battle of Waterloo.

**Below:** The Farm de la Kelle: a view from the bottom of the Lasne defile. Blücher's troops struggled down these steep, muddy slopes to cross the River Lasne.

**Above:** Paris Wood: Bülow's IV Corps formed up along this track and amidst the trees on either side ready to debouch on to the battlefield at 4.30 pm.

**Below:** Prussian infantry at the 1995 re-enactment.

**Above:** General Baron Friedrich Wilhelm Bülow, Count von Dennewitz, issues orders during the battle; his IV Corps bore the brunt of the fighting in the Prussian sector.

**Below:** As the Prussian IV Corps debouched from Paris Wood and advanced towards Plancenoit village, they could see the French cavalry charging against Wellington. This photograph was taken 1500 metres north-east of the Prussian monument. Note the Lion Mound on the horizon and, immediately in front, the farm of La Haie Sainte.

**Opposite page:** The Prussian 15th Infantry of 16th brigade storm into Plancenoit village. The defenders are men of the 1st battalion, 2nd Grenadiers of the Old Guard.

**Above:** Plancenoit village is in flames as Prussian infantry charge across open ground north of the church.

**Below:** Plancenoit village from the north. In the background is the spire of the church; in the foreground stands a monument to the French Young Guard.

**Above:** Plancenoit church as it is today.

**Below:** The Prussian monument north of Plancenoit.

**Above:** The Chapelle Jacques north-east of the battlefield. The advanced guard of the Prussian I Corps reached this point in the evening, minutes before its decisive intervention in the front line. Note the Lion Mound in the background. This chapel is not the one that stood here in 1815.

**Below:** The pursuit after Waterloo: Gneisenau mounted an infantry drummer on horseback to keep the French fugitives running. French prisoners trudge dejectedly northwards on the left.

**Above:** The Bridge of Christ at Wavre. The River Dyle flows beneath the pedestrian precinct in the right foreground. The French infantry attacked from the left.

**Below:** The Farm de la Bourse at Limal.

**Above:** The River Dyle near Bierges mill. Marshal Grouchy's infantry attacked unsuccessfully from the background across marshy meadows.

**Below:** The monument near Bierges mill to Maurice Gérard, who fell severely wounded at the head of the French IV Corps.

**Above:** The site of the Porte de Bruxelles at Namur. On the right, a plaque fixed to the wall of the park commemorates the French rearguard action of 20 June.

**Below:** Namur: looking north over the city from the citadel. On the left is the River Sambre and on the right stands the Cathedral of St Aubain. Beyond the cathedral are the heights on which Marshal Grouchy's troops briefly held their Prussian pursuers at bay before retiring within the ramparts.

**Opposite page:** British Royal Horse Artillery galloping into action.

**Above:** The tomb of Alexander Cavalié Mercer, who commanded 'G' Troop, Royal Horse Artillery at Waterloo.

**Below:** The south side of Strijtem château, where Mercer was staying when Napoleon invaded the United Netherlands on 15 June.

**Above:** Lady Elizabeth Longford unveils a sign commemorating the King's German Legion at the old Barrack Road cemetery in Bexhill, East Sussex, on 23 April 1994.

**Below:** Barrack Hall, Bexhill: it served as the KGL officers' mess.

**Above:** The fall of La Haie Sainte: Major George Baring, on horseback, orders a bayonet charge as the French finally storm into the courtyard. On the right, troops endeavour to extinguish the flames on the barn roof.

**Below:** The courtyard as it is today: a view towards the main gate on the eastern side of the farm.

**Above:** Re-enactors of the 2nd Light battalion, King's German Legion.

**Below:** A view of the battlefield of Waterloo, looking from the crossroads at the centre of Wellington's front line southwards along the Brussels road. The farm of La Haie Sainte stands next to the road on the right; on the horizon immediately to the left of the road are La Belle Alliance and the column of Victor Hugo's monument.

Wavre had fled or hidden, leaving their doors locked.[1] Three battalions under Colonel von Zepelin occupied Wavre and prepared for the coming fight by knocking loopholes in the houses of the north bank adjoining the river.

Throughout the morning of 18 June the rest of the Prussian army had rolled out of the area in long columns towards Waterloo. Intense confusion inevitably attended this march. Indeed, Thielmann's 9th brigade had been unaware that III Corps was remaining at Wavre as a rearguard and had followed Blücher's troops. 9th brigade had left behind only a few battalions in Wavre and Basse-Wavre and a cavalry squadron.

On the other hand, Ziethen's I Corps had left behind the 19th Infantry and three cavalry squadrons; this force went to guard the bridge over the Dyle at Limal, one and a half miles upstream from Bierges. The English historian William Siborne concluded: 'Thielmann's position was certainly a very favourable one and the occupation of it was arranged with great skill.'[2]

Towards 3.00 pm French skirmishers at last arrived on the heights south of Wavre. Lieutenant-General Count Dominique Vandamme's III Corps rolled up in strength towards 4.00 pm and immediately commenced the attack. The hot-headed Vandamme failed to reconnoitre or bombard Wavre before sending in Lieutenant-General Baron Habert's infantry division. The troops paid the penalty of Vandamme's folly in high casualties; Habert himself was among the wounded. Colonel Stoffel's 2nd Swiss regiment, wearing traditional red jackets, was massacred on the Bridge of Christ. Among the wounded of this unit was a woman who had accompanied her officer husband throughout all his campaigns since 1792 and had given him twenty-one children. Her husband was killed at Wavre.[3]

The survivors of Habert's division could not advance into the hail of musketry but, owing to the deluge of Prussian artillery fire striking the open slopes south of Wavre, they could not, or would not, retreat. Marshal Grouchy, who arrived just then, was forced to send in further troops. The French hoped to storm over the barricaded bridge by sheer elan. They failed. Skirmishers of the two armies extended along each bank of the Dyle. They hid behind trees and hedges, sniping and reloading. Lieutenant-General Count Rémy Exelmans' dragoons and an infantry battalion now stood south of Basse-Wavre.

West of Wavre, a French battalion of Lieutenant-General Baron Etienne Lefol's division tried to bypass the town by securing a bridgehead at the mill of Bierges. However, the Prussian position was too strong here as well. Lefol's men fell back; a fresh battalion of the 9th Light infantry from Lieutenant-General Count Maurice Gérard's newly-arrived IV Corps launched a second assault. The heavily burdened French troops dashed across open meadows under a hail of fire only to tumble into deep, water filled ditches. Some of the soldiers were nearly drowned. Gérard renewed the attack in person only to be seriously wounded by a musket-ball in the chest.

## BATTLE OF WAVRE: AFTERNOON, 18 JUNE

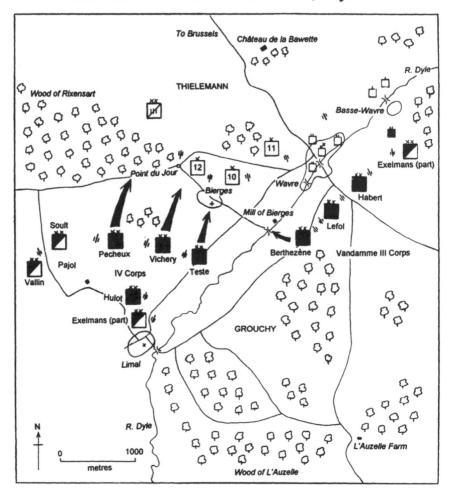

Marshal Grouchy asked Brigadier-General Baron Basile Baltus de Pouilly, commander of Gérard's artillery, to lead a further assault but Baltus refused. Grouchy thereupon dismounted: 'if a soldier can not make his subordinates obey him, he must know how to get himself killed!' he exclaimed.[4] The gallant marshal then led the advance which like its predecessors inevitably failed.

By now it was clear that no crossing could be forced at either Wavre or Bierges mill. So Grouchy left Exelmans, Vandamme and one division of IV Corps south of Wavre to maintain frontal pressure and thereby detain the Prussian forces in this area. He himself set off with the remainder of IV Corps to Limal, 2300 metres upstream from Bierges mill.

Grouchy had already ordered the rearmost units of his command, the 4th and 7th Cavalry and 21st Infantry divisions under Lieutenant-General Count

Claude Pajol, to proceed direct to Limal instead of joining him at Wavre. Grouchy hoped to gain at Limal the bridgehead over the Dyle that still eluded him at Wavre and Bierges mill.

The need to establish a bridgehead at Limal was now even more urgent. All frontal attacks at Wavre had failed, yet at 5.00 pm Grouchy had received a message which Marshal Soult had written on the battlefield of Waterloo at 1.15 pm. Soult's despatch was rambling: Grouchy's plan of marching on Wavre was 'in accordance with the dispositions which have been communicated to you.' But at the same time Grouchy was always to manoeuvre towards the Emperor. This was self-contradictory. The remainder of the despatch was vague: 'it is up to you to see the point where we are, so you can act accordingly, and to link our communications also always to be able to fall on any enemy troops who would seek to worry our right flank and to crush them.' The only firm command Soult gave was the last sentence: 'the centre of the English army is at Mont St Jean, therefore manoeuvre to join our right flank.'

This communication made little sense but Soult's postscript was disturbing: 'a letter which has just been intercepted says that General Bülow [commander of the Prussian IV Corps] is going to attack our flank. We think we can perceive this corps on the heights of [Chapelle] St Lambert. Therefore do not lose a moment to come closer and join us and to crush Bülow whom you will destroy utterly.'

Grouchy seems not to have been as worried by this message as he ought to have been. In his memoirs he claimed he had read one of the sentences as 'the battle is won [gagnée]' rather than 'the battle is engaged [engagée]'. Grouchy was either lying or remarkably careless in reading orders. The original despatch clearly states 'engaged.' Nevertheless Grouchy seems still to have been optimistic that Napoleon would win and that the bulk of the Prussians were northeast of Wavre on the Chyse plain or recoiling on Brussels. Indeed, when Grouchy finally defeated Thielmann on 19 June and could hear no more gunfire from Waterloo, he would commence marching on Brussels. It is clear that Grouchy was too dogmatic to reconsider his original assessments in the light of new evidence.

Towards 7.00 pm Lieutenant-General Count Claude Pajol reached Limal in accordance with Grouchy's orders. Pajol's force comprised the 4th and 7th Cavalry Divisions under Lieutenant-General Baron Pierre Soult and Brigadier-General Baron Louis Vallin and the 21st Infantry Division under Lieutenant-General Baron François Teste, together with three batteries. A small Prussian detachment under Lieutenant-Colonel von Stengel guarded the bridge over the Dyle at Limal but had made no attempt to destroy it. Pajol soon captured the intact bridge with a brisk cavalry attack; Stengel fell back to the north and Grouchy, who arrived from Wavre at 9.00 pm, rushed troops up from Limal to the crest of the plateau to secure his bridgehead.

## BATTLE OF WAVRE: EVENING, 18 JUNE

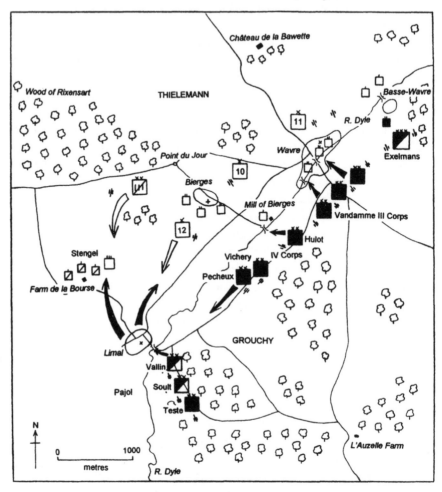

Thielmann shifted his second line of troops to the west and freed 12th brigade and his Reserve Cavalry to contain the breakthrough at Limal. The Prussian forces unwisely mounted a night attack, became disunited and disorientated and were pinned down by French fire. The Prussians left outposts and withdrew 1500 metres northwards to the woods of Rixensart. The French had consolidated their defence line around Limal but were deeply anxious at hearing no more gunfire from Waterloo.

At Wavre, fighting continued until 11.00 pm. Fires started during the action were slowly consuming the town; a number of wounded were unable to escape from blazing houses and were burnt to death. On one occasion, the French seized the Bridge of Christ and gained a temporary foothold on the northern side of the Dyle but were unable to establish any permanent advantage. The

Prussians kept their reserves concealed and sheltered in streets running parallel to the river and drew on them whenever necessary.

During the night, the outposts of both sides were tense and patrols clashed frequently. Thielmann received some unconfirmed news of victory at Waterloo, which caused Stengel's detachment to march away to rejoin its parent I Corps. Thielmann expected that Grouchy had heard of Napoleon's defeat and would fall back. So at daybreak, towards 4.00 am on 19 June, Thielmann launched a cavalry attack in the Limal sector to hasten the French on their way. Prussian gunfire heralded the renewal of combat. French troops awoke to find projectiles raining down into their bivouacs and a French sentry outside Grouchy's headquarters was cut in two by a cannon-ball.[5]

The French recovered quickly and, having heard nothing of Waterloo, had

## BATTLE OF WAVRE: MORNING, 19 JUNE

293

no intention of retreating. A fierce artillery duel developed in the course of which five Prussian guns were disabled. Grouchy organised a general offensive on the west bank of the Dyle. The western flank of this advance was guarded by Pajol's cavalry.

Three infantry columns, each accompanied by an artillery battery and a swarm of skirmishers, ploughed forward. The western two columns, composed of two divisions of IV Corps, drove the outnumbered Thielmann out of Rixensart woods. Captain Charles François of the 30th Line infantry was troubled by Prussian taunts: 'Come with us, brave Frenchmen! You no longer have an army. Napoleon is dead.' François and those of his comrades who understood German did not know what to make of this.[6]

The easternmost French column was Lieutenant-General Baron François Teste's division, detached from VI Corps at Waterloo. Seconded by Vandamme's forces on the east bank, Teste succeeded in capturing Bierges village from two battalions of Kurmark Landwehr in spite of being wounded and losing one of his brigade commanders, Baron Raymond Penne, to a Prussian shell.[7] Bierges was the key of Thielmann's position, for after its capture Grouchy could quickly pass troops over the Dyle without them having to undertake the long march via Limal. Furthermore, Bierges had been an anchor point in the Prussian defence line. The Prussians were able to resist well when ensconced in barns and houses but in open fields the French advantage of numbers soon told.

Thus the fall of Bierges was a turning point and soon afterwards Thielmann ordered a general withdrawal to avoid a crushing defeat. Vandamme, so fiery the day before, hardly harassed the Prussian battalions evacuating Wavre. When his troops finally entered the town, crossed the Dyle and emerged into the open country to the north, they were gallantly checked by two battalions of the 4th Kurmark Landwehr. Prussian cavalry formed a rearguard while Thielmann fell back five miles northwards to St-Agatha-Rode. The French did not pursue fiercely. Indeed, at 10.30 am, an exhausted messenger informed an astounded Grouchy of the disaster of Waterloo. The marshal immediately began a retreat of his own.

Casualties in the battle were not heavy. The Prussians lost around 2400 and the French 2600. The French losses had been suffered in vain for the Prussians had successfully held Grouchy at bay until he had no choice but to retreat. For the French, Wavre was a brave but pointless battle. For the Prussians, as the historian William Siborne commented, it was 'one of the brightest examples of the defence of a town and of the passage of a river, recorded in military history.'[8]

Over the years, the battlefield has suffered the usual encroachments of industry, housing and motorway. Wavre itself has been modernised and expanded. Its population in 1993 was 26,000 whereas in 1815 it was only 4000.[9] The

Germans destroyed much of the town in 1914 and bombed it heavily in May 1940. Nevertheless, a visit is worthwhile to see not just the relics of 1815 that have survived but also the difficult terrain the foes had to fight over in the Wavre area.

Start your tour on the French side of the Dyle valley, south of Wavre. At the junction of the N4 and the N43, you will find a superb view of the slope leading northwards into the town. Vandamme's infantry charged down this street, the rue du pont de Christ, in their first attack. Lieutenant-General Baron Pierre Berthezène related how:

> Wavre was occupied by the Prussians: its houses were garrisoned by skirmishers. Its bridge was barricaded and swept by the fire of numerous guns which were established on the heights dominating the left bank of the Dyle. General Vandamme attacked the town as soon as he arrived before it, without taking any measure to ensure success. He simply ordered Habert's division to enter it in column. In spite of the murderous fire of the enemy, this column reached the bridge but when Habert was wounded, it retired in disorder and came to reform at the entrance of the town. This stupid attack cost us five or six hundred men. ... Besides, the occupation of Wavre could have no influence on the outcome of the campaign.[10]

Follow the route of the French attack into Wavre until you arrive at the Bridge of Christ, on which a metal plaque records simply that this was the site of a fight between Grouchy and the Prussians. The original bridge had to be widened in 1845 and today's version is nothing like the original.[11] A pedestrian precinct covers the Dyle east of the bridge but if you look over the western parapet you gain an idea of the width of the river. The iron crucifix on this side witnessed the battle, as did the first house south-west of the bridge. Colonel Fantin des Odoards, commander of the 22nd Line infantry, vividly described the epic struggle in the vicinity:

> General Vandamme ... wanted ... to capture a bridge that was carefully barricaded and protected by thousands of skirmishers posted in the houses of the other bank. This position should have been turned but the general persisted in attacking it head on with massed troops which, engaged in a long street perpendicular to the bridge, received all the Prussian fire without being able to use their own. We lost many men there fruitlessly.
>
> The 70th Regiment, the same unit which had been thrown into confusion two days before [at the Battle of Ligny], was ordered to clear the bridge under a hail of musketry and was routed there. Brought back by its colonel, it hesitated again but this brave Colonel Maury, seizing its eagle, cried: 'What, rabble, you dishonoured me the day before yesterday and you offend me again today! Forward! Follow me!'
>
> With the eagle in his hand, he rushed on to the bridge; the charge was beaten and the regiment followed. But hardly was he at the barricades than this worthy

## WAVRE AND BIERGES TODAY

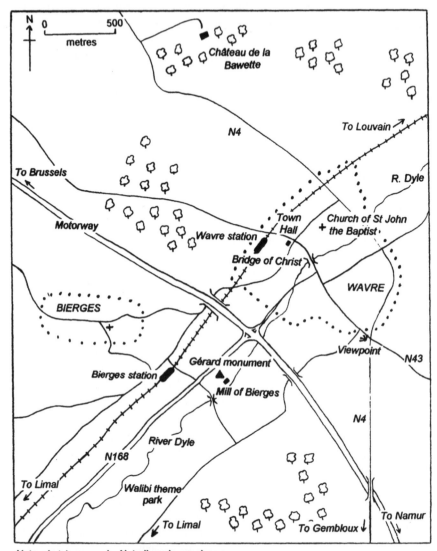

Note: sketch map only. Not all roads are shown.

leader fell dead and the 70th fled ... so rapidly that without the help of my 22nd, the eagle which was lying on the ground in the middle on the bridge beside my lifeless comrade, would have fallen into the hands of the enemy skirmishers who were already trying to seize it ... The following day General Vandamme agreed that he had made a mistake but the damage was done.[12]

Proceed north up the rue du chemin de fer to the Town Hall. The building was restored after being badly damaged in World War Two and had served in 1815 as a hospital for wounded troops. At this point, a road leads east to the Church of St Jean-Baptiste. The church was built in the fifteenth century, except the tower which ascended in stages into the seventeenth century. Embedded in the top of the fourth pillar on your right as you enter the church is a cannon-ball, surrounded by a recently added plaque with a Latin inscription. We can infer from its position that the missile came from the French side of the valley and smashed through a window to find its final destination. The plaque dates from only the 1970s and reads: *quid vis irrita acies contra hanc petram? Ecce nedum plus ultra! Sic inconsulta transit gloria mundi*. This translates as 'what force have you against this stone, violent cannon-ball? Certainly you will go no further! So passes the inconsiderate glory of the world.'

Return to the rue du chemin de fer and walk along it north-westwards to Wavre station, where you can catch a train for Bierges to the south-west. Bierges station lies on the north bank of the Dyle valley; the village occupies the heights above it. If you have time, climb these heights to see the strength of the Prussian position. Thielmann posted six guns of Horse Battery no. 20 immediately east of Bierges village; they had an excellent field of fire. Marshal Grouchy neatly summed up the difficulties he faced:

They [the Prussians] crowned all the heights behind Wavre and extended towards Limal. Numerous artillery pieces defended this strong position, at the foot of which runs the Dyle. The nature of the country hardly allowed me precisely to estimate the enemy numbers ... Shooting went on from one bank to another. The cannonade was very lively and from their dominating position the Prussians were able to judge all the dispositions I was able to make and to delay their execution by attacking the units I had left before them and by worrying my rear.[13]

Now descend to the Dyle and stand on the modern bridge. To the south-east are the marshy meadows in which the French attacks became bogged down. You may find some of the ditches, into which the leading French skirmishers tumbled, but they are much shallower and drier today. The Dyle itself is narrower than it was on 18 June after the thunderstorms of the previous afternoon and night. Captain Thouvenin of the staff of the French IV Corps related how: 'I was sent to reconnoitre the river [at Bierges] above the mill occupied by the enemy. As far as I recollect, its width was about nine metres. Its parallel, low banks gave it the appearance of a miry canal. I pushed my horse in and I had water up to my waist. Captain Pellissier and his voltigeurs helped me to retrieve my horse.'[14]

The failure of the attacks at Bierges was inevitable. General Gérard later commented:

I ordered General [Baron Etienne] Hulot, an officer as intelligent as he was brave, to go with a battalion of the 9th Light infantry to renew the attack already attempted unsuccessfully by the troops of III Corps. This new attack and another which occurred in the presence of the Count de Grouchy met with no more success than had the first. The troops can not be blamed for they showed much courage again and again. But the nature of the terrain offered insurmountable difficulties ... The marshy meadows [south of the Dyle] are cut by very deep ditches which run parallel to the river and are too wide to be jumped over. They were filled by four, five or six feet of water ... The banks of the Dyle are wooded, in addition to which the Prussian infantry were placed under cover even in the mill. Prussians occupied the left bank of the river as well as the slopes of the hills leading down to it. Fire from the strong Prussian artillery joined that of the infantry from the mill and the left bank and fell into this grassland which had to be crossed in order to reach the bridge. These obstacles alone caused all the attacks on this point to fail. I repeat that the troops can not be blamed without the greatest injustice ...[15]

Lieutenant-General Baron Etienne Hulot, commander of one of Gérard's three infantry divisions, reported how he tackled the difficult terrain in front of Bierges mill:

I believed that by moving slighty to the left and passing these ditches higher up, I would find less water. Hence I moved my battalion nearly a musketshot in this direction and unleashed it. I ordered the men to run with their heads down and to throw themselves into the ditches if they could not leap over them. The first troops threw themselves in, were nearly drowned and were unable to climb out without help from their comrades. These numerous obstacles halted and rebuffed the soldiers; I reckoned that this post could not be attacked in this manner.

As I returned towards the height to give General Gérard my opinion, I met him: he had just descended with another battalion. He had seen the failure of my attempt and told me, when I approached him, that he was going to renew the attack and that I must assist it by leading forward my first battalion again. Indeed, the attack was renewed. General Gérard and the officers of his staff participated in these fruitless final efforts which could only have unpleasant results. In fact, it was in these circumstances that the general received a musketball in his chest.[16]

Bierges mill still stands but has been modernised. More recent buildings have been built beside it; today it is more a farm than a mill. Nevertheless, you will appreciate the solidity of this bastion which was garrisoned by a company of the Prussian 31st Infantry. The soldiers of this regiment, although Prussians, wore green Russian uniforms and the unique concave-topped Russian 1812-pattern shako, as they had formerly been part of the Russo-German Legion. The legion had been formed in 1812 from Prussian exiles in Russia; it had helped drive Napoleon from Europe in the campaigns of 1813–14. The soldiers of the 31st Infantry were tough, experienced warriors.

It is impossible to ascertain the exact location where Gérard was wounded; a memorial stone north of the mill does not mark the spot. Its inscription records that the general was wounded 'in this area'. It calls Gérard the 'defender of our national independence'. This is a reference to the Belgian Revolution against the Dutch in 1830–2, during which Gérard led a French army into Belgium to expel a Dutch garrison from Antwerp.

You may have some difficulty in finding Gérard's monument as it is half-hidden in a thick hedge of bushes. The best way to reach it is to walk ninety metres northwards from the modern bridge spanning the Dyle and then to turn right on to the N168. One hundred and fifty metres along the grassy southern edge of this busy road you will see the monument on your right.

Now return to Bierges station to catch a train to the village of Limal, the scene of Count Pajol's brilliant attack which at last secured a French bridgehead over the Dyle towards 7.00 pm. If you prefer to walk to Limal from Bierges, use the road which runs parallel to the Dyle and 350 metres south of it (the N168 is closed to pedestrians and cyclists).

If you walk along this road you will be following the route taken by Marshal Grouchy and two divisions of IV Corps which marched to reinforce Pajol on the west bank at Limal. You reach the village immediately after crossing the Dyle at the Bridge of the 13th Algerian Tirailleurs. In May 1940, the Dyle was employed as a defence line against the Germans and Limal was held for three days by Algerians of the French 1st Army. Further north, from Wavre to Louvain, stood the British Expeditionary Force under Lord Gort. One hundred and one French troops were killed at Limal in 1940; a monument to them stands beside the church.

The Prussian detachment which held Limal in 1815 put up a far less impressive resistance. Fortunately, Count Pajol's ADC, Major Hubert-François Biot, has left a detailed account of the brief action.[17] Pajol's force approached Limal from the east; a local peasant had pointed out the right direction to take. Biot was leading the way with the 7th Cavalry Division under Brigadier-General Baron Louis Vallin and was about to debouch from the woods east of Limal when he was challenged: 'who's there?' Biot replied 'France!' and was told to go no further. The speaker was a French infantry sergeant on outpost duty and he warned Biot that Prussians occupied the houses near Limal bridge. Sure enough, the French cavalry were greeted by two cannon-balls, so Biot proceeded alone towards the river. He successfully ascertained that the wooden bridge was not barricaded and returned to report to his general.

Pajol ordered the attack: 'We must cross. Tell General Vallin to give us the first squadron of the 6th Hussars and then you are to seize the bridge. But do not stop; immediately take the road to the right which you have already described to me and debouch into the plain. I will have you supported as necessary.' Biot galloped over to Vallin to give this order. Prince Joseph-Marie de Savoie Carignan, the commander of 6th Hussars, led his squadron forward at the gallop and the remainder of Pajol's horsemen followed at a trot.

The squadron of the 6th Hussars galloped, four horses abreast, through a harmless volley of musketry and on to the west bank. They swung right and chased stunned Prussian skirmishers before overrunning a Prussian battalion at the cost of just one officer and two men killed. The 6th Hussars and 8th Chasseurs à cheval pursued a good distance along the road towards Bierges before being recalled. Looking across the river, Biot saw two divisions of IV Corps on the opposite bank as they marched southwards to Limal.

In the meantime two regiments of green-coated dragoons, led by Pajol in person, clattered across the bridge into Limal and cleared the village of the remaining Prussians. Lieutenant-Colonel von Stengel's Prussians rallied on the heights to the north. Their musketry checked Pajol's dragoons so Lieutenant-General Baron François Teste brought up one of his infantry regiments and successfully scaled the heights in the obscurity of dusk.[18]

Stengel fell back in the direction of Bierges. If you stand on the eastern platform of Limal station and look along the track in the direction of Louvain, you can identify the spire of Bierges church on the horizon directly above the track. It was from around this church, precisely 2350 metres away as the crow flies, that Thielmann had to rush Prussian troops to Limal to plug the gap the French had made in his defence line.

North of Limal church is a narrow tarmacked road bordered on the right by a red brick wall. It is called the rue du Petit Sart and is so narrow that it is a one way street and you may not drive up it. This road follows the route of the sunken lane the French used to ascend the heights. Houses stand either side of the track today but the slopes would have been open country in 1815. Note the steep gradient and how vulnerable Grouchy's men would have been if Stengel had possessed a larger force. Major Hubert-François Biot vividly remembered the difficult ascent:

> We could climb the steep western slope of the Dyle valley only by a very bad and narrow track. The enemy shot at us with muskets from the edge of the plateau where they were showing off. The dragoons followed this track while the 40th Line infantry[19] marched on both flanks, climbing as best they could. A young drummer of this regiment whom I ordered to beat the charge, was hit in the hand by a musket-ball yet continued to beat on his drum with his other, unhurt, hand. Thus we arrived on the plateau from which the enemy had entirely disappeared. This plateau was covered with heather and was wooded in places; a light skirmish started in the heather ...[20]

Marshal Grouchy remained on the plateau until late in the night, posting his troops as they arrived; two divisions of IV Corps had now joined Pajol's force in the bridgehead. Although Thielmann's 12th brigade and Stengel's detachment united in an attempt to retake the plateau, they were beaten off in the darkness.

The failure of this Prussian counter-attack was inevitable; only the danger posed by the existence of the French bridgehead caused the night attack to be undertaken. The Prussians could judge neither the strength nor dispositions of the French and were unable to co-ordinate the movements of their battalions. Note the uneven ground of the plateau which the Prussians had to cross. The leading two battalions of 12th brigade were checked by a volley as they tried to cross a hollow way while the three battalions in the second wave inclined by mistake to the east and instead of supporting the first wave ran into French skirmisher fire. Stengel's weak detachment had advanced in support to the west of 12th brigade but soon retired when Pajol's cavalry menaced its flank.[21]

Grouchy established his headquarters at the Ferme de la Bourse, which you can still see today 1100 metres north-west of Limal. Above the arched gateway is the date 1702. From this farm the marshal wrote to Vandamme at 11.30 pm:

> I place the whole of Gérard's corps under your command. At dawn we will attack here, we will distract the enemy at Wavre by feint attacks and I hope we will succeed in joining the Emperor as he has ordered. It is said he has beaten the English but I have no more news from him and I am having great difficulty in giving him ours.
>
> I beg you, my dear general, in the name of the fatherland to execute this order immediately. I can see only this method of extricating ourselves from our difficult position and the safety of the army depends on it. I await you.[22]

Captain Charles François of the 30th Line infantry summed up the day's fighting:

> The attack was general and directed against Thielmann's troops. The infantry and cavalry performed prodigies of valour which served only to kill and wound many men ... This action had little use and cost us 1100 men. It hardly honours our generals, who seemed to be groping their way forward and we heard gunfire all day on our left, in the direction of Waterloo. Unlike my usual self, I was depressed and low down, I was furious.[23]

Few relics remain of the fighting that flared up on the morning of 19 June but you may care to follow the path of the French offensive on the west bank of the Dyle over the difficult terrain from Limal to Bierges. You might also visit the Château of La Bawette, 1400 metres north-west of Wavre. The château, restored after war damage this century, had previously served as Thielmann's corps headquarters. Around 10.30 am Grouchy summoned an emergency council of war at La Bawette after receiving the sad tidings of Napoleon's defeat at Waterloo. Soon afterwards, he commenced a retreat to France via Namur and Dinant.

# Notes

1. W. Aerts, *Waterloo. Opérations de l'armée prussienne du Bas-Rhin* (1908), p.276

2. W. Siborne, *History of the Waterloo campaign* (1990), p.403

3. E. Chapuisart, 'Les études napoléoniennes en Suisse: 1913', in *Revue des études napoléoniennes* (Jan–June 1915)

4. H. Houssaye, *Waterloo 1815* (1987), p.454

5. C. François, *Journal du Capitaine François* (1904), v.2, p.889

6. *Ibid*, v.2, p.890

7. H. Biot, *Souvenirs anecdotiques et militaires* (1901), p.255

8. W. Siborne, *History of the Waterloo campaign* (1990), p.410

9. J. Weller, *Wellington at Waterloo* (1967), p.223

10. P. Berthezène, *Souvenirs militaires de la république et de l'empire* (1855), v.2, pp.392–3

11. L. Navez, *Les Quatre-Bras, Ligny, Waterloo et Wavre* (1903), p.266

12. *Journal du général Fantin des Odoards* (1895), pp.433–4; according to A. Martinien, *Tableaux par corps et par batailles des officiers tués et blessés pendant les guerres de l'empire (1808–1815)* (n.d.), pp.280–1, Colonel Maury was killed at Ligny and his successor, Uny, was slain at Wavre.

13. E. Grouchy, *Fragments historiques relatifs à la campagne de 1815 et à la bataille de Waterloo* (1829), pp.12, 14–15

14. L. Navez, *Les Quatre-Bras, Ligny, Waterloo et Wavre* (1903), pp.267–8

15. E. Gérard, *Quelques documents sur la bataille de Waterloo propres à éclairer la question portée devant la publique par M. le Marquis de Grouchy* (1829), pp.42–3

16. *Le Spectateur Militaire* (Jan–March 1884), series 4, v.24, pp.211–13

17. H. Biot, *Souvenirs anecdotiques et militaires* (1901), pp.250–4

18. C. Pajol, *Pajol. Général en chef* (1874), v.3, pp.230–4

19. The actual French text reads '14th' but the 14th Line infantry was not with the Army of the North. The 40th Line, however, was part of Teste's division. It is easy to understand how Biot could have made such an error as the French words for fourteen and forty are 'quatorze' and 'quarante' respectively.

20. H. Biot, *Souvenirs anecdotiques et militaires* (1901), p.254

21. W. Siborne, *History of the Waterloo campaign* (1990), p.408

22. W. Aerts, *Waterloo. Opérations de l'armée prussienne du Bas-Rhin* (1908), p.287

23. C. François, *Journal du Capitaine François* (1904), v.2, pp.888–9; François' assertion that Grouchy seemed to be groping his way forward is confirmed by Grouchy's vague letter to Vandamme written at 11.30 pm, in which he begs rather than orders Vandamme to obey. According to H. Biot (*Souvenirs anecdotiques et militaires* [1901], p.250), in the afternoon of 18 June Pajol received two orders from Grouchy, neither of which bore any indication of time. One of these orders commanded Pajol to march on Wavre, the other to march towards Napoleon. A little later Grouchy's ADC arrived with orders to cross the Dyle at Limal.

# 20

# AFTERMATH

By 10.30 am on 19 June, Marshal Emmanuel de Grouchy had defeated the Prussian III Corps at Wavre and pushed it back north towards Louvain. He himself was near Rosières, three miles north-west of Wavre, preparing to march the ten miles separating him from Brussels. Just then a French staff officer galloped up looking tattered, wild-eyed and exhausted.[1] 'An ADC covered in dust and whose horse seemed literally broken, after being overworked by an excessive ride, passed near me,' remembered Major Hubert-François Biot.[2] The messenger stuttered out an incoherent string of news in a breathless scramble. He must, Grouchy decided, be either mad or drunk or both. But gradually details of disaster at Waterloo were repeated, repeated again and were believed. When Napoleon had reached Quatre Bras from Waterloo at 1.00 am on 19 June he had sent this staff officer to warn Grouchy of the catastrophic outcome of the campaign.

Grouchy summoned an emergency council of war of his senior officers at the Château of La Bawette, 1400 metres north of Wavre. Grouchy announced the terrible news with tears in his eyes. This prompted the insubordinate Lieutenant-General Count Dominique Vandamme later to sneer that 'Grouchy could only cry like an old woman.'[3] Grouchy first defended his refusal the day before to march on the sound of the guns of Waterloo and then turned to future plans.

Lieutenant-General Vandamme daringly suggested marching straight to Brussels, liberating the numerous French prisoners there before sweeping behind Wellington and Blücher's victorious armies to arrive in France via Enghien and Ath.[4] Grouchy swiftly crushed this idea. Wellington had made careful preparations for the defence of the major Belgian towns and cities and sizeable detachments of troops were on garrison duty. Grouchy's command would soon be halted, surrounded and crushed unless it marched quickly and efficiently directly southwards to France via Namur and Dinant. Speed was vital.

For the retreat, Grouchy divided his command into four sections. First, the advanced guard, Lieutenant-General Count Rémy Exelmans' II Cavalry Corps of green-coated dragoons, would lead the retreat twenty-two miles south-eastwards to Namur. Then would follow two columns marching by separate

## MARSHAL GROUCHY'S RETREAT FROM WAVRE: 19 JUNE

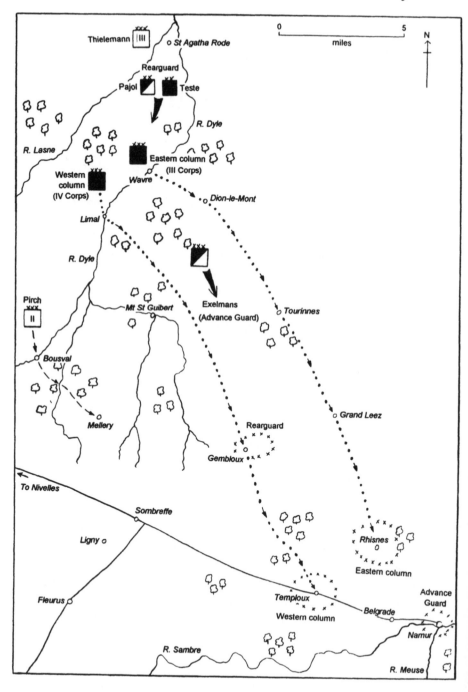

but parallel routes. The IV Corps would form the western column and would be accompanied by Marshal Grouchy in person and by those French troops who had been wounded at the Battle of Wavre and who could be transported. The eastern column comprised Vandamme's III Corps and the 20th Dragoons. The fourth section of Grouchy's detachment was the rearguard, formed by Lieutenant-General Baron François Teste's infantry division and by Lieutenant-General Count Claude Pajol's I Cavalry Corps.

The retreat began between 11.00 am and 12.00 pm. First, Grouchy sent his advanced guard under Exelmans to secure for his force the vital crossing point over the River Sambre at Namur. Exelmans' dragoons performed their task perfectly and swiftly covered the twenty-two miles from Wavre to Namur. The leading French brigade arrived at Namur at 4.00 pm to find the Francophile citizens expecting them.

A French soldier had reached Namur early that morning with news of Napoleon's disaster at Waterloo. Immediately, the citizens had taken measures to help Grouchy salvage his detachment from Napoleon's catastrophe. Since Namur had no garrison, it had formed its own civil guard of forty-nine eminent men. This small but august unit set off to await the French at Belgrade, a village nearly two miles west of Namur.

When Exelmans' leading troops arrived in the afternoon, the civil guard welcomed them at Belgrade and conducted them to the main square of Namur. French dragoons guarded the river bridges and the three city gates on the northern side of Namur. By 7.00 pm the remainder of Exelmans' corps had arrived, thus consolidating the French grip on the bridges over the Sambre. On this crossing point depended the fate of Grouchy's detachment.

Grouchy was busy manoeuvring the two main columns of his force, encumbered by waggons, artillery and the wounded, across over twenty-two miles of poor tracks to Namur. He faced the onerous responsibility of evading Prussian interception attempts, of passing his force over the Sambre and then blocking a pursuit with a fierce rearguard action. By the close of 19 June, Grouchy's western column had marched from Limal to Gembloux and then further south to Temploux, a village on the Nivelles to Namur chaussée, five miles from Namur. Here the column bivouacked, with Grouchy's headquarters in its midst.

The eastern column under Vandamme had fallen back through Wavre before, late in the afternoon, following tracks through Dion-le-Mont, Tourinnes and Grand-Leez. Towards midnight the column halted to rest. Colonel Fantin des Odoards of the 22nd Line recalled that at 1.00 am on 20 June, Vandamme's column began marching again, 'sad and silent . . . The cavalry and artillery, which necessarily followed the tracks, progressed more or less at ease. But the poor infantry, marching across country in a dark night and encountering hedges and ditches at every step, advanced only in disorder and with great difficulty ... If at this moment the enemy had appeared, he would have met no resistance.'[5]

Vandamme's column finally halted in the early hours of 20 June near the village of Rhisnes, three and three-quarter miles north-west of Namur.

Grouchy's rearguard had first followed the mauled Prussian III Corps north-eastwards from Wavre to St-Agatha-Rode. Late on 19 June, when the rest of the French troops were safely to the south, the rearguard began its own retreat and bivouacked at Gembloux for the night. As it fell back it blocked the bridges at Wavre and Limal to delay any pursuit.[6]

So far during the retreat, Grouchy had been fortunate in not having had to contend with any Prussian interference. Lieutenant-General Baron Johann von Thielmann's Prussian III Corps was duped by the presence of Grouchy's rearguard into believing the whole of Grouchy's force was still at Wavre. Thielmann hoped that victorious Prussian units would arrive from Waterloo to sever Grouchy's retreat southwards. He learnt only late on 19 June that Grouchy had marched away and only at 5.00 am on 20 June did he dispatch his reserve cavalry and a horse artillery battery under Major-General von Hobe to pursue the French. Hobe had been reinforced since the Battle of Wavre by two squadrons of the 9th Hussars and two of the 6th Dragoons. These four squadrons had been on the outposts when Napoleon invaded on 15 June and had hitherto been unable to rejoin Blücher's army. Hobe was also joined by the 12th Hussars, a newly formed regiment under Lieutenant-Colonel von Czettritz.

Grouchy would also have to face a second Prussian force coming from another direction. On 18 June Major-General Georg von Pirch's II Corps had marched with Blücher to Waterloo and had arrived in time for its leading units to see action. Pirch's 5th infantry brigade had joined Gneisenau's pursuit of Napoleon but the rest of II Corps was ordered to about turn and march south-eastwards from Plancenoit via Maransart and Bousval to try and cut off Grouchy's retreat. Pirch reached the village of Mellery, three and three-quarter miles north of the battlefield of Ligny, at 11.00 am on 18 June.

Pirch arrived at Mellery while Grouchy, at Wavre, had only just learnt of the outcome of Waterloo. But Pirch had little power to intercept the French retreat. His Prussians had been on the march in atrocious conditions for twenty-four hours without a break: from Wavre to the Battle of Waterloo to Mellery. Furthermore, Pirch had yet to establish operational contact with Thielemann's III Corps and in the absence of this contact, he was outnumbered by Grouchy.

Towards 4.00 pm on 19 June, Pirch did send a cavalry reconnaissance north-eastwards to Mont St Guibert and this confirmed that Grouchy was retreating. But on 19 June the Prussians were too exhausted and disunited to undertake a serious pursuit.

Shots were fired early on 20 June. Grouchy's rearguard completed its march

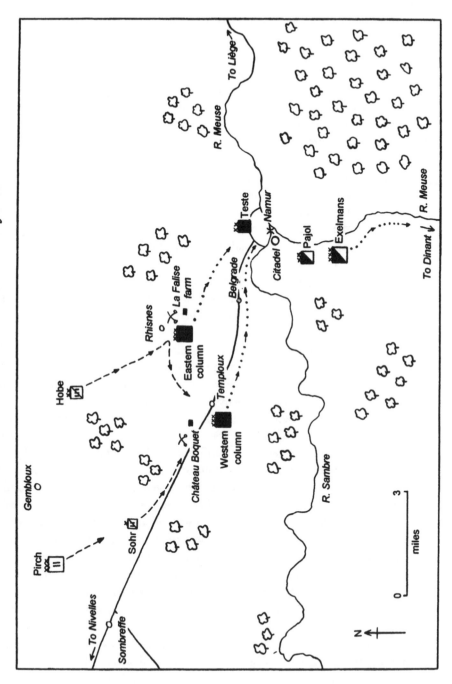

THE FIGHTING AROUND NAMUR: 20 JUNE

to Namur where it began to prepare for a defensive stand. Later, the French western and eastern columns also set off for Namur. Then the Prussians struck. Major-General von Hobe's squadrons from the III Corps had swept from the north to fall on the surprised rearguard of the French eastern column around the farm of La Falise near Rhisnes. Prussian horsemen broke a French infantry unit, captured three guns and sent shocked troops running to shelter in nearby woods. The French 20th Dragoons, accompanying this column, tried to halt the Prussian onslaught by carbine fire but were overwhelmed by the superior numbers of the 7th and 8th Uhlans and 12th Hussars.[7] Major-General von Hobe's men captured fifty of the dragoons' horses. Vandamme was absent, having gone inexcusably to pass the night in Namur.[8]

At the same time, a further Prussian threat appeared from the west. Pirch's II Corps, led by Lieutenant-Colonel von Sohr's cavalry brigade, headed for the French western column and attacked its rearguard around the Château Boquet. The gallant Marshal Grouchy tackled the crisis head-on. 'Be calm', he ordered the anxious waggon loads of wounded from the Battle of Wavre. 'We swear not to desert you. But I am confident that our dispositions will save us.'[9] Then Grouchy took Brigadier-General Baron Louis Vallin's cavalry division from the IV Corps to rescue the eastern column. Vallin united with the 20th Dragoons and drubbed Hobe's Prussians. The French recaptured two guns and even seized a Prussian howitzer.[10]

A fighting retreat to the gates of Namur now started. Hobe's rebuffed horsemen left the French eastern column in peace and linked up with Pirch's II Corps which concentrated its efforts against Grouchy's western column. Nevertheless, the French units all arrived under the ramparts of Namur.

Lieutenant-General Baron François Teste's infantry division, having arrived at Namur with the remainder of the rearguard early in the morning, was preparing to defend the gates and fortifications. Vandamme's eastern column had halted on the heights north of Namur to hold the Prussians at bay until the western column could file through the streets and continue its retreat south towards France. An ADC, Major Hubert-François Biot, left Namur to ask Vandamme how long he could hold on. 'I will remain as short a time as proves necessary, for this place is awfully hot,' was the blunt reply. Indeed, although Biot remained in the vicinity only a few moments, his horse was twice wounded. He returned to Namur, from where he could see the Prussian infantry man-oeuvring on the heights. Fortunately, he noted, 'their artillery contented itself for the moment with sending some shells and cannonballs towards the bridges.'[11]

Shortly before 5.00 pm, Vandamme was able to fall back through Namur leaving Teste's division to fight a stiff rearguard action. Teste's defensive arrangements were masterly and his troops inflicted heavy casualties on the Prussians who strove in vain to seize the three gates on the northern side of

Namur. Nearing the end of his ammunition, Teste finally abandoned Namur, having blocked the road behind him.

On 21 June, Grouchy completed his retreat to France, crossing the frontier north of Givet, a strong fortress town. The Prussian pursuit of Grouchy's detachment soon petered out. The Prussians found the narrow, tortuous track from Namur to Dinant barricaded at every suitable spot. At Dinant, the pursuit had lagged so far behind that it was called off.

Why was Marshal Grouchy's retreat so successful? Firstly, the Prussians were exhausted and consequently slow-moving.

Secondly, until Thielmann's cavalry linked up with Pirch's II Corps on the afternoon of 20 June, the Prussian pursuers were disunited and lacked co-ordination.

Thirdly, the French retreat was well organised. Grouchy marched the bulk of his force by separate but parallel routes, protected them with a rearguard and quickly seized a crossing point at Namur for them with an advanced guard.

Fourthly, the French troops were aware of the peril, hated the Prussians and feared capture by them. Major-General Georg von Pirch wrote that Grouchy's 'masses retired slowly from position to position and showed a great robustness.'[12] Lieutenant-General Baron François Teste's rearguard action at Namur was especially heroic.

Fifthly, the French were retreating through friendly territory. 'We only had to cross a region of friends', recalled Brigadier-General Jean-Baptiste Berton, commander of a brigade of dragoons.[13] Grouchy's forces received food, drink, help and encouragement from the local people, especially in Namur itself. The citizens of Namur gave the French their river boats in which to transport the wounded up the Meuse. Many Belgians were serving in the French army in 1815. One of Grouchy's ADCs had even been born in Namur.[14] By contrast, the Prussians were loathed by the natives because of the burdens and exactions they had imposed when in cantonments before the campaign began. When a British tourist, Captain William Frye, visited Namur in May 1815, he noted that 'we heard at the inn and in the shops which we visited the same complaints against the Prussians.'[15]

Sixthly, Marshal Grouchy demonstrated fine leadership throughout the retreat and exercised the initiative he had lacked on 18 June. He no longer had to follow imprecise and delayed orders from his awesome master, Napoleon. Moreover, Lieutenant-General Count Maurice Gérard, one of his two troublesome subordinates, had been wounded at Wavre and was not present during the retreat to criticise and undermine Grouchy's authority.

You will find most of the relics of Grouchy's retreat in Namur. But if you have time, you may wish to visit the Farm of La Falise near Rhisnes. In the fields around this farm Prussian cavalry fell on the French eastern column on 20 June. Major-General von Hobe opened fire with his battery before hurling his two cavalry brigades at the French. Note the steep, wooded hills in the vicinity. This region did not favour cavalry and once the French infantry hurried into the woods they soon checked the Prussians.[16]

Visit also the Château Boquet near Temploux, where the western column came under attack. Although the château is closed to the public you can spot it peering over surrounding trees. From the château, follow the route of the French column as it marched along the road to Namur. The rearguard of the column was provided by the 30th and 96th Line infantry and in the ranks of the former regiment was Captain Charles François, who recalled the onset of harassment by Lieutenant-Colonel von Sohr's 3rd and 5th Hussars:[17]

> We were dying from exhaustion and hunger ... The regimental sappers killed three oxen found in a farm ... We of the 30th Line had still not left the place where we had halted when we were attacked. The meat was abandoned, the cooking pots overturned and we went into action. The enemy moved off when confronted by our defensive manoeuvres. We set off at the quick march, with the enemy cavalry on our flanks. With a bit more boldness, they would have captured us.
>
> When we arrived on the heights three quarters of a league from Namur we halted. The enemy pressed close to us and cannonaded our flank; we replied in kind. The 96th Line, below us, formed square. The hostile cavalry came, partly in skirmish order, up to one hundred paces away to scoff at us. We [of the 30th] were marching in [two] squares. We arrived on the heights and the road which descends to Namur and sited our batteries; the cannonade resumed on both sides heavier than before. General Rome [our brigade commander] ordered one square to remain on the road and placed the other on the slope of the hill. The numerically superior enemy artillery knocked out three of our guns.
>
> The 96th Line continued its march on Namur and we [of the 30th] remained in our position, formed in two squares. Enemy cavalry charged us three times; three times they were repulsed with loss. Captain Guilleminot was killed, as was another captain in command of the square on the slope of the hill. Two others who replaced him were grievously wounded one after the other. So too were several soldiers who retired on Namur where they were later captured. Rebuffed, the foe moved back. Still formed in two squares, we therefore descended on Namur. The square I commanded was the last. I marched slowly, ... often halting and facing to the front to wait for the enemy cavalry to come to ten or fifteen paces distance. I commanded a fire from two ranks and those Prussian braggarts fled. Finally, with a little loss, we arrived under the walls of Namur.

One of the Frenchmen who failed to make it to safety was Lieutenant Fauville, a Belgian in the 96th Line. Shot in the right leg and chest and dying, he was left in the hands of the Prussians.[18] Captain François and his hungry comrades found welcome refreshments at Namur and were amazed at the generosity of the inhabitants:

While crossing the town, I saw the dismayed inhabitants: they were crying while bidding us farewell. They helped the soldiers ... they gave us bread, beer, stock and meat. The streets we passed through were encumbered with tables laden with foods. The people who were handing these foods out repeatedly said to us: 'Are you abandoning us, then? It is the traitors who have ruined you and us as well ...' These good people still thought of themselves as French.[19]

The 'good people' were Walloons, French-speakers who lived in the southern half of Belgium and had no love either of Dutch rule or of Prussian looting and exactions. Another French eyewitness, Lieutenant-General Baron Pierre Berthezène, praised the Walloons of Namur for their kindness:

It would have been impossible for us to save our wounded without the help and the compassion of the inhabitants of Namur. By their care, our poor comrades were placed in small boats and could sail up the Meuse. May these good inhabitants and those of the Meuse valley find in these pages the expression of my deep gratitude! Their humanity and their touching attention in such a critical time gave them eternal rights to the gratitude of all Frenchmen.[20]

Colonel Fantin des Odoards of the 22nd Line infantry recalled that not one wine cellar was closed:

During this long day of hostilities the people of Namur, without appearing frightened by the din, gave us all imaginable attentions ... The most elegant ladies, most of them pretty, showed themselves to be just as assiduous as the common women. On all sides we heard ... imprecations against the Prussians, so much more sincere demonstrations in that this good population saw well that we were going to leave it ... Oh! when we are more fortunate, we will carry our arms back into Belgium.[21]

Major Hubert-François Biot, ADC to Lieutenant-General Count Claude Pajol, also paid tribute to the citizens:

All their houses opened for our wounded, their inhabitants competing with each other to offer us comforts. I saw women of Namur taking the wounded from the hands of the unharmed soldiers who were carrying them and urging the soldiers to return to the fight. When we left, the people of Namur prayed for our next return, trying to console us for the circumstances of the fortune which they had so often seen favourable to our arms.[22]

Namur was ravaged in both world wars and most of the buildings are recent. But you will find a few that witnessed the passage of Grouchy's troops. The domed Cathedral of St Aubain existed in 1815, as did the ancient Church of St Loup. The Place d'Armes was where the first French dragoons to arrive were welcomed by a local dignitary, the Count of Villers-Masbourg.

## NAMUR TODAY

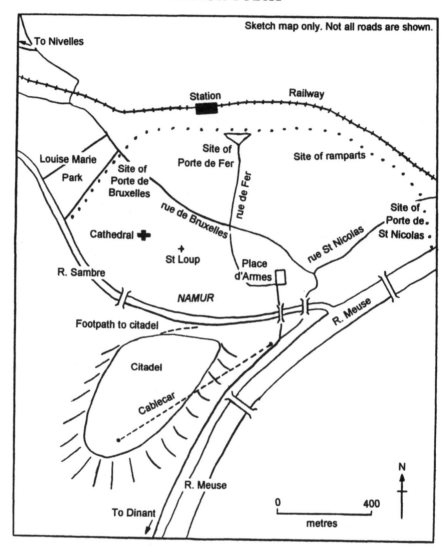

Sketch map only. Not all roads are shown.

To Nivelles

Station   Railway

Louise Marie
Park

Site of
Porte de Fer

Site of ramparts

Site of
Porte de
Bruxelles

rue de Fer

rue de Bruxelles

Cathedral ✠

+
St Loup

Place
d'Armes

rue St Nicolas

Site of
Porte de
St Nicolas

R. Sambre

NAMUR

R. Meuse

Footpath to citadel

Citadel

Cablecar

R. Meuse

To Dinant

N

0      400
metres

Fierce fighting raged around Namur when the Prussians attacked Lieutenant-General Baron François Teste's division covering Grouchy's retreat. Although the city has been modernised, it is possible to follow the action on the actual ground today. In 1815, the ramparts of Namur consisted merely of an earth bank only as high as a man's waist.[23] The French had to plug gaps with makeshift barricades of carts. These ramparts used to follow a line similar to that followed today by the railway.

The Prussians launched their attacks on the three gates on the north side of the city: the Porte de Bruxelles, the Porte de Fer and the Porte St Nicholas.

Unfortunately, these gates have since been demolished. On the gatepost at the north-east corner of Marie-Louise Park is affixed a plaque reading: 'Here stood the Porte de Bruxelles. On 20 June 1815 this gate was the witness of the fights between Marshal Grouchy's rearguard and the Prussian army.'

Five companies of Colonel Mathivet's 75th Line infantry guarded the Brussels gate. Their fierce musketry repulsed all Prussian assaults launched on this point. Sheltered by the ramparts, the French massacred the woefully exposed attackers.

The next gate to the east was the Porte de Fer, the 'Iron Gate', so named owing to its two doors constructed from iron grilles.[24] It used to stand at the northern end of the rue de Fer, 200 metres south-east of the railway station. Here stood two grenadier companies of the 75th regiment with two cannon which were loaded and camouflaged with foliage. Shortly after 5.00 pm five battalions of the Prussian 6th brigade of II Corps advanced on the Porte de Fer with the intention of blowing it up. But, at practically point blank range, the French unmasked their two cannon. A blazing hail of canister and musketry shredded the Prussian formations. The French continued firing as the compact mass of Prussian troops strove to extricate itself from the ambush and to retreat out of range.[25]

Colonel Heinrich von Zastrow, the courageous second-in-command of 6th brigade, was struck full in the chest and died later. Also killed was Colonel von Bismarck, commander of the 1st Elbe Landwehr and uncle of the future Chancellor of united Germany. Colonel von Reuss of the 26th Regiment was seriously wounded and on 20 June the Prussian 6th brigade lost 1318 men. In his subsequent report, Major-General von Pirch's anger was clear: 'Colonel von Zastrow, carried away by his ardour and having imprudently advanced paying no attention to the repeated recalls addressed to him, was struck by a shot in the chest, on the line of skirmishers amidst whom he was standing ... The 6th brigade distinguished itself in this fight but its over-hasty action caused the death of many of our men.'[26]

One and a half miles west of Namur, on the northern side of the road to Nivelles, is the cemetery of the town of St Servais. Here, near the entrance, you will find the tomb of Colonel von Zastrow. Note the maltese crosses carved on each of the four sides of the monument. The German inscription is barely legible: 'Heinrich von Zastrow, superior officer and commander of the Royal Prussian Infantry Regiment, fallen at the head of the regiment near the gate of Namur on 20 June 1815. The corps of officers of the regiment in remembrance of its valorous officer.'

Inside Namur, Baron François Teste's division was fighting magnificently. The officers, seeing that their soldiers needed no orders, themselves picked up the muskets of the dead and wounded and fired at the Prussians. The attacks on all three gates collapsed in tatters. Around 6.00 pm Major-General von Pirch was forced to relieve the shattered 6th brigade with the 7th, to suspend offensive operations and to blockade the northern face of the city. Pirch intended to undertake no further attacks as he realised the French were holding Namur solely to cover their retreat. Sooner or later the city would be abandoned and there was no point in sacrificing hundreds of lives in a second vain attempt to speed up that result.

In fact the French were running low on ammunition and could not retain their obstinate hold on Namur for much longer. In any case, the bulk of Grouchy's army was by now out of the grasp of the Prussians. It was approaching 8.00 pm. Four hundred paces from the Porte de Fer stood Major von Jochens and the 3rd battalion, 22nd Infantry. Suddenly an alarm spread that the French were attempting a sortie from Namur. Immediately, Jochens' brigade commander ordered him to lead his battalion forward to meet the sortie at the Porte de Fer. Jochens was to overthrow the French force and then try to penetrate into Namur in close pursuit. In fact, it seems that the French sortie, if intended, never materialised. Jochens' men found the Porte de Fer firmly shut. Unable to force open the stubborn gate, the Prussians broke in the windows of the adjoining customs house and passed through the building to find themselves in a street inside Namur. Further Prussian units marched up and entered the city.

The customs building has long since vanished but you can follow the route of the exuberant Prussians down the rue de Fer across the market place until they reached the bridge over the River Sambre. A modern bridge crosses the river at this point today. The French had barricaded the old bridge along its entire length and the last of Teste's heroic troops had to run along its parapets. Marshal Grouchy would have blown this bridge up if only he had possessed the means.[27] Nevertheless, French engineers kept the Prussians at bay for a while by firing from loopholed houses on the south bank of the Sambre. The Prussians tried to ford the Sambre but failed.[28]

Teste had posted a company of voltigeurs, or skirmishers, of the 75th Line infantry in observation on the heights of the citadel which overlooks Namur from the south bank. In 1815 the citadel was in ruins and remained like that until rebuilt by the Dutch in 1818.[29] Nonetheless, the heights themselves commanded a magnificent view of Namur, as they still do today. You may ascend either by cable-car or by foot. All the essential features of Namur are visible from the top of the citadel: the Cathedral of St Aubain, the market place, the line where the ramparts used to stand and, on the horizon, the hills where Vandamme's troops had held the Prussians at bay until Grouchy had marched the bulk of his force through Namur and Teste was ready to defend the ramparts.

Only between 8.30 and 9.00 pm did the French withdraw completely, after the Prussians successfully stormed the bridge over the Sambre. Loud cheers announced the Prussian occupation of Namur. At the Dinant gate on the south bank of the city, Teste's troops had piled up wood, straw and pitch. The last Frenchmen passed out of Namur and on to the road towards Dinant before Captain Borremans, a Belgian in the ranks of the 75th Line, lit the pyre. The gate was on fire, nearby houses blazed and the road to Dinant was blocked. With the Prussians powerless and exhausted, Teste followed in Grouchy's footsteps and rejoined him at Dinant towards 4.00 am on 21 June after a three hour rest at Profondeville. In the pocket of one of Teste's officers still lay the key to the Porte de Bruxelles.[30] Teste had lost relatively few men compared with his opponents although 150 Frenchmen had fallen into Prussian hands when Namur finally fell.[31]

If time permits, catch a train along the Meuse valley to Dinant. No relics of Grouchy's retreat are here but you will gain a vivid impression of the tortuous road he marched along and which effectively checked the Prussian pursuit. The Meuse valley has a long association with military history. At Bouvignes, immediately north of Dinant, Major-General Erwin Rommel, commander of the German 7th Panzer Division, crossed the river in May 1940. In Dinant itself the young Charles de Gaulle was wounded in the knee on 15 August 1914 while serving in the 33rd Infantry. A significant skirmish occurred on 24 December 1944 just five miles east of Dinant, for at the village of Celles the 3rd battalion of the British Royal Tank Regiment halted the westernmost push of the German Ardennes offensive.[32]

But at Dinant on the night of 20/21 June 1815, Captain Charles François' thoughts were not on the future: 'some officers and a lot of soldiers stayed in the houses alongside the road. As for me, I remained in the bivouac and I reposed in the centre of the battalion, where the flag was, thinking of our past glory and of our present misfortunes.'[33]

Marshal Grouchy continued his retreat from Dinant and crossed the frontier into France at Givet. On 26 June at Laon he linked up with the remnants of the French formations which had been mauled at Waterloo. Thus the debris of the once Grand Army were reunited and placed under Grouchy's command. They numbered barely 60,000 men. Desertion was rife and Baron Marcellin de Marbot, commander of the 7th Hussars, claimed that only the death penalty could stem the problem. On 23 June Wellington wrote: 'I may be wrong, but my opinion is, that we have given Napoleon his death blow; from all I hear his army is totally destroyed, the men are deserting in parties, even the Generals are withdrawing from him.'[34]

The political repercussions were out-pacing the military consequences of Waterloo. Napoleon had reached Paris early on 21 June. Exhausted and unnerved by his defeat, he had failed immediately to dissolve the Chambers of Peers and Deputies and rule by decree after declaring a state of emergency. The initiative passed to Napoleon's political enemies, including the slippery Joseph

Fouché, and the hostile Chambers declared themselves to be in permanent session. As a result, Napoleon would only be able to regain his authority by force and that would risk civil war. He abdicated on 23 June and a Provisional Government was set up under Fouché. This political turmoil further demoralised the French army.

By now, hostile troops were on French soil. Wellington and Blücher had commenced their 150 mile march from Waterloo to Paris. Further south, vast Austrian and Russian armies were advancing against the skeleton forces guarding France's eastern frontiers.

Wellington had crossed the French frontier at Malplaquet on 21 June and then breached a triple line of French fortresses by seizing Cambrai and Péronne. Blücher had advanced on Wellington's left, via Charleroi, Avesnes, Guise and St Quentin. The Prussians, eager to avenge French atrocities committed in Prussia in 1806, advanced faster than Wellington but left a trail of devastation behind them. Even in Wellington's disciplined army, some barbarities occurred. According to a British officer, 'a Hanoverian soldier entered a house where he had seen children, and running his bayonet into one of them, suspended it in the air, to show, as he said, how the French had served the children of his country when they invaded it.'[35]

Marshal Grouchy fought some skirmishes at Compiègne and Senlis on 27 June and Villers-Cotterêts the next day but could not seriously delay the relentless Prussian advance. He led his remaining troops into Paris on 29 June.

Wellington and Blücher had left sizeable detachments, including the Prussian II Corps, to observe or besiege fortresses and guard their communications. Only around 118,000 of their troops arrived before Paris. The French had about 117,000 in and around Paris under Marshal Davout and Napoleon offered his services as a mere general to the Provisional Government to avenge Waterloo.[36] His offer was rejected in spite of the French soldiers' eagerness to fight for Paris. The Provisional Government, and Davout himself, wanted peace, even at the price of a Bourbon restoration and an Allied occupation of France.

Napoleon thereupon departed for Rochefort on the western coast in a bid to escape to America. He was only just in time, for Blücher arrived north of Paris on 29 June and Prussian hussars swept round west of the city. A series of clashes ended with the Prussian hussars being trapped in a village and nearly all shot down or captured. A local inhabitant, the Countess Hocquart, stood on a terrace and applauded: 'bravo! bravo! Kill all those people for me!'[37]

This fiasco proved no more than a momentary setback. Paris was fortified only on the northern side so Blücher led his army round to the unprotected southern suburbs while Wellington arrived to the north. A British officer described on 2 July how at last 'the domes and spires of the city of Paris were in view: wonderful it appeared to see a British army *there*, after the renown which the French had acquired for twenty-five years back.'[38] Captain Alexander Cavalié Mercer, commander of 'G' Troop, Royal Horse Artillery, on the other hand, was troubled by 'feverish dreams of Paris in flames; of plundering, mutinous soldiers and all sorts of horrors.'[39]

The Prussians encountered heavy fighting on 2 July in Issy and Vanves, at the outskirts of Paris. But the hopelessness of the French position was now apparent and at 7.15 am on 3 July, firing ceased. The Convention of St Cloud was agreed on at 3.00 pm. The French army was to evacuate the capital in three days and retire south of the River Loire. For their part, Wellington and Blücher agreed in Article Twelve that: 'private persons and property shall be equally respected. The inhabitants, and in general all individuals who shall be in the capital, shall continue to enjoy their rights and liberties, without being disturbed or called to account, either as to the situations which they hold, or may have held, or as to their conduct or political opinions.' In the event, neither Wellington nor Blücher would prevent the restored Bourbons launching a cowardly and vindictive White Terror which hunted down and murdered many of Napoleon's officers, including Marshal Ney.

On 4 July the French duly left Paris and three days later allied troops entered it. Louis XVIII returned on 8 July. The Treaty of Paris brought hostilities officially to a close on 20 November 1815. According to its terms, France was to pay large reparations and all art treasures looted by French armies were to be restored. Wellington would command an army of occupation of 150,000 men in France for five years though in the event the period was only three years.

In the meantime, Napoleon had found British ships blocking any passage to America. On 13 July 1815 he had written to England's Prince Regent: 'Your Royal Highness ... I have ended my political career and come, like Themistocles, to seat myself at the hearth of the British people. I put myself under the protection of her laws and address this entreaty to Your Highness as the most steadfast and the most generous of my foes.'[40]

Two days later the fallen Emperor surrendered to Captain Frederick Maitland of HMS *Bellerophon*. On 17 October he landed on the remote island of St Helena, where he was to remain a prisoner until his death in 1821.

The most momentous event of the nineteenth century was Napoleon's invasion of Russia in 1812. The destruction of his Grand Army exhausted French resources and signalled the uprising of Europe against Napoleonic domination. The most decisive battle of the Napoleonic wars was not Waterloo but Leipzig in 1813, where the nations of Europe defeated Napoleon on the battlefield. Within and without the French Empire, dissention grew and Napoleon's fall in April 1814 was but a question of time.

In 1815 Napoleon hoped to re-establish his vision of a Europe dominated by France and run for the benefit of France. This dream could have won only a temporary success. Napoleon's foes had learnt from his method of war and had reformed and modernised Europe's armies. Sooner or later Napoleon would have fallen; he was too weak and his enemies too strong for him to build anew his Empire.

Nonetheless, it was at Waterloo that Napoleon's ambition was shattered once and for all. Henceforth, Napoleon would strive to conquer hearts and minds but never again would he conquer the lands and armies of Europe.

Napoleon's vision of a French-dominated Europe was out of date. 'For Napoleon to have won Waterloo would have been counter to the tide of the nineteenth century,' wrote the French literary giant, Victor Hugo. 'Waterloo was not a battle but a change in the direction of the world.'[41]

Nevertheless, the post-Napoleonic Europe that emerged disappointed many. After so long a period of strife, people hoped that Waterloo would herald the dawn of a golden age. But while international relations were largely peaceful, social frictions accumulated. In central and eastern Europe especially, rulers co-operated in suppressing democracy and national self-determination. At the same time the industrial revolution was changing Europe and producing further social and political stress.

Frustrated forces eventually shattered the European settlement of 1815. The ideals of national independence and liberty nurtured during the Revolutionary and Napoleonic eras inspired the overthrow of Spanish rule in South America by 1825 and the Greek War of Independence against Turkish domination in 1821–9. Two waves of revolutions swept across Europe itself in 1830 and 1848. These disturbances transformed the continent and led to Belgian independence, the final disappearance of the monarchy in France and political reform in western Europe. Meanwhile, Prussia took the lead in central Europe and began mustering the economic and military power it needed to unite a German nation under Prussian leadership by 1871. In the following decades Germany would attempt to create a united Europe under the Teutonic heel and it would take two world wars to destroy this objective.

Waterloo failed to bring true liberty, except from French oppression. It failed to herald social stability and untroubled economic prosperity. It failed to produce a united and permanently stable Europe. But it did provide four decades undisturbed by major European war. Such a long period of peaceful co-existence was remarkable and made the self-sacrifice of those who fell in battle worthwhile.

The victory of Waterloo also marked the ascendancy of Britain's prestige and indicated the industrial and financial power which, allied with command of the seas, would shortly lead to Queen Victoria's empire on which the sun never set.

Furthermore, Waterloo was the last battle between Britain and France. The bitter rivalry between these two great nations had lasted for centuries and now came to a close. Gradually the two former foes became friends. Just forty years after Waterloo, the Crimean War saw British soldiers fighting side by side with

French troops against Russia. By 1914 Britain and France had become, together, the two great defenders of liberty in Europe.

Waterloo failed to achieve the stability Europe now enjoys following two world wars and the collapse of communist Eastern Europe. But it did point the way forward. It was a blood-soaked milestone on the long and tortuous road called progress.

# Notes

1. A Near Observer, *The battle of Waterloo* (1816), p.240
2. H. Biot, *Souvenirs anecdotiques et militaires* (1901), p.256
3. H. Houssaye, *Waterloo 1815* (1987), p.460
4. *Ibid*, p.461
5. F. des Odoards, *Journal du général Fantin des Odoards* (1895), p.436
6. H. Biot, *Souvenirs anecdotiques et militaires* (1901), p.259
7. K. Damitz, *Histoire de la campagne de 1815* (1840), v.1, p.339
8. H. Houssaye, *Waterloo 1815* (1987), p.464
9. *Ibid*, p.465
10. A Near Observer, *The Battle of Waterloo* (1816), p.240
11. H. Biot, *Souvenirs anecdotiques et militaires* (1901), p.262
12. H. Couvreur, *Le drame belge de Waterloo* (1959), p.97
13. *Ibid*, p.100
14. H. Biot, *Souvenirs anecdotiques et militaires* (1901), p.262
15. W. Frye, *After Waterloo. Reminiscences of European travel 1815–1819* (1908), p.14
16. K. Damitz, *Histoire de la campagne de 1815* (1840), v.1, p.339
17. *Ibid*, v.1, p.340
18. H. Couvreur, *Le drame belge de Waterloo* (1959), p.98
19. C. François, *Journal du capitaine François* (1904), v.2, pp.891–2
20. J. Berthezène, *Souvenirs militaires* (1855), v.2, p.400
21. H. Couvreur, *Le drame belge de Waterloo* (1959), p.100
22. H. Biot, *Souvenirs anecdotiques et militaires* (1901), p.263; H. Couvreur, *Le drame belge de Waterloo* (1959), p.100
23. H. Biot, *Souvenirs anecdotiques et militaires* (1901), p.261
24. *Idem*
25. *Ibid*, p.262
26. F. de Bas and J. de Wommerson, *La campagne de 1815 aux Pays-Bas* (1908), v.3, pp.515–7
27. A Near Observer, *The Battle of Waterloo* (1816), p.240
28. K. Damitz, *Histoire de la campagne de 1815* (1840), v.1, pp.343–4
29. W. Frye, *After Waterloo. Reminiscences of European travel 1815–1819* (1908), p.14
30. H. Couvreur, *Le drame belge de Waterloo* (1959), pp.97–101
31. K. Damitz, *Histoire de la campagne de 1815* (1840), v.1, p.345
32. M. Glover, *A new guide to the battlefields of northern France and the Low Countries* (1987), p.43
33. C. François, *Journal du capitaine François* (1904), v.2, p.893
34. J. Gurwood ed., *The dispatches of the Duke of Wellington* (1838), v.12, pp.499–500
35. 'Operations of the Fifth or Picton's Division in the campaign of Waterloo', in *United Service Magazine* (June 1841), p.194
36. D. Chandler, *Waterloo, the hundred days* (1980), pp.179–83
37. H. Houssaye, *1815* (1895), v.3
38. 'Operations of the Fifth or Picton's Division in the campaign of Waterloo', in *United Service Magazine* (June 1841), p.201
39. C. Mercer, Journal of the *Waterloo campaign* (1985), p.236
40. E. Longford, *Wellington: pillar of state* (1972), p.17
41. V. Hugo, *Les Misérables* (1985), pp.302–3

# 21

# ECHOES OF WATERLOO

'Waterloo is one of those monumental landmarks which can never crumble. Its shadow can only grow longer.' With these words Wellington's eminent biographer, Lady Elizabeth Longford, introduced another addition to the scores of books describing the battle.[1] Relics of Waterloo cover the world and it would be impossible in one chapter to include all the echoes of the battle. Indeed it would require more than a lifetime to discover them all and this forms part of the fascination exerted by the titanic battle.

Hundreds of British towns adopted the battle's name, from the English Waterlooville north of Portsmouth to Waterloo with Seaforth near Liverpool. At Waterloo with Seaforth, local tradition contends that the design of a farmhouse called Potter's Barn was inspired by the farm of La Haie Sainte at the centre of Wellington's battlefield.[2] Other places named Waterloo exist in such diverse countries as Australia, Canada, New Zealand, the Caribbean island of Trinidad, Suriname and Guyana in South America, and Sierra Leone in West Africa. The United States of America boasts of a Waterloo in several states, notably Alabama, Arkansas, California, Illinois, Indiana, Iowa, Michigan, Montana, Nebraska, New Jersey, New York, Oregon, South Carolina and Wisconsin.

Scores of English streets bear the name of the great battle, as do Waterloo Station and Waterloo Bridge in London. The present Waterloo Bridge opened in 1945 to replace the original one dating from 1817. In Gwynedd, Wales, a cast iron bridge at Betws-y-Coed over the River Conway bears the inscription 'this arch was constructed in the same year the Battle of Waterloo was fought.' Even a mountain on New Zealand's South Island is called Waterloo Peak.

The great French novelist Victor Hugo saw the irony in all this. The battle ravaged the little known villages and farms of Plancenoit, Papelotte, Hougoumont and La Haie Sainte but left the village of Waterloo, nearly three miles behind the front line, unscarred. Yet it is Waterloo that has reaped all the glory. As the Roman poet Virgil wrote, *sic vos non vobis mellificatis apes*: 'thus do you make honey, but not for yourselves, o bees!'

You will discover the tombs of Waterloo veterans as far afield as America and Australia. For instance, Lieutenant James Crummer fought in the British 28th Foot at Waterloo, settled in Australia and died there in 1867. He rests at Port Macquarie on the coast of New South Wales, 200 miles north-east of Sydney. Countless other British Waterloo veterans served in Australia and many chose, as old soldiers, to fade away there.

The United States of America was a popular haven for French soldiers immediately after their defeat at Waterloo. The restored French Bourbon monarchy launched a White Terror which murdered several hundred Bona-partists and many old soldiers went into exile until the wind of wrath should blow over. Faced with repression in France, these veterans instinctively sought the Land of Liberty. Marshal Emmanuel de Grouchy and Lieutenant-General Count Dominique Vandamme both stayed temporarily in America before returning to their native land.

Philadelphia in Pennsylvannia became the main centre of these French exiles. Grouchy and Napoleon's elder brother, Joseph Bonaparte, the one time King of Spain, both resided there. However, many of the French exiles left Philadelphia and became pioneers in the wilderness of modern day Texas and Alabama. There they founded their own settlements. The pioneer life-style was a tough one and the French settlers failed to adapt to it. Instead of beating their swords into ploughshares they sought to recreate the past by making their settlements in the image of Napoleon's military camps. Nostalgia was not a luxury pioneers could allow themselves in an environment infested with alligators, mosquitoes and yellow fever. Many saw the settlements as merely a temporary base from which to attempt a rescue of their Emperor from captivity on St Helena.[3]

In 1817 around 150 French refugees settled on the banks of the River Tombigbee in what is now the State of Alabama. They called their first set-tlement Demopolis, which is Greek for 'city of the people.' One of the leading colonists was Lieutenant-General Count Charles Lefebvre-Desnouëttes, who commanded Napoleon's Guard light cavalry at Waterloo. His log cabin con-tained a large bronze statue of Napoleon and a collection of swords and pistols on the walls. In 1822 he would drown in a shipwreck on the coast of Ireland while returning from exile. The French colonists also founded Aigleville, 'town of the eagle', but both Demopolis and Aigleville had to be abandoned when it emerged they were built outside the land granted to the French. So the colonists created a third settlement, named Arcola after Napoleon's victory of 1796.

Many of the French settlers returned to France when the political atmosphere there improved. Others went to New Orleans to pursue business interests. Nevertheless, a few of the French colonists remained. Even today at Demopolis, ninety-five miles south-west of Birmingham, you can still see some vines and olive trees descended from the ones the French imported from Bordeaux. French family names are still common in this region of Alabama.

Another expedition to found an agricultural colony on the banks of the River

Trinity in present day Texas was less successful. One of the leaders was General François Lallemand, who had led the Guard Chasseurs à cheval at Waterloo and many of the 300 or 400 settlers were ex-Imperial Guardsmen. They founded the Champ d'Asile in 1818 at a location about forty-five miles north-east of the modern city of Houston. The colony soon dissolved but today a memorial stone at the site of the Champ d'Asile commemorates Lallemand and his fellow veterans. The stone bears the legend 'we wish to remain free, laborious and peaceful.'[4]

It was not only the French who arrived in America. Some former Prussian troops also came to escape repression in the Old World, including Franz Lieber. He had fought in the 9th Infantry of Blücher's II Corps in the 1815 campaign. Later he had to seek political asylum in the States, where he became a professor at South Carolina College and later at Columbia College, New York. Another Prussian soldier, Louis Riep, was born on 5 April 1798 and enlisted at the age of seventeen. He fought under Blücher in 1815 and died in Michigan in 1903 aged 105.[5]

Nevertheless, Europe contains the largest concentration of graves of Waterloo veterans. Count Pierre Durutte, who commanded an infantry division of d'Erlon's French I Corps at Waterloo, was buried at Ypres cemetery in Belgium. He had married at Ypres and sought refuge there following the restoration of King Louis XVIII to the French throne. He died aged fifty-nine in 1827. The inscription on his tomb reads: 'his military career began at Valmy [in 1792] and ended at Waterloo. Under the Republic, under the Consulate, under the Empire, under the Monarchy, he served only France. R.I.P.'[6] At the Belgian Army Museum in Brussels you will see the blood-stained saddlecloth Durutte used at Waterloo. The blood came from two serious wounds, one in his fore-head and the other to his right wrist.

In France, you will find graves of Waterloo veterans all over the country. Captain Jean-Roch Coignet, Napoleon's waggon-master at Waterloo and the author of some entertaining memoirs[7], is at the Saint-Amatre cemetery in Auxerre, ninety miles south-east of Paris while the grave of Count Louis Friant, who was wounded in the evening of 18 June while commanding the grenadiers of the Guard, is at Séraincourt, thirty miles west of Paris.

Père Lachaise cemetery in Paris contains scores of Waterloo veterans' graves. Père Lachaise itself is a relic of the Napoleonic era. As First Consul, Napoleon ordered the Prefect of Paris to buy land outside the city walls for a 'modern and hygenic' cemetery. Named after King Louis XIV's confessor and adviser, Père Lachaise admitted its first resident, a five-year old girl, on 21 May 1804.[8]

Père Lachaise soon became the most fashionable cemetery in France. Today it forms a vast, fascinating outdoor museum and those mausoleums and tombs which are falling into disrepair only add to the historic atmosphere. Victor Hugo described this sprawling cemetery as a 'city of sepulchres'[9] and the inhabitants sleep not in tombs but monuments. The people who roam the cemetery paths come some as mourners, most as pilgrims.

Plans of the cemetery are on sale at the entrances and indicate the locations of the more famous residents. Most of the Waterloo veterans lie in the centre of the southern half of the cemetery. The most prominent of these men is Marshal Michel Ney, who was shot on 7 December 1815 by the restored Bourbon monarchy. Ney sleeps at the western edge of the Chemin Masséna; the tomb itself is a simple stone slab with a cross. This is sheltered on three sides by a stone wall bearing an effigy of the marshal. He is still a hero to the French nation and flowers are often left on his tomb even today.

Walk along the Chemin Masséna and you will find the graves of many other Waterloo veterans, including those of Honoré Reille and Maximilien Foy of Napoleon's II Corps. After Waterloo, Foy entered politics and died of a heart attack in 1825, aged fifty. His tomb is thirty feet high and includes a statue of the general.

Nearby sleeps François Haxo, the commander of the Imperial Guard engineers at Waterloo. Before the battle, he reconnoitred Wellington's battle line to see if it included any entrenchments. The same neighbourhood includes the celebrated surgeon, Dominique Larrey, and André Burthe, commander of a brigade of dragoons in II Cavalry Corps. He served under Marshal Grouchy at the Battle of Wavre.

Follow the Chemin Masséna eastwards into the Chemin Suchet and then the Chemin des Anglais. Here, on the western side of the Chemin des Anglais, you will find Pierre Dejean, one of the ADCs who served Napoleon at Waterloo. On the other side of the chemin lies Jean-Baptiste Jamin, marquis de Bermuy. He fell at Waterloo at the head of the Grenadiers à cheval of the Guard while charging Wellington's batteries.

Another of Napoleon's ADCs buried in the cemetery is Charles de la Bédoyère. Aged only twenty-nine, he was shot by the Bourbons after their restoration to power. His grief-stricken mother had inscribed on the tomb: 'my love for my son alone was able to keep me alive.' A statue of an imperial eagle stands on top of the monument, which you will find in the Chemin de Labédoyère, south of the Carrefour du Grand Rond.

Other Waterloo veterans at Père Lachaise include François Roguet and Joseph Christiani of the Guard, François Kellermann, the commander of III Cavalry Corps, and François Lallemand, who led the Guard Chasseurs à cheval. Marcellin de Marbot, commander of the 7th Hussars, and his brigade commander, Adrien Bruno, also sleep here; you will find Marbot's grave halfway along the eastern edge of the Chemin du Quinconce, near the Columbarium. Marshal Emmanuel de Grouchy rests at the edge of the Avenue latéral du Nord, immediately north of the Monument aux Morts.

Besides veterans of the 1815 campaign, Père Lachaise counts among its eminent guests Henry Houssaye, the foremost French historian of the battle. He is buried near the eastern end of the Avenue Principale, near the Monument aux Morts. Père Lachaise holds scores of other men and women who helped make the Napoleonic era one of the most glittering of history. For instance, the cemetery is home to the talented artists Jean-Louis Géricault and Antoine-Jean Gros and the skilled goldsmith Jean-Baptiste Odiot who decorated the cradle of Napoleon's son the King of Rome. The cemetery also shelters François Joseph Talma, the great tragic actor, and the talented mathematician Gaspard Monge, who at fourteen invented a fire engine and at twenty-seven produced a technique for turning church bells into cannon.

General Joseph Hugo, father of the great French novelist Victor Hugo, is another of the cemetery's inhabitants. He did not fight at Waterloo but was undoubtedly the main reason for his son's fascination with Napoleon's final defeat. Joseph Hugo, the son of a carpenter, became a soldier in 1788 and spent most of his military career fighting bandits and rebels in France and Italy and guerrillas in Spain. Such was his staunch Bonapartism that in both 1814 and 1815 he held the town of Thionville sixteen miles north of Metz long after Napoleon's abdications. Victor Hugo himself lies at the Panthéon in Paris among such luminaries as the novelist and celebrated campaigner Emile Zola and Jean Moulin, the murdered hero of the wartime Resistance.

Napoleon himself rests in a magnificent red porphyry tomb at the Invalides on the south bank of the Seine in Paris. He was buried initially in exile on the island of St Helena but the French King Louis-Philippe had his body brought back to his capital city on 15 December 1840. This fulfilled Napoleon's own request: 'I wish my ashes to rest on the banks of the Seine, in the middle of this French people I have so loved.'

Nearby is the French Emperor's son, the King of Rome, who died in Austria from tuberculosis aged just twenty-one. Napoleon's brother Prince Jérôme Bonaparte, who led the attack on Hougoumont, also sleeps here, as does the Count of Lobau, the stout-hearted commander of VI Corps who defied the Prussians to the end at Waterloo.

The Duke of Wellington sleeps in London, in the crypt of St Paul's Cathedral. Nearby are the tombs of some of Britain's other war heroes, including Admiral Sir Horatio Nelson who fell at the Battle of Trafalgar on 21 October 1805 at the moment of victory over Napoleon's fleet.

Wellington's horse, Copenhagen, lies in the grounds of the Duke's Hampshire palace of Stratfield Saye. The gravestone is inscribed: 'here lies Copenhagen, the charger ridden by the Duke of Wellington the entire day at the Battle of Waterloo. Born 1808 died 1836. God's humbler instrument, though meaner clay should share the glory of that glorious day.'

Many of the British veterans who fought under Wellington at Waterloo sleep in a quiet corner of an English village churchyard. For instance, Joseph

Oliver of the 95th Rifles is buried at the parish church of Stonesfield in Oxfordshire.

Captain Alexander Cavalié Mercer, who commanded 'G' Troop, Royal Horse Artillery, at Waterloo, left a journal which is justly regarded today as the most vivid and detailed eyewitness account of the 1815 campaign.[10] Published posthumously in 1870, it ensured him lasting fame. He never saw active campaigning again after Waterloo but he did serve in Canada in 1837 when a war threatened between Britain and America. Later he commanded the garrison at Dover and became General Mercer in 1865. He spent his last years at Cowley, two miles north-west of Exeter, and died there on 9 November 1868 at the advanced age of eighty-five.

You will find Mercer's simple stone tomb in the graveyard of St David's Church, Exeter, on the right of the entrance path. On 18 June 1915, the Officer Commanding Royal Field Artillery at Topsham Barracks in Exeter placed on Mercer's grave a wreath of laurel leaves with blue flowers and red roses, the colours of the Royal Regiment of Artillery. Elsewhere in the country further representatives of the regiment placed wreaths simultaneously on thirty-nine other graves of artillerymen who had fought at Waterloo.

Among these thirty-nine graves were those of three of Mercer's fellow officers in 'G' Troop. First Lieutenant Henry Leathes lies buried at St Margaret's Church in Herringfleet and First Lieutenant John Breton at Lyndhurst, Hants. The wreath-laying ceremony at Bedale in Yorkshire on the grave of First Lieutenant John Hincks attracted a large crowd. Among others were local schoolboys, hospital patients, curates, one British and two Belgian soldiers invalided from the Western Front and Miss Askey who, as a nine-year-old child, had known Hincks in person.[11]

Hundreds of statues and monuments commemorate the heroes of Waterloo. At the French town of Damvillers, twelve miles north of Verdun, you will find a statue of Marshal Maurice Gérard, who as a lieutenant-general commanded Napoleon's IV Corps in 1815. Two days before Waterloo at the Battle of Ligny, Gérard's troops attacked Blücher's Prussians in Ligny village. One of the happier results of the battle was the decision in 1965 to twin the Belgian village of Ligny with Gérard's birthplace, Damvillers. Ligny also contains a General Gérard Centre which includes a museum about the battle.

In Germany, Prince Blücher and his talented but much maligned chief-of-staff, Augustus von Gneisenau, are both commemorated by larger than life statues in the Unter den Linden in Berlin. One of Gneisenau's descendants was Colonel Count Claus von Stauffenberg, who heroically executed the unsuccessful bomb plot against Adolf Hitler's life in July 1944.[12] Elsewhere in Germany, monuments commemorate the dead soldiers of the German contingents of Wellington's army. At the city of Hanover, 150 miles west of Berlin, a 212-foot high memorial in the Waterlooplatz commemorates the approximately 700 Hanoverian and King's German Legion troops who fell in the 1815 campaign.[13] The memorial was erected between 1826 and 1832 and consists of a column supporting both a viewing platform and a winged figure of Victory.

The Duchy of Nassau was another German state that provided a contingent for Wellington's army. Its lands lay around the town of Wiesbaden, which lies on the north bank of the River Rhine 165 miles south of Hanover. Today, a monument in front of the twin-spired Bonifatiuskirche pays tribute to the 2nd Nassau Infantry and the Orange-Nassau Regiment who at Waterloo defended Wellington's far left flank under Prince Bernhard of Saxe-Weimar. It also remembers the 1st Nassau Infantry under General August von Kruse who helped hold the centre of the line. Detachments of Nassau troops also contributed to the defence of both Hougoumont and La Haie Sainte. Sadly, this monument, a stone obelisk, is often defaced with graffiti.

Many British towns boast of a statue of the Duke of Wellington though often, as at Manchester, such statues portray him as a civilian and commemorate his achievements as a statesman and politician. An enormous equestrian statue of the Duke as a military commander used to stand at Hyde Park Corner but was transferred in 1883 to Aldershot. A more modest statue by Sir J.E. Boehm now stands outside the Duke's London home of Apsley House. Apsley House is today a museum and visitors can see the Waterloo Gallery in which, from 1830 to 1852, Wellington held his famous banquets for his senior subordinates on the anniversary of the battle.

A monument on the Isle of Anglesey near Llanfairpwllgwyngll remembers Lord Uxbridge, Wellington's erstwhile cavalry commander at Waterloo. It consists of a 100-foot column erected in 1817. Six years after Uxbridge died in 1854 a bronze statue of him in uniform as Colonel of the 7th Hussars was added to the summit. A spiral staircase inside the column allows access to a platform offering magnificent views over the Menai Straits towards the Welsh mountains. One and a half miles to the south-west along the A4080 is the house of Plas Newydd. Here, a small museum contains one of Uxbridge's artificial legs made to replace the one amputated after Waterloo. You can also see a leg of his hussar trousers, still splashed with mud from the battlefield.[14]

The Church of St Luke at Gaddesby, six miles south-west of Melton Mowbray in Leicestershire, contains one of the more unusual monuments to a Waterloo hero. A large marble statue depicts Captain Edward Cheney of the Scots Greys astride a fallen horse. He had four horses killed and one wounded under him in the course of the battle and commanded his regiment in the closing stages. Cheney had married Eliza Ayre at Gaddesby in 1811 and died there on 3 March 1848. The local Cheney Arms public house is named in his honour.

Countless national and regimental museums contain weapons wielded at Waterloo or uniforms worn by the combatants. One of the most fascinating relics in the British Household Cavalry Museum at Windsor is the bugle of sixteen-year-old Field-Trumpeter John Edwards of the 1st Life Guards. He sounded the charge when the Household Cavalry, in conjunction with the Union Brigade, launched their devastating counter-attack against Napoleon's attack on Wellington's left flank at about 2.30 pm. John Edwards served for thirty-two years in the 1st Life Guards and received a pension in 1841.[15]

The Rijksmuseum in Amsterdam has a whole room devoted to the battle and the army museums in Brussels and Rastatt in south-west Germany also contain fine collections of Waterloo relics. In Paris, the Invalides houses the French Army Museum, which shows the extent to which Napoleonic nostalgia has pervaded the French military through and beyond the disaster of 1815. The French Napoleonic historian Henry Lachouque, himself a combatant in the two world wars, described how Napoleon's Imperial Guard set a standard and provided an inspiration 'which animated the whole Imperial army and continued to inspire those who came after it in 1854, 1870 and 1914.'[16]

In London, the National Army Museum contains a 'Road to Waterloo' exhibition. One of the relics on display is the eagle of the French 105th Line infantry, which was captured by the Royal Dragoons. But the centre-piece of the exhibition is a 420 square foot model of the battle constructed by William Siborne, the great English historian who collected hundreds of letters from eyewitnesses. His model contains over 70,000 miniature soldiers and depicts the moment of victory as Wellington's infantry repulse the French Middle Guard towards 8.00 pm. Siborne also constructed a smaller model of the repulse of d'Erlon's French I Corps by Wellington's left flank around 2.30 pm and this is now on display at Dover Castle. Another model of Waterloo, showing the battlefield as it appeared at 4.30 pm, is at the Musée de la Figurine Historique at Compiègne in France.

The British Royal Military Academy at Sandhurst contains several fine paintings of the battle as well as some guns used at Waterloo. A French 12-pounder guards the Yorktown Gate while a further two French guns and four British 6-pounder cannon stand in front of the Old College on the edge of the parade ground.

One of the most interesting Waterloo exhibitions is at Bexhill museum on the south coast of England. Situated four miles west of Hastings, in 1804 Bexhill became the main base of the King's German Legion, which won imperishable fame for its gallant defence of La Haie Sainte farm at Waterloo. In 1989 local enthusiasts formed the Bexhill Hanoverian Study Group to research and record the KGL's stay in the town.

Lady Elizabeth Longford, the Duke of Wellington's eminent biographer, opened a temporary exhibition on the KGL at Bexhill museum on 16 June 1990. At the town's Northern Hotel in Sea Road she unveiled a portrait of the 1st Duke of Wellington and a plaque to record her visit. She also dedicated the hotel's Wellington Room to the memory of the heroic KGL troops who stayed in Bexhill between 1804 and 1815. Also present at the ceremony was the great-great-granddaughter of a Waterloo veteran, Lieutenant Stephen Macdonald. She proudly wore his Waterloo medal for the day's events. Stephen Macdonald was an Englishman but since he grew up at Bexhill during the Napoleonic wars, he joined the 1st Light battalion KGL.

In May 1991 a smaller but permanent display replaced the museum's temporary exhibition. This contains information on the famous KGL person-alities and on the relics of the KGL presence in Bexhill. A visit to Bexhill imparts a fascinating insight into the lives of the exiled Hanoverian soldiers who formed the KGL and fought and died under the British flag so bravely at Waterloo. For these homesick troops, Bexhill became an adopted home.

The impact of the KGL's arrival at Bexhill in August 1804 was immense. The town accommodated four KGL battalions, 2673 men, in a twenty-five acre camp. The population of Bexhill at the time was less than 1000. By 1808 the inhabitants numbered just 1091 and in 1811, 1627. Thus the KGL must have overwhelmed Bexhill, which had no facilities for housing more than a handful of officers. At first the soldiers had to live in tents but they soon built simple huts with straw roofs. Even these huts were unsatisfactory. 'They are still a long way from being ready,' noted Christian von Ompteda of the 1st Line battalion in his diary on 20 November 1804. 'Those already inhabited [are] damp, natural consequence of using green wood.' The huts were cold and draughty and sometimes their turf walls subsided in the rain.[17]

Violent storms in October and November 1804 brought flooding and misery to the camp.[18] 'Continued cold and bad weather,' noted Christian von Omp-teda on 5 November. 'Being unwell, find my field-bed only a partial shelter. Ceaseless din of all kinds of bad music; meaningless shoutings and clamour. All this is trying to the patience, and leads to sullen stupefaction. This is the anniversary of the Gunpowder Plot, and Guy Fawkes consequently burnt with huzzas and jubilation in several bonfires in my proximity.'[19]

In the summer of 1805, the troops drilled almost daily at Crowhurst park, which you will find today on the south side of the A2100 between Hastings and Battle. The troops also trained at locations nearer Bexhill.[20]

At first, the KGL received a cool reception from villagers suspicious of all soldiers and especially of foreign ones. Christian von Ompteda, who fell at Waterloo, wrote in his diary on 6 August 1804 that the inhabitants of Bexhill looked on him and his comrades 'much as we do on Cossacks'. But later that same day he added, 'the gentry round called at the camp. They seem to be beginning to discover that we are not quite outlandish bears.'[21]

The passage of time made the KGL troops great favourites with the villagers. Relationships sprang up and the register of St Peter's Church began to record weddings of officers, NCOs and men to Bexhill girls as early as 27 August

1804. The last occurred on 15 August 1814 and in that ten-year span, the parish of St Peter's recorded 108 marriages between KGL men and local brides.[22] When the KGL disbanded in 1816 after the Napoleonic Wars, large numbers of soldiers returned to Hanover with their dutiful English wives.

However, many of the married soldiers remained in England. One was Conrad Olderhausen, a bugler with the 1st Light battalion at Waterloo. He had fought with the KGL during the Peninsular war and when discharged from the legion on 24 August 1815 he joined the 85th Foot for three more years. He then served for five years in the militia and then in the navy in India and China. While at Bexhill he had married an Englishwoman and when he died he was buried at Hastings.

Other liaisons were not legitimised and a warrant issued at Battle Petty Sessions on 13 April 1813 concerns the accusation by one Sophia Brazier that Captain Frederick Rehwinkel of the KGL artillery was the father of her bastard child. The captain unwisely replied that Miss Brazier was a 'lewd girl.' Not surprisingly, further records show that Rehwinkel paid Sophia Brazier two shillings a week for six weeks in August 1813.

Relations between the soldiers and the civilians were also improved by trade. The KGL required food, horses, equipment, fuel and drink and the merchants of Bexhill profited immensely from the consequent boom in the village economy. Local bootmakers quickly mastered the art of making the Hessian style boots popular with the KGL while Pocock's the butchers became the troops' prime supplier of meat.

The KGL's band offered public concerts and quickly became a great favourite with the villagers. Local soldiers attended services at St Peter's and their fine singing impressed everyone. Squire Brook, a famous local figure who died in 1890, said that among his strongest childhood memories were the Germans singing in St Peter's.

The KGL held a grand Ball on 14 January 1805 just two months after their arrival in Bexhill to strengthen ties with the villagers. Soldiers erected an improvised corridor between two of the newly built huts, made it look like an orange grove, festooned it with real fruit and lit it brilliantly. The effect must have been striking for it impressed the local gentry and yeomen whom the KGL had invited to the Ball. They took to the occasion and to the full force of the band and danced English dances and waltzes and the newly adopted French quadrille.

The local people were also fascinated by the strong KGL attachment to horses and the loving care the troops took of them. Thus the relationship between Bexhill and the KGL blossomed into a strong friendship which survived some careless accidents unharmed. 'Out for a walk to-day,' noted Christian von Ompteda on 11 April 1805, 'I was almost grazed by a musket-ball, which was discharged by an Englishman who was letting off a firearm for the first time in his life. On my remonstrating, he assured me that it should not occur again.'[23]

Bexhill museum is near the seafront, in the modern town of Bexhill-on-sea which sprang into being in the Victorian age. During the Napoleonic wars, Bexhill was but a small village three-quarters of a mile to the north. It is to this part of Bexhill – the old town – that the visitor should head to see in person the buildings connected with the KGL.

St Peter's church, founded in 772, lies at the heart of historic Bexhill. Two local people are usually on duty at the church and are eager to describe to the visitor the historic relics, especially the Bexhill stone, part of an eighth century reliquary in classic Celtic design. KGL troops used to worship inside St Peter's and their colonel-in-chief, the Duke of Cambridge, attended a service there. The parish register contains many records of KGL births, marriages and deaths. St Peter's churchyard does contain several military tombstones but none relate to the KGL. One stone is inscribed to the memory of Robert White of the 11th Light Dragoons who apparently slipped from his horse and drowned while riding along Bexhill beach in 1804 shortly before the KGL arrived in the town.

KGL troops who died at Bexhill were buried at a cemetery at Barrack Road, to the north-west of the church. Now disused, it served the town of Bexhill until the end of the nineteeenth century. All the tombstones except a few near the boundary wall have disappeared. The remains of 152 KGL troops and members of their families lie there and the first Bexhill Hanoverian Study Group commemorative signpost was unveiled there by Lady Elizabeth Longford on 23 April 1994. A detachment of re-enactors from Germany attended, uniformed as soldiers of the 2nd Light battalion, KGL. Several re-enactors of the 15th Hussars also attended to represent the British troops stationed at Bexhill in the Napoleonic era. To the mournful sound of hussar bugles the KGL re-enactors respectfully laid a wreath in yellow and white Hanoverian colours. Thus a small corner of an English memorial garden is now forever Hanover. The Study Group plans seven further signs to commemorate other relics of the KGL.

Two hundred and fifty metres south of the cemetery, where Chantry Lane joins Belle Hill, stands Barrack Hall. The hall was built in about 1794, although in the mid-nineteenth century a new facade was added. During the Napoleonic wars, it served as the KGL headquarters and officers' mess.[24] The hall is today a women's refuge but the residents are likely to move to modern accommodation elsewhere. This would leave Barrack Hall empty but hopes to turn it into a museum are unlikely to become reality. The intricate maze of corridors is not suited for museum displays.

Go through the gate to the side of Barrack Hall and proceed down a path to an open grassy space. This is the site of the parade ground and KGL buttons have been recovered here. The future Duke of Wellington was one of the officers who inspected troops on the parade ground during a review in 1806.

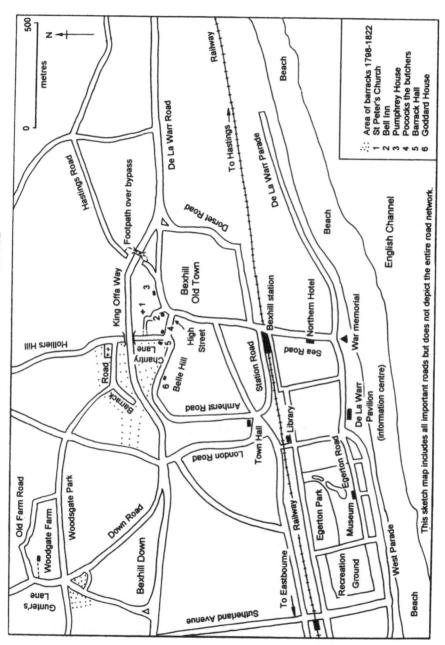

BEXHILL-ON-SEA TODAY

Area of barracks 1798-1822
1 St Peter's Church
2 Bell Inn
3 Pumphrey House
4 Pococks the butchers
5 Barrack Hall
6 Goddard House

This sketch map includes all important roads but does not depict the entire road network.

The barracks inhabited by the KGL used to extend 500 metres to the west of Barrack Hall. Note how these were built on the reverse slope of the hills, out of sight from any French ships in the English Channel. As already mentioned, at first the KGL had to live in tents and Christian von Ompteda complained on 13 November 1804 that:

> Uninterrupted bad weather has turned the clay soil of our encampment into a sticky, miry morass, so slippery that one can scarcely escape the danger of falling down. The wet and stuffiness of my tent delayed my recovery [from a nervous breakdown], and I was obliged, unwilling though I was not to share our common hardships, to obey the warnings of reason and necesssity. A neighbouring farm became my refuge.[25]

The farm Ompteda convalesced in was Woodgate farm north of Bexhill Down. A small cottage of the farm's buildings housed the KGL officer, who remarked in his diary of the politeness of little Miss Mary Lansdale, his hosts' daughter, in showing him over the house:

> Agreeable impression of the innocent mirth of the family after the wild disturbances of the camp. Fresh experience. How easily a man can accustom himself to the sacrifices demanded by a military mode of life, as long as he is in good health, almost as easily as he gets spoiled by luxury. After that life (of hardship) the commonest comforts of life have an enhanced value ... Elegant appointments; mahogany chairs with horse-hair seats, carpet, mirror, a fine fireplace, and exotics in the room I occupy ... No shouting and noise. Four men and two boys do their work as quietly and cleverly as if they were skilled artisans plying a handicraft. The same quietude and goodness seem to prevail over the domestic animals and beasts of burden. No ill-tempered horse to be seen, nor goring horned cattle, and no barking dog to be heard. The female dwellers in this house are industrious, quiet, and cheerful; the tone of their hearty laugh, provoked sometimes by the antics of a favourite dog, does one good, being the expression of *nature's* own joy.[26]

The open expanse of Bexhill Down was occupied in part by cavalry encampments. An old map of Bexhill in the early 1800s shows a path running diagonally across the down, a path that the troops quartered here would have used. Today it has become Down Road. In retracing your steps eastwards to the old town, pass along Belle Hill. The KGL reportedly stored its ammunition in several brick lined tunnels dug into the hillside along Belle Hill. One such tunnel is in the back garden of one of the houses, while on the north side of the road used to stand a large ammunition storage building. Further to the east stands Goddard House, built around 1806 and probably home to Charles von Alten, a German who commanded Wellington's 3rd Division at Waterloo.

In the High Street of the old town you will find Pocock's the butchers, who supplied meat to the KGL. Inside the window you can see a stone sign indicating the shop was built in 1801. A little further on, at the far end of the High Street, stands the Bell Inn, established well before the arrival of the KGL and undoubtedly frequented by the Germans.

Pass from the High Street into De La Warr Road. Numbers 5 and 7 on the north side used to constitute a single house owned at the time of Napoleon by a customs official, Thomas Pumphrey. His daughter married Captain Gottlieb Thilo Holtzermann, an officer of the 1st Light battalion KGL, who fell on the field of honour at Waterloo. Holtzermann served in the expedition to Hanover in 1805, the expedition to the Baltic in 1807–8, the Peninsular war from 1808 to 1809, the expedition to the Scheldt, the campaign in Northern Germany in 1813–14, the Netherlands in 1814 and finally the 1815 campaign.[27]

Captain Holtzermann's name is inscribed on the Hanoverian monument on the battlefield of Waterloo along with that of Colonel Christian von Ompteda and twenty-six other KGL officers. Nearly all of them would have known Bexhill well yet it is only in the last decade that their stay in the town has received the attention it deserves. In the words of Lady Elizabeth Longford, 'to me a local effort like this is worth all the Victoria and Alberts put together. It is very rare that local people are so interested in their own history and it is even rarer that they have the chance to understand it and feel it and see it all around them.'

Such is the interest in Waterloo that more echoes of the battle are certain to come to light in the future. One of the societies which is doing most to encourage research in the Napoleonic era is the Napoleonic Society of America. This flourishing association has now launched an ambitious fund-raising campaign. It hopes to provide a prestigious centre in the United States, to stimulate interest and study in the Napoleonic era and its effects on Western civilisation.

But of all the countless echoes of Waterloo, the most evocative are the weapons and uniforms which bear the marks of battle. In the French Army Museum at the Invalides is the cuirass of François-Antoine Faveau. He was a former butter dealer and was twenty-three years old in 1815. At Waterloo he charged with the carabiniers of François Kellermann's III Cavalry Corps and a gaping hole punched through both plates of the cuirass testify to a cannon-shot which put an abrupt end to his dreams of glory. In England, the Military Heritage Museum at Lewes in Sussex has a helmet worn by Captain Henry Madox of the 6th (Inniskilling) Dragoons. It is scarred by a musket-ball which only just failed to kill the captain. Casualties in the regiment were so great that Madox found himself in command towards 6.30 pm.[28]

Old soldiers never die; they merely fade away. Those of Waterloo have faded into the mists of time and now belong to the ages. Their memorials cover the entire world. The weathered gravestones in churchyards, the dented museum relics, the eyewitness recollections gathering dust in libraries all offer the same message: Waterloo was a vast human tragedy. For the soldiers, 18 June 1815 meant misery, suffering and death while for the bereaved relatives, life afterwards offered nothing but grief and loneliness. From Waterloo, across the hollow expanse of two centuries, thousands of voices speak to us: in battle, there is no glory; in war, there are no victors.

# Notes

1. U. Pericoli and M. Glover, *1815 The armies at Waterloo* (1973), p.7
2. *The official guide to Waterloo with Seaforth* (1928), p.8
3. J. Sutherland, *Men of Waterloo* (1967), pp.265–6
4. J. Rosengarten, *French colonists and exiles in the United States* (1907); A. Moore, *History of Alabama* (1934); J. Sutherland, *Men of Waterloo* (1967)
5. L. van Neck, *Waterloo illustré* (1903), p.44
6. *Ibid*, pp.161–2
7. J. Coignet, *The notebooks of Captain Coignet* (1986)
8. M. Dansel, *Au Père Lachaise* (1973)
9. V. Hugo, *Les Misérables* (1985), pp.1200–1
10. *Journal of the Waterloo Campaign* (reprinted in 1985 by Greenhill Books).
11. J. Leslie, *The centenary of the Battle of Waterloo* (1916)
12. J. Keegan, *Six armies in Normandy* (1982), p.227
13. Eight hundred dead is the figure usually quoted but this appears to be too high.
14. Marquess of Anglesey, *One leg* (1961), p.153
15. C. Dalton, *The Waterloo roll call* (1978), p.267
16. H. Lachouque, *The anatomy of glory* (1961), p.505
17. L. Ompteda, *A Hanoverian-English officer a hundred years ago* (1892), p.179
18. N. Beamish, *History of the King's German Legion* (1832), v.1, p.83
19. L. Ompteda, *A Hanoverian-English officer a hundred years ago* (1892), p.177
20. B. Schwertfeger, *Geschichte der Königlich deutschen Legion, 1803–1816* (1907), v.1, pp.29–30
21. L. Ompteda, *A Hanoverian-English officer a hundred years ago* (1892), p.176
22. P. Vernon, *Marriages at Bexhill of men of the King's German Legion, 1804–1814* (1990)
23. L. Ompteda, *A Hanoverian-English officer a hundred years ago* (1892), p.180
24. *Bexhill Chronicle* (November 1899)
25. L. Ompteda, *A Hanoverian-English officer a hundred years ago* (1892), p.178
26. *Idem*
27. N. Beamish, *History of the King's German Legion* (1837), v.2, p.633
28. BL Add. MSS 34,707/13: 'the Senior Captain Madox had his Helmet perforated by a Musket Shot.'

# APPENDICES

# Appendix 1

# ORDERS OF BATTLE OF THE THREE ARMIES ENGAGED IN THE 1815 CAMPAIGN

Unit strengths are approximate and refer to strengths before casualties began to be taken.

In some cases, units joined their parent formations only in the course of the campaign. For instance, the French 65th Line infantry joined Lieutenant-General Georges Mouton, Count of Lobau's VI Corps on 17 June.[1]

None of the three armies had a rigid order of battle: for example, Lieutenant-General Baron Jean-Baptiste Girard's infantry division was detached from the French II Corps on 15 June and did not fight with its parent corps for the rest of the campaign. In the French IV Cavalry Corps, when Brigadier-General Baron Etienne Travers de Jever was wounded on 18 June, Colonel Michel Ordener, the commander of the 1st Cuirassiers, was given command of a new brigade formed from his own regiment and the 7th Cuirassiers. One reason why the original brigade structure was altered in this case may have been that Ordener's brother, Gaston, was a lieutenant in the 7th Cuirassiers.[2]

In Wellington's army, the corps had little significance at Waterloo and was more an administrative concept than a military unit. As an example, HRH Prince Frederick (the eighteen-year-old younger brother of HRH the Prince of Orange) commanded a formation consisting of the 1st Dutch-Belgian Division and the Netherlands Indian brigade. This formation was a subordinate part of II Corps as Prince Frederick received orders from Lord Hill. Nevertheless, in his dispatches Wellington referred to Prince Frederick's command as 'a corps.'[3]

Wellington's cavalry was seriously weakened by the absence of any divisional organisation. Lord Uxbridge could not be everywhere at once and should have had divisional commanders to help him control his eight British and Hanoverian cavalry brigades.

Wellington's order of battle was further confused by the composite nature of his army. It contained contingents from Britain, the United Netherlands, Hanover, Brunswick and Nassau. Wellington was careful not to allow any lengthy part of his line to be held solely by non-British troops as he feared that they were not as stout as his redcoats. Each Hanoverian infantry brigade was joined to two brigades of the British army to form a division.

337

Wellington was unable to disperse his Dutch-Belgian brigades in a similar manner for political reasons. King William I of the Netherlands insisted that his Dutch-Belgian divisions should not be split up and should be commanded by Netherlands officers. The Dutch-Belgian cavalry division came under Lord Uxbridge's command only on the morning of 18 June, having hitherto belonged to HRH the Prince of Orange's I Corps.

Similarly, the Brunswick contingent formed a self-contained unit under its Duke. At the Battle of Quatre Bras on 16 June, Duke Frederick William personally commanded his infantry and cavalry, which acted in close mutual support. Nevertheless at Waterloo after the Duke's death the Brunswick cavalry seems to have acted more independently of its infantry and in concert with other allied cavalry formations, particularly when counter-attacking Marshal Ney's massed horsemen in the afternoon.[4]

Blücher's infantry brigades were equivalent in strength to British and French divisions. Similarly, his infantry regiments were of brigade strength and his battalions contained approximately 730 men. These large units were too unwieldy to be used effectively: at the Battle of Ligny especially, brigades and even regiments were split up and their individual battalions sent to different sectors of the battlefield. The clumsy Prussian order of battle made for serious problems in command and control.

The most flexible, sophisticated and finely-tuned army structure was that of the French.

## ORDER OF BATTLE OF THE FRENCH ARMY

| | |
|---|---|
| Commander-in-chief: | Emperor Napoleon |
| Chief-of-staff: | Marshal Soult |
| Strength: | 124,000 men and 370 guns |

I CORPS (21,000; 46 guns)
Commander: Lt-Gen Drouet, Count d'Erlon
1st Division (Brig-Gen Quiot)

| | |
|---|---|
| Brigade: | 54th and 55th Line Infantry |
| Bourgeois' brigade: | 28th and 105th Line Infantry |

2nd Division (Lt-Gen Baron Donzelot)

| | |
|---|---|
| Schmitz's brigade: | 13th Light and 17th Line Infantry |
| Aulard's brigade: | 19th and 31st Line Infantry |

3rd Division (Lt-Gen Baron Marcognet)

| | |
|---|---|
| Noguès' brigade: | 21st and 46th Line Infantry |
| Grenier's brigade: | 25th and 45th Line Infantry |

4th Division (Lt-Gen Count Durutte)

| | |
|---|---|
| Pégot's brigade: | 8th and 29th Line Infantry |
| Brue's brigade: | 85th and 95th Line Infantry |

1st Cavalry Division (Lt-Gen Baron Jacquinot)

| | |
|---|---|
| Bruno's brigade: | 7th Hussars and 3rd Chasseurs à cheval |
| Gobrecht's brigade: | 3rd and 4th Lancers |

Five foot and one horse artillery batteries
Five engineer companies

<u>II CORPS</u> (25,000; 46 guns)
Commander: Lt-Gen Count Reille
5th Division (Lt-Gen Baron Bachelu)
    Husson's brigade:          2nd Light and 61st Line Infantry
    Campi's brigade:          72nd and 108th Line Infantry
6th Division (Lt-Gen Prince Jérôme Bonaparte)
    Bauduin's brigade:        1st Light and 3rd Line Infantry
    Soye's brigade:           1st and 2nd Line Infantry
7th Division (Lt-Gen Baron Girard)[5]
    De Villiers' brigade:      11th Light and 82nd Line Infantry
    Piat's brigade:           12th Light and 4th Line Infantry
9th Division (Lt-Gen Baron Foy)
    Gauthier's brigade[6]:      92nd and 93rd Line Infantry
    Jamin's brigade:         4th Light and 100th Line Infantry
2nd Cavalry Division (Lt-Gen Count de Piré)
    Hubert's brigade:        1st and 6th Chasseurs à cheval
    Wathiez's brigade:      5th and 6th Lancers
Five foot and one horse artillery batteries
Five companies of engineers

<u>III CORPS</u> (18,000; 38 guns)
Commander: Lt-Gen Count Vandamme
8th Division (Lt-Gen Baron Lefol)
    Billiard's brigade:       15th Light and 23rd Line Infantry
    Corsin's brigade:        37th and 64th Line Infantry
10th Division (Lt-Gen Baron Habert)
    Gengoult's brigade:     34th and 88th Line Infantry
    Dupeyroux's brigade:    22nd and 70th Line Infantry; 2nd Swiss Infantry
11th Division (Lt-Gen Baron Berthezène)
    Dufour's brigade:        12th and 56th Line Infantry
    Lagarde's brigade:       33rd and 86th Line Infantry
3rd Cavalry Division (Lt-Gen Baron Domon)
    Dommanget's brigade:   4th and 9th Chasseurs à cheval
    Vinot's brigade:         12th Chasseurs à cheval
Four foot and one horse artillery batteries
Two engineer companies

<u>IV CORPS</u> (16,000; 38 guns)
Commander: Lt-Gen Count Gérard
12th Division (Lt-Gen Baron Pêcheux)
    Rome's brigade:          30th and 96th Line Infantry
    Schoeffer's brigade:      6th Light and 63rd Line Infantry
13th Division (Lt-Gen Baron Vichery)
    Le Capitaine's brigade[7]:   59th and 76th Line Infantry
    Desprez's brigade:       48th and 69th Line Infantry

14th Division (Lt-Gen Count de Bourmont) [deserted 15 June; replaced by Brig-Gen Baron Hulot]

| | |
|---|---|
| Hulot's brigade: | 9th Light and 111th Line Infantry |
| Toussaint's brigade: | 44th and 50th Line Infantry |

7th Cavalry Division (Lt-Gen Baron Maurin)[8]

| | |
|---|---|
| Vallin's brigade: | 6th Hussars and 8th Chasseurs à cheval |
| Berruyer's brigade: | 6th and 16th Dragoons |

Four foot and one horse artillery batteries
Three engineer companies

## VI CORPS (11,000; 32 guns)
Commander: Lt-Gen Count de Lobau
19th Division (Lt-Gen Baron Simmer)

| | |
|---|---|
| Bellair's brigade: | 5th and 11th Line Infantry |
| Jamin's brigade: | 27th and 84th Line Infantry |

20th Division (Lt-Gen Baron Jeanin)

| | |
|---|---|
| Bony's brigade: | 5th Light and 10th Line Infantry |
| Tromelin's brigade: | 107th Line and 2nd battalion, 47th Line Infantry |

21st Division (Lt-Gen Baron Teste)

| | |
|---|---|
| Laffitte's brigade: | 8th Light and 40th Line Infantry |
| Penne's brigade: | 65th and 75th Line Infantry |

Four artillery batteries
Two companies of engineers

## RESERVE CAVALRY (13,000; 48 guns)
Commander: Marshal Grouchy

## I CAVALRY CORPS (3000; 12 guns)
Commander: Lt-Gen Count Pajol
4th Cavalry Division (Lt-Gen Baron Soult)

| | |
|---|---|
| Saint-Laurent's brigade: | 1st and 4th Hussars |
| Ameil's brigade: | 5th Hussars |

5th Cavalry Division (Lt-Gen Baron Subervie)

| | |
|---|---|
| De Colbert's brigade: | 1st and 2nd Lancers |
| De Douai's brigade: | 11th Chasseurs à cheval |

Two horse artillery batteries

## II CAVALRY CORPS (3000; 12 guns)
Commander: Lt-Gen Count Exelmans
9th Cavalry Division (Lt-Gen Baron Strolz)

| | |
|---|---|
| Burthe's brigade: | 5th and 13th Dragoons |
| Vincent's brigade: | 15th and 20th Dragoons |

10th Cavalry Division (Lt-Gen Baron Chastel)

| | |
|---|---|
| Bonnemains' brigade: | 4th and 12th Dragoons |
| Berton's brigade: | 14th and 17th Dragoons |

Two horse artillery batteries

<u>III CAVALRY CORPS</u> (4000; 12 guns)
Commander: Lt-Gen Count Kellermann
11th Cavalry Division (Lt-Gen Baron L'Héritier)
   Picquet's brigade:         2nd and 7th Dragoons
   Guiton's brigade:         8th and 11th Cuirassiers
12th Cavalry Division (Lt-Gen Baron Roussel d'Hurbal)
   Blanchard's brigade:      1st and 2nd Carabiniers
   Donop's brigade:         2nd and 3rd Cuirassiers
Two horse artillery batteries

<u>IV CAVALRY CORPS</u> (3000; 12 guns)
Commander: Lt-Gen Count Milhaud
13th Cavalry Division (Lt-Gen Wathier, Count de Saint-Alphonse)
   Dubois' brigade:         1st and 4th Cuirassiers
   Travers' brigade:        7th and 12th Cuirassiers
14th Cavalry Division (Lt-Gen Baron Delort)
   Vial's brigade:           5th and 10th Cuirassiers
   Farine's brigade:        6th and 9th Cuirassiers
Two horse artillery batteries

<u>IMPERIAL GUARD</u> (20,000; 122 guns)
Commander: Lt-Gen Count Drouot[9]

<u>Guard Infantry</u>
Grenadiers (Lt-Gen Count Friant)
   1st, 2nd, 3rd and 4th Grenadiers
Chasseurs (Lt-Gen Count Morand)
   1st, 2nd, 3rd and 4th Chasseurs
Young Guard (Lt-Gen Count Duhesme)
   1st and 3rd Tirailleurs; 1st and 3rd Voltigeurs

<u>Guard Cavalry</u>
Heavy Cavalry (Lt-Gen Count Guyot)
   Grenadiers à cheval; Empress' Dragoons; Gendarmerie d'élite
Light Cavalry (Lt-Gen Count Lefebvre-Desnouëttes)
   Lancers; Chasseurs à cheval

<u>Guard Artillery</u> (Lt-Gen Baron Desvaux de Saint-Maurice)
   Horse Artillery: 3 batteries
   Foot Artillery: 13 batteries
One company of engineers
One company of marines

## ORDER OF BATTLE OF THE ANGLO-DUTCH-GERMAN ARMY

Commander-in-chief: Field Marshal the Duke of Wellington
Deputy Quartermaster General: Col Sir William De Lancey
Adjutant General: Maj-Gen Sir Edward Barnes
Strength: 93,000 men and 204 guns

I CORPS (31,000; 64 guns)
Commander: HRH the Prince of Orange

1st (British) Division (Maj-Gen Cooke)
  1st British brigade (Maj-Gen Maitland)
    2/1st Guards and 3/1st Guards
  2nd British brigade (Maj-Gen Byng)
    2/2nd and 2/3rd Guards
  Artillery (Lt-Col Adye)
    Sandham's battery RFA; Kuhlmann's battery, KGL Horse Artillery

3rd (Anglo-Hanoverian) Division (Lt-Gen Alten)
  5th British brigade (Maj-Gen C. Halkett)
    2/30th; 33rd; 2/69th; 2/73rd
  2nd KGL brigade (Col Ompteda)
    1st and 2nd Light; 5th and 8th Line btns
  1st Hanoverian brigade (Maj-Gen Kielmannsegge)
    Bremen, Verden and York Field Btns; Lüneburg and Grubenhagen Light Btns;
    Field Jäger Corps
  Artillery (Lt-Col Williamson)
    Lloyd's battery, RFA; Cleeve's battery, KGL Foot Artillery

2nd Dutch-Belgian Division (Lt-Gen Perponcher)
  1st brigade (Maj-Gen Bijlandt)
    7th (Belgian) Infantry; 27th (Dutch) Jägers; 5th, 7th and 8th National Militia
  2nd brigade (Prince Bernhard of Saxe-Weimar)
    2nd Nassau Infantry; Regiment of Orange-Nassau
  Artillery (Maj Opstal)
    Bijleveld's battery, Horse Artillery; Stievenaar's battery, Foot Artillery

3rd Dutch-Belgian Division (Lt-Gen Chassé)
  1st brigade (Col Detmers)
    2nd (Belgian) Infantry; 35th (Belgian) Jägers; 4th, 6th, 17th and 19th National
    Militia
  2nd brigade (Maj-Gen d'Aubremé)
    3rd (Dutch), 12th (Dutch) and 13th (Dutch) Infantry; 36th (Belgian) Jägers; 3rd
    and 10th National Militia
  Artillery (Maj Smissen)
    Krahmer's battery, Horse Artillery; Lux's battery, Foot Artillery

Dutch-Belgian Cavalry Division (Lt-Gen Collaërt)
   1st Dutch-Belgian brigade (Maj-Gen Trip)
      1st (Dutch), 2nd (Belgian) and 3rd (Dutch) Carabiniers
   2nd Dutch-Belgian brigade (Maj-Gen Ghigny)
      4th (Dutch) Light Dragoons; 8th (Belgian) Hussars
   3rd Dutch-Belgian brigade (Maj-Gen Merlen)
      5th (Belgian) Light Dragoons; 6th (Dutch) Hussars
   Dutch-Belgian Horse Artillery
      Petter and Gey's battery

II CORPS (27,000; 40 guns)
Commander: Lt-Gen Lord Hill

2nd (Anglo-Hanoverian) Division (Lt-Gen Clinton)
   3rd British brigade (Maj-Gen Adam)
      1/52nd Light Infantry; 1/71st Light Infantry; 2/95th Rifles; 3/95th Rifles
   1st KGL brigade (Col du Plat)
      1st, 2nd, 3rd and 4th Line btns
   3rd Hanoverian brigade (Col H. Halkett)
      Bremervörde, Osnabrück, Quackenbrück and Salzgitter Landwehr btns
   Artillery (Lt-Col Gold)
      Bolton's battery, RFA; Sympher's battery, KGL Horse Artillery

4th (Anglo-Hanoverian) Division (Lt-Gen Colville)
   4th British brigade (Col Mitchell)
      3/14th; 1/23rd Fusiliers; 51st Light Infantry
   6th British brigade (Maj-Gen Johnstone)
      2/35th; 1/54th; 2/59th; 1/91st
   6th Hanoverian brigade (Maj-Gen Lyon)
      Lauenberg and Calenburg Field Btns; Nienburg, Hoya and Bentheim Landwehr Btns
   Artillery (Lt-Col Hawker)
      Brome's battery, RFA; Rettburg's battery, Hanoverian Foot Artillery

HRH Prince Frederick of Orange's command

1st Dutch-Belgian Division (Lt-Gen Stedmann)
   1st brigade (Maj-Gen Hauw)
      4th (Belgian) and 6th (Dutch) Infantry; 16th (Dutch) Jägers; 9th, 14th and 15th National Militia
   2nd brigade (Maj-Gen Eerens)
      1st (Belgian) Infantry; 18th (Dutch) Jägers; 1st, 2nd and 18th National Militia
   Artillery
      Wynaud's battery, Foot Artillery

Netherlands Indian brigade (Lt-Gen Anthing)
  5th (East Indies) Infantry; Flanquer btn; 10th and 11th Indies Light Infantry
Artillery
  Riesz's battery, Foot Artillery

## RESERVE CORPS (24,000; 64 guns)

5th (Anglo-Hanoverian) Division (Lt-Gen Picton)
  8th British brigade (Maj-Gen Kempt)
    1/28th; 1/32nd; 1/79th Highlanders; 1/95th Rifles
  9th British brigade (Maj-Gen Pack)
    3/1st; 1/42nd Highlanders; 2/44th; 1/92nd Highlanders
  5th Hanoverian brigade (Col Vincke)
    Gifhorn, Hameln, Hildesheim and Peine Landwehr Btns
  Artillery (Maj Heise)
    Roger's battery, RFA; Braun's battery, Hanoverian Foot Artillery

6th (Anglo-Hanoverian) Division (Lt-Gen Cole)
  10th British brigade (Maj-Gen Lambert)
    1/4th; 1/27th; 1/40th; 2/81st [81st detached on 18 June to help garrison
    Brussels]
  4th Hanoverian brigade (Col Best)
    Lüneburg, Münden, Osterode and Verden Landwehr Btns
  Artillery (Lt-Col Bruckmann)
    Unett's battery, RFA; Sinclair's battery, RFA

The Brunswick Contingent (Duke of Brunswick)
  Infantry
    Advanced Guard Btn
    Light brigade (Lt-Col Buttlar)
      Leib Btn; 1st, 2nd and 3rd Light Btns
    Line brigade (Lt-Col Specht)
      1st, 2nd and 3rd Line Btns
  Cavalry
    One squadron of Uhlans; four squadrons of Hussars
  Artillery (Maj Mahn)
    Heinemann's battery, Horse Artillery; Moll's battery, Foot Artillery

The Nassau Contingent (Gen Kruse)
  1st Nassau Infantry

British Reserve Artillery (Maj Drummond)
  Ross' 'A' Troop, RHA; Beane's 'D' Troop, RHA; Morrisson's battery, RFA;
  Hutchesson's battery, RFA; Ilbert's battery, RFA[10]

<u>CAVALRY CORPS</u> (11,000; 36 guns)
Commander: Lord Uxbridge

British Horse Artillery (attached to cavalry)
Bull's 'I' Troop, RHA; Webber Smith's 'F' Troop, RHA; Gardiner's 'E' Troop, RHA; Whinyates' 2nd Rocket Troop, RHA; Mercer's 'G' Troop, RHA; Ramsay's 'H' Troop, RHA

1st British brigade (Maj-Gen Somerset)
1st and 2nd Life Guards; Royal Horse Guards (Blues); 1st (King's) Dragoon Guards
2nd British brigade (Maj-Gen Ponsonby)
1st (Royals), 2nd ('Scots Greys') and 6th (Inniskilling) Dragoons
3rd British brigade (Maj-Gen Dörnberg)
23rd Light Dragoons; 1st and 2nd Light Dragoons, KGL
4th British brigade (Maj-Gen Vandeleur)
11th, 12th and 16th Light Dragoons
5th British brigade (Maj-Gen Grant)
7th and 15th Hussars; 13th Light Dragoons
6th British brigade (Maj-Gen Vivian)
10th and 18th Hussars; 1st Hussars, KGL
7th British brigade (Col Arentsschildt)
3rd Hussars, KGL
1st Hanoverian brigade (Col Estorff)
Duke of Cumberland's Hussars; Bremen and Verden Hussars; Prince Regent's Hussars

*Note:* The 2nd Hussars, KGL, were guarding the frontier. This regiment belonged to the 5th British cavalry brigade and in its absence it was replaced by the 13th Light Dragoons from the 7th brigade. Wellington also had garrison formations in important towns, cities and ports such as Ypres, Brussels and Ostend; these garrisons are not included in the total strength of 93,000.

<u>ORDER OF BATTLE OF THE PRUSSIAN ARMY</u>

| | |
|---|---|
| Commander-in-chief: | Field Marshal Prince Blücher |
| Chief-of-staff: | Lt-Gen Gneisenau |
| Quartermaster-General: | Maj-Gen Grolmann |
| Strength: | 117,000 men and 312 guns |

<u>I CORPS</u> (31,000; 96 guns)
Commander: Lt-Gen Ziethen
Chief-of-staff: Lt-Col Reiche

Infantry
1st brigade (Maj-Gen Steinmetz)
12th and 24th Infantry; 1st Westphalian Landwehr; 1st and 3rd Silesian sharpshooter companies

2nd brigade (Maj-Gen Pirch II)
    6th and 28th Infantry; 2nd Westphalian Landwehr
3rd brigade (Maj-Gen Jägow)
    7th and 29th Infantry; 3rd Westphalian Landwehr
4th brigade (Maj-Gen Henckel von Donnersmarck)
    19th Infantry; 4th Westphalian Landwehr; 2nd and 4th Silesian sharpshooter companies

Cavalry (Maj-Gen Röder)
Brigade cavalry[11]
    4th Hussars; 1st Westphalian Landwehr Cavalry
Lützow's brigade[12]
    6th Uhlans; 1st and 2nd Kurmark Landwehr Cavalry
Tresckow's brigade
        2nd and 5th Dragoons; 4th Uhlans

Artillery (Lt-Col Lehmann)
Brigade artillery
    Foot artillery:    6-pounder batteries nos. 3, 7, 8, 15
Reserve artillery
    Foot artillery:    12-pounder batteries nos. 2, 6, 9;
                       6-pounder battery no. 1;
                       Howitzer battery no. 1
    Horse artillery:   Batteries nos. 2, 7, 10
1st Engineer company

II CORPS (32,000; 80 guns)
Commander: Maj-Gen Pirch I
Chief-of-staff: Col Aster

Infantry
5th brigade (Maj-Gen Tippelskirch)
    2nd and 25th Infantry; 5th Westphalian Landwehr
6th brigade (Maj-Gen Krafft)
    9th and 26th Infantry; 1st Elbe Landwehr
7th brigade (Maj-Gen Brause)
    14th and 22nd Infantry; 2nd Elbe Landwehr
8th brigade (Col Langen)[13]
    21st and 23rd Infantry; 3rd Elbe Landwehr

Cavalry (Maj-Gen Jürgass)[14]
Brigade cavalry
    5th Kurmark Landwehr Cavalry; Elbe Landwehr Cavalry
Thümen's brigade[15]
    6th Dragoons; 11th Hussars; 2nd Uhlans
Schulenburg's brigade
    1st Dragoons; 4th Kurmark Landwehr Cavalry

Sohr's brigade
   3rd and 5th Hussars

Artillery (Lt-Col Röhl)
Brigade artillery
   Foot artillery:    6-pounder batteries nos. 5, 10, 12, 34
Reserve artillery
   Foot artillery:    12-pounder batteries nos. 4, 8;
                      6-pounder battery no. 37
   Horse artillery:   Batteries nos. 5, 6, 14
7th Engineer Company


III CORPS (24,000; 48 guns)
Commander: Lt-Gen Thielmann

Infantry
9th brigade (Maj-Gen Borcke)
   8th and 30th Infantry; 1st Kurmark Landwehr
10th brigade (Col Kemphen)
   27th Infantry; 2nd Kurmark Landwehr
11th brigade (Col Luck)
   3rd and 4th Kurmark Landwehr
12th brigade (Col Stülpnagel)
   31st Infantry; 5th and 6th Kurmark Landwehr

Cavalry (Maj-Gen Hobe)
Brigade cavalry
   3rd and 6th Kurmark Landwehr Cavalry
Marwitz's brigade
   7th and 8th Uhlans
Lottum's brigade
   4th Dragoons; 5th Uhlans

Artillery (Col Mohnhaupt)
Brigade artillery
   Foot artillery:    6-pounder batteries nos. 18, 35
Reserve artillery
   Foot artillery:    12-pounder battery no. 7
   Horse artillery:   Batteries nos. 18, 19, 20
5th Engineer Company


IV CORPS (30,000; 88 guns)
Commander: Gen Count Bülow von Dennewitz
Chief-of-staff: Maj-Gen Valentini

Infantry
13th brigade (Maj-Gen Hake)
   10th Infantry; 2nd and 3rd Neumark Landwehr

14th brigade (Maj-Gen Ryssel)
11th Infantry; 1st and 2nd Pommeranian Landwehr
15th brigade (Maj-Gen Losthin)
18th Infantry; 3rd and 4th Silesian Landwehr
16th brigade (Col Hiller von Gärtringen)
15th Infantry; 1st and 2nd Silesian Landwehr

Cavalry (Prince William of Prussia)
Brigade cavalry
2nd and 3rd Silesian Landwehr Cavalry
Schwerin's brigade
1st Uhlans; 6th Hussars
Watzdorff's brigade
8th and 10th Hussars
Sydow's brigade
1st and 2nd Neumark Landwehr Cavalry; 1st and 2nd Pommeranian Landwehr
cavalry; 1st Silesian Landwehr Cavalry

Artillery (Maj Bardeleben)[16]
Brigade artillery
Foot artillery:      6-pounder batteries nos. 2, 13, 14, 21
Reserve Artillery
Foot artillery:      12-pounder batteries nos. 3, 5, 13;
                     6-pounder battery no. 11
Horse artillery:  Batteries nos. 1, 11, 12
4th Engineer company

# Notes

1. H. Lachouque, *Le secret de Waterloo* (1952), p.304
2. H. Lot, *Les deux généraux Ordener* (1910), p.92–3
3. J. Gurwood ed., *The dispatches of the Duke of Wellington* (1838), v.12, pp.472–6
4. H. Lachouque, *Le secret de Waterloo* (1952), p.310; H. Siborne ed., *The Waterloo letters* (1983), pp.3–4
5. Girard fell mortally wounded at the Battle of Ligny on 16 June.
6. Gauthier fell mortally wounded at the Battle of Quatre Bras on 16 June.
7. Le Capitaine was killed at the Battle of Ligny.
8. Maurin was seriously wounded at the Battle of Ligny and replaced by Vallin.
9. Marshal Mortier, the original commander of the Guard, fell ill on the eve of the campaign.
10. The last three of these batteries did not see action in Belgium.
11. Prussian 'brigade cavalry' and 'brigade artillery' were units attached to specific infantry brigades. The remaining cavalry and artillery regiments formed the corps' reserve cavalry and reserve artillery.
12. Lützow was captured at the Battle of Ligny.
13. Langen was mortally wounded at the Battle of Ligny and replaced by Lt-Col Reckow.
14. Jürgass was wounded at the Battle of Ligny.
15. Thümen was killed at the Battle of Ligny and replaced by Lt-Col Schmiedeberg
16. Bardeleben apparently assumed command of Bülow's artillery only after the Battle of Waterloo.

# Appendix 2

# MUSEUM ADDRESSES AND OPENING TIMES

Note: opening times are subject to variation. Confirmation can be obtained from the Tourist Information Office in the town of Waterloo:

Syndicat d'initiative et du Tourisme de Waterloo, Chaussée de Bruxelles 149, 1410 Waterloo, Belgium. *Tel: 02 354 99 10*

Open:  1 April to 15 November: 09.30–18.30

16 November to 31 March: 10.30–17.00

Closed:  1 January and 25 December

If you intend to visit all of the main attractions at Waterloo (Wellington Museum, Lion Mound, Visitors' Centre, Panorama, Waxworks Museum and Le Caillou), buy a *ticket commun* at the tourist information office, which adjoins the Wellington Museum. This ticket is cheaper than paying separate entrance fees at the individual attractions.

Wellington Museum

Musée de Wellington, Chaussée de Bruxelles 147, 1410 Waterloo. *Tel: 32 2 354 78 06*

Open:  1 April to 15 November: 09.30–18.30

16 November to 31 March: 10.30–17.00

Closed:  1 January and 25 December

Napoleon's Headquarters, Le Caillou

Musée Provincial du Caillou, Chaussée de Bruxelles 66, 1472 Vieux-Genappe. *Tel: 32 2 384 24 24*

Open:  1 April to 31 October: 10.30–18.00

1 November to 31 March: 13.30–17.00

Closed:  January and Mondays (except bank holidays)

Visitors' Centre

Centre du Visiteur, Route du Lion 254, 1420 Braine-l'Alleud. *Tel: 32 2 385 19 12*

Open:  1 April to 31 October: 09.30–18.30

1 November to 31 March: 10.30–16.00

Note: access to the Lion Mound is through the Visitors' Centre, so the same opening times apply for the Mound.

## Panorama
Panorama de la bataille, Chemin des Vertes Bournes 90, 1420 Braine-l'Alleud.
*Tel: 32 2 384 31 39*
    Open:   Monday to Saturday: 09.30–18.00
               Sunday and Bank Holiday: 09.30–18.30

## Waxworks Museum
Musée de Cires, Route du Lion 315, 1410 Waterloo. *Tel: 32 2 384 67 40*
    Open:   1 April to 31 October: 09.00–18.30
               1 November to 31 March: Saturday and Sunday, 10.00–16.45

## Brussels Army Museum
Musée Royal de l'Armée et d'Histoire Militaire, Parc du Cinquantenaire, Bruxelles
    Open:   Tuesday–Sunday, 09.00–12.00 and 13.00–16.45
    Closed:  Mondays, 1 January, 1 May, 1 November, 25 December, election days

For a guided tour of the battlefield, contact:
Guides 1815 A.S.B.L., Route de Lion 250, 1420 Braine-l'Alleud. *Tel: 02 385 06 25*

## Accommodation
Brussels is only twelve miles north of the battlefield and has numerous hotels, though most of these are expensive. The city does have a good Youth Hostel in the Boulevard de l'Empereur.

The tourist information office at Waterloo can advise of local hotels and restaurants. One five star hotel, *Le 1815*, is actually on the battlefield, immediately west of the crossroads. Its rooms, which enjoy magnificent views of the battlefield, are named after the famous generals of the 1815 campaign: Napoleon, Ney, Reille, Lobau, Grouchy, Cambronne, Soult, d'Erlon, Wellington, Picton, Hill, Uxbridge, the Prince of Orange, Blücher, Gneisenau and Thielmann. It even boasts of a miniature golf course involving models of the farms and monuments of the battlefield.

You can find a few campsites in the campaign area, such as Renipont at Ohain, two and a half miles east of the battlefield of Waterloo.

# Appendix 3

# SOURCES

The bibliographies in Antony Brett-James and Jac Weller give an idea of the vast literature available on the 1815 campaign. Some of the best titles are given below; further sources, especially eyewitness accounts, will be found in the footnotes of this book:

Aerts, W. and Wilmet, L., *18 Juin 1815. Waterloo. L'attaque de la Garde. Les derniers carrés. La déroute* (Brussels, 1904)

Aerts, W., *Waterloo. Opérations de l'armée prussienne du Bas-Rhin pendant la campagne de 1815 en Belgique* (Brussels, 1908)

Anglesey, Marquis of, *One-leg, the life and letters of Henry William Paget* (London, 1961)

Barral, G., *Itinéraire illustré de l'épopée de Waterloo* (Paris, 1896)

Bernard, H., *La campagne de 1815 en Belgique ou la faillite des transmissions* (Brussels, 1954)

Bernard, H., *Le duc de Wellington et la Belgique* (Brussels, 1973)

Brett-James, A., *The hundred days* (London, 1964)

Chalfont, Lord, ed., *Waterloo: battle of three armies* (London, 1979)

Chandler, D., *Waterloo: the hundred days* (London, 1980)

Charras, J., *Histoire de la campagne de 1815* (Paris, 1857, 1869)

Cotton, E., *A voice from Waterloo* (Brussels, 9th ed., 1900; reprinted 1974)

Dalton, C., *The Waterloo roll call* (London, 2nd ed., 1904; reprinted 1978)

Damitz, K., *Histoire de la campagne de 1815* (Berlin, 1837–8; French translation published Paris, 1840–1)

De Bas, J., and de Wommersom, *La campagne de 1815 aux Pays-Bas* (Brussels, 3 vols, 1908–9)

Fleischmann, T., *Histoire de la ferme du Caillou* (Brussels, 1958; reprinted 1984)

Fleischmann, T., *Le quartier général de Wellington à Waterloo* (Charleroi, 1964)

Fleischmann, T. and W. Aerts, *Bruxelles pendant la bataille de Waterloo* (Brussels, 1956)

Fletcher, I., *Wellington's regiments* (Staplehurst, 1994)

Glover, M., *A new guide to the battlefields of northern France and the Low Countries* (London, 1987)

Hamilton-Williams, D., *Waterloo: new perspectives* (London, 1993)

Haythornthwaite, P., *Uniforms of Waterloo* (Poole, 1974)

Haythornthwaite, P., *The armies of Wellington* (London, 1994)

Haythornthwaite, P., *The Napoleonic source book* (London, 1990)

Haythornthwaite, P., *The armies of Wellington* (London, 1994)

Howarth, D., *A near run thing* (London, 1968)

Houssaye, H., *1815: Waterloo* (English translation of 31st French ed. published London, 1900)

Keegan, J., *The face of battle* (Harmondsworth, 1976)

Lachouque, H., *Waterloo* (London, 1975)

Lettow-Vorbeck, O., *Napoleons Untergang 1815* (Berlin, 1904), v.1

Logie, J., *Waterloo: l'évitable défaite* (Paris and Louvain-la-Neuve, 1989)

Longford, E., *Wellington: the years of the sword* (London, 1969)

Mauduit, H. de, *Les derniers jours de la grande armée* (Paris, 1848), v.2

Mercer, A., *Journal of the Waterloo campaign* (London, 1870, 1927, 1985)

Navez, L., *Les Quatre Bras, Ligny, Waterloo et Wavre* (Paris, 1910)

Nofi, A., *The Waterloo campaign, June 1815* (London, 1993)

Offord, P., *An introduction to historic Bexhill* (Bexhill, 1992)

Ollech, C., *Geschichte des Feldzuges von 1815 nach archivalischen Quellen* (Berlin, 1876)

Parker, H., *Three Napoleonic battles* (Durham, N.C., 1944; reprinted 1983)

Parkinson, R., *The hussar general* (London, 1975)

Pflugk-Harttung, J., *Belle Alliance* (Berlin, 1915)

Siborne, H. ed., *The Waterloo letters* (London, 1891, 1983, 1993)

Siborne, W., *History of the Waterloo campaign* (London, 1844; reprinted in 1990 from 2nd, revised, ed. of 1848)

Six, G., *Dictionnaire biographique des généraux et amiraux français de la Révolution et de l'Empire* (Paris, 2 vols, 1934)

Treuenfeld, B., *Die Tage von Ligny und Belle-Alliance* (Hanover, 1880)

Weller, J., *Wellington at Waterloo* (London, 1967, 1992)

Wellington and his staff at Waterloo

# INDEX

Adam, Maj-Gen Frederick, 119, 186
Aerts, Winand, 34
Aigleville, 321
Ali, Mameluke, 31, 147, 155, 218
Alost, 246
Alten, Lt-Gen Sir Charles von, 332
Amsterdam:
  Rijksmuseum, 327
Anglo–Dutch–German Army:
  casualty figures, 40
  contingents: British, *passim*; Brunswick, 37, 48, 56, 94, 117, 128,
    250, 253, 258, 337–8; Dutch-Belgian, 36–7, 54–5, 62, 74–
    5, 77, 79, 83, 92, 132, 137, 165, 167, 173, 176, 179, 222,
    240; Hanoverian, 36–7, 49, 55, 64, 70, 72, 83, 89, 125, 138,
    156, 178, 184, 191, 255, 316, 326, 337; King's German
    Legion, 36, 52, 115, 119–25, 130, 178, 184, 222, 326–33,
    337; Nassau, 22, 36–7, 64, 67, 70, 73, 88–90, 92, 114, 121,
    125–6, 130, 184, 228, 230, 232, 240, 326
  quality of troops, 37
  surgeons, 56–8, 251, 257
*Corps:*
  I, 18, 56, 125, 338
  II, 18, 337
  Reserve Corps, 18, 248, 250
  Cavalry Corps, 18, 36
*Divisions:*
  *(British):*
  1st (Guards), 36, 48
  2nd, 115
  3rd, 36, 116, 332
  5th, 36–7, 74–84, 114–16, 127, 165, 248, 250
  *(Dutch-Belgian):*
  1st Dutch-Belgian, 337
  2nd Dutch-Belgian, 55, 240
*Brigades (see also name of commander):*
  *(British):*
  Household Brigade, 40, 79, 128, 173, 327
  Union Brigade, 40, 79, 128, 168, 171–3, 327
  5th Brigade, 90
*Regiments:*
  *(British):*
  1st (King's) Dragoon Guards, 51, 82
  1st Life Guards, 57–8, 60, 173, 327
  2nd Life Guards, 60
  1st Dragoons, or Royals, 30, 79–80, 168, 327
  2nd Dragoons, or Scots Greys, 30, 61, 79–82, 84, 168, 326
  6th Dragoons, or Inniskillings, 30, 79–80, 82, 128, 333
  7th Hussars, 55, 60, 71, 89, 91, 95, 113, 127, 247, 264, 326
  10th Hussars, 139, 207, 216
  11th Light Dragoons, 330
  12th Light Dragoons, 58
  15th Hussars, 25, 50, 330
  16th Light Dragoons, 43, 51, 58, 81
  18th Hussars, 32, 128, 139, 235.
  23rd Light Dragoons, 30, 139
  1st Guards, 36, 58, 64, 70, 86, 93, 113, 132, 136–7, 234,
    263–5
  2nd (Coldstream) Guards, 36, 64, 67, 71, 263
  3rd (Scots) Guards, 36, 64–7, 69–71, 263
  1st Foot, 53, 79, 83
  4th Foot, 113
  14th Foot, 265
  23rd Royal Welsh Fusiliers, 49, 264
  27th Foot, 113, 126–7
  28th Foot, 77–8, 172, 321
  30th Foot, 51–2, 90, 94, 114, 125, 128, 133

32nd Foot, 80
33rd Foot, 42, 51, 53–4, 62, 90, 96, 135, 137
40th Foot, 49, 96, 113, 127
42nd Highlanders, 78–9, 83, 90, 249
44th Foot, 77, 83, 114, 155, 248, 258
51st Light Infantry, 69, 180
52nd Light Infantry, 119, 136–8, 225, 235
69th Foot, 90, 126, 135
71st Light Infantry, 119
73rd Foot, 42, 51–2, 89–90, 94, 114, 129, 133, 263
79th Highlanders, 78–9, 83, 90
81st Foot, 255
92nd Highlanders, 60, 74, 77, 79–81, 83–4, 90, 96, 114, 116,
  246, 248–9, 258
95th Rifles, 44, 57, 74–5, 121, 125, 127, 129, 138, 248, 252,
  325
1st Light battalion, KGL, 121, 328–9, 333
2nd Light battalion, KGL, 36, 120–4, 130, 330
5th Line battalion, KGL, 121, 124–5
8th Line battalion, KGL, 178
*(Dutch-Belgian):*
  1st (Dutch) Carabiniers, 54
  3rd (Dutch) Carabiniers, 55
  4th (Dutch) Light Dragoons, 92
  8th (Belgian) Hussars, 54, 92
  Orange-Nassau Regiment, 228, 326
  1st Nassau Infantry, 88, 130, 326
  2nd Nassau Infantry, 54–5, 64, 70, 73, 228, 326
  7th (Belgian) Infantry, 75, 83
  35th (Belgian) Jägers, 135
*(Hanoverian):*
  Duke of Cumberland's Hussars, 55, 255
  Field-Jäger Corps, 72
  Grubenhagen Light battalion, 72
  Lüneburg Light battalion, 72, 174, 178
  Osnabrück battalion of Hanoverian landwehr, 191
*Batteries:*
  *(British):*
  'E' Troop, RHA, 213, 253
  'G' Troop, RHA, 41–2, 90, 113–14, 117, 128, 317, 325
  'H' Troop, RHA, 50, 52
  Rocket Battery, 172–3
  *(Dutch-Belgian):*
  Krahmer's Dutch-Belgian Battery, 133
*Supporting units:*
  Royal Staff Corps, 53, 140, 248
  Royal Waggon Train, 64
Angoulême, Duke of, 215
Antwerp, 219, 252–5, 258, 262, 266, 299
Arcola, 321
Ardennes offensive 1944, 315
Asquith, Herbert, 250
Ath, 303
Auerstädt, 250
Austerlitz, 149, 176, 195
Auxerre, 322
Avesnes, 18, 236, 316
Aywiers, Abbey of, 213

Bachelu, Lt-Gen Baron Gilbert, 152, 160–1, 180–2, 186
Badajoz, 43
Bagration, Gen, 159
Baltus de Pouilly, Brig-Gen Basile, 290
Barail, Capt de, 132
Baring, Maj George, 120–3, 125, 130
Barral, Lt, 20, 24

Barrington, Lt the Hon. Samuel Shute, 263, 266
Basse-Wavre, 271, 289
Battersby, Capt George, 51
Batty, Ensign Robert, 94–5, 137, 266
Bauduin, Brig-Gen Baron Pierre-François, 71, 157
Beaumont, 18
Bedale, 325
Belcher, Lt Robert, 80
Belcourt, Maj, 191
Belgrade, 305
Bell, Charles, 257
Bellair, Brig-Gen Baron Antoine de, 217
*Bellerophon*, HMS, 317
Berger, Capt, 124
Berlin, 325
Bernard, Cornet the Hon. Henry, 51
Bernard, Gen Baron Simon, 206
Berthezène, Lt-Gen Baron Pierre, 295, 311
Berton, Brig-Gen Jean-Baptiste, 309
Bertrand, Lt-Gen Count, 155
Best, Col, 61, 83, 138, 156
Betws-y-Coed, 320
Bexhill, 120, 327–33
  Barrack Hall, 330, 332
  Barrack Road cemetery, 330
  Bexhill Down, 332
  Bexhill Hanoverian Study Group, 327, 330
  Museum, 120, 327–8, 330
  Northern Hotel, 327–8
  St Peter's Church, 328–30
  Woodgate Farm, 332
Bierges, 203–4, 271, 289–91, 294, 297–301
Bijlandt, Maj-Gen Count van, 36, 55, 62, 74–5, 77–9, 83, 165
Biot, Maj Hubert-François, 299–300, 302–3, 308, 311
Birtwhistle, Ensign John, 80
Bismarck, Col von, 313
Blackman, Capt John Lucie, 71, 263
Blancard, Brig-Gen Baron Amable, 177
Blücher, Col Count Francis von, 235
Blücher, Field Marshal Gebhard von, Prince of Wahlstadt, *passim*
Boehm, Mr and Mrs Edmund, Ball of, 48
Bolton, Capt Samuel, 52
Bonaparte, Prince Jérôme, 148, 157, 159–61, 173, 188, 324
Bonaparte, Joseph, 321
Boquet, Château, 308, 310
Borodino (La Moskowa), 85, 149, 155
Borremans, Capt, 315
Bossu wood, 53, 266
Bousval, 306
Bouvignes, 315
Boyce, Lt John, 54
Braine-l'Alleud, 56, 132, 188–90, 253, 265
  Church of St Etienne, 56, 226
Brandis, Lt von, 125
Brazier, Sophia, 329
Breton, First Lt John, 325
Brieske, Dr, 236
Bringhurst, Maj John, 51
Bro de Commères, Col, 171
Brock, Irving, 151
Brooke, Lt Francis, 51
Brown, Capt Thomas, 263, 266
Browne, Maj Fielding, 127
Bruno, Brig-Gen Adrien, 323
Brunswick, Frederick William, Duke of, 94, 250
Brussels, *passim*
  Cathedral of Saints Michael and Gudule, 257
  Evere cemetery, 71, 261–7
  Grand'Place, 251, 255
  Hôtel de Ville (Town Hall), 33, 251
  Musée de l'armée et d'histoire militaire, 233, 322, 327, 350
  Park, 245–50, 255, 258

Petit-Château barracks, 255, 257
Place Royale, 248–9, 255
rue de la Blanchisserie, 247
rue des Cendres, 247
St Josse Ten Noode cemetery, 267
Wellington's residence, 245–6, 256
Bruylant, Gen, 189
Buck, Lt Henry, 54
Buckley, Lt Henry, 50
Bull, Capt Robert, 70
Bullen, Ensign James, 51
Bülow, Gen Baron Friedrich Wilhelm, Count von Dennewitz, 40, 201–4, 206–7, 209–11, 213, 215–19, 221–2, 225–6, 231–4, 239–40, 252, 291
Burney, Fanny (Mme d'Arblay), 249–50, 254, 258
Burthe, Brig-Gen Baron André, 323
Büsgen, Maj, 70, 72
Bussaco, 78
Bussy windmill, 235
Byron, Lord, 246–7

Caesar, Julius, 48
Cambrai, 316
Cambridge, Duke of, 261–3
Cambronne, Gen Count Pierre, 149, 191, 350
Cameron, Pipe-Major Alexander, 80, 248
Cameron, Lt John, 54
Canler, Louis, 151–2, 165, 167–8, 170
Canning, Lt-Col Charles, 52–3
Capel, Caroline, 245, 250, 253, 265
Capel, Maria, 265
Capellen, Baron de, 251–2, 254, 256, 259
Caulaincourt, Duke of Vicenza, Gen Armand, 17
Celles, 315
Chaboulon, Count Fleury de, 179
Chambers, Major Thomas, 51–2
Champ d'Asile, 322
Chantelet, 150, 221, 234
Chapelle Jacques, 231
Chapelle-lez-Herlaimont, 190
Chapelle Notre Dame de Bon Secours, 231
Chapelle St Lambert, 202–4, 206–7, 209, 222, 291
Chapelle St Robert, 204, 206, 238
Chapuis, Capt, 170
Charleroi, 18, 20, 22, 24, 149, 178, 190–1, 246, 316
  Belle Vue tavern, 22
Charles II, King of Spain, 50
Chartrand, Brig-Gen, 220
Chassé, Lt-Gen Baron David, 132–3, 135
Chasseriau, Baron, 179
Cheney, Capt Edward, 326
Christiani, Brig-Gen Joseph, 323
Churchill, Sir Winston, 259
Civrieux, Larreguy de, 159–60
Clark, Capt Alexander Kennedy, 80–1
Clay, Pvte Matthew, 67
Clinton, Lt-Gen Sir Henry, 115
Clusky, Adjt Michael, 81
Clyde, Lt John, 264
Coenegracht, Lt-Col, 54
Coignet, Maj Jean-Roch, 156, 322
Colborne, Lt-Col Sir John, 136, 138, 225
Colomb, Maj von, 215
Compiègne, 316, 327
Congress of Vienna, 18
Congreve, Sir William, 172
Constant-Rebecque, Baron Jean-Victor de, 83, 88, 92, 114, 131, 137, 173, 222, 240
Constant-Rebecque de Villars, Capt Baron Jules de, 126, 131, 141
Copenhagen, 92, 140, 324
Costello, Sergt Edward, 252
Cotton, Edward, 71, 89, 91, 95, 113–14, 264–5

Courtrai, 18
Couture, 222
Crammond, Driver, 42
Crawfurd, Capt Thomas, 71
Creevey, Thomas, 81, 246, 254–6
Cretté, Capt, 221
Cromie, Lt Michael, 263
Crowhurst, 328
Crummer, Lt James, 321
Cruyce, Monsieur van den, 245
Cubières, Col Despans de, 67
Curzon, Capt the Hon. William, 126
Czettritz, Lt-Col von, 306

D'Erlon, Lt-Gen Jean-Baptiste Drouet, Count, 24–5, 37, 40, 78,
    153, 155, 165, 170–1, 173, 178, 183–4, 216, 221, 232,
    238, 322, 327, 350
D'Hooghvorst, Baron Vanderlinden, 251
Dahrendorf, Pvte, 123
Damvillers, 325
Davout, Marshal Louis-Nicolas, 167, 316
Debienne, Monsieur, 203
Decoster, Jean-Baptiste, 154
De Gaulle, Charles, 315
Dejean, Lt-Gen Count Pierre, 170, 323
De Lancey, Lady Magdalene, 266–7
De Lancey, Col Sir William Howe, 263–4, 266–7
Delhaize, Jules, 34
Delort, Lt-Gen Baron Jacques, 152, 170, 175–6, 179, 188
Demopolis, 321
Demulder, Lt Augustin, 118, 175
Desirée, 145
Desvaux de Saint-Maurice, Lt-Gen Baron Jean, 154
Desvreux, Monsieur, 85
Détaille, Edouard, 189
Detmer, Col Henri, 135
Dickens, Charles, 267
Dickson, Corpl John, 61, 80–2
Dighton, Denis, 72
Dinant, 301, 303, 309, 315
Dion-le-Mont, 202, 238, 305
Domon, Lt-Gen Baron Jean-Simon, 206–7, 209–10, 216, 238
Donop, Brig-Gen Frédéric de, 94, 179
Donzelot, Lt-Gen Baron François, 83, 184
Dörnberg, Gen Wilhelm von, 139
Dover, 262, 325, 327
Drouot, Lt-Gen Count Antoine, 147, 149, 155
Dubois, Brig-Gen Baron Jacques, 173
Duchastel de la Howarderie, Count Camille, 54
Duhesme, Lt-Gen Count Philippe, 190, 218, 220, 236
Dullart, Capt, 135
Dumoulin, Louis, 85
Dunkirk, 18
Duperier, Lt Henry, 32
Du Plat, Col, 115, 119
Dupuis, Mme Thérèse, 190
Durutte, Lt-Gen Count Pierre, 83, 170–1, 184, 190, 228, 233,
    322
Duuring, Maj Jean, 149
Dyle, R., 201, 204, 206, 236, 271, 289, 291–2, 294–5, 297–302
Dyneley, Capt Thomas, 213

Edinburgh, 52
Edwards, Field-Trumpeter John, 327
Elba, 18, 193
Ellis, Lt-Col Sir Henry, 49
Enghien, 303
Essling, 149
Evere cemetery, see Brussels
Ewart, Sergt Charles, 81
Exelmans, Lt-Gen Count Rémy, 289–90, 303, 305
Exeter, 325

Eylau, 176, 185

Falconer, Rev William, 34
Falkenhausen, Maj von, 203, 215
Fantin des Odoards, Col Louis, 295, 305, 311
Faré, Lt, 221
Farine, Brig-Gen Count Pierre, 170, 175
Fauville, Lt, 310
Faveau, François-Antoine, 333
Fichermont convent, 35, 74
Fisher, Capt William, 96
Flameng, François, 146
Fleurus, 22, 24, 148
Folgersberg, Maj-Gen von, 233
Forbes, Lt Alexander, 83
Forbes, Capt the Hon. Hastings, 263–4
Fouché, Joseph, 316
Foy, Lt-Gen Count Maximilien, 20, 154, 157, 160–1, 177–8, 180–
    2, 186, 237, 323
François, Capt Charles, 294, 301–2, 310, 315
Frank, Ensign George, 123–4
Fraser, Sir William, 47, 62
Frasnes, 238
Frazer, Lt-Col Sir Augustus, 52, 137
French Army:
    casualty figures, 40, 294
    quality of troops, 37
    surgeons, 150, 160
    *Corps:*
        I, 24, 30, 37, 40, 78, 151, 153, 164–5, 171, 183–4, 190, 206,
            216, 228, 232, 238, 322, 327
        II, 37, 93, 118, 148, 151–3, 156–7, 164, 177–8, 180, 182, 237,
            323, 337
        III, 289, 298, 305
        IV, 219, 289–90, 294, 297, 299–300, 305, 308, 325
        VI, 22, 37, 40, 151, 153, 164, 190, 207, 209, 215, 220, 225,
            238, 240, 294, 324, 337
        Reserve Cavalry, 22
        I Cavalry Corps, 305
        II Cavalry Corps, 303, 323
        III Cavalry Corps, 37, 86, 151, 161, 177, 323, 333
        IV Cavalry Corps, 31, 37, 86, 89, 165, 170, 175, 337
        Imperial Guard, 20, 22, 24–6, 37, 40, 44, 51, 54, 86, 88, 94,
            113, 130, 145, 147–51, 153–4, 176–9, 184–5, 187–8, 191,
            193, 196, 220, 225–6, 233, 239–40, 321–3, 327
            Old Guard, 132, 149, 188, 191, 220, 222, 225, 227, 231, 239
            Middle Guard, 52, 88, 132–7, 185, 187–8, 191, 221, 232,
                239, 327
            Young Guard, 25, 190, 218–20, 225
            Guard artillery, 37, 154, 164, 218
            Guard engineers, 151, 323
    *Divisions: see name of commander*
    *Regiments:*
        Chasseurs à cheval of the Guard, 88, 148, 154, 179, 322–3
        Dragoons of the Guard, 94
        Gendarmerie d'élite of the Guard, 113
        Grenadiers à cheval of the Guard, 113, 179, 323
        Polish Lancers of the Guard, 22, 193
        Red Lancers of the Guard, 88, 93–4, 150
        1st Cuirassiers, 88, 173, 176, 178, 183, 185, 239, 337
        1st Lancers, 216
        2nd Carabiniers, 132
        3rd Chasseurs à cheval, 171
        3rd Cuirassiers, 179
        3rd Lancers, 171
        4th Cuirassiers, 173, 179
        4th Lancers, 171
        5th Cuirassiers, 118, 175, 179
        6th Chasseurs à cheval, 151, 156
        6th Cuirassiers, 170, 179
        6th Hussars, 299–300
        7th Cuirassiers, 92, 173, 185, 337

7th Dragoons, 178–9
7th Hussars, 30, 203, 206, 209–10, 315, 323
8th Chasseurs à cheval, 300
8th Cuirassiers, 93
9th Cuirassiers, 170
12th Cuirassiers, 88, 173
20th Dragoons, 305, 308
1st Chasseurs, 149–50, 191, 221
2nd Chasseurs, 220, 225
3rd Chasseurs, 136, 191
4th Chasseurs, 136, 141, 187
1st Grenadiers, 25–6, 44, 147, 153, 191, 221
2nd Grenadiers, 150, 221, 226
3rd Grenadiers, 133, 135, 187, 191
4th Grenadiers, 135, 187
3rd Tirailleurs, 218
1st Light, 67, 154, 157, 161, 257
2nd Swiss, 289
3rd Line, 157, 161
5th Line, 217–18
8th Line, 184
9th Light, 289, 297
10th Line, 215
11th Line, 217
13th Light, 123, 183–4
14th Line, 302
22nd Line, 295–6, 305, 311
28th Line, 83, 151–2, 165, 168
29th Line, 184
30th Line, 294, 301, 310
40th Line, 300, 302
45th Line, 30, 81, 152, 167–8, 184
47th Line, 220
54th Line, 165
55th Line, 84, 165
65th Line, 337
70th Line, 295–6
75th Line, 313–15
85th Line, 170, 174
96th Line, 310
105th Line, 80, 83, 165, 168, 170, 327
1st Regiment of Engineers, 183
6th Regiment of Foot Artillery, 164
Friant, Lt-Gen Count Louis, 187, 322
Frichermont, 36, 83, 171, 210–11, 213, 215–16, 228, 230–2,
   240–1; see also Fichermont convent
Friedland, 149, 176
Fritz, Capt, 26
Froidmont, 204
Frye, Capt William, 41, 254, 259, 309
Fuentes d'Onoro, 52
Fuller, Lt-Col William, 51

Gaddesby, 326
Garcia Hernandez, 120
Garland, Capt John, 129, 131
Gembloux, 204, 253, 305–6
Genappe, 148, 151, 156, 190–1, 203, 236–7, 256
   Auberge du roi d'espagne, 148, 236, 257
Genval, 204
George III, King, 120
Gérard, Lt-Gen Count Maurice, 219, 289–90, 297–9, 301, 309,
   325
Gérard, Monsieur, 190
Géricault, Jean-Louis, 324
Gerke, Lucien, 47
Gérôme, Jean-Léon, 188–9
Gettysburg, 35, 85
Ghent, 18, 245
Ghigny, Maj-Gen Charles-Etienne de, 82, 172
Gibney, Assistant-Surgeon William, 25, 50, 55, 58, 128
Gilmore, Hussar, 264

Girard, Lt-Gen Baron Jean-Baptiste, 337
Givet, 309, 315
Gneisenau, Lt-Gen Count August von, passim
Gobert, Col Baron, 175, 179
Golzio, Lt-Col, 221
Gordon, Lt-Col the Hon. Sir Alexander, 48–9, 94, 263–4
   monument, 48
Gore, Lt Arthur, 53, 62
Gore, Capt Ralph, 53
Gosselies, 237
Graeme, Lt George, 124, 174
Graham, Capt Henry, 51
Grammont, 265
Grand-Leez, 305
Grandmaison, Baron de, 189
Great Battery, 74, 81, 83, 163–5, 170, 173
Grenoble, 218
Gröben, Maj, 204
Gronow, Ensign Rees, 58, 60, 86, 91, 93–5, 115
Gros, Antoine-Jean, 324
Grose, Capt Edward, 263, 265
Grouchy, Marshal Emmanuel de, 22, 26, 323
   at Battle of Wavre, 271–302
   retreats to France, 303–16
   exile, 321
Grove, Capt Henry, 139
Guilleminot, Capt, 310
Guise, 316
Gunning, Deputy Inspector, 56–7
Guyot, Capt, 135
Guyot, Lt-Gen Baron Claude, 86, 177, 185

Habert, Lt-Gen Baron, 289, 295
Haig, FM Sir Douglas, 171
Haigh, Capt John, 54
Haigh, Lt Thomas, 53–4
Hal, 197
Halkett, Maj-Gen Sir Colin, 90, 93–4, 129, 133
Halkett, Lt-Gen Hugh, 191
Hamilton, Lt Archibald, 61
Hanau, 149
Hanover, 120, 325–6
Hardt, Lt A., 54
Hare, Capt John, 127
Haren, 1st Lt Baron van, 55, 77
Harlet, Gen Baron Louis, 187
Harris, Lt-Col William, 114
Hart, Lt James, 54
Hastings, 120, 327–9
Haxo, Lt-Gen Baron François Nicolas, 151, 156, 323
Hay, Alexander, Esquire of Nunraw, 51
Hay, Ensign James Lord, 264–5
Hay, Lt William, 58
Haydon, Benjamin, 133
Healey, Edward, 248, 255
Hechmann, Maj, 55
Henckens, Lt J., 151, 156
Henrion, Gen Baron Christophe, 187
Hepburn, Maj Francis, 71
Herringfleet, 325
Heyland, Maj Arthur, 49
Heymès, Col, 86, 168, 172, 185
Hibbert, Lt John, 51
Hill, Lt-Gen Lord, 337, 350
Hiller von Gärtringen, Col, 219–20
Hincks, First Lt John, 325
Hobe, Maj-Gen von, 271, 306, 308–9
Hocquart, Countess, 316
Holtzermann, Capt Gottleib Thilo, 333
Hooper, William, 96
Hope, Lt James, 77, 79, 83, 116
Hougoumont, 35–7, 43, 54, 64–72, 75, 86, 94, 113, 119, 130,

135, 137, 139, 150, 153–4, 157–61, 163, 173, 176–8, 180,
  185, 191, 195, 225, 237, 263, 265, 320, 324, 326
Chapel, 69–70
Château, 69–70, 72
  French monument, 71
  Garden, 64, 70–1, 157, 161
  Gardener's House, 71–2
  Great Barn, 64, 67, 69
  Hollow way, 71
  North Gate, 64, 67, 161
  Orchard, 64, 66, 71, 119, 161, 177, 180–1
  Wood, 64, 70–2, 157, 159–61, 178, 180, 182
Houssaye, Henry, 188–9, 197, 324
Howard, Maj the Hon. Frederick, 139–40
Hugo, Gen Joseph, 324
Hugo, Victor, 40, 88, 193–6, 318, 320, 322, 324
  monument, 193
Hulot, Col, 164
Hulot, Lt-Gen Baron Etienne, 297–8
Hume, Dr John, 48

Ingilby, Lt William, 253
Inveresk, 52
Issy, 317

Jackson, Lt Basil, 53, 56, 62, 93, 140, 235, 248
Jacquinot, Col, 216
Jacquinot, Lt-Gen Baron Charles, 171–2, 216
James, Ensign John, 51
James, Assistant-Surgeon John Haddy, 57–8, 60
Jamin de Bermuy, Gen Jean-Baptiste, 179, 323
Janot, Capt, 114
Jena, 149, 176, 237–8
Jerzmanowski, Maj Baron Jean-Paul, 193
Jochens, Maj von, 314
Johnston, Lt Elliot, 57
Joli-Bois, 264
Jolyet, Maj Jean-Baptiste, 154, 161, 257–8

Kellermann, Lt-Gen François, 86, 161, 177, 185, 323, 333
Kelly, Lt-Col Dawson, 52
Kempt, Maj-Gen Sir James, 74
Kennedy, Ensign James Grant, 53
Keppel, Ensign George, 78, 265
Kielmannsegge, Maj-Gen Count, 72, 89, 132, 178, 184
Kincaid, Lt Johnny, 75, 125, 127, 138–9, 248
Knollys, Col Henry, 35
Krahmer de Bichin, Capt Charles, 133
Kruse, Gen August von, 88, 114, 121, 326

L'Héritier, Lt-Gen Baron Samuel, 177
L'Olivier, Capt Henry, 77
La Bédoyère, Gen Count Charles de, 323
La Belle Alliance, 30, 37, 119, 136–7, 140, 150–1, 157, 163–5,
  171, 173, 175, 180, 188–9, 191, 193, 215, 219, 226, 231,
  234–5
La Falise, 308–9
La Haie Sainte, 34, 36–7, 40, 43, 48, 51, 65, 74–5, 86, 88, 119–
  26, 130, 132, 139, 165, 173–6, 178, 183–4, 187, 191, 213,
  239, 320, 326–7
La Haye (Battle of Ligny), 24–5
La Haye (Battle of Waterloo), 36, 83, 140, 165, 170, 184, 228,
  230–3
La Marache, see Smohain
Le Caillou, 141, 145–51, 155, 218, 221, 251, 349
  monument to 1st Chasseurs, 149
  orchard, 149–50
  ossuary, 150
  skeleton of slain soldier, 145–6
  Victor Hugo's balcony, 194
Le Hameau, 24
Le Hardy de Beaulieu, Count Jean-Charles, 230

Le Havre, 258
Lachouque, Henry, 327
Lacroix, Col, 179
Lacy, Pvte, 80
Laeken, 250, 253
Lalaing, Count Jacques de, 262
Lallemand, Gen Baron François, 179, 322–3
Lamare, Col J., 183, 186
Lambert, Maj-Gen Sir John, 113, 126
Lansdale, Mary, 332
Laon, 18, 315
Larrey, Baron Dominique, 160, 323
Larroumet, Gustave, 188
Lasne, 207, 209–11, 218, 220
  Ferme de la Kelle, 209
Lasne, R., 27, 201, 203, 206–7, 209–10, 215, 221–2, 238
Laudy, Lucien, 145, 150
Lawrence, Sergt William, 96, 116
Leathes, First Lt Henry, 325
Lebedur, Lt-Col von, 201, 226
Lechleitner, Lt-Col, 55
Leeke, Ensign William, 119, 133, 137–8, 235
Lefebvre-Desnouëttes, Lt-Gen Charles, 86, 176, 193, 321
Lefol, Lt-Gen Baron Etienne, 289
Legros, Sub-Lt, 66
Leipzig, 173, 237, 317
Lemonnier-Delafosse, Maj, 25, 154, 161, 180–1, 186, 237
Lennox, Lady Georgiana, 255–6, 265
Léopold, Col, 178–9
Leopold II, King of the Belgians, 189, 262
Letang, Maj, 178
Lettow-Vorbeck, Oscar von, 239
Levavasseur, Col Octave, 159, 173, 183, 187, 236
Lewes:
  Military Heritage Museum, 333
Lieber, Rifleman Franz, 322
Liège, 18, 20, 24, 26
Ligny, 22, 24–7, 148, 175, 188, 201, 203–4, 224, 234–5, 237,
  250, 252, 271, 295, 302, 306, 325, 338
Limal, 289–94, 297, 299–302, 305–6
  Ferme de la Bourse, 301
Lindau, Pvte Frederick, 120, 123
Lindhorst, Pvte, 121
Lion Mound, see Waterloo
Llanfairpwllgwyngll, 326
Lloyd, Maj William John, 89, 263
Lobau, Lt-Gen Georges Mouton, Count of, 37, 149, 190, 207,
  209–11, 215–18, 220, 225, 240, 324, 337, 350
Loire, R., 317
London:
  Apsley House, 69, 326
  National Army Museum, 78, 80, 145, 327
Longford, Lady Elizabeth, 320, 327, 330, 333
Loisthin, Maj-Gen von, 239
Louis XVIII, 17–18, 37, 246, 317, 322
Louis, Lt M., 218
Louis-Philippe, King, 324
Louvain, 197, 299–300, 303
Lützow, Lt-Col Baron Ludwig von, 233
Lyndhurst, 325
Lyons, 218

Macdonald, Maj Donald, 96, 113
Macdonald, Lt Stephen, 328
Macdonell, Lt-Col James, 67, 70
Maclean, Maj Archibald John, 263
McNab, Capt Alexander, 51
Macready, Ensign Edward, 51, 125, 128–9, 133, 135
Maczek, Maj-Gen Stanislaw, 193
Madox, Capt Henry, 333
Maison du Roi, 140–1, 234
Maitland, Capt Frederick, 317

Maitland, Maj-Gen Peregrine, 70, 93, 133, 136
Malespina, Monsieur, 85
Malines, 256, 259
Mallet, Col, 191
Malplaquet, 141, 316
Manchester, 326
Maransart, 222, 225, 306
Marbot, Col Baron Marcellin de, 30, 206, 209–10, 315, 323
March, Captain the Earl of, 126
Marchand, Louis-Joseph-Narcisse, 147, 149, 155
Marcognet, Lt-Gen Pierre Binet de, 83, 167, 184
Marengo, 145, 149
Marie, 145, 149
Marlborough, Duke of, 141, 230
Marquiaud, Capt, 236
Marshall, Troop Sergt-Maj Matthew, 82
Martigue, Col, 171
Martin, Lt Jacques, 30, 152, 167–8, 184
Mathivet, Col, 313
Mauduit, Sergt Hippolyte de, 26, 147, 153, 226
Mauroy, Count Albert de, 188
Maury, Col, 295, 302
May, Lt-Col Sir John, 90
Meir, Monsieur, 85
Mellery, 234, 306
Mercer, Capt Alexander Cavalié, 41, 90, 113, 117–18, 128, 130, 317, 325
Merlen, Maj-Gen Baron Jean-Baptiste van, 92–3
Metz, 324
Meuse, R., 311, 315
Michel, Gen Count Claude, 187
Milhaud, Lt-Gen Count Edouard, 31, 86, 89, 165, 170–1, 175–6, 179
Mill, Lt James, 113, 115
Milnes, Lt-Col William Henry, 263
Monge, Gaspard, 324
Mons, 18
Mont St Guibert, 201, 226, 306
Mont St Jean, 27, 30, 56, 60, 92, 132, 153, 163, 180, 264, 291
 Farm, 36, 56–8, 60, 89
 Hotel des Colonnes, 194
Montmirail, 149
Morris, Sergt Tom, 42, 89, 91, 129
Möser, Col Hans, 210
Motet, Maj, 172
Moulin, Jean, 324
Mountsteven, Ensign William, 77, 172
Müffling, Baron Carl von, 31, 138, 204, 211, 231–2, 240–1
Müller, Corpl Henry, 121
Murat, Marshal Joachim, 185
Murray, Lt-Col the Hon. Henry, 128, 139
Muter, Lt-Col Joseph, 128

Nalinnes, 20
Namur, 20, 22, 34, 301, 303, 305–6, 308–15
 Cathedral of St Aubain, 311, 314
 Church of St Loup, 311
 citadel, 314
 Parc Marie-Louise, 313
 Place d'Armes, 311
 Porte de Bruxelles, 312–13, 315
 Porte de Fer, 312–14
 Porte St Nicholas, 312
Nantes, 191
Napoleon I, passim
Napoleon III, 197
Nelson, Admiral Horatio, 33, 324
New Orleans, 43, 321
Ney, Marshal Michel, passim
Nieman, Volunteer Henri, 233
Niemen, R., 152
Nivelles, 20, 22, 118, 132, 178, 180, 196, 313

Nivelles–Namur highroad, 20, 22, 25, 253, 259, 305
Normandy, 50, 193, 259
Northern, Adolf, 123
Nostitz, Lt-Col Count von, 211, 213
Nyevelt, Col Zuylen van, 77

O'Grady, Lt Standish, 113
Odiot, Jean-Baptiste, 324
Ohain, 32, 195, 230–1, 350
Olderhausen, Conrad, 329
Oliver, Joseph, 325
Ompteda, Col Christian von, 61, 88, 94, 120–1, 124–5, 132, 184, 328–9, 332–3
Orange, Prince William of, 33, 92, 124–6, 130, 251–2, 256, 259, 337–8, 350
Ord, Miss Elizabeth, 254, 257
Ordener, Lt Gaston, 179, 337
Ordener, Col Count Michel, 88, 92, 176–7, 179, 183, 185, 233, 239, 337
Orkney, Lord, 141
Osten, Maj von, 233
Ostend, 22, 27, 262

Pack, Maj-Gen Sir Denis, 74, 79
Pagan, Lt Samuel, 96
Pajol, Lt-Gen Count Claude, 291, 294, 299–302, 305, 311
Panorama, see Waterloo
Papelotte, 36–7, 75, 83, 127, 130, 140, 164–5, 170–1, 184, 211, 228, 230, 232, 240, 320
Paris, 17, 18, 141, 150, 167, 171, 191, 193, 218, 258, 315–17, 322
 Invalides, 324, 327, 333
 Panthéon, 324
 Père Lachaise cemetery, 322–4
Paris, Monsieur Hyacinthe, 49, 62
Paris, Wood of, 209–11, 213, 222, 240
Pattison, Lt Frederick, 42, 51, 54, 62, 96, 135, 137
Pégot, Brig-Gen Jean, 184
Pelet, Brig-Gen Baron Jean, 220–1, 225
Pellissier, Capt, 297
Penne, Brig-Gen Baron Raymond, 294
Pepin, Monsieur, 33
Percy, Maj Henry, 48
Péronne, 316
Perponcher-Sedlnitsky, Baron Henri-Georges, 55, 77
Perrot, Maj, 172
Pétiet, Col Auguste, 216
Petit, Gen Baron Jean-Martin, 191
Philadelphia, 321
Philippeville, 18
Picton, Lt-Gen Sir Thomas, 36–7, 74–5, 77–8, 80–1, 83–4, 156, 248, 250, 350
Pirch, Maj-Gen Georg von, 201, 204, 222, 225, 234, 236, 306, 308–9, 313
Piré, Lt-Gen Count de, 156
Pirenne, Count Jacques-Henri, 47
Plancenoit, 40, 132, 151, 153, 175, 185, 211, 213, 216–22, 224–6, 231–2, 234, 236, 239–40, 306, 320
 Church of St Catherine, 40, 153, 188, 213, 217–22, 224–25
 French Young Guard monument, 218
 plaques, 218
 Prussian monument, 189, 218–19
 significance to Blücher, 239–40
Plas Newydd, 326
Pleunes, Lucien, 85
Ponsonby, Maj-Gen the Hon Sir William, 79, 171–2, 179
Poret de Morvan, Gen Baron Paul, 187
Port Macquarie, 326
Portarlington, Lt-Col John, Earl of, 30
Poulet, Corpl, 150
Powell, Capt Harry Weyland, 132, 136
Prendergast, Lt Edmund, 51

Prince Regent, 48–9, 317
Pringle, Lt George, 136
Profondeville, 315
Prussian Army:
 casualty figures, 40, 219, 294
 *Corps:*
 I, 22, 27, 201–2, 204, 228, 230–3, 240, 289, 293
 II, 24, 27, 201, 203–4, 222, 232, 234, 240, 306, 308–9, 313, 316, 322
 III, 27, 201–2, 206, 217, 222, 271, 289, 303, 306, 308
 IV, 26–7, 40, 201–4, 209, 216–17, 222, 231–2, 234, 236, 238, 240, 291
 *Infantry brigades:*
 1st, 232–3
 5th, 222, 234, 306
 6th, 313–14
 7th, 222, 314
 9th, 289
 10th, 271
 11th, 271
 12th, 271, 292, 300–1
 13th, 210, 217, 220, 225, 228, 239–40
 14th, 201, 206, 210, 217, 219–21, 226, 239–40
 15th, 203, 210, 213–17, 220, 225, 228, 239–40
 16th, 210, 213, 215–17, 219–21, 239–40
 *Regiments:*
 1st Uhlans, 216
 3rd Hussars, 310
 4th Hussars, 235
 5th Dragoons, 233
 5th Hussars, 310
 6th Dragoons, 306
 6th Hussars, 203, 209–10, 213, 215, 221
 6th Uhlans, 233
 7th Uhlans, 308
 8th Hussars, 215
 8th Uhlans, 308
 9th Hussars, 306
 10th Hussars, 201, 226
 12th Hussars, 306, 308
 Westphalian Landwehr Cavalry, 26
 1st Pommeranian Landwehr Cavalry, 216
 2nd Neumark Landwehr Cavalry, 215
 4th Kurmark Landwehr Cavalry, 222
 2nd Infantry, 222, 224
 9th Infantry, 322
 11th Infantry, 219, 222, 226
 14th Infantry, 203
 15th Infantry, 219–20, 222, 234, 236, 238–9
 18th Infantry, 203, 239–40
 19th Infantry, 289
 22nd Infantry, 314
 25th Infantry, 222, 234
 26th Infantry, 313
 31st Infantry, 271, 298
 1st Elbe Landwehr, 313
 1st Pommeranian Landwehr, 219, 226
 1st Silesian Landwehr, 219, 222
 2nd Pommeranian Landwehr, 222
 2nd Silesian Landwehr, 219
 3rd Silesian Landwehr, 239
 4th Kurmark Landwehr, 294
 5th Westphalian Landwehr, 222
 *Sharpshooter companies:*
 1st and 3rd Silesian Schützen companies, 232
 *Batteries:*
 Horse Bty no.20, 297
 *Engineers:*
 7th engineer company, 203
Pumphrey, Thomas, 333

Quatre Bras, 22, 24–5, 27, 30, 53–4, 67, 78, 151, 159, 236–7,
247, 250–1, 253, 263, 265–6, 303, 338
Quiot du Passage, Brig-Gen Baron Joachim, 83

Ramsay, Maj William Norman, 52
Rastatt, 327
Rebecque, *see Constant-Rebecque*
Reeve, Capt John, 136
Rehwinkel, Capt Frederick, 329
Reiche, Lt-Col Ludwig von, 204, 230–2, 241
Reille, Lt-Gen Honoré, 37, 118, 148, 153–4, 157, 159, 180, 323, 350
Rennette, Gen Baron de, 261
Rettberg, Capt von, 228, 230, 240
Reuss, Col von, 313
Reuter, Capt von, 206, 233
Reynier, Sergt, 179
Rhisnes, 306, 308–9
Richmond: Duchess of Richmond's Ball, 48, 246–7, 265
Richmond, Duke of, 256
Riddock, Lt Alexander, 83, 114, 155, 248, 258
Riep, Louis, 322
Rixensart, 190, 292, 294
Robe, Lt William, 50
Roberts, FM Earl, 35
Robertson, Ensign Alexander, 53
Robertson, Sergt Duncan, 60, 74, 114
Robertson, Lt John, 53
Robiquet, Monsieur, 85
Robson, Assistant-Surgeon James, 57
Rochefort, 316
Rogers, Maj Thomas, 83
Roguet, Lt-Gen Baron François, 323
Roland, Thérèse, *see Dupuis, Thérèse*
Rome, Brig-Gen, 310
Rommel, FM Erwin, 315
Rosières, 303
Ross, Lt James Kerr, 84, 116
Rossomme, 151, 153–4, 185, 191–2, 206
Roussille, Col, 217–18
Roy, Sergt, 92
Royal Irish Rangers, 127
Rudyard, Capt Samuel, 89
Ruelle, Col, 184

St-Agatha-Rode, 294, 306
St Amand, 24–6
St Cloud, Convention of, 317
St Helena, 177, 317, 321, 324
St Quentin, 316
St Servais, 313
Saltoun, Lt-Col Alexander, Lord, 70, 136, 265
Sambre, R., 20, 22, 188, 305, 314
Sandhurst, Royal Military Academy, 327
Savoie-Carignan, Prince Joseph-Marie de, 300
Saxe-Weimar, Prince Bernhard of, 72, 228, 231, 326
Scharnhorst, Capt von, 231, 241
Scheltens, Lt Chretien, 75, 79
Schlemm, Corpl Diedrich, 121
Schmidt, Maj, 150
Schwerin, Count Wilhelm von, 209–12, 220
Seine, R., 324
Senlis, 316
Séraincourt, 322
Seymour, Capt Horace, 65, 78, 240
Sharpin, Lt William, 52
Shaw, Corpl John, 60
Shelver, Lt Thomas, 51
Siborne, William, 83–4, 194, 225, 289, 294, 327
Simmer, Lt-Gen Baron François, 217
Simmons, Lt George, 57
Smith, Volunteer Charles, 44
Smith, Maj Harry, 43

Smohain, 36, 75, 83, 165, 170, 184, 215–16, 228, 230–4, 240
Smolensk, 149
Sohr, Lt-Col von, 308, 310
Soignes, Forest of, 31, 89, 148, 230, 253, 257
Sombreffe, 22, 26
Somerset, Maj-Gen Lord Edward, 79
Somerset, Lord Fitzroy, 32, 57
Somosierra, 193
Soult, Marshal Nicolas, 148, 153–4, 167, 207, 291, 350
Soult, Lt-Gen Baron Pierre, 291
Soye, Brig-Gen Baron Jean-Louis, 157
Spa, 258
Spearman, Lt Charles, 263
Stables, Lt-Col Edward, 264
Standen, Ensign George, 69
Stanhope, Capt the Hon. James, 113, 234
Stanislas, Sister, 265
Stauffenberg, Col Count Claus von, 325
Steinmetz, Gen Karl von, 232
Stengel, Lt-Col von, 291, 293, 300–1
Stiles, Corpl Francis, 80
Stoffel, Col, 289
Stothert, Capt William, 263
Stratfield Saye, 324
Stretton, Capt Sempronius, 96, 113
Stubert, Drum Maj, 221
Subervie, Lt-Gen Baron Jacques, 206–7, 209–10, 216, 238
Switzer, Covering Colour-Sergt Christopher, 80

Talma, François Joseph, 324
Tar, Corpl Sam, 82
Tattet, Lt Jacques, 218
Taylor, Capt Thomas, 216
Templer, FM Sir Gerald, 36
Temploux, 305, 310
Teste, Lt-Gen Baron François, 207, 291, 294, 300, 302, 305, 308–9, 312–15
Tête-du-bois, Marie, 44
Thielmann, Lt-Gen Baron Johann von, 206, 217, 271, 289, 292–4, 297, 300–1, 306, 309, 350
Thionville, 324
Thouvenin, Capt, 297
Tilsit, Treaty of, 193
Tombigbee, R., 321
Torakinson, Capt William, 43, 58, 71, 81
Toole, Capt William, 80
Tourinnes, 305
Tournai, 18
Trafalgar, 33, 324
Travers de Jever, Brig-Gen Baron Etienne, 173, 185, 337
Trefçon, Col Toussaint-Jean, 152, 161, 177–8, 182, 237
Tresigny familly, 255
Trinity, R., 322
Trip, Maj-Gen, 92
Tuileries, 154, 156

Ulm, 149
Urban, Sergt, 171–2
Uxbridge, Lord (later Marquis of Anglesey), 30, 36, 49, 79, 90, 92, 240, 265, 326, 337–8, 350

Vallin, Brig-Gen Baron Louis, 291, 299, 308
Vandamme, Lt-Gen Count Dominique, 289–90, 294–6, 301–3, 305–6, 308, 314, 321
Vandeleur, Maj-Gen Sir John, 82, 128, 139, 172, 230
Vanves, 317
Vatry, Capt Bourdon de, 160
Vaux, Monsieur Barbet de, 171
Venta del Pozo, 120
Verdun, 191, 325
Verdurel, Fusilier, 220
Verner, Capt William, 55, 60, 127, 247
Verrand, Second Lt, 172

Victoria, Queen, 261–2, 318
Vienna, Congress of, see Congress of Vienna
Vietnam war, 185
Vieux, Lt, 183
Vieux-Sart, 201
Villers-Cotterêts, 316
Villers-Masbourg, Count of, 311
Vincent, Baron de, 256
Vinck, Monsieur, 85
Vittoria, 245
Vivian, Lord, 262–3
Vivian, Maj-Gen Sir Hussey, 32, 115, 128, 139, 230, 240, 262, 264

Wagnelée, 24–5
Wagram, 149, 176
Waldie, Miss Charlotte Ann (later Charlotte Eaton), 41, 48, 50, 67, 72, 248–50, 252
Waterloo, passim
  Belgian monument, 77, 197
  Gordon monument, see Gordon, Lt-Col the Hon. Sir Alexander
  Hanoverian monument, 75, 125, 184, 189, 333
  Lion Mound, 33–6, 40, 44, 48, 56, 64, 74, 85, 126, 132–3, 135, 148, 187, 189–90, 197, 213, 264
  Panorama, 85–94, 117–18, 135, 350
  Protection of the Battlefield Law 1914, 35–6, 74, 217
  Prussian monument, see Plancenoit
  Royal Chapel and Church of St Joseph, 47, 50–5, 261
  significance of the battle, 317–19
  Sunken lane, 88, 114, 195
  Visitors' Centre, 35, 349
  Waxworks museum, 35, 148, 350
  Wellington Museum, 47–9, 140, 349
  Wounded Eagle monument, 154, 188–90, 192
Watzdorff, Lt-Col von, 220
Wavre, 40, 201–4, 206, 253, 259, 294–7, 303, 305–6
  Bridge of Christ, 271, 289, 292, 295–6
  Château de la Bawette, 271, 301, 303
  Church of St Jean-Baptiste, 297
  Prussian regrouping at, 26–7, 201, 252
  accidental fire at, 203
  Battle of, 206, 217, 222, 271, 289–303, 305–6, 308, 323
Ways, 190, 236
Webster, Lt Henry, 130
Weiterhausen, Capt von, 130
Wellington, Arthur Wellesley, First Duke of, passim
Wellington, Fourth Duke of, 35
Wellington, Eighth Duke of, 36, 54
Wheatley, Lt Edmund, 43, 61, 74, 88, 94–5, 125, 222
Wheeler, Pvte William, 69
Whinyates, Capt Edward, 172–3
White, Robert, 330
Wiesbaden, 326
William I, King of United Netherlands, 33, 126, 338
William of Prussia, Prince (later Emperor William I of Germany), 216, 220, 234
Winchester, Lt Robert, 81, 83–4, 258
Windsor:
  Household Cavalry Museum, 327
Woestine, Marquis de la, 171
Wolff, Capt von, 221
Woodford, Maj Alexander, 67, 70
Wounded Eagle monument, see Waterloo
Wurmb, Capt Ernest von, 121
Wyndham, Lt Charles, 79, 82, 84

Ypres, 50, 227, 322

Zastrow, Col Heinrich von, 313
Zepelin, Col von, 289
Ziethen, Lt-Gen Count Hans von, 22, 201, 204, 228–34, 240–1, 289
Zola, Emile, 324